STUDY GUIDE

Jeannie Shearer-Gillmore
University of Western Ontario

Foundations of Microeconomics

Second Edition

Robin Bade

Michael Parkin
University of Western Ontario

Brian Lyons
Sheridan Institute of Technology and Advanced Learning

PEARSON

Addison
Wesley

Original edition published by Addison Wesley, Inc., a division of Pearson Education, Boston, MA. Copyright © 2004. This edition is authorized for sale in Canada only.

We'd like to thank the original authors of the U.S. edition of the Study Guide:
• Thomas Meyer, *Patrick Henry Community College*
• Mark Rush, *University of Florida*

Study Guide multiple-choice questions authored by:
• Seema Ahmad, *Dutchess Community College*
• Sue Bartlett, *University of South Florida*
• Jack Chambless, *Valencia Community College*
• Paul Harris, *Camden County Community College*
• William Mosher, *Assumption College*
• Terry Sutton, *Southeast Missouri State University*

ISBN 0-321-24301-3

Senior Acquisitions Editor: Gary Bennett
Developmental Editor: Michelle Harrington
Production Editor: Jennifer Handel
Production Coordinator: Deborah Starks

1 2 3 4 5   09 08 07 06 05

Printed and bound in Canada.

Table of Contents

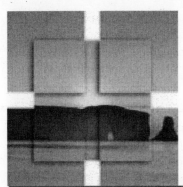

Your Complete Learning Package

■ The Complete Package

Your *Foundations of Microeconomics* package consists of

- Textbook
- Study Guide
- Foundations Web site

The Foundations Web site is a powerful and tightly integrated online learning environment. For students, the site includes

- eText—the entire textbook in PDF format with hyperlinks to all the other components of the Web site and with Flash animations of all the textbook figures accompanied by audio explanations prepared by us
- eStudy Guide—the entire Study Guide online
- *Foundations Interactive*—tutorials, quizzes, and graphing tools that make curves shift and graphs come to life with the click of a mouse
- Diagnostic Quiz for every Checkpoint with feedback that includes hyperlinks to the eText, the tutorial and quiz in *Foundations Interactive*, and the eStudy Guide
- Economics in the News updated twice a week (or more often) during the school year
- Online "Office Hours"—ask a question via e-mail, and one of us will respond with 24 hours!
- Economic links—links to sites that keep students up to date with what's going on in the economy and that enable them to work end-of-chapter Web Exercises

■ Checklist and Checkpoints: The Glue That Holds Your Tools Together

Each chapter of your textbook opens with a Chapter Checklist that tells you what you'll be able to do when you've completed the chapter. The number of tasks varies from two to five and most often is three or four. Begin by reviewing this list thoughtfully and get a good sense of what you are about to learn.

Your Study Guide provides an Expanded Chapter Checklist that breaks down your tasks into detailed bite-size pieces.

Each part of a chapter in the textbook, Study Guide, and Foundations Web site is linked directly to a Checklist item to enable you to know exactly what you're studying and how it will enable you to accomplish your learning objective.

Each part of a chapter in the textbook ends with a Checkpoint—a page that offers you a practice problem, a worked and illustrated solution to the practice problem, and a further (parallel) exercise. The Checkpoints enable you to review what you've read when it's fresh in your mind—the most effective and productive time to do so. The Checkpoints guide you in a step-by-step approach that takes the guesswork out of learning. The Study Guide reinforces each Checkpoint by providing a more detailed solution to the textbook practice problem and an additional practice problem.

Self-test questions in the Study Guide, the Diagnostic Quiz on the Foundations Web site, and the tutorials and quizzes in *Foundations Interactive* are organized by Checkpoint. The Study Guide page numbers are listed at every textbook Checkpoint.

■ Practice Makes Perfect

As you study, distinguish between *practice* and *self-test*. Practice is part of the learning process—learning by doing. Self-test is a check. It shows you where you need to go back and reinforce your understanding, and it helps you build your confidence.

The Checkpoint Practice Problems and Exercises, the end-of-chapter Exercises, and the quizzes in *Foundations Interactive* are designed for practice. The self-test questions in the Study Guide, the Diagnostic Quiz on the Web site, and the practice exam in *Foundations Interactive* are designed to reveal your gaps in understanding and to target your final examination of the material.

■ Learn Your Learning Style

It is unlikely that you'll need to use all the tools that we've created all of the time. Try to discover how you learn best. If you learn best by reading with a marker or pencil in your hand, you'll use the textbook and Study Guide more often than the other items. If you learn best by seeing the action, you'll often use the *e*Text and Foundations Interactive Demos with their animated graphics. If you learn best by hearing, you'll use the *e*Text audio explanations of the action in key figures. If you learn best by participating and acting, you'll often use the Action and Quiz in *Foundations Interactive*.

■ Tell Us What Works for You

Please tell us the tools that you find most helpful and what you think we can improve. Email us at robin@econ100.com or michael.parkin@uwo.ca, or use the Office Hours in your Foundations Web site.

Robin Bade
Michael Parkin
Ontario, Canada
February, 2004

Your Learning Tools at a Glance

Activity	Print		eFoundations	
	Textbook	**Study Guide**	**eText and eStudy Guide**	**Foundations Interactive**
Getting into a chapter	Chapter opener— previews and places chapter in context	Chapter in perspective—a short summary of the core material		
	Chapter checklist tells you what you'll be able to do when you've completed the chapter	Expanded chapter checklist breaks down your tasks into detailed bite-size pieces		
Learning the material	Explanations; matched tables and figures; figures with numbered captions		eText has exactly the same content as the print textbook plus: dynamic figures and audio explanations	Fast track summarizes each topic. Textbook figures are interactive in Action and animated in Demo
	Key terms defined in text and in margin	Key terms list for review	Key terms with hyperlinks to definitions, examples, and related terms in both tools	
	Chapter checkpoint • Key points • Key terms list			
Practice makes perfect	Checkpoints • Practice problem • Exercise • Solution to practice problem	Checkpoints • Practice problem • Additional practice problem • Expanded solution to practice problem	eText practice problems, exercises and solutions; eStudy Guide additional practice problems and expanded solutions	Five question types in Interactive Quiz: • Fill in the blanks • True or False • Multiple Choice • Numeric • Complete the graph
	Chapter checkpoint exercises		Chapter checkpoint exercises link to external sites	
Self Test		Self Test: • Fill in the blanks • True or False • Multiple Choice • Complete the graph • Short Answer	eStudy Guide has the same content as the print Study Guide. Online quizzes with hyperlinks to eText for further review: • True or False • Multiple Choice	Self Test version of Interactive Quiz: • Fill in the blanks • True or False • Multiple Choice • Numeric • Complete the graph
Enrichment, Critical Thinking, and Applications	Eye On ... • The Canadian economy • The global economy • The past			
	Economics in the News		Economics in the News hyperlinks to news article and related sites	

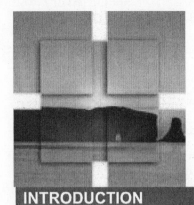

Your Course and Your Study Guide

INTRODUCTION

The goal of this Study Guide is to help you to understand the course material presented by your teacher and by your textbook. The Study Guide is just one of the tools that you will use to reach your peak performance on examinations. Using this Study Guide alone is not enough to guarantee that you will earn an A. To help you overcome the problems and difficulties that many students encounter, I have some general advice on how to study economics and some specific advice on how to use this Study Guide.

Economics is difficult for many students because it studies familiar things in an unfamiliar way. Economics doesn't *describe* the economic world: it *explains* it. And to do so, economists make extensive use of *models* that are simpler than the world in which we live. In an economic model, everything remains the same except for the tiny part of the world that we are trying to explain. We make assumptions about what people and businesses are trying to achieve. Then we figure out the decisions that people will make. This approach can be demanding. It feels unfamiliar to most students and requires practice.

It is not as easy to do well in economics on the basis of your raw intelligence and high-school knowledge as it is in many other courses. Many students are frustrated and puzzled that they are receiving As and Bs in their other courses but only a C or worse in economics. They have not recognized that economics is different and requires practice.

To avoid a frustrating visit to your instructor after your first exam, I suggest you do the following.

HOW TO STUDY ECONOMICS

■ Don't rely solely on your high-school economics

If you took high-school economics, you've already studied demand and supply, which your instructor will lecture on in the first few weeks. Don't be lulled into feeling that the course will be easy. Your high-school knowledge of economic concepts will be useful, but it will not be enough to guarantee high scores on exams. Your college instructor will demand more detailed knowledge of concepts and ask you to apply them in new circumstances.

■ Keep up with the course material on a weekly basis

Read the appropriate textbook chapter before your instructor lectures on it. You'll be amazed at how your instructor's teaching ability improves when you come to class prepared. After class, work the practice problems and exercise and Foundations Interactive quiz for practice. Then use the Study Guide quiz to test your understanding. Economics requires lots of practice and self testing.

■ Make a good set of notes

Good notes are vital to focus your studying. Writing the notes is more important than reading them! The note-writing process begins when you read the textbook *before* the lecture. Make an outline set of notes at that time. List all the key terms and be sure you know their definitions. Take the outline to class and fill in the details. After class, rewrite the notes clearly so that you can easily review them later. At this time, elaborate any items that your instructor emphasizes.

■ Use your instructor and/or teaching assistants for help

When you have questions or problems with course material, ask questions. Your instructor is here to help you learn. Instructors like to be asked questions. And there are no stupid questions! So try not to be shy. The personal contact that comes from one-on-one tutoring is rewarding for instructors as well as beneficial for you.

■ Form a study group

A useful way to motivate your studying and to learn economics is to discuss the course material and problems with other students. Explaining the answer to a question out loud is a very effective way of discovering how well you understand the question. When you answer a question only in your head, you often skip steps in the chain of reasoning without realizing it. When you are forced to explain your reasoning aloud, gaps and mistakes quickly appear, and you and your fellow group members can quickly correct your reasoning. The Checkpoint practice problems and exercises are extremely good study group material.

■ Work old exams intelligently

You can usually obtain old exam papers in your school library, from your instructor, or from students who have already taken the course. Past exams give you a feel for the style of question your instructor might ask, and working them under a time constraint helps you to pace yourself and do the exam in the allotted time. But remember that you are preparing for the *next* exam that your instructor will set, not the *last* one. You must *understand* the answer to each question. If you *memorize* answers, you are likely to fail. Every year, instructors hear students who tell them that this year's exam was much harder than last year's. In truth, it was the same paper with a few numbers and examples changed!

■ Use All Your Tools

The authors of your book, Robin Bade, Michael Parkin, and Brian Lyons, have created a rich array of learning tools that they describe in the preceding section, "Your Complete Learning Package." Make sure that you read this section and use *all* your tools! You should attempt to complete a chapter in the Study Guide only after you have read the corresponding textbook chapter and listened to your instructor lecture on the material.

HOW TO USE THE STUDY GUIDE

Each Study Guide chapter contains:

Chapter in Perspective

This first section is a short summary of the key material. It is designed to focus you quickly and precisely on the core material that you must master. You can use it to help you organize you own notes when you first read the textbook chapter. And you can use it before your exam to serve as a final check of the key concepts you have studied.

Expanded Chapter Checklist

A key point of the textbook is its use of Chapter Checklist and Checkpoints. Each Checklist item is explained in the textbook and is followed by a Checkpoint where you will work practice problems and exercises. The Study Guide repeats the Checklist learning objective and then breaks it down into a list of smaller objectives. Use this more detailed list to organize your study and for review. If you have mastered each of the detailed checklist objectives, you can be confident that you understand the material.

Key Terms

One aspect many students find difficult about economics is its vocabulary. To understand economics you must learn its vocabulary. The Study Guide lists the key terms in each chapter and gives the page in the textbook on which they are found. You can use this list to help you review for a test. Be sure that you can define each term and that you understand its definition.

After the Key Terms, the Study Guide is divided into topics that correspond to each Checkpoint in your text. At the beginning of each Checkpoint the learning objective is repeated. Always keep this objective in mind because it helps place the material in the Checkpoint into perspective.

Practice Problem

Each Checkpoint in the text contains a practice problem with answers. These practice problems are repeated in the Study Guide, but the explanations of the solutions are more detailed than in the textbook. Use these solutions to enhance your understanding of the topic.

Additional Practice Problem

After the original practice problem is explained, the Study Guide presents an additional practice problem. The additional practice problem either extends the original one or covers a related topic. Although the solution to the additional practice problem is given, try to solve it on your own first.

Following the additional practice problem is the Self Test. This section has fill in the blank, true or false, multiple choice, complete the graph, and short answer questions. The questions are designed to test your understanding of each topic.

Do the Self Test questions as if they were real exam questions, which means do them without looking at the answers. Struggling to work out the answers to a question that you find difficult is one of the most effective ways to learn. You will learn the most from right answers you had to struggle to work out and from your wrong answers and mistakes. Look at the answers, only

after you have attempted all the questions in a Checkpoint. When you finally do check the answers, be sure to understand where you went wrong and why the answer given is correct.

Fill in the Blanks

Fill in the blank questions will help you with the economics vocabulary and allow you to check that you know the definitions of the key terms and how to use them. These questions will also help you review for a test because, once completed, they serve as a *very* brief list of the main points within a Checklist item.

True or False

Some instructors use true or false questions on exams or quizzes, so these questions can prove very valuable exam practice. The answers to the questions are given along with a textbook page reference. If you do not understand the answer, turn to the textbook and study the topic. Reviewing the textbook page at this time will enable you to improve your understanding and perhaps ensure that you will not miss a similar question on your exams.

Multiple Choice

Many exams contain multiple choice questions, so pay particular attention to these questions. The answers to each of these questions also contain a textbook page reference. If you have difficulty with a question, use this page reference to review the topic in the textbook and improve your understanding. Remember that multiple choice is not multiple guess. Work out the answer. Know why an incorrect option is incorrect.

Complete the Graph

The complete the graph questions allow you to practice using one of economists' major tools, graphs. If there are essay questions on your exams, it is a safe bet that you will be expected to use some graphs in your essay. Complete the graph questions are designed to ensure that you are well prepared to draw graphs correctly.

Use the graph in the Study Guide to answer the questions. Although the answer is given, do *not* look at it before you attempt to solve the problem. It is much too easy to deceive yourself into thinking that you understand the answer when you simply look at the question and then read the answer. Involve yourself in the material by answering the question and then looking at the answer. If you cannot answer the question or if you got the answer wrong, the Study Guide gives the textbook reference. Use the text and study the material!

Short Answer

The last set of questions are short answer questions. Approach them in the same way as you approach the other question types. Answer them before you look at the answers in the Study Guide. These questions make good discussion questions for your study group. Use them to check how well your study group members understand the topic. If your group disagrees about the answer, use the textbook page references to settle the disagreements and be sure that everyone has a solid grasp of the topic.

FINAL COMMENTS

This Study Guide could not have been written without the help of many people.

Robin Bade, Michael Parkin, and Brian Lyons have written an outstanding textbook. Their intense interest in their students and their dedication to producing the best learning package possible is inspirational. It was my privilege to be one of Michael Parkin's graduate students at the University of Western Ontario. I know from experience his outstanding pedagogical principles. And Robin Bade has taught me over the last eight years that details are important and that we should always strive for excellence—a lesson we can use in all aspects of life, not just economics!

Mark Rush from the University of Florida provided the initial files upon which this Study Guide is based.

Jane McAndrew, my friend in the Economics Reference Centre at the University of Western Ontario continues to help me in my quests for data. She also managed to mitigate my stress level with her well-timed gift of the Potato-Head Family.

Richard Parkin produced all of the artwork and maintained a wonderful sense of humour when deadlines seem insurmountable.

I made two good e-mail buddies during the work on this Study Guide. My thanks to Gary Bennett and Michelle Harrington for their support during this project.

My son Andy, who is now a grade 10 student continues to inspire me with dedication to his academic responsibilities. He always manages to meet his deadlines and I try to do likewise.

Thanks go to my husband Marvin and his parents Bernice and Ross who kept the Gillmore family afloat this past holiday season while I was so busy with work. A special thank you to my mother-in-law who not only decorated my tree but also did much of my Christmas shopping!

And finally my parents, Ve and Bill Shearer, who continue to be the rocks of support behind my endeavours. My parents believe that if I set my mind to doing something, then the thing will be done. Thank you for your faith in me.

I have tried to make the Study Guide as helpful and useful as possible. Undoubtedly I have made some mistakes—mistakes that you might find. If you do find a mistake, please let me know so that I can correct any errors. If you have a question, suggestion, or comment, please contact me. My address follows, or you can e-mail me at

jeannie.gillmore@uwo.ca.

Jeannie Gillmore
Department of Economics
University of Western Ontario
London, Ontario
N6A 5C2
February, 2004.

Getting Started

Chapter

1

Chapter 1 defines economics, discusses the three major questions of microeconomics, and examines methods used by economists to study the economic world. In this chapter you will discover why even those who do not plan on becoming economists should learn the essential elements of this discipline.

■ **Define economics, distinguish between microeconomics and macroeconomics, and explain the questions of microeconomics.**

Economic questions exist because of scarcity, the condition that arises because the available resources are insufficient to satisfy wants. Economics is the social science that studies the choices that we make as we cope with scarcity and the incentives that influence and reconcile our choices. Microeconomics is the study of the choices that individuals and businesses make and the way these choices respond to incentives, interact, and are influenced by governments. Macroeconomics is the study of the aggregate (or total) effects on the national economy and the global economy of the choices that individuals, businesses, and governments make. The three major microeconomic questions are "*What* goods and services get produced and in what quantities?", "*How* are goods and services produced?", and "*For whom* are goods and services produced?"

■ **Describe the work of economists as social scientists.**

Statements about what *is* are *positive* statements; statements about what *ought to be* are *normative* statements. Economists use observing and measuring, model building, and testing to develop their theories. An economic model simplifies reality by including only those features needed for the purpose at hand. *Ceteris paribus* is a Latin term that means "other things being equal" or "if all other relevant things remain the same." Correlation is the tendency for the values of two variables to move in a predictable and related way. The *post hoc* fallacy is the error of reasoning that a first event *causes* a second event because the first occurred before the second.

■ **Explain five core ideas that define the economic way of thinking.**

The five core ideas that form the basis of all microeconomic models are: people make rational choices by comparing costs and benefits; cost is what you must give up to get something; benefit is what you gain when you get something and is measured by what you are willing to give up to get it; a rational choice is made on the margin; and people respond to incentives.

■ **Explain why economics is worth studying.**

Studying economics provides understanding and expanded career opportunities. The costs of studying economics are forgone knowledge of some other subject and forgone leisure time.

EXPANDED CHAPTER CHECKLIST

When you have completed this chapter, you will be able to

1 Define economics, distinguish between microeconomics and macroeconomics, and explain the questions of microeconomics.

- Define economics and explain the meaning of scarcity.
- Distinguish between macroeconomics and microeconomics and discuss the subjects each study.
- List and discuss the three major microeconomic questions.

2 Describe the work of economists as social scientists.

- Explain the difference between a positive statement and a normative statement.
- Describe the task of economic science.
- Define *ceteris paribus* and explain why it is used in economic models.
- Discuss the correlation between two variables.
- Describe natural experiments, statistical investigations, and economic experiments.
- Define and give examples of the *post hoc* fallacy.

3 Explain five core ideas that define the economic way of thinking.

- Define rational choice and explain why a rational choice is made on the margin.
- Define opportunity cost and distinguish between an opportunity cost and a sunk cost.
- Define benefit.
- Define marginal cost and marginal benefit.

- Explain the role of incentives in making rational choices.

4 Explain why economics is worth studying.

- State two benefits from studying economics.
- State two costs of studying economics.

KEY TERMS

- Benefit (page 12)
- *Ceteris paribus* (page 8)
- Correlation (page 9)
- Economic model (page 7)
- Economic theory (page 7)
- Economics (page 3)
- Goods and services (page 4)
- Incentive (page 2)
- Macroeconomics (page 3)
- Margin (page 13)
- Marginal benefit (page 13)
- Marginal cost (page 13)
- Microeconomics (page 3)
- Opportunity cost (page 11)
- *Post hoc* fallacy (page 9)
- Rational choice (page 11)
- Scarcity (page 2)
- Sunk cost (page 12)

CHECKPOINT 1.1

■ **Define economics, distinguish between microeconomics and macroeconomics, and explain the questions of microeconomics.**

Practice Problems 1.1

1. Economics studies choices that arise from one fact. What is that fact?

2. Provide three examples of wants in Canada today that are especially pressing but not satisfied.

3. Provide an example of an incentive that is like a carrot and one that is like a stick.

4. Sort the following issues into microeconomic and macroeconomic issues:

a. People must install catalytic converters in their cars.

b. Canadian unemployment should be much lower.

c. Your local county opens a neighbourhood gym for teenagers.

5. Match the following headlines with the What, How, and For whom questions:

a. With more research, we will cure cancer.

b. A good education is the right of every child.

c. What will the government do with its budget surplus—increase welfare or cut taxes?

Solution to Practice Problems 1.1

These practice problems use several definitions. You must know the distinction between microeconomics and macroeconomics, and understand the three major microeconomic questions.

Quick Review

• *Microeconomics* The study of the choices that individuals and businesses make and the way these choices respond to incentives, interact, and are influenced by governments.

• *Macroeconomics* The study of the aggregate (or total) effects on the national economy and the global economy of the choices that individuals, businesses, and governments make.

• *What?* What goods and services get produced and in what quantities?

• *How?* How are goods and services produced?

• *For Whom?* For whom are goods and services produced?

1. Economics studies choices that arise from one fact. What is that fact?

The fact is scarcity. The available resources are insufficient to satisfy wants. Scarcity influences all of economics.

2. Provide three examples of wants in Canada today that are especially pressing but not satisfied.

A cure for AIDS, a cure for cancer, and affordable housing for everyone are three examples of pressing wants that are not satisfied.

3. Provide an example of an incentive that is like a carrot and one that is like a stick.

Receiving a scholarship that pays your college fees because your high school average is above 90 percent is a carrot. Receiving a $150 fine for speeding is a stick.

4. Sort the following issues into microeconomic and macroeconomic issues:

a. People must install catalytic converters in their cars.

Installing a catalytic converter is a microeconomic issue because it deals with choices made by individual people.

b. Canadian unemployment should be much lower.

Canadian unemployment is a macroeconomic issue because it refers to the national economy.

c. Your local county opens a neighbourhood gym for teenagers.

Opening a neighbourhood gym for teenagers is a microeconomic issue because it deals with the interaction of the decisions of local county government and individuals. It is not on a national, macroeconomic scale.

5.   Match the following headlines with the What, How, and For whom questions:

a.   With more research, we will cure cancer.

The statement involves two of the three questions. First, we do not yet know how to cure cancer, so more research is a How question. Second, we could conduct research to find a cure for cancer or, say, a cure for diabetes, so a cure for cancer is a What question.

b.   A good education is the right of every child.

Similar to part (a), this statement also involves two of the three questions. The production of good education instead of, say, more hospitals, is a What question. And "every child" receiving the education is a For whom question.

c.   What will the government do with its budget surplus—increase welfare or cut taxes?

The question asks who will get the surplus, so it is a For whom question.

Additional Practice Problem 1.1a

Tell whether each product is a good or a service.

a.   E.D. Smith strawberry jam

b.   A dishwasher

c.   A cup of coffee from Tim Horton's

d.   A hair cut at your local salon

e.   H&R Block completing your taxes

f.   Plywood purchased at Home Hardware

Solution to Additional Practice Problem 1.1a

a.   E.D. Smith strawberry jam

E.D. Smith strawberry jam is a good.

b.   A dishwasher

A dishwasher is a good.

c.   A cup of coffee from Tim Horton's

A cup of coffee from Tim Horton's is a good.

d.   A hair cut at your local salon

A hair cut at your local salon is a service.

e.   H&R Block completing your taxes

H&R Block completing your taxes is a service.

f.   Plywood purchased at Home Hardware

Plywood purchased at Home Hardware is a good.

■ Self Test 1.1

Fill in the blanks

Economic questions arise because ____ (wants; resources) exceed the ____ (wants; resources) available to satisfy them. Faced with ____, people must make choices. ____ (Macroeconomics; Microeconomics) is the study of the choices that individuals and businesses make and the way these choices respond to incentives, interact, and are influenced by governments. The three major microeconomic questions are: ____, ____, ____.

True or false

1.   Faced with scarcity we must make choices.

2.   "Why are people buying more orange juice this winter than last winter?" is a macroeconomic question.

3.   The subject of economics divides into two main parts, which are macroeconomics and microeconomics.

4.   The three major questions of microeconomics are what, how, and why.

Multiple choice

1. The characteristic from which all economic problems arise is
a. political decisions.
b. lack of adequate incentives.
c. how to make a profit.
d. scarcity.

2. Scarcity results from the fact that
a. the available resources are insufficient to satisfy wants.
b. not all goals are desirable.
c. all goals are desirable.
d. the population keeps growing.

3. Scarcity
a. can be eliminated by politicians.
b. existed in the 18th and 19th centuries throughout the world but exists today only in third world countries.
c. occurs only when incentives discourage actions.
d. exists for rich people and poor people.

4. Which of the following is a microeconomic issue?
a. Why has unemployment risen nationwide?
b. Why has economic growth been rapid in China?
c. What is the impact on the quantity of regular coffee purchased if consumers' tastes change in favour of specialty coffee beverages?
d. All of the above are microeconomic issues.

5. The major microeconomic questions exist because
a. economic science hasn't yet determined the best answers.
b. of growing world population.
c. the federal government typically makes bad economic decisions.
d. of scarcity.

6. The question "Should we produce MP3 discs or CDs?" is an example of a ____ question.
a. what
b. how
c. for whom
d. why

Short answer

1. Will there ever come a time without scarcity?
2. Explain the difference between microeconomics and macroeconomics.
3. What are the three major microeconomic questions? Give an example of each.

CHECKPOINT 1.2

■ **Describe the work of economists as social scientists.**

Practice Problems 1.2

1. Classify each of the following statements as positive or normative:
a. There is too much poverty in Canada.
b. An increase in the gas tax will cut pollution.
c. Cuts to social programs in Canada have been too large.

2. Provide two examples of the *post hoc* fallacy.

Solution to Practice Problems 1.2

The key to whether a statement is positive or normative is whether the statement can be tested. If we can test the statement, it is positive; if we cannot test the statement, it is normative.

Quick Review

- *Positive statement* A positive statement tells what is currently understood about the way the world operates.

- *Normative statement* A normative statement tells what ought to be. It depends on values.

- *Post hoc* fallacy The error of reasoning that a first event *causes* a second event because the first occurred *before* the second.

a. **There is too much poverty in Canada.**

This statement cannot be tested. It depends on the values of the person making the statement. It is a normative statement.

b. **An increase in the gas tax will cut pollution.**

This statement can be tested by increasing the gas tax and then measuring the change in pollution. It is a positive statement.

c. **Cuts to social programs in Canada have been too large.**

This statement cannot be tested. It depends on the values of the person making the statement. It is a normative statement.

2. **Provide two examples of the *post hoc* fallacy.**

Your examples will differ. The key is that the first event does not cause the second.

i) The Bay runs a sale on swimsuits in April and it is warm in June.

ii) I buy 100 shares of Bell Canada stock today and its price falls tomorrow.

Additional Practice Problem 1.2a

What is the relationship between *ceteris paribus*, a controlled experiment, and the approaches economists must take to test their theories?

Solution to Additional Practice Problem 1.2a

Ceteris paribus is a Latin term that means "if all other relevant things remain the same." Similar to other scientists, economists develop models that predict the effect of the change of one factor when all other factors remain the same. The model predicts the effect of a change in one factor, *ceteris paribus*. Laboratory sciences can conduct controlled experiments in which only the one factor under investigation changes. Economists cannot conduct such controlled experiments. So economists use natural experiments, in which in the ordinary course of economic life, only one factor changes; statistical investigations, in which economists look for correlations; and, economic experiments, in which real subjects are placed in a decision-making situation and the influence of interest is varied to discover how the subjects respond to one factor at a time.

■ **Self Test 1.2**

Fill in the blanks

A statement that tells what *is* is a ____ (positive; normative) statement. A statement that tells what *ought to be* is a ____ (positive; normative) statement. An economic ____ (model; theory) simplifies the reality it describes. The process of building and testing models creates ____. The Latin term meaning "other things being equal" is ____ (*ceteris paribus; post hoc*).

True or false

1. The statement, "When more people volunteer in their communities, crime rates decrease" is a positive statement.

2. An economic model must include all the details about the real world.

3. A situation that arises in the ordinary course of economic life in which the one factor of interest is different and other things are equal is an economic experiment.

4. Assuming that one event causes another because the first occurs before the second is sound economic reasoning.

Multiple choice

1. A positive statement

a. must always be right.

b. cannot be tested.

c. might be right or wrong.

d. cannot be negative.

2. Which of the following is an example of a normative statement?

a. If cars become more expensive, fewer people will buy them.

b. Car prices should be affordable.

c. If wages increase, firms will fire some workers.

d. Cars emit pollution.

3. If an economic theory conflicts with actual data,

a. it is a good theory.

b. the model needs adjustment.

c. it becomes an economic law.

d. the subject matter must be normative.

4. The Latin term *ceteris paribus* means

a. after this, therefore because of this.

b. other things being equal.

c. what is correct for the part is not correct for the whole.

d. when one variable increases, the other variable decreases.

5. Economists are scientists and so want to construct and test economic models to help understand the economic world. Consequently, economists must use which of the following to construct economic models?

a. natural experiments

b. statistical investigations

c. economic experiments

d. all of the above

6. "The rooster crows every morning and then the sun comes out. Therefore, sunrise is caused by the rooster's crowing." This statement is a

a. true statement.

b. *post hoc* fallacy.

c. normative statement.

d. negative statement.

Short answer

1. Becky is writing an essay about the effectiveness of the law that requires all passengers in a car to use a seat belt. What might be a positive statement and a normative statement that she will include in her essay?

2. The task of economic science is broken into three steps. List these three steps.

CHECKPOINT 1.3

■ **Explain five core ideas that define the economic way of thinking.**

Practice Problem 1.3

Kate usually plays tennis for two hours a week and her grade on each math test is usually 70 percent. Last week, after playing two hours of tennis, Kate thought long and hard about playing for another hour. She decided to play another hour of tennis and cut her study time by one additional hour. But the grade on last week's math test was 60 percent.

a. What was Kate's opportunity cost of the third hour of tennis?

b. Given that Kate made the decision to play the third hour of tennis, what can you conclude about the comparison of her marginal benefit and marginal cost of the second hour of tennis?

c. Was Kate's decision to play the third hour of tennis rational?

d. Did Kate make her decision on the margin?

Solution to Practice Problem 1.3

This practice problem uses several ideas, including rational choice. To understand rational choice, you also need to understand marginal benefit and marginal cost because a rational choice compares the marginal benefit to the marginal cost.

Quick Review

- *Marginal cost* The opportunity cost that arises from a one-unit increase in an activity. The marginal cost of something is what you *must* give up to get *one more* unit of it.

- *Marginal benefit* The benefit that arises from a one-unit increase in an activity. The marginal benefit of something is *measured* by what you are *willing* to give up to get *one more* unit of it.

- *Rational choice* A choice that uses the available resources to most effectively satisfy the wants of the person making the choice.

a. What was Kate's opportunity cost of the third hour of tennis?

The opportunity cost of the third hour of tennis was the ten-percentage point drop on her math test grade because she cut her studying by one hour to play an additional hour of tennis. If Kate had not played tennis for the third hour, she would have studied and her grade would not have dropped.

b. Given that Kate made the decision to play the third hour of tennis, what can you conclude about the comparison of her marginal benefit and marginal cost of the second hour of tennis?

Kate chose to play the third hour of tennis, so the marginal benefit of the second hour of tennis was greater than the marginal cost of the second hour of tennis. If the marginal benefit of the second hour of tennis was not greater than the marginal cost of the second hour of tennis, Kate would have studied rather than played tennis in the third hour.

c. Was Kate's decision to play the third hour of tennis rational?

Kate's decision was rational if the marginal benefit of the third hour of playing tennis was greater than the marginal cost of the third hour of playing tennis.

d. Did Kate make her decision on the margin?

Kate's decision to play was made at the margin because she compared the cost and benefit of playing tennis for one additional hour.

Additional Practice Problem 1.3a

Tom over slept this morning and he may be late for work. When Tom reaches an intersection the traffic light turns yellow. Tom can (1) apply the brake, (2) accelerate and (hopefully) make the light, (3) drive through the parking lot on the corner to get around the light.

a. Analyze his choices on the margin.

b. Describe the outcome in terms of making a rational choice.

Solution to Additional Practice Problem 1.3a

a. Analyze his choices on the margin.

Braking preserves safety, order, and polite expectations, which are marginal benefits, while risking delay and the potential consequences of arriving late for work are marginal costs. Accelerating might get Tom to work on time, a marginal benefit, but is done at higher risk to self and others, a marginal cost. Cutting through the parking lot might reduce Tom's chances of getting fired, a marginal benefit, but if there is a police officer nearby, it might get him a ticket, a marginal cost.

b. Describe the outcome in terms of making a rational choice.

The choice Tom makes is rational if it is the strategy for which the marginal benefit exceeds or equals the marginal cost.

■ Self Test 1.3

Fill in the blanks

A _____ (marginal; rational) choice uses the available resources to most effectively satisfy the wants of the person making the choice. The opportunity cost of an activity is _____ (all of the activities forgone; the highest-valued alternative forgone). The benefit of an activity is measured by what you _____ (are willing to; must) give up. A choice on the margin is made by comparing all the relevant alternatives ____ (incrementally; together). We make a rational choice when the marginal benefit of the activity ____ (exceeds or equals; is less than) the marginal cost.

True or false

1. In the next two hours, Kim can play a game of tennis, watch a movie, or attend class. For Kim the opportunity cost of attending class is forgoing the game of tennis *and* watching the movie.

2. Marginal cost is what you gain when you get one more unit of something.

3. A rational choice involves comparing the marginal benefit of an action to its marginal cost.

4. A change in marginal benefit or a change in marginal cost brings a change in the incentives and leads us to change our actions.

Multiple choice

1. When Jane makes a rational choice, she

a. behaves selfishly.

b. does not consider her emotions.

c. weighs the costs and benefits of her options and acts to satisfy her wants.

d. is necessarily making the best decision.

2. Jamie has enough money to buy a Mountain Dew, or a Pepsi, or a bag of chips. He chooses to buy the Mountain Dew. The opportunity cost of the Mountain Dew is

a. the Pepsi and the bag of chips.

b. the Pepsi or the bag of chips, whichever is the highest-valued alternative forgone.

c. the Mountain Dew.

d. zero because he enjoys the Mountain Dew.

3. The benefit of something is

a. purely objective and measured in dollars.

b. how a person feels about something or the gain or pleasure that it brings.

c. the value of its sunk cost.

d. not measurable on the margin.

4. The opportunity cost of a one-unit increase in an activity

a. is the total one-unit cost.

b. is the marginal cost.

c. decreases as you do more of the activity.

d. Answers a and c are correct.

5. Marginal benefit

a. is the benefit from a one-unit increase in an activity.

b. means the benefit of some small activity.

c. is measured by what a person pays.

d. All of the above answers are correct.

6. If the marginal benefit of the next slice of pizza exceeds the marginal cost, you will

a. eat the next slice of pizza.

b. not eat the next slice of pizza.

c. be indecisive about eating or not eating.

d. eat half of the next slice.

Short answer

1. What is a sunk cost?

2. What is benefit and how is it measured?

3. What is a marginal cost? A marginal benefit? How do they relate to rational choice?

CHECKPOINT 1.4

■ **Explain why economics is worth studying.**

Practice Problem 1.4

A student is choosing between an economics course and a popular music course. List two opportunity costs and two benefits from taking a course in economics.

Solution to Practice Problem 1.4

This practice problem uses the idea of making a rational choice, which is a choice that uses the available resources to most effectively satisfy the wants of the person making the choice.

Quick Review

- *Opportunity cost* The opportunity cost of something is what you *must* give up to get it.

  A student is choosing between an economics course and a popular music course. List two opportunity costs and two benefits from taking a course in economics.

The opportunity cost of taking the economics course is the forgone knowledge from the popular music course. If the popular music course does not involve as much time studying, forgone leisure is another opportunity cost.

Benefits from taking the economics course are knowledge gained from the class, a better understanding of the world, better problem-solving skills, and expanded career opportunities.

Additional Practice Problem 1.4a

What are the opportunity costs and benefits of using this *Study Guide*?

Solution to Additional Practice Problem 1.4a

The opportunity cost is the highest-valued activity, be it studying for another class, sleeping, or some other activity, which is forgone because of the time spent using the *Study Guide*.

The benefits from the *Study Guide* are an enhanced understanding of the important topics in the book, which likely will lead to a higher grade in the class. Over a longer time horizon, an increased understanding might influence the future courses you take and lead to career benefits.

■ **Self Test 1.4**

Fill in the blanks

A better understanding of important issues is one of the ____ (benefits; costs) from studying economics. The cost of buying textbooks ____ (is; is not) an opportunity cost of studying economics rather than another subject.

True or false

1. Economics requires thinking abstractly about concrete issues.

2. Economics graduates are among the highest paid professionals.

3. The benefits of studying economics are forgone knowledge of some other subject.

4. Most students of economics do not go on to major in the subject.

Multiple choice

1. A benefit from studying economics is
   a. forgone knowledge of another subject.
   b. an understanding of many of today's events.
   c. increased leisure time.
   d. that you will become as rich as Mick Jagger.

2. Economics is a good major for a ____
   a. pre-med student.
   b. pre-law student.
   c. pre-MBA student.
   d. All of the above answers are correct.

3. On average, economics graduates earn less than ____ graduates and more than ____ graduates.
   a. engineering and computer science; commerce
   b. commerce; fine arts and humanities
   c. commerce; engineering and computer science
   d. fine arts and humanities; engineering and computer science

4. An opportunity cost of studying economics rather than another subject is the

a. money you spent on textbooks and tuition.

b. tuition you pay but not the expense of the textbooks you buy.

c. the decreased leisure time from the choice of economics as a major.

d. increased salary you earn after you graduate.

5. Economics says that you should major in economics if

a. your instructor tells you that the benefits from the major exceed the costs.

b. you think the benefits from the major exceed the costs.

c. you think you will make lots of money regardless of the costs.

d. you are very good at memorization.

Short answer

1. What are the career benefits from taking economics courses?

2. Why do some students decide not to major in economics?

SELF TEST ANSWERS

■ CHECKPOINT 1.1

Fill in the blanks

Economic questions arise because <u>wants</u> exceed the <u>resources</u> available to satisfy them. Faced with <u>scarcity</u>, people must make choices. <u>Microeconomics</u> is the study of the choices that individuals and businesses make and the way these choices respond to incentives, interact, and are influenced by governments. The three major microeconomic questions are: <u>what</u>, <u>how</u>, and <u>for whom</u>.

True or false

1. True; page 2
2. False; page 3
3. True; page 3
4. False; pages 3-4

Multiple choice

1. d; page 2
2. a; page 2
3. d; page 2
4. c; page 3
5. d; page 3
6. a; pages 3-4

Short answer

1. There will never be a time without scarcity because human wants exceed the resources available to satisfy them; page 2.

2. Microeconomics is the study of the choices that individuals and businesses make and the way these choices respond to incentives, interact, and are influenced by governments. Macroeconomics is the study of the aggregate (or total) effects on the national economy and the global economy of the choices that individuals, businesses, and governments make; page 3.

3. The questions are "*What* goods and services get produced and in what quantities?", "*How* are goods and services produced?", and "*For whom* are goods and services produced?" An example of the "What" question is "Should more MP3 discs or CDs be produced?" An example of the "How" question is "Should car washes use more people or more machinery to wash cars?" An example of the "For Whom" question is "Should college graduates earn higher incomes than high school graduates?" pages 3-4.

■ CHECKPOINT 1.2

Fill in the blanks

A statement that tells what *is* is a <u>positive</u> statement. A statement that tells what *ought to be* is a <u>normative</u> statement. An economic <u>model</u> simplifies the reality it describes. The process of building and testing models creates <u>theories</u>. The Latin term meaning "other things being equal" is <u>*ceteris paribus*</u>.

True or false

1. True; page 6
2. False; page 7
3. False; page 9
4. False; page 9

Multiple choice

1. c; page 6
2. b; page 6
3. b; page 7
4. b; page 8
5. d; pages 9-10
6. b; page 9

Short answer

1. A positive statement is "People who obey the law and wear seat belts are involved in fewer road deaths." This statement can be tested. A normative statement is "People should be free to choose whether to wear a seat belt or not." This statement cannot be tested; page 6.

2. The three steps are observing and measuring, model building, and testing; pages 6-7.

■ CHECKPOINT 1.3

Fill in the blanks

A <u>rational</u> choice uses the available resources to most effectively satisfy the wants of the person making the choice. The opportunity cost of an activity is <u>the highest-valued alternative forgone</u>. The benefit of an activity is measured by what you <u>are willing to</u> give up. A choice on the margin is made by comparing all the relevant alternatives <u>incrementally</u>. We make a rational choice when the marginal benefit of the activity <u>exceeds or equals</u> the marginal cost.

True or false

1. False; page 11
2. False; page 13
3. True; page 14
4. True; page 14

Multiple choice

1. c; page 11
2. b; page 11
3. b; page 12
4. b; page 13
5. a; page 13
6. a; page 14

Short answer

1. A sunk cost is a previously incurred and irreversible cost; page 12.

2. The benefit of something is the gain or pleasure that it brings. Economists measure the benefit of something by what a person is wiling to give up to get it; page 12.

3. Marginal cost is the cost that arises from a one-unit increase in an activity. The marginal cost of something is what you *must* give up to get *one more* unit of it. Marginal benefit is the benefit that arises from a one-unit increase in an activity. The marginal benefit of something is measured by what you are *willing* to give up to get *one more* unit of it. A rational choice is made by comparing the marginal cost and marginal benefit. If the marginal benefit of an activity exceeds or equals the marginal cost, the activity is undertaken; pages 13-14.

■ CHECKPOINT 1.4

Fill in the blanks

A better understanding of important issues is one of the <u>benefits</u> from studying economics. The cost of buying textbooks <u>is not</u> an opportunity cost of studying economics rather than another subject.

True or false

1. True; page 17
2. True; page 17
3. False; page 18
4. True; page 17

Multiple choice

1. b; page 16
2. d; page 17
3. a; page 17
4. c; page 18
5. b; page 18

Short answer

1. Economics courses stress thinking abstractly
    and logically about important subjects,
    which are valuable skills to possess. In addi-
    tion, economics courses discuss many impor-
    tant economic concepts. A student's career
    benefits from the style of thought gained in
    economics classes and from the economic
    concepts covered in the classes; pages 16-17.

2. There are students for whom the benefit of
    economics as a major is less than the cost.
    The costs might be high because the student
    does not enjoy economics or because the stu-
    dent finds the subject difficult. These stu-
    dents should not major in economics;
    page 18.

Appendix: Making and Using Graphs

Chapter

1

This appendix reviews the graphs used in your economics course.

◼ **Making and using graphs.**

A graph represents a quantity as a distance. The vertical axis is the *y*-axis and the horizontal axis is the *x*-axis. A scatter diagram is a graph of the value of one variable against the value of another variable. A time-series graph measures time on the *x*-axis and the variable or variables of interest on the *y*-axis. A cross-section graph shows the values of an economic variable for different groups in a population at a point in time. A relationship between two variables that move in the same direction is a positive or direct relationship. A relationship between two variables that move in opposite directions is a negative or inverse relationship. Some relationships have minimum or maximum points. The slope of a relationship is the change in the value of the variable measured on the *y*-axis divided by the change in the value of the variable measured on the *x*-axis. To graph a relationship among more than two variables, we use the *ceteris paribus* assumption and graph the relationship between two of the variables holding the other variables constant.

EXPANDED APPENDIX CHECKLIST

When you have completed this chapter, you will be able to

1 Interpret a scatter diagram, time-series graph, and cross-section graph.

- Identify the *x*-axis, the *y*-axis, and the origin in a graph.

- Explain what is plotted and identify a scatter diagram, a time-series graph, and a cross-section graph.

2 Interpret the graphs used in economic models.

- Identify a positive or direct relationship between two variables.

- Identify a negative or inverse relationship between two variables.

- Identify a relationship that has a maximum or a minimum.

- Identify when variables are unrelated.

3 Define and calculate slope.

- Present the formula used to calculate the slope of a relationship and use it to calculate slope.

4 Graph relationships among more than two variables.

- Describe how the *ceteris paribus* assumption is used to allow us to illustrate the relationship among more than two variables.

KEY TERMS

- Cross-section graph (page 24)

- Direct relationship (page 26)

- Inverse relationship (page 27)

- Linear relationship (page 26)

- Negative relationship (page 27)

- Positive relationship (page 26)

- Scatter diagram (page 24)

- Slope (page 29)

- Time-series graph (page 24)

- Trend (page 24)

CHECKPOINT A1.1

■ **Making and using graphs.**

Additional Practice Problems A1.1

1. You have data on the average monthly rainfall and the monthly expenditure on umbrellas in Halifax. What type of graph would be the best to reveal if any relationship exists between these variables?

2. The table in the next column shows the average price of a litre of gas in Ottawa for the decade of the 1990s. In Figure A1.1, label the axes and then plot these data. What type of graph are you creating? What is the trend of gas prices during this decade?

3. In Figure A1.2, draw a straight line that shows a positive relationship and another straight line that shows a negative relationship.

4. Figure A1.3 shows the relationship between the price of a paperback book and the quantity of paperback books a publisher is willing to sell. What is the slope of the line in Figure A1.3?

Year	Price (cents per litre)
1990	58.9
1991	59.2
1992	57.3
1993	54.2
1994	52.5
1995	53.8
1996	55.1
1997	56.0
1998	51.3
1999	56.2

■ **FIGURE A1.1**

■ **FIGURE A1.2**

■ **FIGURE A1.3**

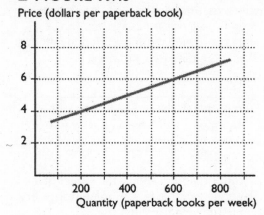

Price (dollars per paperback book)

Quantity (paperback books per week)

■ **FIGURE A1.4**

Price (cents per litre)

Year

Solution to Additional Practice Problems A1.1

1. **You have data on the average monthly rainfall and the monthly expenditure on umbrellas in Halifax. What type of graph would be the best to reveal if any relationship exists between these variables?**

A scatter diagram would be the best graph to use. A scatter diagram plots average monthly rainfall on the vertical axis (the *y*-axis) and the monthly expenditure on umbrellas on the horizontal axis (the *x*-axis).

2. **The table shows the average price of a litre of gas in Ottawa for the decade of the 1990s. In Figure A1.1, label the axes and then plot these data. What type of graph are you creating? What is the trend of gas prices during this decade?**

Figure A1.4 labels the axes and plots the data in the table. The graph is a time-series graph. The trend is negative because the price of gas has generally been decreasing during 1990s.

3. **In Figure A1.2, draw a straight line that shows a positive relationship and another straight line that shows a negative relationship.**

Figure A1.5 has two lines, one that shows a positive relationship and another that shows a negative relationship. Your figure might not show exactly these lines. The key point is that the line for the positive relationship slopes up as *x* increases along it and the line for the negative relationship slopes down as *x* increases along it.

■ **FIGURE A1.5**

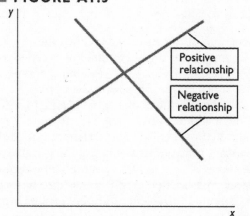

y

Positive relationship

Negative relationship

x

4. What is the slope of the line in Figure A1.3?

The slope of a line is the change in the variable measured on the *y*-axis divided by the change in the variable measured on the *x*-axis. To calculate the slope of the line in the figure, use points *A* and *B* in Figure A1.6. Between *A* and *B*, *y* rises by 2, from 4 to 6. And *x* increases by 400, from 200 to 600. The slope equals 2 ÷ 400, which is 0.005.

■ **FIGURE A1.6**

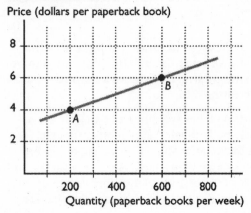

Price (dollars per paperback book)

Quantity (paperback books per week)

■ **Self Test A1.1**

Fill in the blanks

In a graph, the vertical line is called the ____ (*x*-axis; *y*-axis) and the horizontal line is called the ____ (*x*-axis; *y*-axis). A ____ (scatter diagram; time-series graph; cross-section graph) is a graph of the value of one variable against the value of another variable. A ____ (scatter diagram; time-series graph; cross-section graph) measures time on the *x*-axis and the variable on the *y*-axis. A ____ (scatter diagram; time-series graph; cross-section graph) shows the values of an economic variable for different groups in a population at a point in time. If the graph of a relationship between two variables slopes up to the right, the two variables have a ____ (positive; negative) relationship. If the graph between two variables is a vertical line, the two variables ____ (are; are not) related. The slope of a relationship is the change in the value of the variable measured on the ____ (*x*-axis; *y*-axis)

divided by the change in the value of the variable measured on the ____ (*x*-axis; *y*-axis). By using the *ceteris paribus* assumption, it ____ (is; is not) possible to graph a relationship that involves more than two variables.

True or false

1. A point that is above and to the right of another point will have a larger value of the *x*-axis variable and a larger value of the *y*-axis variable.

2. A scatter diagram shows the values of an economic variable for different groups in a population at a point in time.

3. A time-series graph compares values of a variable for different groups at a single point in time.

4. A trend is a measure of the closeness of the points on a graph.

5. A positive relationship is always a linear relationship.

6. A relationship that starts out sloping upward and then slopes downward has a maximum.

7. A graph that shows a horizontal line indicates variables that are unrelated.

8. The slope of a relationship is calculated as the change in the value of the variable measured on the *x*-axis divided by the change in the value of the variable measured on the *y*-axis.

9. The slope at a point on a curve equals the slope of the straight line that touches the point and no other point on the curve.

Multiple choice

1. The best way to demonstrate how a variable changes from one year to the next is to use a

a. scatter diagram.

b. time-series graph.

c. linear graph.

d. cross-section graph.

2. To show the values of a variable for different groups in a population at a point in time, it is best to use a

    a. scatter diagram.
    b. time-series graph.
    c. linear graph.
    d. cross-section graph.

3. If whenever one variable increases, another variable also increases, then these two variables have a ____ relationship.

    a. positive
    b. negative
    c. inverse
    d. cross-sectional

4. A graph of the relationship between two variables is a line that slopes down to the right. These two variables have ____ relationship.

    a. a positive
    b. a direct
    c. a negative
    d. no

5. Two variables are unrelated if the relationship is illustrated by

    a. a vertical line.
    b. a 45° line.
    c. a horizontal line.
    d. Both (a) and (c) are correct.

6. Figure A1.7 shows the relationship between the price of rutabagas and the quantity purchased. Between points A and B, what is the slope of the line?

    a. 4
    b. 1
    c. 3
    d. –3

■ FIGURE A1.7

Price (dollars per kilogram)

Quantity (rutabagas purchased per month)

7. In Figure A1.8 an increase in z leads to a

    a. movement up along one of the lines that shows the relationship between x and y.
    b. movement down along one of the lines that shows the relationship between x and y.
    c. rightward shift of the line that shows the relationship between x and y.
    d. leftward shift of the line that shows the relationship between x and y.

■ FIGURE A1.8

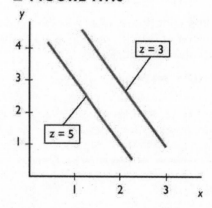

8. In Figure A1.8, *ceteris paribus*, an increase in *x* is associated with

a. an increase in *y*.

b. a decrease in *y*.

c. an increase in *z*.

d. a decrease in *z*.

Complete the graph

1. The table below gives the number of people working in agriculture in Saskatchewan during the decade of the 1990s. In Figure A1.9, measure time on the horizontal axis and the number of workers on the vertical axis, and then plot these data.

Year	Workers (thousands)
1990	83.0
1991	83.5
1992	81.6
1993	82.2
1994	75.3
1995	72.6
1996	71.4
1997	70.0
1998	71.6
1999	67.5

a. What type of graph are you creating?

b. Using your figure, what was the trend in the number of people working in agriculture in Saskatchewan during the 1990s?

■ **FIGURE A1.9**

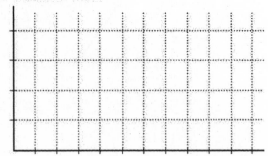

2. The table below gives the average annual value of the TSE composite index and the interest rate for the decade of the 1990s. In Figure A1.10, measure the interest rate along the *x*-axis and the TSE composite index along the *y*-axis. Then plot these data.

Year	Interest rate (percent per year)	TSE composite index
1990	10.9	3421
1991	9.8	3469
1992	8.8	3402
1993	7.8	3904
1994	8.6	4284
1995	8.3	4433
1996	7.5	5268
1997	6.4	6458
1998	5.5	6757
1999	5.7	7059

a. What type of graph are you creating?

b. What is the relationship between the interest rate and the TSE composite index that you see in your figure?

■ **FIGURE A1.10**

3. The number of sacks of premium cat food that cat lovers buy depends on the price of a sack of cat food. The relationship is given in the table. In Figure A1.11, plot this relationship, putting the price on the vertical axis and the quantity on the horizontal axis.

Price (dollars per sack of cat food)	Quantity (sacks of cat food per month)
1	10,000
2	8,000
3	7,000
4	4,000

a. If the price of a sack of cat food is $2, how many sacks are purchased in a month?

b. If the price of a sack of cat food is $3, how many sacks are purchased in a month?

c. Is the relationship between the price and the quantity positive or negative?

■ **FIGURE A1.11**

4. In Figure A1.12, label the maximum and minimum points.

■ **FIGURE A1.12**

5. In Figure A1.13, draw a line through point *A* with a slope of 2. Label the line "1." Draw another line through point *A* with a slope of –2. Label this line "2."

■ **FIGURE A1.13**

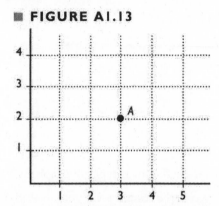

6. Bobby says that he buys fewer compact discs when the price of a compact disc is higher. Bobby also says that he will buy more compact discs after he graduates and his income is higher. The table below shows the number of compact discs Bobby buys in a month at different prices when his income is low and when his income is high.

Price (dollars per compact disc)	Quantity of compact discs purchased, low income	Quantity of compact discs purchased, high income
11	4	5
12	3	4
13	1	3
14	0	2

a. In Figure A1.14, put the price on the vertical axis and the quantity purchased on the horizontal axis. Show the relationship between the number of discs purchased and the price when Bobby's income is low.

b. On the same figure, draw the relationship between the number of discs purchased and the price when his income is high.

c. When Bobby's income increases, does the curve that graphs the relationship between the price of a compact disc and the number purchased shift rightward or leftward?

■ **FIGURE A1.14**

Short answer

1. What are the three types of graphs?

2. If two variables are positively related, will the slope of a graph of the two variables be positive or negative?

3. If a line slopes downward to the right, is its slope positive or negative?

4. In Figure A1.15, what is the slope of the curved line at point *A*? At point *B*?

■ **FIGURE A1.15**

SELF TEST ANSWERS

■ **CHECKPOINT A1.1**

Fill in the blanks

In a graph, the vertical line is called the y-axis and the horizontal line is called the x-axis. A scatter diagram is a graph of the value of one variable against the value of another variable. A time-series graph measures time on the x-axis and the variable on the y-axis. A cross-section graph shows the values of an economic variable for different groups in a population at a point in time. If the graph of a relationship between two variables slopes up to the right, the two variables have a positive relationship. If the graph between two variables is a vertical line, the two variables are not related. The slope of a relationship is the change in the value of the variable measured on the y-axis divided by the change in the value of the variable measured on the x-axis. By using the *ceteris paribus* assumption, it is possible to graph a relationship that involves more than two variables.

True or false

1. True; page 23
2. False; page 24
3. False; page 24
4. False; page 24
5. False; page 26
6. True; page 28
7. True; page 28
8. False; page 29
9. True; page 29

Multiple choice

1. b; page 24
2. d; page 24
3. a; page 26
4. c; page 27
5. d; page 28
6. d; page 29
7. d; page 30
8. b; page 30

Complete the graph

■ **FIGURE A1.16**

Workers (thousands)

1. Figure A1.16 plots the data.
a. This is a time-series graph; page 24.
b. The trend is negative; page 24

■ **FIGURE A1.17**

TSE composite index

2. Figure A1.17 plots the data.
a. The figure is a scatter diagram; page 24.
b. The relationship is negative; page 27.

■ **FIGURE A1.18**
Price (dollars per sack)

Sacks of cat food (thousands per month)

3. Figure A1.18 plots the relationship.

a. If the price is $2 a sack, 8,000 sacks are purchased in a month.

b. If the price is $3 a sack, 7,000 sacks are purchased in a month.

c. The relationship between the price and quantity of sacks is negative; page 27

■ **FIGURE A1.19**

4. Figure A1.19 labels the two maximum points and one minimum point; page 28.

5. Figure A1.20 shows the two lines; page 29.

6a. Figure A1.21 plots the relationship.

b. Figure A1.21 plots the relationship.

c. An increase in Bobby's income shifts the relationship rightward; page 30.

■ **FIGURE A1.20**

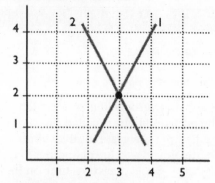

■ **FIGURE A1.21**
Price (dollars per compact disc)

Compact discs

Short answer

1. The three types of graphs are scatter diagram, time-series graph, and cross-section graph; page 24.

2. If two variables are positively related, a graph of the relationship will have a positive slope; pages 26, 29.

3. If a line slopes downward to the right, its slope is negative; page 29.

4. The slope of the curved line at point A is -2 and the slope of the curved line at point B is 1; page 29.

The Canadian Economy

Chapter 2

CHAPTER IN PERSPECTIVE

As in other countries, the economic activities of people in Canada answer the questions of what to produce, how to produce, and for whom to produce. Chapter 2 explores these questions and develops the circular flow model to show how the answers to these questions are determined.

■ **Describe the patterns and changes in *what* goods and services are produced in Canada.**

Shelter, transportation, and food are the items on which Canadians spend the largest share of their income. Over time, as incomes have increased, expenditure on necessities has taken a smaller percentage of income and expenditure on services has taken a larger percentage of income. We produce more services than goods. Machinery and equipment and automotive products are large categories of goods we buy from other countries.

■ **Describe the patterns and changes in *how* goods and services are produced in Canada.**

Goods and services are produced using the factors of production: land, labour, capital, and entrepreneurship. Land includes all the gifts of nature. Labour is the work time and work effort that people devote to producing goods and services. Capital is the tools, instruments, machines, buildings, and other constructions that have been produced in the past and that businesses now use to produce goods and services. Entrepreneurship is the human resource that organizes labour, land, and capital.

■ **Describe *for whom* goods and services are produced in Canada.**

The functional distribution of income is the percentage distribution of income among the factors of production. In Canada, labour earns most of the income. The personal distribution of income is the percentage distribution of income among households. In Canada, the richest 20 percent of households earn about 43 percent of total income; the poorest 20 percent of households earn only about 5 percent of total income.

■ **Use the circular flow model to show how households, firms, and governments interact to determine what, how, and for whom goods and services are produced.**

The circular flow model shows that households provide factors of production and firms hire factors of production in factor markets and that households purchase goods and services and firms sell goods and services in goods markets. The federal government provides goods and services such as national defence and pays benefits to unemployed people and pensions to retired people. In the circular flow model, the government buys goods and services in goods markets. It makes transfers to firms and households and receives taxes from them. The federal government's largest payment is health and social services, and its largest source of receipts is personal income taxes. 43 percent of provincial and local governments' payments are for health care. 10 percent of provincial and local governments' receipts come from sales taxes and 19 percent come from personal income taxes.

EXPANDED CHAPTER CHECKLIST

When you have completed this chapter, you will be able to

1 Describe the patterns and changes in *what* goods and services are produced in Canada.

- List the six largest items on which Canadians spend their incomes.
- Explain how consumption patterns have changed over time.
- List the largest categories of goods and services produced in Canada and the relative size of each.
- Describe the major categories of goods imported into Canada.

2 Describe the patterns and changes in *how* goods and services are produced in Canada.

- List the four factors of production
- Provide examples of what economists mean when they use the term "land."
- Give examples of renewable and nonrenewable resources.
- Define labour and human capital and explain what factors increase human capital.
- Define capital and explain why stocks and bonds are not capital goods.
- Define entrepreneurship.

3 Describe *for whom* goods and services are produced in Canada.

- List the type of income earned by each factor of production.
- Discuss the functional distribution of income and tell what factor earns most of the income in Canada.
- Discuss the personal distribution of income and categorize the amount of income earned by each 20 percent group of households.

4 Use the circular flow model to show how households, firms, and governments interact to determine what, how, and for whom goods and services are produced.

- Tell what is bought and sold in goods markets and in factor markets.
- Draw the circular flow between households and firms and between households, firms, and the government.
- Discuss the magnitude of the federal government's payments and receipts.
- Discuss the magnitude of the provincial and local governments' payments and receipts.
- Define national debt.

KEY TERMS

- Capital (page 41)
- Circular flow model (page 46)
- Entrepreneurship (page 42)
- Factor markets (page 46)
- Factors of production (page 38)
- Firms (page 46)
- Functional distribution of income (page 44)
- Goods markets (page 46)
- Households (page 46)
- Human capital (page 40)
- Interest (page 44)
- Labour (page 40)
- Land (page 38)
- Market (page 46)
- National debt (page 50)
- Personal distribution of income (page 44)
- Profit (or loss) (page 44)
- Rent (page 44)
- Wages (page 44)

CHECKPOINT 2.1

■ **Describe the patterns and changes in *what* goods and services are produced in Canada.**

Practice Problems 2.1

1. On which goods and services do Canadians spend most of their incomes?

2. How have the goods and services on which Canadians spend most of their incomes changed between 1947 and 2002?

Solution to Practice Problems 2.1

These questions study trends and facts about the goods and services on which we spend our income.

1. On which goods and services do Canadians spend most of their incomes?

The six largest items of goods and services on which Canadians spend their income are shelter (29 percent of household expenditure), transportation (19 percent of household expenditure), food (16 percent of household expenditure), recreation (8 percent of household expenditure), household operations (6.4 percent of household expenditure) and clothing and footwear (just over 6 percent of household expenditure).

2. How have the goods and services on which Canadians spend most of their incomes changed between 1947 and 2002?

Over time, incomes have increased, and as they have done so, expenditure on the necessities of life has taken a smaller percentage of income and expenditure on services has taken a larger percentage of income.

For example, total expenditure on food has fallen from 27 percent of household expenditure in 1947 to 16 percent in 2002. But the amount that we spend on restaurant food has increased from 10 percent of total food expenditure in 1947 to nearly 31 percent of food expenditure in 2002.

Additional Practice Problem 2.1a

What is the country to which Canada exports the most? Among consumer goods, what is Canada's largest import?

Solution to Additional Practice Problem 2.1a

Canada exports much of its output to the rest of the world, and exports mostly to the United States. Among consumer goods, automobiles are Canada's largest single import.

■ **Self Test 2.1**

Fill in the blanks

In Canada, the largest single category of expenditure is ____ (food; shelter; transportation) and the second largest is ____ (food; shelter; transportation). Between 1947 and 2002, as a percentage of total consumer spending, expenditure on food ____ (fell; rose). Canada produces ____ (more; fewer) services than goods.

True or false

1. In Canada, shelter and transportation are the two largest categories of household expenditure.

2. In Canada as incomes have increased, expenditure on services has taken a larger percentage of income.

3. Most of the goods and services that people in Canada buy are produced in Canada.

4. Canada produces more goods than services.

Multiple choice

1. Which of the following is the largest category of expenditure in Canada?

a. shelter

b. recreation

c. transportation

d. food

2. In Canada as incomes have increased, expenditure on necessities as a percentage of income has

a. risen more rapidly than has expenditure on services.

b. risen but less rapidly than has expenditure on services.

c. fallen.

d. not been affected.

3. In Canada as incomes have increased, expenditure on services as a percentage of income has

a. risen.

b. fallen.

c. not changed.

d. risen but in recent years has fallen dramatically.

4. Canada produces

a. more services than goods.

b. a smaller percentage of services now than in previous years.

c. wholesale trade and retail trade, which represent nearly 12 percent of the value of total production.

d. Both answers (a) and (c) are correct.

5. Most of the goods and services bought by people in Canada are produced

a. abroad and imported into the country.

b. by businesses located in Canada.

c. by the government.

d. by child labour.

6. Most of our manufactured imports, such as clothing, DVD players, toys, and sporting goods come from

a. Asia.

b. Australia.

c. Africa.

d. South America.

Short answer

1. Describe the goods and services produced in Canada today.

2. As incomes in Canada have increased, what has happened to expenditure on services?

CHECKPOINT 2.2

■ **Describe the patterns and changes in *how* goods and services are produced in Canada.**

Practice Problems 2.2

1. Name three different types of natural resources that Canada possesses in abundance.

2. Which energy resources will Canada run out of first? Which of Canada's proven reserves of gas, oil, and coal is the largest?

3. Classify each of the following as one of the four factors of production:

a. The St. Lawrence River.

b. School teachers.

c. A car-park attendant.

d. A robot owned by General Motors.

e. A cruise ship.

Solution to Practice Problems 2.2

The first two problems emphasize facts that will help shape your view of the Canadian economy and the nation's use of different resources.

Quick Review

• *Land* The "gifts of nature" or *natural resources*, that we use to produce goods and services.

1. **Name three different types of natural resources that Canada possesses in abundance.**

Canada has very large amounts of crude oil (300 billion barrels in the Alberta Tar Sands alone), fresh water (nearly 900,000 square kilometres of surface area), and forest land (over 4 million square kilometres).

2. Which energy resources will Canada run out of first? Which of Canada's proven reserves of gas, oil, and coal is the largest?

If actual reserves equal currently proven reserves, and the current growth rate of use persists, Canada will run out of natural gas first.

Canada's proven reserves of oil are larger than the proven reserves of natural gas and coal.

3. Classify each of the following as one of the four factors of production:

a. The St. Lawrence River.

The St. Lawrence River is a gift of nature and is classified as land.

b. School teachers.

School teachers are classified as labour.

c. A car-park attendant.

A car-park attendant is classified as labour.

d. A robot owned by General Motors.

A robot is used to produce other goods and services, so it is classified as capital.

e. A cruise ship.

A cruise ship is used to produce other goods and services, for example recreation, so it is classified as capital.

Additional Practice Problem 2.2a

What are the four factors of production?

Solution to Additional Practice Problem 2.2a

The four factors of production are land, labour, capital, and entrepreneurship.

Land is the "gifts of nature" or *natural resources*, that we use to produce goods and services.

Labour is the work time and work effort that people devote to producing goods and services.

Capital is the tools, instruments, machines, buildings, and other constructions that have been produced in the past and that businesses now use to produce goods and services.

Entrepreneurship is the human resource that organizes labour, land, and capital.

■ Self Test 2.2

Fill in the blanks

Productive resources are called ____ and are grouped into four categories: ____, ____, ____, and ____. In Canada, ____ (more; less) land is devoted to agricultural use than to urban use. The knowledge and skill that people obtain from education, on-the-job training, and work experience is called ____ (labour; human capital; human resources). Money, stocks, and bonds ____ (are; are not) productive resources.

True or false

1. In Canada between 1971 and 2001, built-up urban land increased from 16,000 square kilometres to more than 30,000 square kilometres.

2. Among natural gas, oil, and coal, the world's known resources of coal will last the greatest number of years.

3. There are more women than men in the Canadian labour force today.

4. Economists categorize money, stocks, and bonds as capital.

Multiple choice

1. Factors of production include

a. labour, capital, and entrepreneurship.

b. money, labour, land, and capital.

c. buyers and sellers.

d. land, labour, and markets.

2. Which of the following is classified as part of the "land" factor of production?

a. houses

b. commercial buildings

c. mineral resources

d. capital

3. Which of the following statements is true?

a. Almost 10 percent of Canada's land surface is water.

b. Less than 20 percent of Canada's land surface is forest land.

c. One-half of the Canadian population lives in the three largest cities.

d. 20 percent of Canada's population lives in 14 cities with populations that exceed 100,000.

4. Which of the following gifts of nature is non-renewable?

a. land surface

b. water

c. air

d. oil

5. _____ improves the quality of labour.

a. Capital

b. Entrepreneurship

c. Human capital

d. Financial capital

6. To an economist, the term "capital" includes

a. natural resources.

b. stocks, bonds, and money.

c. tools, machines, and buildings.

d. labour productivity.

Short answer

1. Describe how the surface area of Canada is used.

2. Describe the trend in the Canadian labour force between 1982 and 2002.

3. What is "capital"? Explain whether stocks, bonds, and money are capital.

CHECKPOINT 2.3

■ Describe *for whom* goods and services are produced in Canada.

Practice Problems 2.3

1. Distinguish between the functional distribution of income and the personal distribution of income.

2. How can wages account for 68 percent of all incomes when the 20 percent of households with the highest incomes receive 43 percent of total income?

Solution to Practice Problems 2.3

The distribution of income is a topic of interest to almost everyone, and this checkpoint gives you some basic facts about it. We will return to the topic in later chapters, so for now concentrate on learning the facts about the distribution of income.

Quick Review

- *Functional distribution of income* The percentage distribution of income among the factors of production.

- *Personal distribution of income* The percentage distribution of income among households.

1. **Distinguish between the functional distribution of income and the personal distribution of income.**

The two distributions of income differ in the groups into which they divide total income. The functional distribution of income is the percentage distribution of income among the factors of production. The personal distribution of income is the percentage distribution of income among households.

2. How can wages account for 68 percent of all incomes when the 20 percent of households with the highest incomes receive 43 percent of total income?

Many of the richest households earn much of their income from rent, interest, and profit, while most of the other 80 percent of households earn primarily wage income. And many of the richest 20 percent of households also earn high salaries.

Additional Practice Problem 2.3a

If income was distributed equally among households, what percentage of total income would the poorest 20 percent of households earn and what percentage would the richest 20 percent of households earn? How do those percentages compare with the actual Canadian personal distribution of income?

Solution to Additional Practice Problem 2.3a

If income was distributed equally, each household would earn the same income. The poorest 20 percent of households and the richest 20 percent of households would each earn 20 percent of total income. The actual personal distribution of income is far from equal, with the poorest 20 percent of households earning only about 5 percent of total income and the richest 20 percent of households earning 43 percent of total income.

■ Self Test 2.3

Fill in the blanks

____ (Interest; Rent) is paid for the use of land, ____ (profits; wages) are paid for the services of labour, ____ (interest; profit) is paid for the use of capital, and entrepreneurs receive a ____ (dividend; profit or incur a loss). The factor of production that earns the largest share of total income is ____ (labour; capital; entrepreneurship). The richest 20 percent of households earn about ____ (23; 43; 73) percent of total income.

True or false

1. The income earned by an entrepreneur is interest.

2. The functional distribution of income is the percentage distribution of income among the factors of production.

3. Among factors of production in Canada in 2002, labour earned the highest amount of income and capital earned the second highest.

4. In Canada in 2001, the richest 20 percent of households earned about 43 percent of total income and the other 80 percent earned about 57 percent of total income.

Multiple choice

1. Payments received by the factors of production
a. are measured by the personal functional distribution of income.
b. include rent, interest, wages, and profit.
c. are always in cash.
d. are mainly made to businesses.

2. Profit is earned by
a. land.
b. labour.
c. capital.
d. entrepreneurs.

3. Interest is paid for the use of
a. land.
b. labour.
c. capital.
d. entrepreneurial ability.

4. Which factor of production earns the largest share of total income?
a. land
b. labour
c. capital
d. entrepreneurship

5. Income in Canada is distributed such that the poorest 80 percent of households receive about ____ percent of total income.

a. 69

b. 57

c. 46

d. 10

6. About 43 percent of Canada's total income is earned by the _____ percent of households.

a. poorest 20

b. poorest 40

c. richest 20

d. richest 40

Short answer

1. What is the functional distribution of income?

2. What is the difference between the functional and the personal distribution of income?

CHECKPOINT 2.4

■ Use the circular flow model to show how households, firms, and governments interact to determine what, how, and for whom goods and services are produced.

Practice Problem 2.4

What are the real flows and money flows that run between households, firms, and government in the circular flow model?

Solution to Practice Problem 2.4

The circular flow model shows the interactions between firms, households, and the government in goods markets and in factor markets.

Quick Review

• *Circular flow model* A model of the economy that shows the circular flow of expenditures and incomes that result from decision mak-

ers' choices, and the way those choices interact to determine what, how, and for whom goods and services are produced.

What are the real flows and money flows that run between households, firms, and government in the circular flow model?

Start with the circular flow diagram, illustrated in Figure 2.1. The circular flow diagram illustrates the flows between households, firms, and the government. The real flows are in orange. They are the flows of the services of the factors of production through factor markets and the flows of goods and services through goods markets. In the goods markets, households and the government buy goods and services from firms. In the factor markets, households provide land, labour, capital, and entrepreneurship to firms. The money flows are in red, blue, and green. The money flows are incomes earned by factors of production (rent, wages, interest, and profit or loss), expenditures made by households and the government on goods and services, and transfers from the government to households and firms and taxes from households and firms to the government.

■ FIGURE 2.1

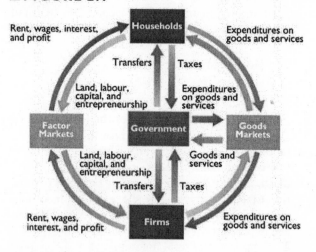

Additional Practice Problem 2.4a

In the circular flow model, describe the flow of money between households and firms and the government.

Solution to Additional Practice Problem 2.4a

Households and firms pay taxes to the government. The government makes cash payments to households and firms, which are called transfers. Taxes and transfers are direct transactions with government and do not go through the goods markets and factor markets.

■ Self Test 2.4

Fill in the blanks

The ____ (circular; economic) flow model shows the flow of expenditures and incomes. An arrangement that brings buyers and sellers together is a ____ (firm; household; market). A market in which goods and services are bought and sold is a ____ (goods; factor) market and a market in which factors of production are bought and sold is a ____ (goods; factor) market. In 2003, the federal government's receipts were equal to nearly _____ (20; 38; 75) percent of the total value of all the goods and services produced in Canada that year. In 2003, local and provincial governments spent _____ (20; 50; 75) percent more than was spent by the federal government. _____ is the largest source of federal receipts. In 2003, transfers from the federal government provided _____ (13; 38; 75) percent of provincial and local government receipts.

True or false

1. Firms own the factors of production.

2. A market is any arrangement where buyers and sellers meet face-to-face.

3. Factors of production flow from households to firms through goods markets.

4. The largest source of provincial and local government receipts is the GST.

Multiple choice

1. A market is
   a. the physical place where goods are sold.
   b. the physical place where goods and services are sold.
   c. any arrangement that brings buyers and sellers together.
   d. another name for a store such as a grocery store.

2. In the circular flow model,
   a. only firms sell in markets.
   b. only households buy from markets.
   c. the government does not transact in either the goods market or the factor market.
   d. firms sell and firms buy.

3. In the circular flow model, ____ choose the quantities of goods and services to produce, and ____ choose the quantities of goods and services to buy.
   a. households; firms
   b. firms; households and the government
   c. the government; firms
   d. households; the government

4. In the circular flow model, the expenditures on goods and services flow in the
   a. same direction as goods and services.
   b. opposite direction as goods and services.
   c. same direction as factor markets.
   d. None of the above answers are correct.

5. The largest payment that the federal government makes is
   a. education and training.
   b. health and social services.
   c. payments to provinces.
   d. interest on the national debt.

6. The largest source of receipts for the federal government is

a. personal income taxes.

b. GST.

c. corporate income taxes.

d. lotteries.

Complete the graph

1. Figure 2.2 ignores the government and shows the flows into and out of households.

▪ FIGURE 2.2

Label the flows and identify who they come from and who they go to.

2. Figure 2.3 ignores the government and shows the flows into and out of firms.

▪ FIGURE 2.3

Label the flows and identify who they come from and who they go to.

▪ FIGURE 2.4

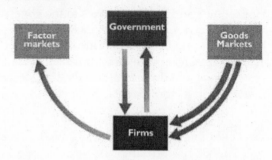

3. Figure 2.4 now includes the government and shows some of the flows into and out of firms. Label the flows.

Short answer

1. Ignoring taxes and transfer payments, what funds flow into firms and what funds flow out of firms?

2. In what markets do households earn their incomes? In what markets do households spend their income?

3. Compare the magnitude of the payments of local and provincial governments with the payments of the federal government in 2003.

4. Compare the amount of the federal government's spending on interest on the national debt to its spending on defence, law, and order.

SELF TEST ANSWERS

■ CHECKPOINT 2.1

Fill in the blanks

In Canada, the largest single category of expenditure is shelter and the second largest is transportation. Between 1947 and 2002, as a percentage of total consumer spending, expenditure on food fell. Canada produces more services than goods.

True or false

1. True; page 34

2. True; page 35

3. True; page 35

4. False; page 35

Multiple choice

1. a; page 34

2. c; page 35

3. a; page 35

4. d; page 35

5. b; page 35

6. a; page 36

Short answer

1. Today in Canada, 67 percent of what we produce is services and 33 percent is goods. The largest five service items produced in Canada are wholesale trade, health, retail trade, education, and financial services. Construction, motor vehicles, crude oil and natural gas, food, and electrical and electronic products are the largest five goods produced; page 35.

2. As incomes have increased, expenditure on the necessities of life has taken a smaller percentage of income and expenditure on services has taken a larger percentage of income; page 35.

■ CHECKPOINT 2.2

Fill in the blanks

Productive resources are called factors of production and are grouped into four categories: land, labour, capital, and entrepreneurship. In Canada, more land is devoted to agricultural use than to urban use. The knowledge and skill that people obtain from education, on-the-job training, and work experience is called human capital. Money, stocks, and bonds are not productive resources.

True or false

1. True; pages 38-39

2. True; page 39

3. False; page 40

4. False; page 41

Multiple choice

1. a; page 38

2. c; page 38

3. a; pages 38-39

4. d; page 39

5. c; page 40

6. c; page 41

Short answer

1. Canada covers 9.9 million square kilometres. Almost 10 percent of Canada's land surface is water, more than 30 percent is forest land, and more than 50 percent is wildland. In 2001, 650,000 square kilometres or 6.5 percent of the land was in agricultural use.

   People live on a very small proportion of Canada's land area. Between 1971 and 2001, built-up urban land increased from 16,000 square kilometres to more than 30,000 square kilometres; pages 38-39.

2. From 1982 to 2002, for every 10 men added to the labour force, more than 15 women

were added, raising the proportion of the labour force consisting of women from less than 41 percent to 46 percent. Over this period, women accounted for 60 percent of the growth of the labour force; page 40

3. Capital consists of the tools, instruments, machines, buildings, and other constructions that have been produced in the past and that businesses now use to produce goods and services. Stocks, bonds, and money are financial capital but are not capital; page 41.

■ CHECKPOINT 2.3

Fill in the blanks

Rent is paid for the use of land, wages are paid for the services of labour, interest is paid for the use of capital, and entrepreneurs receive a profit or incur a loss. The factor of production that earns the largest share of total income is labour. The richest 20 percent of households earn about 43 percent of total income.

True or false

1. False; page 44
2. True; page 44
3. True; page 44
4. True; page 44

Multiple choice

1. b; page 44
2. d; page 44
3. c; page 44
4. b; page 44
5. b; page 44
6. c; page 44

Short answer

1. The functional distribution of income is the percentage distribution of income among the factors of production; page 44.

2. The difference between the two income distributions is in how they divide total income.

The functional distribution of income is the percentage distribution of income among the factors of production. The personal distribution of income is the percentage distribution of income among households; page 44.

■ CHECKPOINT 2.4

Fill in the blanks

The circular flow model shows the flow of expenditures and incomes. An arrangement that brings buyers and sellers together is a market. A market in which goods and services are bought and sold is a goods market and a market in which factors of production are bought and sold is a factor market. In 2003, the federal government's receipts were equal to nearly 20 percent of the total value of all the goods and services produced in Canada that year. In 2003, local and provincial governments spent 50 percent more than was spent by the federal government. Personal income taxes is the largest source of federal receipts. In 2003, transfers from the federal government provided 13 percent of provincial and local receipts.

True or false

1. False; page 46
2. False; page 46
3. False; page 46
4. False; page 51

Multiple choice

1. c; page 46
2. d; page 46
3. b; pages 46, 49
4. b; page 47
5. b; page 50
6. a; page 50

Complete the graph

1.   Figure 2.5 labels the flows.

■ FIGURE 2.5

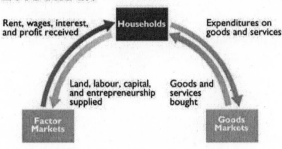

Rent, wages, interest, and profit (or loss) flow from factor markets while land, labour, capital, and entrepreneurship flow to factor markets. Expenditures on goods and services flow to goods markets and goods and services flow from goods markets; page 47

2.   Figure 2.6 labels the flows.

■ FIGURE 2.6

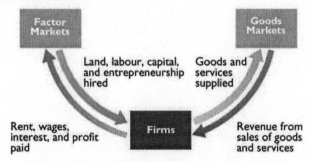

Revenue from the sale of goods and services flows into firms from goods markets and goods and services flow from firms to goods markets. Land, labour, capital, and entrepreneurship flow into firms from factor markets and rent, wages, interest, and profit (or loss) flow from firms to factor markets; page 47.

3.   Figure 2.7 labels the flows into and out of firms; pages 47, 49.

■ FIGURE 2.7

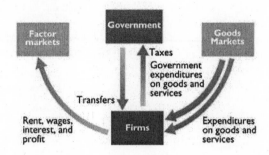

Short answer

1.   Funds that flow into firms are household and government expenditures on goods and services. Funds that flow out of firms are payments for rent, wages, interest, and profit to households in exchange for the factors of production; pages 46, 47, 49.

2.   Households earn their incomes by supplying factors of production in factor markets. Households spend their incomes on goods and services in goods markets; page 46.

3.   In 2003, provincial and local governments spent about $290 billion—50 percent more than was spent by the federal government; page 48.

4.   The federal government spends more on interest on the national debt than on defence, law, and order. In 2003, 13 percent of government payments was spent on interest on the national debt and 11 percent was spent on defence, law, and order; page 46.

The Economic Problem

CHAPTER IN PERSPECTIVE

Chapter 3 studies the production possibilities frontier, *PPF*. The *PPF* shows how the opportunity cost of a good or service increases as more of the good or service is produced. The *PPF* also shows how people gain by specializing according to comparative advantage.

■ **Use the production possibilities frontier to illustrate the economic problem.**

The production possibilities frontier is the boundary between the combinations of goods and services that can be produced and the combinations that cannot be produced, given the available factors of production and the state of technology. A production point outside the *PPF* is unattainable. Points on and inside the *PPF* are attainable. When resources are fully employed, production occurs at a point on the *PPF*. With unemployed resources, production occurs at a point inside the *PPF*. As we move along the *PPF* producing more of one good, less of another good is produced—a tradeoff. When we move from a point inside the *PPF* to a point on the *PPF* more of some goods and services can be produced without producing less of some other goods and services—a free lunch.

■ **Calculate opportunity cost.**

Along the *PPF* all choices involve a tradeoff. The *PPF* enables us to calculate opportunity cost—how much of one good we have to give up to get an additional unit of another good. Along the *PPF*, the opportunity cost of the good on the *x*-axis is equal to the decrease in the good on the *y*-axis divided by the increase in the good on the *x*-axis. As more of a good is produced, its opportunity cost increases.

■ **Define efficiency and describe an efficient use of resources.**

Efficiency occurs when we produce the quantities of goods and services that people value most highly. Efficiency is achieved when the conditions of production efficiency and allocative efficiency are met. Production efficiency is a situation in which we cannot produce more of one good or service without producing less of some other good or service—production is at a point on the *PPF*. Allocative efficiency is the combination of goods and services on the *PPF* that we value most highly.

■ **Explain how people gain from specialization and trade.**

A person has a comparative advantage in an activity if that person can perform the activity at a lower opportunity cost than someone else. People gain from specializing in the production of the good in which they have comparative advantage and then trading with others. Absolute advantage occurs when one person is more productive than another person in several or even all activities. A person can have an absolute advantage in all activities but cannot have a comparative advantage in all activities.

EXPANDED CHAPTER CHECKLIST

When you have completed this chapter, you will be able to

1 Use the production possibilities frontier to illustrate the economic problem.

- Define the production possibilities frontier, *PPF*, and explain the relationship between the *PPF* and the available factors of production and the state of technology.

- State which production points are attainable and which are unattainable.

- Discuss production when resources are fully employed and when resources are unemployed.

- Discuss the difference between tradeoff and free lunch.

2 Calculate opportunity cost.

- Measure opportunity cost along the *PPF*.

- Describe how increasing opportunity cost is reflected in the shape of the *PPF*.

3 Define efficiency and describe an efficient use of resources.

- Define production efficiency and allocative efficiency.

- Use a marginal benefit curve and marginal cost curve to find the efficient use of resources.

4 Explain how people gain from specialization and trade.

- Define comparative advantage and explain its relationship to the gains from trade.

- Determine which of two people will specialize in the production of a good.

- Define absolute advantage and explain why it is different from comparative advantage.

KEY TERMS

- Absolute advantage (page 77)
- Allocative efficiency (page 69)
- Comparative advantage (page 75)
- Efficiency (page 68)
- Production efficiency (page 68)
- Production possibilities frontier (page 58)
- Tradeoff (page 61)

CHECKPOINT 3.1

■ Use the production possibilities frontier to illustrate the economic problem.

Practice Problems 3.1

1. Robinson Crusoe, the forerunner of the television program *Survivor*, lived alone on a deserted island. He spent his day fishing and picking fruit. He varied the time spent on these two activities and kept a record of his production. The table shows the numbers that Crusoe wrote in the sand. Use these numbers to make Crusoe's *PPF* if he can work only 8 hours a day.

Hours	Fish (kilograms)		Fruit (kilograms)
0	0.0		0
1	4.0	or	8
2	7.5	or	15
3	10.5	or	21
4	13.0	or	26
5	15.0	or	30
6	16.5	or	33
7	17.5	or	35
8	18.0	or	36

2. Which combinations (kilograms of each) are attainable and which are unattainable: (i) 10 fish and 30 fruit, (ii) 13 fish and 26 fruit, (iii) 20 fish and 21 fruit?

3. Which combinations (kilograms of each) use all of Crusoe's available 8 hours a day: (i) 15

fish and 21 fruit, (ii) 7 fish and 30 fruit, (iii) 18 fish and 0 fruit?

4. Which combinations (kilograms of each) provide Crusoe with a free lunch and which confront him with a tradeoff when he increases fruit by 1 kilogram: (i) 18 fish and 0 fruit, (ii) 15 fish and 15 fruit, (iii) 13 fish and 26 fruit?

Solution to Practice Problems 3.1

These Practice Problems involve the construction and interpretation of a production possibilities frontier.

Quick Review

*   *Production possibilities frontier* The boundary between the combinations of goods and services that can be produced and the combinations that cannot be produced, given the available factors of production and the state of technology.

*   *Unattainable points* Production points outside the *PPF* are unattainable.

*   *Full employment* At full employment, production occurs at a point on the *PPF*.

*   *Unemployment* At production points inside the *PPF* some resources are unemployed.

1. **Make Crusoe's *PPF* if he can work only 8 hours a day.**

The table shows Crusoe's *PPF*.

Possibility	Fish (kilograms)		Fruit (kilograms)
A	0.0	and	36
B	4.0	and	35
C	7.5	and	33
D	10.5	and	30
E	13.0	and	26
F	15.0	and	21
G	16.5	and	15
H	17.5	and	8
I	18.0	and	0

To calculate the *PPF*, suppose that Crusoe puts all 8 hours into gathering fruit, so that he gathers 36 kilograms—row *A*. But there is no time left for fishing, so he gets 0 kilograms of fish. If he takes an hour off from gathering fruit, he gathers 35

kilograms of fruit and has an hour in which to fish, so he gets 4 kilograms of fish—row *B*. The rest of the *PPF* is constructed similarly.

2. **Which combinations (kilograms of each) are attainable and which are unattainable: (i) 10 fish and 30 fruit, (ii) 13 fish and 26 fruit, (iii) 20 fish and 21 fruit?**

i) Row *D* shows that Crusoe can produce 10.5 fish and 30 fruit, so he can produce 10 fish and 30 fruit. So (i) is attainable.

ii) 13 fish and 26 fruit is on the production possibilities frontier—row *E*. So (ii) is attainable.

iii) 20 fish and 21 fruit is unattainable because when Crusoe spends the entire 8 hours fishing he can catch only 18 kilograms of fish—row *I*.

3. **Which combinations (kilograms of each) use all of Crusoe's available 8 hours a day: (i) 15 fish and 21 fruit, (ii) 7 fish and 30 fruit, (iii) 18 fish and 0 fruit?**

i) If Crusoe spends enough time to pick 21 fruit, he can also catch 15 fish. This combination uses all his time and is on the *PPF*—row *F*.

ii) Row *C* shows that he can get 7.5 fish and 33 fruit if he works 8 hours, so combination (ii) does not require the full 8 hours. This combination is inside the *PPF*.

iii) Catching 18 fish takes 8 hours, leaving no time for picking fruit. So this combination uses all the 8 hours and is row *I* on the *PPF*.

4. **Which combinations (kilograms of each) provide Crusoe with a free lunch and which confront him with a tradeoff when he increases fruit by 1 kilogram: (i) 18 fish and 0 fruit, (ii) 15 fish and 15 fruit, (iii) 13 fish and 26 fruit?**

i) 18 fish and 0 fruit is on the *PPF*—row *I*—so there is a tradeoff but no free lunch.

ii) The combination of 15 fish and 21 fruit is on the *PPF*—row *F*—so the combination of 15 fish and 15 fruit is inside the *PPF* and there is a free lunch.

iii) 13 fish and 26 fruit is on the *PPF* — row *E* — so there is a tradeoff but no free lunch.

Additional Practice Problem 3.1a

Use the *PPF* from Practice Problem 3.1. Can Crusoe gather 21 kilograms of fruit and catch 30 kilograms of fish? Explain your answer. Suppose that Crusoe discovers another fishing pond with more fish, so that he can catch twice as many fish as before. Now can Crusoe gather 21 kilograms of fruit and catch 30 kilograms of fish? Explain your answer.

Solution to Additional Practice Problem 3.1a

Initially, Crusoe cannot gather 21 kilograms of fruit and catch 30 kilograms of fish. This production point lies outside his *PPF* and is unattainable. He can gather 21 kilograms of fruit and 15 kilograms of fish — row *F* on his *PPF*. When Crusoe discovers the new pond, he doubles the quantity of fish he catches at each production point. He can now gather 21 kilograms of fruit and catch 30 kilograms of fish. The *PPF* depends on the factors of production available and when the factors of production increase, Crusoe's production possibilities change.

■ Self Test 3.1

Fill in the blanks

The ____ (production possibilities; consumption) frontier is the boundary between the combinations of goods and services that can be produced and the combinations that cannot be produced given the available ____ (goods; factors of production) and ____ (number of services; state of technology). Production points outside the *PPF* ____ (are unattainable; are attainable; represent a free lunch). Society has the possibility of a free lunch if production occurs ____ (inside; on; outside) the *PPF*. When resources are fully employed, we face a ____ (free lunch; tradeoff).

True or false

1. Our production capacity is limited by our available resources and by technology.

2. A point outside the production possibilities frontier is unattainable.

3. If all the factors of production are fully employed, production occurs at a point on the production possibilities frontier.

4. Moving from one point on the *PPF* to another point on the *PPF* illustrates a free lunch.

Multiple choice

1. A reason the production possibilities frontier exists is
   a. unlimited resources and technology.
   b. scarcity of resources.
   c. scarcity of resources and unlimited technology.
   d. unemployment.

2. The production possibilities frontier is a graph that shows the
   a. exact point of greatest efficiency for producing goods and services.
   b. combinations of goods and services that can be consumed.
   c. maximum combinations of goods and services that can be produced.
   d. minimum combinations of goods and services that can be produced.

3. The production possibilities frontier is a boundary that separates
   a. the combinations of goods that can be produced from the combinations of services.
   b. attainable combinations of goods and services that can be produced from unattainable combinations.
   c. equitable combinations of goods that can be produced from inequitable combinations.
   d. reasonable combinations of goods that can be consumed from unreasonable combinations.

4. Points inside the *PPF* are all

a. unattainable and use fully employed resources.

b. attainable and use fully employed resources.

c. unattainable and have some unemployed resources.

d. attainable and have some unemployed resources.

5. During a period of time with high unemployment, a country can increase the production of one good or service

a. without decreasing the production of something else.

b. but must decrease the production of something else.

c. and must increase the production of something else.

d. by using resources in the production process twice.

6. A movement along the production possibilities frontier illustrates

a. the existence of tradeoffs.

b. the existence of unemployment of factors of production.

c. the benefit of a free lunch.

d. how free lunches can be exploited through trade.

Complete the graph

1. In Figure 3.1, draw a production possibilities frontier. Label the points that are attainable and unattainable. Label the points that have full employment and the points that have unemployment.

■ FIGURE 3.1

Computers (millions per year)

Food (tonnes per year)

Short answer

1. What factors limit the amount of our production?

2. What is the relationship between unemployment and a free lunch? Between full employment and a tradeoff?

CHECKPOINT 3.2

■ Calculate opportunity cost.

Practice Problems 3.2

1. Use Robinson Crusoe's production possibilities shown in the table to calculate his opportunity cost of a kilogram of fish. Make a table that shows Crusoe's opportunity cost of a kilogram of fish as he increases the time he spends fishing and decreases the time that he spends picking fruit.

Possibil-ity	Fish (kilograms)	Fruit (kilograms)
A	0.0	36
B	4.0	35
C	7.5	33
D	10.5	30
E	13.0	26
F	15.0	21
G	16.5	15
H	17.5	8
I	18.0	0

2. If Crusoe increases his production of fruit from 21 kilograms to 26 kilograms and decreases his production of fish from 15 kilograms to 13 kilograms, what is his opportunity cost of a kilogram of fruit? Explain your answer.

3. If Crusoe is producing 10 kilograms of fish and 20 kilograms of fruit, what is his opportunity cost of a kilogram of fruit and a kilogram of fish? Explain your answer.

Solution to Practice Problems 3.2

Remember that opportunity cost is the highest-valued alternative forgone.

Quick Review

• *Opportunity cost is a ratio* Along a *PPF*, the opportunity cost of one good equals the quantity of the other good forgone divided by the increase in the quantity of the good.

1. **Make a table that shows Crusoe's opportunity cost of a kilogram of fish as he increases the time he spends fishing and decreases the that time he spends picking fruit.**

The opportunity cost of a kilogram of fish is the decrease in fruit divided by the increase in fish as Crusoe moves along his *PPF*. If he increases his time fishing and moves from point *A* to point *B*, he gets 4 kilograms more fish (from 0 kilograms to 4 kilograms) and he picks 1 less kilogram of fruit (he picks 35 kilograms of fruit instead of 36

kilograms). The opportunity cost of 4 kilograms of fish is 1 kilogram of fruit. The opportunity cost of 1 kilogram of fish is (1 kilogram of fruit ÷ 4 kilograms of fish), which is 0.25 kilograms of fruit. The rest of the answers in the table are calculated similarly.

Move from	Increase in fish (kilograms)	Decrease in fruit (kilograms)	Opportunity cost of a kilogram fish (kilograms of fruit)
A to B	4.0	1	0.25
B to C	3.5	2	0.57
C to D	3.0	3	1.00
D to E	2.5	4	1.60
E to F	2.0	5	2.50
F to G	1.5	6	4.00
G to H	1.0	7	7.00
H to I	0.5	8	16.00

2. **If Crusoe increases his production of fruit from 21 kilograms to 26 kilograms and decreases his production of fish from 15 kilograms to 13 kilograms, what is his opportunity cost of a kilogram of fruit? Explain your answer.**

If he increases fruit production from 21 kilograms to 26 kilograms, he gains 5 kilograms of fruit. Production of fish decreases from 15 kilograms to 13 kilograms, a decrease of 2 kilograms. The 5 additional kilograms of fruit cost 2 kilograms of fish. The opportunity cost of 1 kilogram of fruit equals 2 kilograms of fish forgone divided by the gain of 5 kilograms of fruit, which is 2/5 kilograms of fish.

3. **If Crusoe is producing 10 kilograms of fish and 20 kilograms of fruit, what is his opportunity cost of a kilogram of fruit and a kilogram of fish? Explain your answer.**

This combination of fish and fruit lies inside his *PPF* so Crusoe enjoys a free lunch. He can gather more fruit without giving up fish and catch more fish without giving up fruit. His opportunity cost of fruit and of fish are zero.

Additional Practice Problem 3.2a

How does Crusoe's opportunity cost of a kilogram of fish change as he catches more fish?

Solution to Additional Practice Problem 3.2a

Crusoe's opportunity cost of a kilogram of fish increases as he catches more fish. In the table, as Crusoe moves from point *A* to point *B* and increases his quantity of fish from zero to 4 kilograms, the opportunity cost is only 0.25 kilograms of fruit per kilogram of fish. But as he catches more fish, the opportunity cost increases. For example, as he moves from point *H* to point *I* and increases his quantity of fish from 17.5 kilograms to 18 kilograms, the opportunity cost increases to 16.0 kilograms of fruit per kilogram of fish.

■ Self Test 3.2

Fill in the blanks

Along a production possibilities frontier, the opportunity cost of obtaining one more unit of a good is the amount of another good that is ____ (forgone; gained). The opportunity cost of a good is equal to the quantity of the other good forgone ____ (plus; divided by) the increase in the quantity of the good. As more of a good is produced, its opportunity cost ____ (decreases; increases).

True or false

1. Moving from one point on the *PPF* to another point on the *PPF* has no opportunity cost.

2. When we move along the *PPF*, the quantity of CDs increases by 2 and the quantity of DVDs decreases by 1, so the opportunity cost is 2 CDs minus 1 DVD.

3. The opportunity cost of a good increases as more of the good is produced.

4. Increasing opportunity costs are common.

Multiple choice

1. The opportunity cost of one more slice of pizza in terms of pop is the
   a. number of pizza slices we have to give up to get one extra pop.
   b. number of pops we have to give up to get one extra slice of pizza.
   c. total number of pops that we have divided by the total number of pizza slices that we have.
   d. total number of pizza slices that we have divided by the total number of pops that we have.

2. Moving between two points on a *PPF*, a country gains 6 automobiles and forgoes 3 trucks. The opportunity cost of 1 automobile is
   a. 3 trucks.
   b. 6 automobiles – 3 trucks.
   c. 2 trucks.
   d. ½ of a truck.

3. A country produces only cans of soup and pens. If the country produces on its *PPF* and increases the production of cans of soup, the opportunity cost of a
   a. can of soup is increasing.
   b. can of soup is decreasing.
   c. can of soup remains unchanged.
   d. pen is increasing.

4. The bowed-out shape of the *PPF* reflects
   a. different rates of unemployment.
   b. increasing availability of factors of production and improved technology.
   c. decreasing opportunity costs.
   d. increasing opportunity costs.

5. Moving along a country's *PPF*, a reason opportunity cost increases is that

a. unemployment decreases as a country produces more and more of one good.

b. unemployment increases as a country produces more and more of one good.

c. technology declines as a country produces more and more of one good.

d. some resources are better suited for producing one good rather than anther.

6. Increasing opportunity costs exist

a. in the real world.

b. as long as there is high unemployment.

c. only in theory but not in real life.

d. for a country but not for an individual.

Complete the graph

1. The table shows the production possibilities for a nation.

Possibility	MP3 players (millions per year)		DVD players (millions per year)
A	4	and	0.0
B	3	and	3.0
C	2	and	4.0
D	1	and	4.7
E	0	and	5.0

a. Placing MP3 players on the vertical axis, label the axes in Figure 3.2 and graph the production possibilities frontier.

b. What is the opportunity cost of a DVD player when moving from point *A* to point *B*? *B* to *C*? *C* to *D*? *D* to *E*? How does the opportunity cost change as more DVD players are produced?

■ **FIGURE 3.2**

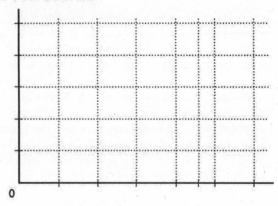

0

Short answer

1. What is the opportunity cost of increasing the production of a good while moving along a *PPF*? Why does this opportunity cost increase?

2. What does it mean for the opportunity cost to be a ratio?

CHECKPOINT 3.3

■ Define efficiency and describe an efficient use of resources.

Practice Problems 3.3

1. The table shows a nation's production possibilities of bananas and coffee.

Possibility	Bananas (bunches)	Coffee (kilograms)
A	70	40
B	50	100
C	30	140
D	10	160

Use the table to calculate the nation's marginal cost of a bunch of bananas. Draw the marginal cost curve.

2. Use the following data to draw the nation's marginal benefit curve for a bunch of bananas:

i) When 20 bunches of bananas are available, people are willing to give up 3 kilograms of coffee to get an additional bunch of bananas.

ii) When 40 bunches of bananas are available, people are willing to give up 2 kilograms of coffee to get an additional bunch of bananas.

iii) When 60 bunches of bananas are available, people are willing to give up 1 kilogram of coffee to get an additional bunch of bananas.

3. Use the data in Practice Problems 1 and 2 to calculate the efficient use of the nation's resources.

Solution to Practice Problems 3.3

This Practice Problem uses marginal benefit and marginal cost to find the efficient use of resources.

Quick Review

• *Marginal benefit* The benefit that a person receives from consuming one more unit of a good or service.

• *Marginal cost* The opportunity cost of producing one more unit of a good or service.

• *Production efficiency* A situation in which we cannot produce more of one good or service without producing less of some other good or service—production is at a point *on* the *PPF*.

• *Allocative efficiency* The combination of goods and services on the *PPF* that we value most highly.

As you move from point *D* to point *C* along the *PPF*, the quantity of bananas increases from 10 bunches to 30 bunches, an increase of 20 bunches, and the quantity of coffee decreases from 160 kilograms to 140 kilograms, a decrease of 20 kilograms. So the opportunity cost of 1 bunch of bananas is 1 kilogram of coffee.

On the average, when the quantity of bananas increases from 10 bunches to 30 bunches, 1 bunch of bananas costs 1 kilogram of coffee. We graph this cost midway between 10 bunches and 30 bunches, at 20 bunches on the *MC* curve.

As you move from point *C* to point *B* along the *PPF*, the quantity of bananas increases from 30 bunches to 50 bunches, an increase of 20 bunches, and the quantity of coffee decreases from 140 kilograms to 100 kilograms, a decrease of 40 kilograms. So the opportunity cost of 1 bunch of bananas is 2 kilograms of coffee.

On the average, when the quantity of bananas increases from 30 bunches to 50 bunches, 1 bunch of bananas costs 2 kilograms of coffee. We graph this cost midway between 30 bunches and 50 bunches, at 40 bunches on the *MC* curve.

Similarly, as you move from point *B* to point *A* along the *PPF*, the quantity of bananas increases from 50 bunches to 70 bunches and the quantity of coffee decreases from 100 kilograms to 40 kilograms. So the opportunity cost of 1 bunch of bananas is 3 kilograms of coffee. We graph this cost midway between 50 bunches and 70 bunches, at 60 bunches on the *MC* curve.

1. Use the table to calculate the nation's marginal cost of a bunch of bananas. Draw the marginal cost curve.

The figure plots the marginal cost curve.

2. Draw the nation's marginal benefit curve for a bunch of bananas.

The marginal benefit of a bunch of bananas is the amount of coffee people are willing to give up to get a bunch of bananas. The figure shows the *MB* curve, which graphs the data given in the problem.

3. Use the data in Practice Problems 1 and 2 to calculate the efficient use of the nation's resources.

The figure shows the *MC* curve and the *MB* curve. The nation uses its resources efficiently when it produces 40 bunches of bananas at the intersection of the *MC*

curve and the *MB* curve. From the *PPF*, when the nation produces 40 bunches of bananas, it also produces 120 kilograms of coffee.

All combinations on the *PPF* are combinations of production efficiency, so when the nation produces 40 bunches of bananas and 120 kilograms of coffee, it is achieving production efficiency. And this combination is also the combination of allocative efficiency because marginal benefit equals marginal cost.

Additional Practice Problem 3.3a

Explain the relationship between production efficiency and allocative efficiency.

Solution to Additional Practice Problem 3.3a

Production efficiency is a situation in which we cannot produce more of one good or service without producing less of some other good or service—production is at a point *on* the *PPF*. Allocative efficiency is the combination of goods and services on the *PPF* that we value most highly.

All the combinations of goods and services on the *PPF* achieve production efficiency. But only one combination is the most highly valued. And the combination that is most highly valued is the combination where marginal benefit equals marginal cost.

■ Self Test 3.3

Fill in the blanks

____ (Production; Allocative) efficiency occurs at each combination of goods and services on the *PPF*. ____ (Production; Allocative) efficiency occurs when we produce the most highly valued combination of goods and services on the *PPF*. As more of a good is consumed, its marginal benefit ____ (increases; decreases), and as more of a good is produced, its marginal cost ____ (increases; decreases). Allocative efficiency occurs when the marginal benefit of a good is ____ (greater than; equal to; less than) the marginal cost of the good.

True or false

1. All combinations of goods and services on the production possibilities frontier are combinations of allocative efficiency.

2. The marginal benefit of a good increases as more of the good is consumed.

3. Marginal benefit is derived from the production possibilities frontier.

4. Resource use is efficient when we achieve production and allocative efficiency.

Multiple choice

1. Efficiency occurs when

a. we produce the quantities of goods and services that people value most highly.

b. all citizens have equal access to all goods.

c. the environment is protected at all cost.

d. goods and services are free.

2. Production efficiency occurs

a. anywhere inside or on the production possibilities frontier.

b. when the total cost of production is minimized.

c. at all points on the production possibilities frontier.

d. at only one point on the production possibilities frontier.

3. Marginal benefit is the _____ one more unit of a good or service.

a. benefit that a person receives from consuming

b. additional efficiency from producing

c. increase in profit from producing

d. cost of producing

4. In general, the marginal cost curve

a. has a positive slope.

b. has a negative slope.

c. is horizontal.

d. is vertical.

5. For resource use to be efficient, when the marginal benefit of a slice of pizza exceeds the marginal cost,

a. more slices of pizza should be produced.

b. fewer slices of pizza should be produced

c. no more slices of pizza should be produced.

d. None of the above answers is correct.

6. Allocative efficiency is achieved when the marginal benefit of a good

a. exceeds its marginal cost by as much as possible.

b. exceeds its marginal cost but not by as much as possible.

c. is less than its marginal cost.

d. equals its marginal cost.

Complete the graph

1. Figure 3.3 shows a production possibilities frontier. Indicate on the *PPF* the combinations of production efficiency. Can you indicate the combination of allocative efficiency?

■ **FIGURE 3.3**
Computers (millions per year)

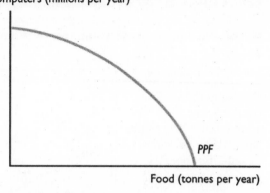

Food (tonnes per year)

2. In Figure 3.4, how many tractors are produced at the point of allocative efficiency?

■ **FIGURE 3.4**
Marginal benefit and marginal cost (T.V. sets per tractor)

Quantity (tractors per week)

Short answer

1. Along a production possibilities frontier, to produce the first skateboard, 1 pair of roller blades must be forgone. To produce the second skateboard, 2 more pairs of roller blades must be forgone. Is the marginal cost of the second skate board 2 or 3 pairs of roller blades?

2. Is it possible to derive the marginal benefit schedule from the production possibilities frontier?

CHECKPOINT 3.4

■ **Explain how people gain from specialization and trade.**

Practice Problem 3.4

Tony and Patty produce scooters and snowboards. The figure shows their production possibilities per day.

a. Calculate Tony's opportunity cost of a snowboard.

b. Calculate Patty's opportunity cost of a snowboard.

c. Who has a comparative advantage in producing snowboards?

d. Who has a comparative advantage in producing scooters?

e. If they specialize and trade, how many snowboards and scooters will they produce?

Solution to Practice Problem 3.4

To answer this Practice Problem, you need to know how to measure opportunity cost along a *PPF* and the definition of comparative advantage.

Quick Review

• *Comparative advantage* The ability of a person to perform an activity or produce a good or service at a lower opportunity cost than someone else.

a. **Calculate Tony's opportunity cost of a snowboard.**

In the figure Tony has a constant opportunity cost because the *PPF* is a straight line. If he uses all his resources to produce scooters he can make 20, and if he uses all his resources to produce snowboards, he can make 10. Each snowboard produced decreases his scooter production by 2. The opportunity cost of a snowboard is 2 scooters.

b. **Calculate Patty's opportunity cost of a snowboard.**

If Patty uses all her resources to produce scooters she can make 10, and if she uses all her resources to produce snowboards, she can make 20. Each snowboard produced decreases her scooter production by ½. The opportunity cost of a snowboard is ½ of a scooter.

c. **Who has the comparative advantage in producing snowboards?**

The opportunity cost of a snowboard for Patty is ½ of a scooter and for Tony is 2 scooters. Patty has a lower opportunity cost. Comparative advantage is the ability of a person to perform an activity or produce a good or service at a lower opportunity cost than someone else. So Patty has the comparative advantage in snowboards.

d. **Who has the comparative advantage in producing scooters?**

The opportunity cost of a scooter for Patty is 2 snowboards and the opportunity cost of a scooter for Tony is ½ of a snowboard. Tony has a lower opportunity cost and so he has the comparative advantage in scooters.

e. **If they specialize and trade, how many snowboards and scooters will they produce?**

Patty specializes in snowboards and Tony specializes in scooters. Patty can produce 20 snowboards and Tony can produce 20 scooters. A total of 20 snowboards and 20 scooters will be produced.

Additional Practice Problem 3.4a

Patty buys new equipment for scooter production that lets her produce 60 scooters a day. Should Patty and Tony specialize and trade?

Solution to Additional Practice Problem 3.4a

When Patty can produce 60 scooters a day, her opportunity cost of a scooter falls to 1/3 snowboards per scooter and her opportunity cost of a snowboard rises to 3 scooters per snowboard. Patty now has the comparative advantage in scooters and Tony in snowboards. Patty and Tony should still specialize and trade, only now Patty will specialize in scooters and Tony will specialize in snowboards.

■ Self Test 3.4

Fill in the blanks

A person has _____ (a comparative; an absolute) advantage in an activity if that person can perform the activity at a lower opportunity cost than someone else. If people specialize according to _____ (comparative; absolute) advantage and then trade, they can consume at a point _____ (outside; inside) their production possibilities frontiers. A person has _____ (a comparative; an absolute) advantage if she is more productive than someone else in several or even all activities. It _____ (is; is not) possible for someone to have a comparative advantage in all activities. It _____ (is; is not) possible for someone to have an absolute advantage in all activities.

True or false

1. Martin has an absolute advantage in an activity if he can perform the activity at a lower opportunity cost than someone else.

2. If Kevin can produce ice cream at a lower opportunity cost than Pat, Kevin has a comparative advantage in ice cream only if he produces more ice cream than Pat in an hour.

3. To achieve the gains from trade, a producer specializes in the product in which he or she has a comparative advantage and then trades with others.

4. Specialization and trade can make both producers better off even if one of them has an absolute advantage in producing all goods.

Multiple choice

1. Norman has a comparative advantage in the production of a good if he can produce
   a. more of all goods than another person.
   b. more of the good in which he has a comparative advantage than another person.
   c. the good in which he has a comparative advantage for a lower dollar cost than another person.
   d. that good at a lower opportunity cost than another person.

2. Bob produces baseballs and softballs. In one hour he produces 10 baseballs or 2 softballs. Bob's opportunity cost of producing 1 softball is
   a. 2 softballs.
   b. 10 baseballs.
   c. 5 baseballs.
   d. 1 baseball.

For the next three questions, use the following information: Scott and Cindy produce only tacos and pizzas. In one hour, Scott can produce 20 pizzas or 40 tacos and Cindy can produce 30 pizzas or 40 tacos.

3. Scott's opportunity cost of producing 1 taco is
   a. 1/2 of a pizza.
   b. 1 pizza.
   c. 2 pizzas.
   d. 20 pizzas.

4. Cindy's opportunity cost of producing 1 taco is
   a. 3/4 of a pizza.
   b. 1 pizza.
   c. 30 pizzas.
   d. 40 pizzas.

5. Based on the data given,

a. Cindy has a comparative advantage in producing tacos.

b. Scott has a comparative advantage in producing tacos.

c. Cindy and Scott have the same comparative advantage when producing tacos.

d. neither Cindy nor Scott has a comparative advantage when producing tacos.

6. In one hour John can produce 20 loaves of bread or 8 cakes. In one hour Phyllis can produce 30 loaves of bread or 15 cakes. Which of the following statements is true?

a. Phyllis has a comparative advantage in producing bread.

b. John has a comparative advantage in producing cakes.

c. Phyllis has an absolute advantage in both goods.

d. John has an absolute advantage in both goods.

Complete the graph

1. Figure 3.5 shows Mark's *PPF* and Sue's *PPF*.

■ FIGURE 3.5

a. Who has the comparative advantage in producing shirts and who has the comparative advantage in producing blouses?

b. Who should specialize in producing blouses and who should specialize in producing shirts?

c. If Mark and Sue specialize according to their comparative advantage, indicate the total production of shirts and blouses by putting a point in Figure 3.5 that shows total production. Label the point *A*.

d. How does point *A* show the gains from trade?

Short answer

1. Why should people specialize according to their comparative advantage?

2. To achieve gains from trade, the opportunity costs of the trading partners must diverge. Why?

3. When it comes to trading one good for another, why is comparative advantage crucial and absolute advantage unimportant?

SELF TEST ANSWERS

■ CHECKPOINT 3.1

Fill in the blanks

The <u>production possibilities</u> frontier is the boundary between the combinations of goods and services that can be produced and the combinations that cannot be produced given the available <u>factors of production</u> and <u>state of technology</u>. Production points outside the *PPF* <u>are unattainable</u>. Society has the possibility of a free lunch if production occurs <u>inside</u> the *PPF*. When resources are fully employed we face a <u>tradeoff</u>.

True or false

1. True;   page 58
2. True;   page 60
3. True;   pages 60-61
4. False; pages 61-62

Multiple choice

1. b; page 58
2. c; page 58
3. b; page 60
4. d; pages 60-61
5. a; pages 61-62
6. a; page 61

Complete the graph

1. Figure 3.6 shows a production possibilities frontier between computers and food and labels the points; pages 58-61.

■ FIGURE 3.6
Computers (millions per year)

Points outside the *PPF* are unattainable

Points on the *PPF* are attainable and have full employment

Points inside the *PPF* are attainable and have unemployed resources

Food (tonnes per year)

Short answer

1. The factors that limit the amount of our production are the available factors of production and the state of technology; page 58.

2. When we are producing at a point with unemployment, a free lunch is possible because the production of some goods and services can be increased without decreasing the production of anything else. When we are producing at full employment, we are on the *PPF* and an increase in the production of one good or service requires a tradeoff. If the production of one good or service is increased, the production of something else must be decreased; pages 60-62.

■ CHECKPOINT 3.2

Fill in the blanks

Along a production possibilities frontier, the opportunity cost of obtaining one more unit of a good is the amount of another good that is <u>forgone</u>. The opportunity cost is equal to the quantity of the other good forgone <u>divided by</u> the increase in the quantity of the good. As more of a good is produced, its opportunity cost <u>increases</u>.

True or false

1. False; page 64

2. False; page 65

3. True; page 66

4. True; page 66

Multiple choice

1. b; page 64

2. d; page 64

3. a; page 66

4. d; page 66

5. d; page 66

6. a; page 66

Complete the graph

1. a. Figure 3.7 illustrates the production possibilities frontier; page 64.

■ **FIGURE 3.7**

MP3 players (millions per year)

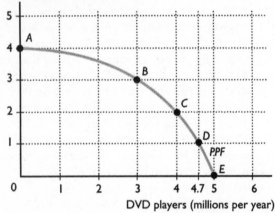

b. The opportunity cost of moving from point *A* to point *B* to is 0.33 MP3 players per DVD player; from *B* to *C* is 1.00 MP3 player per DVD player; from *C* to *D* is 1.43 MP3 players per DVD player; and, from *D* to *E* is 3.33 MP3 players per DVD player. The opportunity cost increases as more DVD players are produced; page 66.

Short answer

1. The opportunity cost of increasing production of one good is the production of some other good forgone. The opportunity cost increases because resources are not equally productive in all activities. When initially increasing the production of one good, resources that are well suited for its production are used. When still more of the good is produced, resources that are less well suited must be used. Because the resources are ill suited, more are necessary to increase the production of the first good, and the forgone amount of the other good increases; page 66.

2. The opportunity cost of a good is the amount of the other good forgone to gain an additional unit of the good. We divide the quantity of the other good forgone by the increase in the good. So opportunity cost is a ratio—the change in the quantity of one good divided by the change in the quantity of another good; pages 65-66.

■ **CHECKPOINT 3.3**

Fill in the blanks

Production efficiency occurs at each combination of goods and services on the *PPF*. Allocative efficiency occurs when we produce the most highly valued combination of goods and services on the *PPF*. As more of a good is consumed, its marginal benefit decreases, and as more of a good is produced, its marginal cost increases. Allocative efficiency occurs when the marginal benefit of a good is equal to the marginal cost of the good.

True or false

1. False; page 69

2. False; page 69

3. False   page 70

4. True; page 72

Multiple choice

1. a; page 68

2. c; page 68

3. a; page 69

4. a; page 71

5. a; page 72

6. d; page 72

Complete the graph

1. Figure 3.8 labels the points on the *PPF* that are combinations of production efficiency.

■ FIGURE 3.8
Computers (millions per year)

Each combination of computers and food on the *PPF* is production efficient. Although the combination of allocative efficiency is a point on the *PPF*, it is not possible to determine that combination without additional information about the marginal benefit of the goods; pages 68-69.

2. Allocative efficiency is the combination of goods and services on the *PPF* that we value most highly. It is the combination where marginal cost equals marginal benefit. In Figure 3.9, allocative efficiency is achieved when 30 tractors a week are produced; pages 69, 72.

■ FIGURE 3.9

Marginal benefit and marginal cost (T.V. sets per tractor)

Short answer

1. The marginal cost of the second skateboard is 2 pairs of roller blades. Marginal cost is the opportunity cost of producing one more unit of a good or service. It is not the cost of all the units produced; page 71.

2. It is not possible to derive the marginal benefit schedule from the production possibilities frontier. The marginal benefit is the benefit that a person receives from consuming one more unit of a good or service. The production possibilities frontier does not give us any information about benefit. The production possibilities frontier is used to derive the marginal cost schedule; pages 70-71.

■ CHECKPOINT 3.4

Fill in the blanks

A person has <u>a comparative</u> advantage in an activity if that person can perform the activity at a lower opportunity cost than someone else. If people specialize according to <u>comparative</u> advantage and then trade, they can consume at a point <u>outside</u> their production possibilities frontiers. A person has <u>an absolute</u> advantage if she is more productive than someone else in several or even all activities. It <u>is not</u> possible for someone to have a comparative advantage in all activities. It <u>is</u> possible for someone to have an absolute advantage in all activities.

True or false

1. False; page 75
2. False; page 75
3. True; page 76
4. True; page 77

Multiple choice

1. d; page 75
2. c; page 75
3. a; page 75
4. a; page 75
5. b; page 75
6. c; page 77

Complete the graph

1. a. Sue has the comparative advantage in producing shirts. Her opportunity cost of a shirt is 1/2 of a blouse and Mark's opportunity cost of a shirt is 2 blouses. Mark has the comparative advantage in producing blouses. His opportunity cost of a blouse is 1/2 of a shirt and Sue's opportunity cost of a blouse is 2 shirts; page 75.

   b. Mark should specialize in producing blouses and Sue should specialize in producing shirts; page 76.

   c. Mark produces 4 blouses and Sue produces 4 shirts, so a total of 4 shirts and 4 blouses are produced. Figure 3.10 shows this production as point *A*; page 76.

   d. If the total production at point *A* is divided evenly, both Mark and Sue have 2 shirts and 2 blouses. When both were producing only for themselves, they could not produce 2 shirts and 2 blouses because this point is beyond both their *PPFs*. By specializing and trading, Mark and Sue get outside their *PPFs*; page 76.

■ **FIGURE 3.10**

Short answer

1. A person has a comparative advantage in the production of a good when the person can produce that good at a lower opportunity cost than other people. By having this person specialize in the production of the good, it is produced at the lowest cost; page 75.

2. If the trading partners' opportunity costs are the same, there is no incentive for them to trade. For example, if two people produce gum and pop and both have the same opportunity cost of producing gum and pop, neither is willing to buy or sell to the other. Only when opportunity costs diverge will one person be willing to buy (the person with the higher opportunity cost) and the other willing to sell (the person with the lower opportunity cost); page 76.

3. People are willing to trade if they can obtain a good at a lower opportunity cost than what it cost them to produce. Even if a person has an absolute advantage in all goods, he does not have a comparative advantage in all goods. Comparative advantage determines who produces a good and who buys it; page 77.

Chapter 4

Demand and Supply

Chapter 4 studies the tools of demand and supply, which determine the quantities and prices of the goods and services produced and consumed and the quantities of the factors of production employed.

■ **Distinguish between quantity demanded and demand and explain what determines demand.**

The quantity demanded is the amount of any good, service, or resource that people are willing and able to buy during a specified period at a specified price. Demand is the relationship between the quantity demanded and the price of a good when all other influences on buying plans remain the same. The law of demand states that other things remaining the same, if the price of a good rises, the quantity demanded of that good decreases; and if the price of a good falls, the quantity demanded of that good increases. A demand curve is a graph of the relationship between the quantity demanded of a good and its price when all other influences on buying plans remain the same. A change in price leads to a *change in the quantity demanded* and a movement along the demand curve. Factors that *change demand* and shift the demand curve are prices of related goods; income; expectations; number of buyers; and preferences.

■ **Distinguish between quantity supplied and supply and explain what determines supply.**

The quantity supplied is the amount of any good, service, or resource that people are willing and able to sell during a specified period at a specified price. Supply is the relationship between the quantity supplied and the price of a good when all other influences on selling plans remain the same. The law of supply states that other things remaining the same, if the price of a good rises, the quantity supplied of that good increases; and if the price of a good falls, the quantity supplied of that good decreases. A supply curve is a graph of the relationship between the quantity supplied of a good and its price when all other influences on selling plans remain the same. A change in price leads to a *change in the quantity supplied* and a movement along the supply curve. Factors that *change supply* and shift the supply curve are prices of related goods; prices of resources and other inputs; expectations; number of sellers; and productivity.

■ **Explain how demand and supply determine price and quantity in a market and explain the effects of changes in demand and supply.**

The equilibrium price and equilibrium quantity occur when the quantity demanded equals the quantity supplied. An increase in demand raises the price and increases the quantity. An increase in supply lowers the price and increases the quantity. An increase in both demand and supply increases the quantity and the price might rise, fall, or not change. An increase in demand and a decrease in supply raises the price and the quantity might increase, decrease, or not change. Changes in demand and supply in the opposite direction lead to reverse changes in price and quantity.

EXPANDED CHAPTER CHECKLIST

When you have completed this chapter, you will be able to

1 **Distinguish between quantity demanded and demand and explain what determines demand.**

- Define quantity demanded and demand.
- State and explain the law of demand.
- Illustrate the law of demand using a demand schedule and a demand curve.
- Define market demand and derive the market demand curve from individual demand curves.
- List the influences on buying plans that change demand.
- Distinguish between a change in the quantity demanded and a change in demand.

2 **Distinguish between quantity supplied and supply and explain what determines supply.**

- Define quantity supplied and supply.
- State and explain the law of supply.
- Illustrate the law of supply using a supply schedule and a supply curve.
- Define market supply and derive the market supply curve from individual supply curves.
- List the influences on selling plans that change supply.
- Distinguish between a change in the quantity supplied and a change in supply.

3 **Explain how demand and supply determine price and quantity in a market and explain the effects of changes in demand and supply.**

- Find the equilibrium price and equilibrium quantity in a demand-supply graph.
- Indicate the amount of a surplus or shortage if the price is not the equilibrium price.

- Illustrate the effects of a change in demand and a change in supply separately and simultaneously.

KEY TERMS

- Change in demand (page 88)
- Change in the quantity demanded (page 88)
- Change in the quantity supplied (page 95)
- Change in supply (page 95)
- Complement (page 89)
- Complement in production (page 96)
- Demand (page 85)
- Demand curve (page 86)
- Demand schedule (page 86)
- Equilibrium price (page 99)
- Equilibrium quantity (page 99)
- Inferior good (page 89)
- Law of demand (page 85)
- Law of market forces (page 100)
- Law of supply (page 92)
- Market demand (page 87)
- Market equilibrium (page 99)
- Market supply (page 94)
- Normal good (page 89)
- Quantity demanded (page 85)
- Quantity supplied (page 92)
- Shortage or excess demand (page 100)
- Substitute (page 88)
- Substitute in production (page 95)
- Supply (page 92)
- Supply curve (page 93)
- Supply schedule (page 93)
- Surplus or excess supply (page 100)

CHECKPOINT 4.1

■ **Distinguish between quantity demanded and demand and explain what determines demand.**

Practice Problem 4.1

In the market for scooters, several events occur one at a time. Explain the influence of each event on the quantity demanded of scooters and on the demand for scooters. Illustrate the effects of each event by either a movement along the demand curve or a shift in the demand curve for scooters, and say which event (or events) illustrates the law of demand in action. These events are

a. The price of a scooter falls.

b. The price of a bicycle falls.

c. Citing rising injury rates, cities and towns ban scooters from sidewalks.

d. Income increases.

e. Rumour has it that the price of a scooter will rise next month.

f. Scooters become unfashionable and the number of buyers decreases.

Solution to Practice Problem 4.1

This problem studies the difference between a change in the quantity demanded and a change in demand.

Quick Review

*   *Change in the quantity demanded* A change in the quantity of a good that people plan to buy that results from a change in the price of the good.

*   *Change in demand* A change in the quantity that people plan to buy when any influence on buying plans other than the price of the good changes.

a. **The price of a scooter falls.**

A fall in the price of a scooter increases the quantity of scooters demanded, which is shown in the figure as a movement down along the demand curve. This event illustrates the law of demand in action.

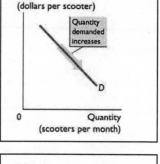

b. **The price of a bicycle falls.**

A fall in the price of a bicycle, which is a substitute for a scooter, decreases the demand for scooters. The demand curve for scooters shifts leftward in the figure from D_0 to D_1.

c. **Citing rising injury rates, cities and towns ban scooters from sidewalks.**

The ban on scooters changes preferences. The demand for scooters decreases and the demand curve for the scooters shifts leftward in the figure from D_0 to D_1.

d. **Income increases.**

The demand for scooters increases when income increases because a scooter is (likely) a normal good. The demand curve shifts rightward in the figure from D_0 to D_2.

e. **Rumour has it that the price of a scooter will rise next month.**

A rise in the expected future price of a scooter increases the demand for scooters now. The demand curve shifts rightward in the figure from D_0 to D_2.

f.   Scooters become unfashionable and the number of buyers decreases.

When the number of buyers decrease, the demand for scooters decreases. The demand curve shifts leftward in the figure from D_0 to D_1.

Additional Practice Problem 4.1a

Each year Anna, Ben, Carol, and Dana are willing and able to buy scooters for the neighbourhood children as shown in the following table.

Price (dollars per scooter)	Quantity demanded (scooters per year)			
	Anna	Ben	Carol	Dana
100	0	0	0	0
75	10	0	0	0
50	20	10	10	0
25	20	10	20	10

Using the information in the table:

a. Label the axes in Figure 4.1.

b. Graph the market demand curve.

■ FIGURE 4.1

Solution to Additional Practice Problem 4.1a

a.   Label the axes in Figure 4.1.

The axes are labelled in Figure 4.2

b.   Graph the market demand curve.

The market demand curve is derived by adding the quantities demanded by Anna, Ben, Carol, and Dana at each price. The market demand curve is illustrated in Figure 4.2.

■ FIGURE 4.2
Price (dollars per scooter)

Quantity (scooters per week)

■   Self Test 4.1

Fill in the blanks

The _____ (demand schedule; law of demand) states that other things remaining the same, if the price of a good rises, the _____ (quantity demanded of; demand for) that good decreases. A _____ (demand; quantity) curve is a graph of the relationship between the quantity demanded of a good and the price when all other influences on buying plans remain the same. An increase in demand shifts the demand curve _____ (leftward; rightward). A rise in the price of a good _____ (does; does not) shift its demand curve.

True or false

1.   The law of demand states that other things remaining the same, if the price of a good rises, the quantity demanded of that good increases.

2.   If the quantity of ice cream demanded at each price increases and other influences on buying plans do not change, there is a movement along the demand curve for ice cream.

3.   When Elizabeth's income increases, her demand for movies increases. For Elizabeth, movies are a normal good.

4.   A rise in the price of a computer increases the demand for computers because a computer is a normal good.

5. If income falls and all other influences on buying plans remain the same, the demand for computers will decrease and there will be a movement along the demand curve.

Multiple choice

1. The law of demand indicates that if Seneca College increases the price of tuition, all other things remaining the same _____ at Seneca College.

a. the demand for classes will decrease

b. the demand for classes will increase

c. the quantity of classes demanded will increase

d. the quantity of classes demanded will decrease

2. Other things remaining the same, the quantity of a good or service demanded will increase if the price of that good or service

a. rises.

b. falls.

c. does not change.

d. rises or falls.

3. If Phillip's demand for pop increases, everything else remaining the same

a. market demand increases.

b. market demand decreases.

c. market demand does not change.

d. there is a movement along the market demand curve.

4. One reason the demand for Dell laptop computers might increase is a

a. decrease in the price of a Dell laptop computer.

b. decrease in price of an Apple computer.

c. change in preferences as laptops have become more portable.

d. poor quality performance record for Dell laptop computers.

5. The number of buyers in the market for sport utility vehicles decreases sharply. As a result,

a. the demand curve for sport utility vehicles shifts leftward.

b. the demand curve for sport utility vehicles shifts rightward.

c. there is neither a shift nor a movement along the demand curve for sport utility vehicles.

d. there is a movement down along the demand curve for sport utility vehicles.

6. When moving along a demand curve, which of the following changes?

a. the consumers' incomes

b. the prices of other goods

c. the number of buyers

d. the price of the good

7. If the price of a CD falls,

a. the demand for CDs will increase and the demand curve for CDs will shift rightward.

b. the demand for CDs will be unaffected, so the demand curve for CDs will not shift.

c. the quantity of CDs demanded will increase and there will be a movement along the demand curve for CDs.

d. Both answers (b) and (c) are correct.

8. Pizza and tacos are substitutes. The price of a pizza rises. Which of the following correctly indicates what happens?

a. The demand for pizzas decreases and the demand for tacos increases.

b. The demand for both goods decreases.

c. The quantity of tacos demanded increases and the quantity of pizza demanded decreases.

d. The quantity of pizza demanded decreases and the demand for tacos increases.

Complete the graph

1. The demand schedule for cotton candy is given in the following table. In Figure 4.3, label the axes and draw the demand curve.

Price (dollars per bag of cotton candy)	Quantity (bags of cotton candy per month)
1	10,000
2	8,000
3	7,000
4	4,000

a. If the price of cotton candy is $2 a bag, what is the quantity of cotton candy demanded?

b. If the price of cotton candy is $3 a bag, what is the quantity of cotton candy demanded?

c. Does the demand curve slope upward or downward?

■ **FIGURE 4.3**

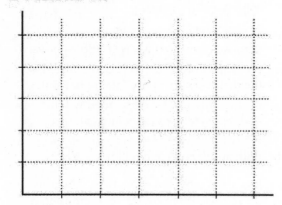

Short answer

1. Explain the difference between a change in the quantity demanded and a change in demand.

2. Explain the difference between a movement along a demand curve and a shift of a demand curve.

CHECKPOINT 4.2

■ Distinguish between quantity supplied and supply and explain what determines supply.

Practice Problem 4.2

In the market for timber beams, several events occur one at a time. Explain the influence of each event on the quantity supplied of timber beams and the supply of timber beams. Illustrate the effects of each event by either a movement along the supply curve or a shift in the supply curve of timber beams, and say which event (or events) illustrates the law of supply in action. These events are

a. The wage rate of sawmill workers rises.

b. The price of sawdust rises.

c. The price of a timber beam rises.

d. The price of a timber beam is expected to rise next year.

e. Environmentalists convince Parliament to introduce a new law that reduces the amount of forest that can be cut for timber products.

f. A new technology lowers the cost of producing timber beams.

Solution to Practice Problem 4.2

This problem studies the difference between a change in the quantity supplied and a change in supply.

Quick Review

• *Change in the quantity supplied* A change in the quantity of a good that suppliers plan to sell that results from a change in the price of the good.

• *Change in supply* A change in the quantity that suppliers plan to sell when any influence on selling plans other than the price of the good changes.

a. The wage rate of sawmill workers rises.

Sawmill workers are a resource used to produce timber beams. A rise in their wage rate decreases the supply of timber beams. The supply curve in the figure shifts leftward from S_0 to S_1.

b. The price of sawdust rises.

Sawdust is produced when timber beams are produced, so sawdust and timber beams are complements in production. A rise in the price of a complement in production increases the supply of timber beams and the supply curve of timber beams in the figure shifts rightward from S_0 to S_2.

c. The price of a timber beam rises.

A rise in the price of a timber beam increases the quantity of timber beams supplied. There is a movement up along the supply curve in the figure. This event illustrates the law of supply in action.

d. The price of a timber beam is expected to rise next year.

The higher expected price decreases the current supply of timber beams because producers plan to sell their timber beams next year when the price is higher. The supply curve in the figure shifts leftward from S_0 to S_1.

e. Environmentalists convince Parliament to introduce a new law that reduces the amount of forest that can be cut for timber products.

The new law decreases the supply of timber beams. The price of a tree, a resource for timber beams, rises. The supply curve of timber beams in the figure shifts leftward from S_0 to S_1.

f. A new technology lowers the cost of producing timber beams.

With the lower cost of production from the new technology, the supply of timber beams increases. The supply curve of timber beams in the figure shifts rightward from S_0 to S_2.

Additional Practice Problem 4.2a

Each month Eddy, Franco, George, and Helen are willing and able to sell plywood as shown in the following table.

Price (dollars per tonne of plywood)	Quantity supplied (tonnes of plywood per month)			
	Eddy	Franco	George	Helen
100	2	2	1	1
75	2	1	1	1
50	1	1	1	0
25	0	0	1	0

a. Label the axes in Figure 4.4.

b. Graph the market supply curve.

■ FIGURE 4.4

Solution to Additional Practice Problem 4.2a

a.   Label the axes in Figure 4.4.

The axes are labelled in Figure 4.5.

a.   Graph the market supply curve.

The market supply curve is derived by adding the quantities supplied by Eddy, Franco, George, and Helen at each price.

■ FIGURE 4.5
Price (dollars per tonne of plywood)

Quantity (tonnes of plywood per month)

■ Self Test 4.2

Fill in the blanks

The _____ (quantity supplied; supply) of a good is the amount people are willing and able to sell during a specified period at a specified price. The law of supply states that other things remaining the same, if the price of a good rises, the quantity supplied _____ (decreases; increases). A change in the price of a good changes _____ (supply; the quantity supplied) and is illustrated by a _____ (movement along; shift of) the supply curve. A decrease in supply shifts the supply curve _____ (leftward; rightward). A fall in the price of a good _____ (does; does not) shift its supply curve.

True or false

1.   The law of supply states that other things remaining the same, if the price of a good rises, the supply of the good increases.

2.   When new technology for producing computers is used by manufacturers, the supply of computers increases.

3.   If the wage rate paid to chefs rises and all other influences on selling plans remain the same, the supply of restaurant meals will increase.

4.   If the price of coffee is expected to rise next month, the supply of coffee this month will decrease.

5.   The supply of a good will increase and there will be a movement up along the supply curve of the good if the price of one of its substitutes in production falls.

Multiple choice

1.   The quantity supplied is the amount that people are _____ during a specified period at a specified price.

a.   able to sell

b.   willing to sell

c.   able and willing to sell

d.   willing and able to buy

2.   One reason a supply curve has an upward slope is because

a.   increased supply will require increased technology.

b.   people will pay a higher price when less is supplied.

c.   a higher price brings a greater return than before, so people want to sell more of that good.

d.   None of the above because supply curves have a downward slope.

3. Which of the following indicates that the law of supply applies to makers of pop?

a. An increase in the price of a pop leads to an increase in the demand for pop.

b. An increase in the price of a pop leads to an increase in the supply of pop.

c. An increase in the price of a pop leads to an increase in the quantity of pop supplied.

d. A decrease in the price of a pop leads to an increase in the quantity of pop demanded.

4. The market supply curve is the

a. horizontal sum of the individual supply curves.

b. vertical sum of the individual supply curves.

c. horizontal sum of the individual supply curves minus the market demand.

d. vertical sum of the individual supply curves minus the market demand.

5. If the price of pepperoni and cheese, ingredients used in the production of pizza, rise what will happen in the market for pizza?

a. The supply of pizza will decrease.

b. The quantity of pizzas supplied will increase as sellers try to cover their costs.

c. Pizza will cease to be produced and sold.

d. The demand curve for pizza will shift leftward when the price of a pizza increases.

6. A rise in the price of a substitute in production for a good will lead to

a. an increase in the supply of that good.

b. a decrease in the supply of that good.

c. no change in the supply of that good.

d. a decrease in the quantity of that good supplied.

7. A technological advance in the production of jeans will bring about which of the following?

a. The quantity of jeans supplied will increase.

b. The supply of jeans will increase.

c. The demand for jeans increases because they are now more efficiently produced.

d. The impact on the supply of jeans is impossible to predict.

8. Suppose the price of leather used to produce shoes increases. As a result, there is ____ in the supply of shoes and the supply curve of shoes shifts ____.

a. an increase; rightward

b. an increase; leftward

c. a decrease; rightward

d. a decrease; leftward

Complete the graph

1. The supply schedule for cotton candy is given in the following table. In Figure 4.6, label the axes and draw the supply curve.

Price (dollars per bag of cotton candy)	Quantity (bags of cotton candy per month)
1	4,000
2	8,000
3	10,000
4	12,000

a. If the price of cotton candy is $2 a bag, what is the quantity supplied?

b. If the price of cotton candy is $3 a bag, what is the quantity supplied?

c. Does the supply curve slope upward or downward?

■ **FIGURE 4.6**

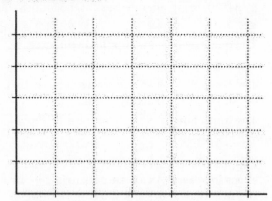

2. Figure 4.7 shows a supply curve of rubber bands. In Figure 4.7, illustrate the effect of a technological advance in the production of rubber bands.

■ **FIGURE 4.7**
Price (dollars per box of rubber bands)

Quantity (boxes of rubber bands per year)

3. Figure 4.8 shows a supply curve for copper. The cost of the natural gas used to refine copper ore into copper rises. In Figure 4.8, show the effect of this event.

■ **FIGURE 4.8**
Price (dollars per tonne of copper)

Quantity (tonnes of copper per year)

Short answer

1. What is the law of supply?

2. The following table gives the supply schedules for the three pizza producers in a small town.

Price (dollars per pizza)	Quantity supplied (pizzas per day)			
	Tom	Bob	Kate	Market supply
14	20	12	15	____
12	16	10	10	____
10	12	8	5	____
8	8	6	0	____

Calculate the market supply schedule in the last column.

3. What influence or influences cause a change in the quantity supplied?

4. What influence or influences cause a change in supply?

CHECKPOINT 4.3

■ **Explain how demand and supply determine price and quantity in a market and explain the effects of changes in demand and supply.**

Practice Problem 4.3

The table shows the demand and supply schedules for milk.

Price (dollars per carton)	Quantity demanded	Quantity supplied
	(cartons per day)	
1.00	200	110
1.25	175	130
1.50	150	150
1.75	125	170
2.00	100	190

a. What is the market equilibrium in the milk market?

b. Describe the situation in the milk market if the price were $1.75 a carton.

c. If the price is $1.75 a carton, explain how the market reaches equilibrium.

d. A drought decreases the quantity supplied by 45 cartons a day at each price. What is the new equilibrium and how does the market adjust to it?

e. Milk becomes more popular, and the quantity demanded increases by 5 cartons a day at each price. Improved feeds for dairy cows increase the quantity of milk supplied by 50 cartons a day at each price. If there is no drought, what is the new equilibrium, and how does the market adjust to it?

Solution to Practice Problem 4.3

This Practice Problem studies market equilibrium and shows how changes in demand and supply change the equilibrium price and equilibrium quantity.

Quick Review

• *Market equilibrium* When the quantity demanded equals the quantity supplied—when buyers' and sellers' plans are consistent.

a. What is the market equilibrium in the milk market?

Find the row in which the quantity supplied and the quantity demanded are equal. The quantity is 150 cartons a day, which is the equilibrium quantity, and the equilibrium price is $1.50 a carton.

b. Describe the situation in the milk market if the price were $1.75 a carton.

When the price is higher than the equilibrium price, the quantity supplied exceeds the quantity demanded, so there is a surplus. At a price of $1.75 a carton, the surplus is 170 cartons minus 125 cartons, which is 45 cartons a day.

c. If the price is $1.75 a carton, explain how the market reaches equilibrium.

At $1.75 a carton, there is a surplus of milk. The price begins to fall, the quantity demanded increases, the quantity supplied decreases, and the surplus decreases. The price falls until the surplus disappears at a price of $1.50 a carton.

d. A drought decreases the quantity supplied by 45 cartons a day at each price. What is the new equilibrium and how does the market adjust to it?

Supply decreases by 45 cartons a day at each price. The table shows the new supply schedule and the original demand schedule.

Price (dollars per carton)	Quantity demanded	New quantity supplied
	(cartons per day)	
1.00	200	65
1.25	175	85
1.50	150	105
1.75	125	125
2.00	100	145

At the original equilibrium price of $1.50 a carton, there is a shortage of milk. The price rises, the quantity of milk demanded decreases, and the quantity supplied increases. The new equilibrium price is $1.75 a carton and the new equilibrium quantity is 125 cartons a day.

e. **Milk becomes more popular and the quantity demanded increases by 5 cartons a day at each price. Improved feeds for dairy cows increase the quantity of milk supplied by 50 cartons a day at each price. If there is no drought, what is the new equilibrium, and how does the market adjust to it?**

The change in preferences increases demand by 5 cartons a day at each price and the improved feeds increase supply by 50 cartons a day at each price. The table shows the new quantity demanded and the new quantity supplied.

Price (dollars per carton)	New quantity demanded	New quantity supplied
	(cartons per day)	
1.00	205	160
1.25	180	180
1.50	155	200
1.75	130	220
2.00	105	240

A surplus exists at the initial equilibrium price of $1.50 a carton. The price falls, the quantity of milk demanded increases, and the quantity of milk supplied decreases. The new equilibrium price is $1.25 a carton and the new equilibrium quantity is 180 cartons a day.

Additional Practice Problem 4.3a

In the market for hot dogs, the price of a hot dog bun falls and the number of hot dog producers increases. The effect of the fall in the price of a hot dog bun is less than the effect of the increase in the number of producers. Describe the new market equilibrium.

Solution to Additional Practice Problem 4.3a

The fall in the price of a complement, hot dog buns, increases the demand for hot dogs. The demand curve for hot dogs shifts rightward in the figure from D_0 to D_1. The increase in
the number of producers increases the supply of hot dogs and the supply curve of hot dogs shifts rightward in the figure from S_0 to S_1. Because the increase in supply exceeds the increase in demand, the price of a hot dog falls and the quantity increases, as shown in the figure.

■ Self Test 4.3

Fill in the blanks

The price at which the quantity demanded equals the quantity supplied is the ____ (demand; equilibrium) price. If price exceeds the equilibrium price, the price ____ (rises; falls). An increase in demand ____ (raises; lowers) the equilibrium price and ____ (increases; decreases) the equilibrium quantity. An increase in supply ____ (raises; lowers) the equilibrium price and ____ (increases; decreases) the equilibrium quantity. If both the demand and supply increase, the equilibrium ____ (price; quantity) increases but the equilibrium ____ (price; quantity) rises, falls, or remains the same.

True or false

1. If the price of asparagus is below the equilibrium price, there is a shortage of asparagus and the price of asparagus will rise until the shortage disappears.

2. When the demand for skateboards decreases and the supply of skateboards remains unchanged, the quantity supplied of skateboards decreases as the price rises.

3. Automakers expect the price of a SUV to fall next season. If the demand for SUVs does not change, the equilibrium price of a SUV today will fall and the equilibrium quantity today will increase.

4. As winter sets in, the demand for and supply of hamburger buns decrease. The price of a hamburger bun will definitely remain the same.

5. The number of buyers of grapefruit juice increases and at the same time severe frost decreases the supply of grapefruit. The price of grapefruit juice will rise.

Multiple choice

1. At the equilibrium price, the

a. quantity of the good demanded equals the quantity of the good supplied.

b. quantity of the good demanded is greater than the quantity of the good supplied.

c. quantity of the good demanded is less than the quantity of the good supplied.

d. demand for the good is equal to the supply of the good.

2. Which of the following is correct?

a. A surplus puts downward pressure on the price of a good.

b. A shortage puts upward pressure on the price of a good.

c. There is no surplus or shortage at equilibrium.

d. All of the above answers are correct.

3. The number of buyers of ceiling fans increases. This increase leads to an increase in

a. the quantity of ceiling fans demanded and a surplus of ceiling fans.

b. the demand for ceiling fans and a rise in the price of a ceiling fan.

c. the demand for ceiling fans and a surplus of ceiling fans.

d. the supply of ceiling fans and no change in the price of a ceiling fan.

4. Which of the following is the best explanation for why the price of gasoline rises during the summer months?

a. Oil producers have lower costs of production in the summer.

b. More people walk or ride their bicycles to work in the summer.

c. Car travel increases in the summer as families go on their annual vacations.

d. Oil refineries increase production in the summer.

5. The price of lettuce used to produce tacos increases. The equilibrium price of a taco ____ and the equilibrium quantity ____.

a. rises; increases

b. rises; decreases

c. falls; increases

d. falls; decreases

6. Advances in technology associated with manufacturing computers have led to a _____ in the equilibrium price of a computer and ____ in the equilibrium quantity.

a. rise; an increase

b. rise; a decrease

c. fall; an increase

d. fall; a decrease

7. If the demand for Christmas trees and the supply of Christmas trees increase by the same amount, then the price of a Christmas tree ____ and the quantity of Christmas trees ____.

a. rises; does not change

b. falls; increases

c. does not change; increases

d. does not change; does not change

8. If the supply of gasoline decreases by a greater amount than the demand for gasoline increases, then the equilibrium price of gasoline _____ and the equilibrium quantity _____.

a. rises; decreases

b. rises; increases

c. rises; does not change

d. falls; does not change

Complete the graph

1. Figure 4.9 shows the demand and supply curves for cotton candy.

a. Describe the market for cotton candy when the price of cotton candy is $1 a bag.

b. Describe the market for cotton candy when the price of cotton candy is $3 a bag.

c. What is the equilibrium price and equilibrium quantity of cotton candy?

■ FIGURE 4.9

Price (dollars per bag of cotton candy)

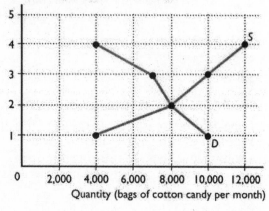

Quantity (bags of cotton candy per month)

Short answer

1. Define shortage and surplus.

2. The table gives the demand and supply schedules for sweatshirts.

Price (dollars per sweatshirt)	Quantity demanded (sweatshirts per season)	Quantity supplied (sweatshirts per season)
35	13	32
30	15	25
25	19	19
20	27	12
15	37	8

What is the equilibrium quantity and the equilibrium price of sweatshirts?

3. People read that drinking orange juice helps prevent heart disease. What is the effect on the equilibrium price and the equilibrium quantity of orange juice?

4. The cost of memory chips used in computers falls. What is the effect on the equilibrium price and equilibrium quantity of computers?

5. New cars are a normal good. Suppose autoworkers receive a pay increase. What is the effect on the price and quantity of new cars?

SELF TEST ANSWERS

■ **CHECKPOINT 4.1**

Fill in the blanks

The <u>law of demand</u> states that other things remaining the same, if the price of a good rises, the <u>quantity demanded of</u> that good decreases. A <u>demand</u> curve is a graph of the relationship between the quantity demanded of a good and the price when all other influences on buying plans remain the same. An increase in demand shifts the demand curve <u>rightward</u>. A rise in the price of a good <u>does not</u> shift its demand curve.

True or false

1. False; page 85
2. False; page 90
3. True; page 89
4. False; page 89
5. False; page 89

Multiple choice

1. d; page 85
2. b; page 85
3. a; page 87
4. c; page 89
5. a; page 90
6. d; page 90
7. d; page 90
8. d; pages 88-89

Complete the graph

1. Figure 4.10 shows the demand curve.
   a. 8,000 bags a month
   b. 7,000 bags a month
   c. The demand curve slopes downward; pages 85-86

Short answer

1. A change in the quantity demanded is a change in the quantity of a good that people plan to buy that results from a change in the price of the good. A change in demand is a change in the quantity that people plan to buy when any influence on buying plans other than the price of the good changes; page 88.

2. A movement along a demand curve shows a change in the quantity demanded. A shift of a demand curve shows a change in demand; page 90.

■ **FIGURE 4.10**

Price (dollars per bag of cotton candy)

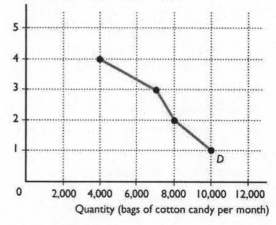

■ **CHECKPOINT 4.2**

Fill in the blanks

The <u>quantity supplied</u> of a good is the amount people are willing and able to sell during a specified period at a specified price. The law of supply states that other things remaining the same, if the price of a good rises, the quantity supplied <u>increases</u>. A change in the price of a good changes <u>the quantity supplied</u> and is illustrated by a <u>movement along</u> the supply curve. A decrease in supply shifts the supply curve <u>leftward</u>. A fall in the price of a good <u>does not</u> shift its supply curve.

True or false

1. False; page 92
2. True; page 96
3. False; page 96
4. True; page 96
5. False; page 97

Multiple choice

1. c; page 92
2. c; page 92
3. c; page 92
4. a; page 94
5. a; page 96
6. b; page 95
7. b; page 96
8. d; page 97

Complete the graph

1. Figure 4.11 shows the supply curve.

   a. 8,000 bags a month.

   b. 10,000 bags a month.

   c. The supply curve slopes upward; page 93

■ FIGURE 4.11

Price (dollars per bag of cotton candy)

Quantity (bags of cotton candy per month)

2. An advance in technology increases supply. Figure 4.12 shows the rightward shift of the supply curve from S_0 to S_1; pages 96-97.

■ FIGURE 4.12

Price (dollars per box of rubber bands)

Quantity (boxes of rubber bands per year)

3. A rise in the price of a resource decreases supply. Figure 4.13 shows the leftward shift of the supply curve from S_0 to S_1; pages 96-97

■ FIGURE 4.13

Price (dollars per tonne of copper)

Quantity (tonnes of copper per year)

Short answer

1. Other things remaining the same, if the price of a good rises, the quantity supplied of that good increases; and if the price of a good falls, the quantity supplied of that good decreases ; page 92.

2. The market supply schedule is in the following table; page 94.

Price (dollars per pizza)	Market supply (pizzas per day)
14	47
12	36
10	25
8	14

3. Change in the price of the good; page 95.

4. Changes in: prices of related goods; prices of resources and other inputs; expectations; number of sellers; and productivity; page 95.

■ CHECKPOINT 4.3

Fill in the blanks

The price at which the quantity demanded equals the quantity supplied is the equilibrium price. If price exceeds the equilibrium price, the price falls. An increase in demand raises the equilibrium price and increases the equilibrium quantity. An increase in supply lowers the equilibrium price and increases the equilibrium quantity. If both the demand and supply increase, the equilibrium quantity increases but the equilibrium price rises, falls, or remains the same.

True or false

1. True; page 100
2. False; page 101
3. True; page 102
4. False; page 104
5. True; page 105

Multiple choice

1. a; page 99
2. d; page 100
3. b; page 101
4. c; page 101
5. b; page 102
6. c; page 102

7. c; page 104
8. a; page 105

Complete the graph

1. a. A shortage of 6,000 bags a month; page 100.

   b. A surplus of 3,000 bags a month; page 100.

   c. The equilibrium price is $2 a bag of cotton candy and the equilibrium quantity is 8,000 bags a month; page 99.

Short answer

1. A shortage is a situation in which the quantity demanded exceeds the quantity supplied. A surplus is a situation in which the quantity supplied exceeds the quantity demanded; page 100.

2. The equilibrium price is $25 a sweatshirt. The equilibrium quantity is 19 sweatshirts a season; page 99.

3. The change in preferences increases the demand for orange juice. The equilibrium price of orange juice rises and the equilibrium quantity increases; page 101.

4. The fall in the cost of the memory chips increases the supply of computers. The equilibrium price of a computer falls and the equilibrium quantity increases; page 102.

5. The pay increase received by autoworkers increases income and the demand for new cars increases. The autoworkers are a resource used to produce cars, so the increase in pay decreases the supply of new cars. When demand increases and supply decreases, the price of a new car rises, but the equilibrium quantity can increase, decrease, or remain the same; page 105.

Elasticities of Demand and Supply

Chapter

5

In Chapter 5 we study the price elasticity of demand, the price elasticity of supply, the cross elasticity of demand, and the income elasticity of demand.

■ **Define price elasticity of demand, explain the factors that influence it, and calculate it.**

The price elasticity of demand is a measure of the extent to which the quantity demanded of a good changes when the price of the good changes and all other influences on buyers' plans remain the same. The price elasticity of demand equals the percentage change in the quantity demanded divided by the percentage change in price. Demand is elastic if the percentage change in the quantity demanded exceeds the percentage change in price. Demand is unit elastic if the percentage change in the quantity demanded equals the percentage change in price. Demand is inelastic if the percentage change in the quantity demanded is less than the percentage change in price. Elasticity is a *units-free* measure. Along a linear demand curve demand is unit elastic at the midpoint of the curve, demand is elastic at all points above the midpoint of the curve, and demand is inelastic at all points below the midpoint of the curve. The total revenue from the sale of a good equals the price of the good multiplied by the quantity sold. If price and total revenue change in opposite directions, demand is elastic. If a price change leaves total revenue unchanged, demand is unit elastic. If price and total revenue change in the same direction, demand is inelastic.

■ **Define price elasticity of supply, explain the factors that influence it, and calculate it.**

The price elasticity of supply is a measure of the extent to which the quantity supplied of a good changes when the price of the good changes and all other influences on sellers' plans remain the same. The two main influences on the price elasticity of supply are production possibilities and storage possibilities. The price elasticity of supply equals the percentage change in the quantity supplied divided by the percentage change in the price. If the price elasticity of supply is greater than 1, supply is elastic. If the price elasticity of supply equals 1, supply is unit elastic. If the price elasticity of supply is less than 1, supply is inelastic.

■ **Define cross elasticity of demand and income elasticity of demand and explain the factors that influence them.**

The cross elasticity of demand is a measure of the extent to which the demand for a good changes when the price of a substitute or complement changes, other things remaining the same. The cross elasticity of demand is positive for a substitute and negative for a complement. The income elasticity of demand is a measure of the extent to which the demand for a good changes when income changes, other things remaining the same. The income elasticity of demand is positive for a normal good and negative for an inferior good.

EXPANDED CHAPTER CHECKLIST

When you have completed this chapter, you will be able to

1 **Define price elasticity of demand, explain the factors that influence it, and calculate it.**

- Define price elasticity of demand.
- Use the midpoint method to calculate the percentage change in price and the percentage change in the quantity demanded.
- Define elastic demand, unit elastic demand, and inelastic demand.
- Use a graph to illustrate perfectly elastic demand and perfectly inelastic demand.
- List and explain the influences on the price elasticity of demand.
- Calculate price elasticity of demand.
- Discuss elasticity along a linear demand curve.
- Use the total revenue test to estimate the price elasticity of demand.
- Discuss the relationship between farm prices and total revenue.
- Explain how we can use price elasticity of demand to design effective policies for dealing with addiction to drugs.

2 **Define price elasticity of supply, explain the factors that influence it, and calculate it.**

- Define price elasticity of supply.
- Define elastic supply, unit elastic supply, and inelastic supply.
- Use a graph to illustrate perfectly elastic supply and perfectly inelastic supply.
- List and explain the influences on the price elasticity of supply.
- Calculate price elasticity of supply.

3 **Define cross elasticity of demand and income elasticity of demand and explain the factors that influence them.**

- Define and calculate the cross elasticity of demand and explain when the cross elasticity of demand is positive and when it is negative.
- Define and calculate the income elasticity of demand and discuss the three ranges into which the income elasticity of demand falls.

KEY TERMS

- Cross elasticity of demand (page 129)
- Elastic demand (page 114)
- Elastic supply (page 124)
- Income elasticity of demand (page 130)
- Inelastic demand (page 114)
- Inelastic supply (page 124)
- Perfectly elastic demand (page 114)
- Perfectly elastic supply (page 124)
- Perfectly inelastic demand (page 114)
- Perfectly inelastic supply (page 124)
- Price elasticity of demand (page 112)
- Price elasticity of supply (page 124)
- Total revenue (page 120)
- Total revenue test (page 120)
- Unit elastic demand (page 114)
- Unit elastic supply (page 124)

CHECKPOINT 5.1

■ **Define price elasticity of demand, explain the factors that influence it, and calculate it.**

Practice Problem 5.1

A 10 percent increase in the price of a good has led to a 2 percent decrease in the quantity demanded of that good.

a. How would you describe the demand for this good?

b. Are substitutes for this good easy to find or does it have poor substitutes?

c. Is this good more likely to be a necessity or a luxury? Why?

d. Is this good more likely to be narrowly or broadly defined? Why?

e. Calculate the price elasticity of demand for this good.

f. Has the total revenue from the sale of the good changed? Explain your answer.

g. The good might be which of the following goods: orange juice, bread, toothpaste, concert tickets, clothing, blue jeans, Stanley Cup tickets? Why?

Solution to Practice Problem 5.1

The practice problem concentrates on the differences between elastic and inelastic demand.

Quick Review

• *Elastic demand* When the percentage change in the quantity demanded exceeds the percentage change in price.

• *Inelastic demand* When the percentage change in the quantity demanded is less than the percentage change in price.

a. How would you describe the demand for this good?

The demand for the good is inelastic because the percentage change in the quantity demanded is less than the percentage change in the price.

b. Are substitutes for this good easy to find or does it have poor substitutes?

The demand for a good is inelastic when a substitute for it is hard to find. Because demand is inelastic, this good probably has poor substitutes.

c. Is this good more likely to be a necessity or a luxury? Why?

This good is probably a necessity. An example of a necessity is food. A necessity has poor substitutes — you must eat — so the demand for a necessity is inelastic.

d. Is this good more likely to be narrowly or broadly defined? Why?

The good is probably broadly defined. The demand for a broadly defined good is inelastic. For example, the demand for a particular brand of coffee is elastic because another brand of coffee is a good substitute. But the demand for coffee is inelastic because tea is a poor substitute for it.

e. Calculate the price elasticity of demand for this good.

Price elasticity of demand equals the percentage change in the quantity demanded divided by the percentage change in the price, which is (2 percent) ÷ (10 percent) = 0.2.

f. Has the total revenue from the sale of the good changed? Explain your answer.

When demand for a good is inelastic, price and total revenue change in the same direction. So when the price rises, total revenue increases.

g. The good might be which of the following goods: orange juice, bread, toothpaste, concert tickets, clothing, blue jeans, Stanley Cup tickets? Why?

The good might be bread because bread is a necessity. The good might be toothpaste because toothpaste has poor substitutes. Or the good might be clothing because clothing is broadly defined.

Additional Practice Problem 5.1a

The table gives the demand schedule for bags of cat food.

Price (dollars per bag of cat food)	Quantity demanded (bags of cat food per year)	Total revenue (dollars)
5	4	____
4	8	____
3	12	____
2	16	____
1	20	____

A graph of this demand schedule gives a linear demand curve.

a. Finish the table by calculating the total revenue for each row.

b. When is the demand elastic? inelastic? unit elastic?

c. Explain your answers to part (b).

Solution to Additional Practice Problem 5.1a

a. Finish the table by calculating the total revenue for each row.

The completed table is below.

Price (dollars per bag of cat food)	Quantity demanded (bags of cat food per year)	Total revenue (dollars)
5	4	20
4	8	32
3	12	36
2	16	32
1	20	20

Total revenue equals price times the quantity sold.

b. When is the demand elastic? inelastic? unit elastic?

The demand is elastic at prices greater than $3 a bag. The demand is inelastic at prices less than $3 a bag. The demand is unit elastic at a price of $3 a bag.

c. Explain your answers to part (b).

Demand is unit elastic at the midpoint of the demand curve. When demand is unit elastic, a price change leaves total revenue unchanged. The midpoint of the curve occurs when the price is $3 a bag, so demand is unit elastic at a price of $3 a bag.

Demand is elastic at all points above the midpoint of the demand curve. When demand is elastic, price and total revenue change in opposite directions. So when the price is greater than $3 a bag, demand is elastic. For example, when the price rises from $4 a bag to $5 a bag, total revenue decreases from $32 to $20.

Demand is inelastic at all points below the midpoint of the demand curve. When demand is inelastic, price and total revenue change in the same direction. So when the price is less than $3 a bag, demand is inelastic. For example, when the price rises from $1 a bag to $2 a bag, total revenue increases from $20 to $32.

■ Self Test 5.1

Fill in the blanks

To calculate the percentage change in price, the midpoint formula divides the change in price by the _____ (initial price; new price; average of the initial and the new price) and then multiplies by 100. If the percentage change in the quantity demanded exceeds the percentage change in the price, demand is _____ (elastic; inelastic). The demand for a good is elastic if a substitute for it is _____ (difficult; easy) to find. The price elasticity of demand equals the percentage change in the _____ (price; quantity demanded) divided by the percentage change in the _____ (price; quantity demanded). Moving along a straight-line demand curve, the slope _____ (is constant; varies) and the elasticity _____ (is constant; varies). If demand is elastic, an increase in price _____ (increases; decreases) total revenue.

True or false

1. The price elasticity of demand equals the magnitude of the slope of the demand curve.

2. If the price increases by 10 percent and the quantity demanded decreases by 8 percent, the price elasticity of demand equals 1.25.

3. If as the price of a good increases, the quantity demanded of it remains the same, then demand for the good is perfectly inelastic.

4. Above the midpoint of a straight-line demand curve, demand is elastic.

5. When the price of a service increases by 5 percent the quantity demanded decreases by 5 percent. Total revenue remains unchanged.

Multiple choice

1. The price elasticity of demand is a measure of the extent to which the quantity demanded of a good changes when ____ changes and all other influences on buyers' plans remain the same.

a. income changes
b. the price of a related good
c. the price of the good
d. the demand

2. According to the midpoint method, what is the percentage change in the price of a movie when the price falls from $9 to $7?

a. 33 percent
b. –33 percent
c. 25 percent
d. –25 percent

3. Demand for a good is elastic if

a. the percentage change in the quantity demanded exceeds the percentage change in price.
b. a large percentage change in price brings about a small percentage change in quantity demanded.
c. a small percentage change in price brings about a small percentage change in quantity demanded.
d. the quantity demanded does not change when the price changes.

4. If when the price of natural gas increases the quantity demanded decreases only a little, the demand for natural gas is

a. inelastic.
b. elastic.
c. unit elastic.
d. perfectly elastic.

5. If substitutes for a good are readily available, the demand for that good will

a. be small.
b. be elastic.
c. be inelastic.
d. not change substantially if the price changes.

6. If the price of a good increases by 5 percent and the quantity demanded decreases by 5 percent, then the elasticity of demand is

a. 0.
b. 1.
c. indeterminate.
d. 5.

7. The price of a bag of pretzels rises from $2 to $3 and the quantity demanded decreases from 100 to 60. What is the price elasticity of demand?

a. 1.0
b. 1.25
c. 40.0
d. 20.0

8. When a firm raises the price of its product, what happens to total revenue?

a. If demand is elastic, total revenue will decrease.
b. If demand is unit elastic, total revenue will increase.
c. If demand is inelastic, total revenue will decrease.
d. If demand is elastic, total revenue will increase.

Complete the graph

1. In Figure 5.1, label the axes and draw a demand curve for a good that has a perfectly elastic demand.

■ **FIGURE 5.1**

2. In Figure 5.2, label the point on the demand curve at which demand is unit elastic.

■ **FIGURE 5.2**

Price (dollars per unit)

Quantity (units per month)

Short answer

1. Complete the table below by calculating the price elasticity of demand.

	Percentage change in price	Percentage change in quantity demanded	Price elasticity of demand
A	5	10	____
B	8	4	____
C	3	0	____
D	6	6	____
E	1	8	____

a. Which row has the most elastic demand?

b. Which row has the least elastic demand?

2. Suppose the price elasticity of demand for oil is 0.3. If the quantity of oil demanded decreases by 6 percent, what will be the effect on the price of oil?

3. What does it mean when the demand for a good is inelastic?

4. What is the relationship between how narrowly a good is defined and the number of substitutes it has?

5. What is the relationship between a rise in price, the elasticity of demand for the good, and the change in total revenue?

CHECKPOINT 5.2

■ **Define price elasticity of supply, explain the factors that influence it, and calculate it.**

Practice Problem 5.2

You are told that a 10 percent increase in the price of a good has led to a 1 percent increase in the quantity supplied of the good after one month. Use this information to answer the following questions:

a. How would you describe the supply of this good?

b. What can you say about the production possibilities of this good?

c. Calculate the price elasticity of supply.

d. If after one year, the quantity supplied has increased by 25 percent, describe how the supply has changed over the year.

e. Calculate the elasticity of supply after one year.

Solution to Practice Problem 5.2

To calculate the price elasticity of supply we divide the percentage change in the quantity supplied by the percentage change in price.

Quick Review

- *Price elasticity of supply* A measure of the extent to which the quantity supplied of a good changes when the price of the good changes and all other influences on sellers' plans remain the same.

a. **How would you describe the supply of this good?**

The supply of this good is inelastic because the percentage change in the quantity supplied is less than the percentage change in the price.

b. **What can you say about the production possibilities of this good?**

The factors of production that are used to produce this good are likely to be quite unique because the percentage increase in the quantity supplied after one month is not large.

c. **Calculate the price elasticity of supply.**

The price elasticity of supply is the percentage change in the quantity supplied divided by the percentage change in price, which is (1 percent) ÷ (10 percent) = 0.1.

d. **If after one year, the quantity supplied has increased by 25 percent, describe how the supply has changed over the year.**

The supply of the good has become more elastic during the year. With the increase in price more producers have entered the market.

e. **Calculate the elasticity of supply after one year.**

The price elasticity of supply equals the percentage change in the quantity supplied divided by percentage change in price, which is (25 percent) ÷ (10 percent) = 2.5.

Additional Practice Problem 5.2a

Over one month the elasticity of supply of avocados is 0.1 and over 5 years the elasticity of supply of avocados is 2.0. If the price of an avocado rises 10 percent, what is the percentage increase in the quantity supplied in one month and in 5 years? Why is there a difference in the quantities?

Solution to Additional Practice Problem 5.2a

The percentage increase in the quantity supplied equals the percentage change in the price times the elasticity of supply. In one month, the quantity supplied increases by (10 percent) × (0.1), which is 1 percent. In 5 years, the quantity supplied increases by (10 percent) × (2.0), which is 20 percent. The increase in the quantity supplied is much greater after 5 years because eventually, additional avocado trees can be planted, mature, and then be harvested. The supply of avocados becomes more elastic as time passes.

■ Self Test 5.2

Fill in the blanks

When a good has a vertical supply curve, then the supply of the good is perfectly ____ (elastic; inelastic). Goods that can be produced at an almost constant opportunity cost have an ____ (elastic; inelastic) supply. As time passes, the elasticity of supply ____ (increases; decreases). The price elasticity of supply equals the percentage change in the ____ (price; quantity supplied) divided by the percentage change in the ____ (price; quantity supplied).

True or false

1. If the percentage change in the quantity supplied is zero when the price changes, supply is perfectly elastic.

2. Goods that are produced at a constant opportunity cost have an elastic supply.

3. The supply of apples is perfectly elastic on the day of a price change.

4. The supply of a storable good is perfectly inelastic.

5. When the price of a pizza is $20, 10 pizzas are supplied and when the price rises to $30 a pizza, 14 pizzas are supplied. The price elasticity of supply of pizzas is 0.83.

Multiple choice

1. The price elasticity of supply is a measure of the extent to which the quantity supplied of a good changes when the _____ and all other influences on sellers' plans remain the same.

   a. cost of producing the product increases
   b. quantity of the good demanded increases
   c. supply increases
   d. price of the good changes

2. When the percentage change in the quantity supplied exceeds the percentage change in price, then the good has _____ supply.

   a. an elastic
   b. an inelastic
   c. a unit elastic
   d. a perfectly inelastic

3. The supply of lakefront property in Muskoka is

   a. elastic.
   b. unit elastic.
   c. negative.
   d. inelastic.

4. If a good has a rapidly increasing opportunity cost of producing additional units, we would expect that _____ that good is _____.

   a. demand for; elastic
   b. supply of; elastic
   c. demand for; inelastic
   d. supply of; inelastic

5. The greater the amount of time that passes after a price change, the

   a. less elastic supply becomes.
   b. more elastic supply becomes.
   c. more negative supply becomes.
   d. more positive supply becomes.

6. The price elasticity of supply equals the percentage change in the

   a. quantity demanded divided by the percentage change in the price of a substitute.
   b. quantity supplied divided by the percentage change in price.
   c. quantity demanded divided by the percentage change in price.
   d. quantity demanded divided by the percentage change in income.

7. If a firm supplies 200 units at a price of $50 and 100 units at a price of $40, what is the price elasticity of supply?

   a. 0.33
   b. 1.00
   c. 3.00
   d. 0

8. If the price of a good increases by 10 percent and the quantity supplied increases by 5 percent, then the elasticity of supply is

   a. greater than one and supply is elastic.
   b. negative and supply is inelastic.
   c. less than one and supply is elastic.
   d. less than one and supply is inelastic.

Complete the graph

1. In Figure 5.3, label the axes and then draw a supply curve for a good that has a perfectly inelastic supply.

■ **FIGURE 5.3**

Short answer

1. If the elasticity of supply of wheat is 0.3 and the price of wheat rises 10 percent, what is the increase in the quantity of wheat supplied? If the elasticity of supply of magazines is 1.3 and the price of a magazine rises 10 percent, what is the increase in the quantity of magazines supplied?

2. The table gives a supply schedule.

	Price (dollars)	Quantity supplied (units per week)
A	5	10
B	15	30
C	25	50
D	35	90

    Calculate the price elasticity of supply between points A and B; between points B and C; and between points C and D.

3. Describe the elasticity of supply of a good that can be stored.

4. Why does the elasticity of supply increase as time passes after a price change?

CHECKPOINT 5.3

■ **Define cross elasticity of demand and income elasticity of demand and explain the factors that influence them.**

Practice Problem 5.3

1. If the quantity demanded of good A increases by 5 percent when the price of good B rises by 10 percent and other things remain the same,

a. Are goods A and B complements or substitutes? Why?

b. Describe how the demand for good A changes.

c. Calculate the cross elasticity of demand of good A with respect to good B.

2. If, when income rises by 5 percent and other things remain the same, the quantity demanded of good C increases by 1 percent,

a. Is good C a normal good or an inferior good? Why?

b. Describe how the demand for good C changes when income increases.

c. Calculate the income elasticity of demand for good C.

Solution to Practice Problem 5.3

This practice problem studies cross elasticity of demand and income elasticity of demand. Remember that when you calculate the cross elasticity of demand for a good that you must divide by the percentage change in the price of one of the good's substitutes or complements.

Quick Review

*   *Cross elasticity of demand* A measure of the extent to which the demand for a good changes when the price of a substitute or complement changes, other things remaining the same.

*   *Income elasticity of demand* A measure of the extent to which the demand for a good changes when income changes, other things remaining the same.

1a. Are goods A and B complements or substitutes? Why?

A rise in the price of a substitute brings an increase in the quantity demanded of the good. A rise in the price of good B increases the quantity of good A demanded, so A and B are substitutes.

1b. Describe how the demand for good A changes.

As the price of good B rises, the demand for good A increases and the demand curve for good A shifts rightward.

1c. Calculate the cross elasticity of demand of good A with respect to good B.

The cross elasticity of demand equals the percentage change in the quantity demanded of good *A* divided by the percentage change in the price of good *B*, which is (5 percent) ÷ (10 percent) = 0.50.

2a. Is good *C* a normal good or an inferior good? Why?

Good *C* is a normal good because when income increases the quantity demanded increases.

2b. Describe how the demand for good *C* changes when income increases.

As income increases, the demand for good *C* increases and its demand curve shifts rightward.

2c. Calculate the income elasticity of demand for good *C*.

The income elasticity of demand equals the percentage change in the quantity demanded divided by the percentage change in income, which is (1 percent) ÷ (5 percent) = 0.20.

Additional Practice Problem 5.3a

Pepsi and Coke are substitutes. Pepsi and Tropicana juice also are substitutes. Which pair of substitutes has the larger cross elasticity of demand?

Solution to Additional Practice Problem 5.3a

For many people, Pepsi and Coke are close substitutes. A slight rise in the price of a Coke increases the quantity of Pepsi demanded significantly. The cross elasticity is large. Pepsi and Tropicana juice are less close substitutes. An increase in the price of Tropicana orange increases the demand for Pepsi by a small amount and the cross elasticity is small.

■ **Self Test 5.3**

Fill in the blanks

The _____ (price; cross; income) elasticity of demand is a measure of the extent to which the demand for a good changes when the price of a substitute or complement changes, other things remaining the same. The cross elasticity of demand is _____ (positive; negative) for a complement. The income elasticity of demand equals the percentage change in _____ (quantity demanded;

income) divided by the percentage change in _____ (the quantity demanded; income). The income elasticity of demand is _____ (positive; negative) for a normal good.

True or false

1. If the cross elasticity of demand is negative, the two goods are substitutes.

2. If the cross elasticity between hamburgers and hot dogs is positive, then hamburgers and hot dogs are substitutes.

3. An inferior good has a negative income elasticity of demand.

4. When the income elasticity of demand of a good is positive, the good is a normal good.

5. A normal good is a good that has a positive cross elasticity of demand

Multiple choice

1. The measure used to determine whether two goods are complements or substitutes is the

    a. price elasticity of supply.

    b. cross elasticity of demand.

    c. price elasticity of demand.

    d. income elasticity.

2. If beef and pork are substitutes, the cross elasticity of demand between the two goods

    a. is negative.

    b. is positive.

    c. cannot be determined.

    d. is elastic.

3. When the price of a pizza is $10, the quantity of pop demanded is 300 cans. When the price of pizza is $15, the quantity of pop demanded is 100 cans. The cross elasticity of demand of pop with respect to pizza is

    a. –0.25.

    b. –0.40.

    c. –2.50.

    d. –25.00.

4. If two goods have a cross elasticity of –2, then when the price of one good increases, the demand curve of the other good

a. shifts rightward.

b. shifts leftward.

c. remains unchanged.

d. may shift rightward, leftward or remain unchanged.

5. Income elasticity of demand equals the percentage change in

a. quantity demanded divided by the percentage change in the price of a substitute.

b. quantity supplied divided by the percentage change in price.

c. quantity demanded divided by the percentage change in price.

d. quantity demanded divided by the percentage change in income.

6. When income increases from $20,000 to $30,000 the number of home delivered pizzas per evening increases from 22 to 40. The income elasticity of demand for home delivered pizza equals

a. 1.45.

b 0.69.

c. 0.58.

d. 0.40.

7. If a good is a normal good, then its income elasticity of demand is

a. zero.

b. positive.

c. negative.

d. indeterminate.

8. The income elasticity of demand for used cars is less than zero. A used car is

a. an inferior good.

b. a normal good.

c. an inelastic good.

d. a perfectly inelastic good.

Complete the graph

1. The income elasticity of demand for large screen televisions is positive. In Figure 5.4, show how the demand for large screen televisions changes when income increases.

■ **FIGURE 5.4**

Price (dollars per large screen television)

Quantity (large screen televisions per year)

Short answer

1. The income elasticity of demand for inter-city bus trips is negative. What does this fact tell you about inter-city bus trips?

2. Complete the table below.

	Percentage change in income	Percentage change in quantity demanded	Income elasticity of demand
A	5	10	____
B	5	–10	____
C	5	2	____
D	6	6	____

Which row indicates an inferior good and which row indicates a good that is income elastic?

SELF TEST ANSWERS

■ CHECKPOINT 5.1

Fill in the blanks

To calculate the percentage change in price, the midpoint formula divides the change in price by the <u>average of the initial and the new price</u> and then multiplies by 100. If the percentage change in the quantity demanded exceeds the percentage change in the price, demand is <u>elastic</u>. The demand for a good is elastic if a substitute for it is <u>easy</u> to find. The price elasticity of demand equals the percentage change in the <u>quantity demanded</u> divided by the percentage change in the <u>price</u>. Moving along a straight-line demand curve, the slope <u>is constant</u> and the elasticity <u>varies</u>. If demand is elastic, an increase in price <u>decreases</u> total revenue.

True or false

1. False; page 116
2. False; page 116
3. True; page 114
4. True; page 118
5. True; page 120

Multiple choice

1. c; page 112
2. d; page 112
3. a; page 114
4. a; page 114
5. b; page 114
6. b; page 116
7. b; page 116
8. a; page 120

Complete the graph

1. Figure 5.5 labels the axes and illustrates a demand curve for a good with perfectly elastic demand; page 115.

■ **FIGURE 5.5**

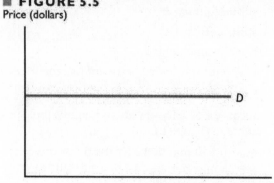

Price (dollars)

Quantity (units per year)

2. In Figure 5.6, demand is unit elastic at the midpoint of the curve; page 118.

■ **FIGURE 5.6**

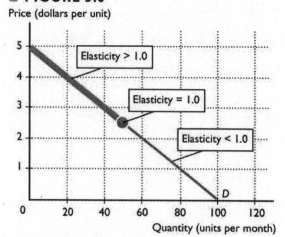

Price (dollars per unit)

Short answer

1. The complete table is below; page 116.

	Percentage change in price	Percentage change in quantity demanded	Price elasticity of demand
A	5	10	2.0
B	8	4	0.5
C	3	0	0.0
D	6	6	1.0
E	1	8	8.0

a. The most elastic demand is in row E; page 116.

b. The least elastic demand is in row C (the demand is perfectly inelastic); page 116.

2. The price rises by 20 percent; page 116.

3. Demand is inelastic if the percentage change in the quantity demanded is less than the percentage change in price; page 114.

4. The more narrow the definition of the good, the more substitutes exist. For example, there are more substitutes for a slice of Pizza Hut pizza than for pizza in general; page 116.

5. When the price of a good rises, total revenue increases if demand is inelastic, total revenue does not change if demand is unit elastic, and total revenue decreases if demand is elastic; page 120.

■ CHECKPOINT 5.2

Fill in the blanks

When a good has a vertical supply curve, then the supply of the good is perfectly <u>inelastic</u>. Goods that can be produced at an almost constant opportunity cost have an <u>elastic</u> supply. As time passes, the elasticity of supply <u>increases</u>. The price elasticity of supply equals the percentage change in the <u>quantity supplied</u> divided by the percentage change in the <u>price</u>.

True or false

1. False; page 124

2. True; page 124

3. False; page 126

4. False; page 126

5. True; page 126

Multiple choice

1. d; page 124

2. a; page 124

3. d; page 124

4. d; page 124

5. b; page 126

6. b; page 126

7. c; page 126

8. d; page 126

Complete the graph

1. Figure 5.7 labels the axes and illustrates a supply curve for a good with a perfectly inelastic supply; page 125.

■ FIGURE 5.7

Price (dollars)

Quantity (units per year)

Short answer

1. If the price of wheat rises 10 percent, the increase in the quantity supplied equals (10 percent) × (0.3) = 3 percent. If the price of a magazine rises 10 percent, the increase in the quantity supplied equals (10 percent) × (1.3) = 13 percent; page 126.

2. The price elasticity of supply between points *A* and *B* is 1.00; between points *B* and *C* is 1.00; and between points *C* and *D* is 1.71; page 126.

3. The elasticity of supply of a good that can be stored depends on the decision to keep the good in storage or offer it for sale. A small price change can make a big difference to this decision, so the supply of a storable good is highly elastic; page 126.

4. As time passes after a price change, it becomes easier to change production plans and supply becomes more elastic. For example, many manufactured goods have an inelastic supply if production plans have had only a short period in which to change. But after all

the technologically possible ways of adjusting production have been exploited, supply is extremely elastic for most manufactured items; page 126.

■ CHECKPOINT 5.3

Fill in the blanks

The <u>cross</u> elasticity of demand is a measure of the extent to which the demand for a good changes when the price of a substitute or complement changes, other things remaining the same. The cross elasticity of demand is <u>negative</u> for a complement. The income elasticity of demand equals the percentage change in <u>quantity demanded</u> divided by the percentage change in <u>income</u>. The income elasticity of demand is <u>positive</u> for a normal good.

True or false

1. False; page 129
2. True; page 129
3. True; page 130
4. True; page 130
5. False; page 130

Multiple choice

1. b; page 129
2. b; page 129
3. c; page 129
4. b; pages 129-130
5. d; page 130
6. a; page 130
7. b; page 130
8. a; page 130

Complete the graph

1. Because the income elasticity of demand is positive, large screen televisions are a normal good. In Figure 5.8 an increase in income shifts the demand curve rightward from D_0 to D_1; page 130.

■ FIGURE 5.8

Price (dollars per large screen television)

Quantity (large screen televisions per year)

Short answer

1. The fact that the income elasticity of demand for inter-city bus trips is negative indicates that an inter-city bus trip is an inferior good. When people's incomes increase, they take fewer inter-city bus trips and instead fly, drive, or take the train; page 130.

2. The completed table is below. The good in Row B is an inferior good. The good in row A is income elastic; page 130.

	Percentage change in income	Percentage change in quantity demanded	Income elasticity of demand
A	5	10	2.0
B	5	−10	−2.0
C	5	2	0.4
D	6	6	1.0

Efficiency and Fairness of Markets

Chapter 6

In Chapter 6 we study the equilibrium quantities of goods, services, and factors of production to determine if markets are efficient. Chapter 6 also studies the main ideas about fairness and determines if competitive markets result in fair outcomes.

■ **Distinguish between value and price and define consumer surplus.**

Value is what we get, and price is what we pay. In economics, the everyday idea of value is *marginal benefit*, which is the maximum price that people are willing to pay for another unit of the good or service. The demand curve tells us this price. A demand curve is a marginal benefit curve. When people buy something for less than it is worth to them, they receive a consumer surplus. Consumer surplus is the marginal benefit from a good or service minus the price paid for it, summed over the quantity consumed.

■ **Distinguish between cost and price and define producer surplus.**

Cost is what a seller must give up to produce a good, and price is what a seller receives when the good is sold. The cost of producing one more unit of a good or service is its *marginal cost*. It is just worth producing one more unit of a good or service if the price for which it can be sold equals marginal cost. The supply curve tells us this price. A supply curve is a marginal cost curve. When the price exceeds marginal cost, the firm obtains a producer surplus. Producer surplus is the price of a good minus the marginal cost of producing it, summed over the quantity produced.

■ **Explain the conditions in which markets are efficient and inefficient.**

A market is efficient when resources are used to produce the goods and services people value most highly. When marginal benefit equals marginal cost, the efficient quantity is produced. The sum of consumer surplus and producer surplus is maximized at a competitive equilibrium. According to Adam Smith, each participant in a competitive market is "led by an invisible hand to promote an end [the efficient use of resources] which was no part of his intention." Obstacles to achieving an efficient allocation of resources include externalities, public goods and common resources, monopoly, price ceilings, price floors, and production quotas, and taxes and subsidies.

■ **Explain the main ideas about fairness and evaluate claims that competitive markets result in unfair outcomes.**

The symmetry principle is the requirement that people in similar situations be treated similarly. Two views of fairness are it's not fair if the *result* isn't fair and it's not fair if the *rules* aren't fair. Utilitarianism is a principle that states that we should strive to achieve "the greatest happiness for the greatest number." The utilitarian idea of complete equality ignores the cost of making income transfers, which leads to the big tradeoff—a tradeoff between efficiency and fairness.

EXPANDED CHAPTER CHECKLIST

When you have completed this chapter, you will be able to

1 Distinguish between value and price and define consumer surplus.

- Discuss the difference between value and price.
- Explain why a demand curve is a marginal benefit curve.
- Define consumer surplus and illustrate it in a figure.

2 Distinguish between cost and price and define producer surplus.

- Discuss the difference between cost and price.
- Explain why a supply curve is a marginal cost curve.
- Define producer surplus and illustrate it in a figure.

3 Explain the conditions in which markets are efficient and inefficient.

- Explain why a competitive equilibrium is efficient.
- Discuss Adam Smith and the "invisible hand".
- List the obstacles to achieving an efficient allocation of resources.
- Define and illustrate deadweight loss.

4 Explain the main ideas about fairness and evaluate claims that competitive markets result in unfair outcomes.

- Define the symmetry principle.
- Discuss the two broad views of fairness.

- Define utilitarianism and discuss the one big problem with the utilitarian idea of complete equality.
- Discuss fairness in the face of a natural disaster.

KEY TERMS

- Big tradeoff (page 152)
- Consumer surplus (page 139)
- Deadweight loss (page 148)
- Producer surplus (page 142)
- Symmetry principle (page 151)
- Utilitarianism (page 152)

CHECKPOINT 6.1

■ **Distinguish between value and price and define consumer surplus.**

Practice Problem 6.1

The figure shows the demand curve for CDs and the market price of a CD. Use the figure to answer the following questions.

a. What is the value of the 10th CD?

b. What is the willingness to pay for the 20th CD?

c. What is the consumer surplus on the 10th CD?

d. What are the quantity of CDs bought and the consumer surplus?

e. What is the amount paid for CDs in part **d**?

f. What is the total benefit from the CDs in part **d**?

g. If the price of a CD rises to $20, what is the change in consumer surplus?

Solution to Practice Problem 6.1

This practice problem illustrates the relationship between the demand curve and the marginal benefit curve. A demand curve is a marginal benefit curve. Marginal benefit is the maximum price that people are willing to pay for another unit of a good or service. The demand curve tells us this price.

Quick Review

- *Value* In economics, the everyday idea of value is *marginal benefit*, which we measure as the maximum price that people are willing to pay for another unit of a good or service.

- *Consumer surplus* The marginal benefit from a good or service minus the price paid for it, summed over the quantity consumed.

a. What is the value of the 10th CD?

The value of the 10th CD is the marginal benefit of the 10th CD. The value of the 10th CD is also equal to the maximum price that someone is willing to pay for it. In the figure, the demand curve shows that if 10 CDs are available, the maximum price willingly paid for the 10th CD is $20.

b. What is the willingness to pay for the 20th CD?

The willingness to pay for the 20th CD is equal to the maximum price that someone is willing to pay for the 20th CD. In the figure, the demand curve shows that if 20 CDs are available, the maximum price willingly paid for the 20th CD is $15.

c. What is the consumer surplus on the 10th CD?

The consumer surplus on the 10th CD is the marginal benefit of 10th CD minus the price of a CD. In the figure, the marginal benefit of the 10th CD is $20 and the price is $15, so consumer surplus is $20 − $15, which is $5.

d. What are the quantity of CDs bought and the consumer surplus?

In the figure, the quantity of CDs bought is 20, which is the quantity where the market price line and the demand curve intersect.

The consumer surplus equals the area of the green triangle in the figure. The area of the triangle is $1/2 \times (\$25 - \$15) \times 20$, which is $100.

e. What is the amount paid for the CDs in part d?

The amount paid for the CDs equals the price multiplied by the quantity bought. The amount paid is $15 × 20, which is $300.

f. What is the total benefit from the CDs in part d?

The total benefit from the CDs is the amount paid for the CDs, which is $300, plus the consumer surplus, which is $100. The total benefit is $400.

g. If the price of a CD rises to $20, what is the consumer surplus?

When the price is $20, the quantity of CDs bought decreases to 10 a day. The consumer surplus equals the area of the green triangle in the figure. The area of the triangle is ½ × ($25 − $20) × 10, which is $25. The change in consumer surplus is $100 – $25, which is $75.

Additional Practice Problem 6.1a

Estelle pays a lawyer $50 to write a letter to settle a rent dispute. What is Estelle's value of this service, her marginal benefit, and consumer surplus?

Solution to Additional Practice Problem 6.1a

The value that Estelle receives from the service provided by the lawyer is the same as her marginal benefit. And Estelle's marginal benefit is the maximum price that she is willing to pay to have the letter prepared. The consumer surplus from the service provided by the lawyer is equal to Estelle's marginal benefit minus the price she pays. If the price that Estelle pays for the letter is less than her marginal benefit, then Estelle receives a consumer surplus.

■ Self Test 6.1

Fill in the blanks

_____ (Price; value) is what we get and _____ (price; value) is what we pay. The benefit a person receives from consuming one more unit of a good is its ____ (marginal; opportunity) benefit. The demand curve ____ (is; is not) a marginal benefit curve. The consumer surplus equals the marginal benefit of a good ____ (plus; multiplied by; minus) the price paid for it, summed over the quantity consumed.

True or false

1. The demand curve for lip gloss tells us the dollars' worth of other goods and services that people are willing to forgo to consume one more lip gloss.

2. Value and price refer to the same thing.

3. A demand curve is a marginal benefit curve.

4. Consumer surplus is the marginal benefit from a good or service minus the price paid for it, summed over the quantity consumed.

Multiple choice

1. In general, as the consumption of a good increases, the marginal benefit from consuming that good
   a. increases.
   b. decreases.
   c. stays the same.
   d. at first increases and then decreases.

2. If the price of a pizza is $10, the consumer surplus from the first pizza consumed ____ the consumer surplus from the second pizza consumed.
   a. equals
   b. is greater than
   c. is less than
   d. cannot be compared to

3. Value is
   a. the price we pay for a good.
   b. the cost of resources used to produce a good.
   c. objective so that it is determined by market forces, not preferences.
   d. the marginal benefit we get from consuming another unit of a good or service.

4. A marginal benefit curve
   a. is the same as a demand curve.
   b. is the same as a supply curve.
   c. slopes upwards.
   d. is a vertical line.

5. The difference between the marginal benefit from a new pair of shoes and the price of the new pair of shoes is

    a. the consumer surplus from that pair of shoes.

    b. what we get.

    c. what we have to pay.

    d. the price when the marginal benefit is maximized.

6. Suppose the price of a scooter is $199 and Cora Lee is willing to pay $250 for a scooter. Cora Lee's

    a. consumer surplus from that scooter is $199.

    b. consumer surplus from that scooter is $51.

    c. total benefit from that scooter is $199.

    d. None of the above answers are correct.

Complete the graph

1. Figure 6.1 shows the marginal benefit curve for roller blades.

■ FIGURE 6.1

Price (dollars per pair of roller blades)

Quantity (thousands of pairs of roller blades per year)

    a. What is the marginal benefit from the 20,000th pair of roller blades?

    b. What is the marginal benefit from the 40,000th pair of roller blades?

2. Figure 6.2 shows the demand curve for bags of potato chips.

■ FIGURE 6.2

Price (dollars per bag of potato chips)

Quantity (millions of bags of potato chips per week)

    a. What is the maximum price a consumer is willing to pay for the 2 millionth bag of chips?

    b. What is the marginal benefit from the 2 millionth bag of chips? What is the relationship between your answer to part (a) and your answer to this part?

    c. If the price of a bag of chips equals $2, in Figure 6.2 shade the area that equals the amount of the consumer surplus.

    d. If the price of a bag of chips equals $2, what is the amount of the consumer surplus?

Short answer

1. The table gives the demand schedule for MP3 players.

Price (dollars per MP3 player)	Quantity (millions of MP3 players per year)	Consumer surplus (dollars)
500	4	_____
400	8	_____
300	12	_____
200	16	_____
100	20	_____

Suppose the price of an MP3 player is $200.

    a. Complete the table by calculating the consumer surplus. In the first row, calculate the consumer surplus for the 4 millionth MP3 player; in the second row, calculate the consumer surplus for the 8 millionth MP3 player; and so on.

b. As more MP3 players are purchased, what happens to the consumer surplus of the last unit purchased? Why?

2. What is the relationship between the value of a good, the maximum price a consumer is willing to pay for the good, and the marginal benefit from the good?

3. What is the relationship between the marginal benefit of a slice of pizza, the price paid for the slice, and its consumer surplus?

CHECKPOINT 6.2

■ **Distinguish between cost and price and define producer surplus.**

Practice Problem 6.2

The figure shows the supply curve of CDs and the market price of a CD. Use the figure to answer the following questions.

b. What is the marginal cost of the 10th CD?

b. What is the minimum supply price of the 20th CD?

c. What is the producer surplus on the 10th CD?

d. What are the quantity of CDs sold and the producer surplus?

e. What is the total revenue from the CDs sold in part **d**?

f. What is the cost of producing the CDs sold in part **d**?

g. If the price of a CD falls to $10, what is the change in the producer surplus?

Solution to Practice Problem 6.2

This practice problem illustrates the relationship between the supply curve and the marginal cost

curve. A supply curve is a marginal cost curve. It is just worth producing one more unit of a good or service if the price for which it can be sold equals marginal cost. The supply curve tells us this price.

Quick Review

*   *Cost* Cost is what the seller must give up to produce a good.

*   *Producer surplus* The price of a good minus the marginal cost of producing it, summed over the quantity produced.

a. **What is the marginal cost of the 10th CD?**

The marginal cost of the 10th CD is equal to the minimum supply price of the 10th CD. The supply curve tells us this price. In the figure, the supply curve shows that the marginal cost of the 10th CD is $10.

b. **What is the minimum supply price of the 20th CD?**

The minimum supply price of the 20th CD is the marginal cost of producing the 20th CD. In the figure, the supply curve shows that the minimum supply price of the 20th CD is $15.

c. **What is the producer surplus on the 10th CD?**

The producer surplus on the 10th CD is the price of the 10th CD minus the marginal cost of producing it. In the figure the producer surplus is $15 – $10, which is $5.

d. What are the quantity of CDs sold and the producer surplus?

At the market price of $15, 20 CDs a day are sold. The producer surplus equals the area of the blue triangle in the figure. The area of the triangle is $1/2 \times 20 \times$ ($15 – $5), which equals $100.

e. What is the total revenue from the CDs sold in part d?

Total revenue equals price multiplied by quantity sold. Total revenue is $15 \times 20 = $300.

f. What is the cost of producing the CDs sold in part d?
The total cost of producing 20 CDs equals the total revenue minus the producer surplus. The total cost is $300 – $100, which is $200.

g. If the price of a CD falls to $10, what is the change in the producer surplus?

When the price falls to $10, the quantity of CDs sold decreases to 10 a day. The producer surplus equals the area of the blue triangle in the figure, which equals $1/2 \times 10 \times$ ($10 – $5)= $25. Producer surplus decreases by $100 – $25, which is $75.

Additional Practice Problem 6.2a

Why is the minimum price that a seller will produce a good equal to the good's marginal cost?

Solution to Additional Practice Problem 6.2a

A seller is willing to produce a good when the price he receives covers all the costs of producing the good. So the minimum price for which a seller is willing to produce a unit of a good is the

amount that just equals the cost of producing that unit. The cost of producing a unit of a good is its marginal cost, so the minimum supply price equals the marginal cost.

■ Self Test 6.2

Fill in the blanks

_____ (Price; Cost) is what a seller must give up to produce a good and _____ (price; cost) is what a seller receives when the good is sold. A _____ (demand; supply) curve is a marginal cost curve. A firm receives a producer surplus when price is _____ (greater; less) than marginal cost.

True or false

1. In economics, cost and price are the same.

2. The minimum price for which Bob will grow another bag of carrots is 50¢, so the marginal cost of an additional bag of carrots is 50¢.

3. A supply curve is a marginal benefit curve.

4. Producer surplus equals the marginal benefit of a good minus the cost of producing it.

Multiple choice

1. Cost is

a. what the buyer pays to get the good.

b. always equal to marginal benefit.

c. what the seller must give up to produce the good.

d. greater than market price.

2. If a firm is willing to supply the 1,000th unit of a good at a price of $23 or more, we know that $23 is the

a. highest price the seller hopes to realize for this output.

b. minimum price the seller must receive to produce this unit.

c. average price the seller could charge.

d. price that sets the marginal benefit equal to the marginal cost.

3. A supply curve shows the _____ of producing one more unit of a good or service.

a. producer surplus

b. consumer surplus

c. total benefit

d. marginal cost

4. Producer surplus is

a. equal to the marginal benefit from a good minus its price.

b. equal to the price of a good minus the marginal cost of producing it, summed over the quantity produced.

c. always equal to consumer surplus.

d. Both answers (a) and (c) are correct.

5. You are willing to tutor your friend for $10 an hour. Your friend pays you $15 an hour. What is your producer surplus?

a. $5 an hour

b. $10 an hour

c. $15 an hour

d. $25 an hour

6. In a figure that shows a supply curve and a demand curve, producer surplus is the area

a. below the demand curve and above the market price.

b. below the supply curve and above the market price.

c. above the demand curve and below the market price.

d. above the supply curve and below the market price.

Complete the graph

1. Figure 6.3 shows the supply curve for bags of potato chips.

■ FIGURE 6.3

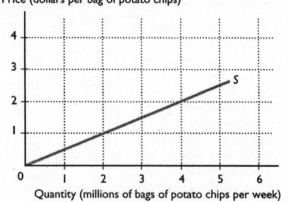

Price (dollars per bag of potato chips)

Quantity (millions of bags of potato chips per week)

a. What is the minimum price for which a supplier is willing to produce the 2 millionth bag of chips?

b. What is the marginal cost of the 2 millionth bag of chips? What is the relationship between your answer to part (a) and your answer to this part?

c. If the price of a bag of chips equals $2, in Figure 6.3 shade the area that equals the amount of the producer surplus.

d. If the price of a bag of chips equals $2, calculate the producer surplus.

Short answer

1. What is the relationship between the minimum price a supplier must receive to produce a slice of pizza and the marginal cost of producing that slice of pizza? What is the relationship between the marginal cost curve and the supply curve?

2. What is producer surplus? As the price of a good or service rises and the supply curve does not shift, what happens to the amount of the producer surplus?

CHECKPOINT 6.3

■ **Explain the conditions in which markets are efficient and inefficient.**

Practice Problem 6.3

The figure shows the market for paper. Use the figure to answer the following questions.

a. What are the equilibrium price and the equilibrium quantity of paper?

b. In market equilibrium, what is the consumer surplus?

c. In market equilibrium, what is the producer surplus?

d. Is the market for paper efficient? Why or why not?

e. If a news magazine lobby group persuaded the government to pass a law requiring paper producers to sell 50 tonnes of paper a day, would the market for paper be efficient? Why or why not?

f. In the situation described in part **e**, shade the deadweight loss on the figure.

g. If an environmental lobby group persuaded the government to pass a law restricting producers of paper to sell only 20 tonnes of paper a day, would the market for paper be efficient? Why or why not?

h. In the situation described in part **g**, shade the deadweight loss on the figure.

Solution to Practice Problem 6.3

The efficient use of resources occurs when marginal benefit equals marginal cost. When produc-

tion in a market occurs at an inefficient level, a deadweight loss occurs.

Quick Review

• *Efficiency of competitive equilibrium* The condition that marginal benefit equals marginal cost delivers an efficient use of resources. It allocates resources to the activities that create the greatest possible value. So a competitive equilibrium is efficient.

• *Deadweight loss* The decrease in consumer surplus and producer surplus that results from an inefficient level of production.

a. **What are the equilibrium price and the equilibrium quantity of paper?**

In the figure, the equilibrium price and the equilibrium quantity of paper occur at the intersection of the demand curve, *D*, and the supply curve, *S*. The equilibrium quantity is 40 tonnes a day and the equilibrium price is $3 a tonne.

b. **In market equilibrium, what is the consumer surplus?**

The consumer surplus equals the area of the green triangle. Consumer surplus equals $1/2 \times (40 \text{ tonnes}) \times (\$9 - \$3)$, which is $120.

c. **In market equilibrium, what is the producer surplus?**

The producer surplus equals the area of the blue triangle. Producer surplus equals 1/2 × (40 tonnes) × ($3 − $1), which is $40.

d. **Is the market for paper efficient? Why or why not?**

The market equilibrium is efficient because marginal benefit equals marginal cost and the sum of consumer surplus and producer surplus is maximized.

e. **If a news magazine lobby group persuaded the government to pass a law requiring paper producers to sell 50 tonnes of paper a day, would the market be efficient? Why or why not?**

When producers produce 50 tonnes of paper a day the market is inefficient because the marginal cost of the 50th tonne exceeds the marginal benefit of the 50th tonne.

f. **In the situation described in part e, shade the deadweight loss on the figure.**

The deadweight loss is shown by the grey triangle. The deadweight loss arises because consumers are willing to pay less for the last tonne of paper than the marginal cost of producing that tonne.

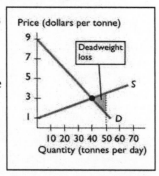

g. **If an environmental lobby group persuaded the government to pass a law restricting producers of paper to sell only 20 tonnes of paper a day, would the market for paper be efficient? Why or why not?**

When producers sell 20 tonnes of paper a day the market is inefficient because the marginal cost of the 20th tonne is less than the marginal benefit of the 20th tonne.

h. **In the situation described in part g, shade the deadweight loss on the figure.**

The deadweight loss is shown by the grey triangle. The deadweight loss arises because consumers are willing to pay more for the last tonne of paper than the marginal cost of producing that tonne.

Additional Practice Problem 6.3a

Who gains from a deadweight loss?

Solution to Additional Practice Problem 6.3a

No one gains from a deadweight loss. Deadweight loss is the decrease in consumer surplus and producer surplus that results from an inefficient level of production. The deadweight loss is borne by the entire society. It is not a loss for the consumers and a gain for the producer. It is a social loss.

■ **Self Test 6.3**

Fill in the blanks

Equilibrium in a competitive market _____ (is; is not) efficient. Adam Smith believed that each participant in a competitive market is "led by _____" (an invisible hand; market forces). _____ (An externality; A public good) is a good or service that is consumed simultaneously by everyone, even if they don't pay for it. A price _____ (ceiling; floor) is a regulation that makes it illegal to charge a price higher than a specified level. Deadweight loss is the decrease in _____ (consumer surplus; consumer surplus and producer surplus; producer surplus) that results from an inefficient level of production.

True or false

1. In a competitive equilibrium, resource use is efficient.

2. When the efficient quantity of a good is produced, the consumer surplus is always zero.

3. According to Adam Smith, competitive markets require government action to ensure that resources are allocated efficiently.

4. Producing less than the efficient quantity of a good results in a deadweight loss but producing more than the efficient quantity does not result in a deadweight loss.

Multiple choice

1. When a market is efficient
a. the sum of consumer surplus and producer surplus is maximized.
b. the consumer surplus is as large as possible.
c. the quantity produced is maximized.
d. marginal cost is less than marginal benefit.

2. When a market is efficient
a. producers earn the highest income possible.
b. production costs equal total benefit.
c. consumer surplus equals producer surplus.
d. resources are used to produce the goods and services that people value most highly

3. The concept of "the invisible hand" suggests that markets
a. do not produce the efficient quantity.
b. are always fair.
c. produce the efficient quantity.
d. are unfair.

4. What can cause a market to produce an inefficient quantity of a good?
a. a monopoly
b. an external cost or an external benefit
c. a public good
d. All of the above.

5. When underproduction occurs,
a. producers realize more surplus at the expense of consumers.
b. marginal cost is greater than marginal benefit.
c. consumer surplus grows to a harmful amount.
d. there is a deadweight loss that is borne by the entire society.

6. When production moves from the efficient quantity to a point of overproduction
a. consumer surplus definitely increases.
b. the sum of producer surplus and consumer surplus increases.
c. there is a deadweight loss.
d. consumers lose and producers gain.

Complete the graph

1. In Figure 6.4, what is the equilibrium quantity of automobiles? What is the efficient quantity of automobiles? Show the consumer surplus and the producer surplus.

■ **FIGURE 6.4**
Price (thousands of dollars per automobile)

2. Figure 6.5 is identical to Figure 6.4. Now, suppose that 80,000 automobiles are produced. If there is a deadweight loss, shade it light grey. Next suppose that 40,000 automobiles are produced. If there is a deadweight loss, shade it dark grey.

■ FIGURE 6.5

Price (thousands of dollars per automobile)

Quantity (thousands of automobiles per week)

Short answer

1. What is the relationship between a competitive market, efficiency, and the invisible hand?

2. Suppose the demand for cotton clothing increases. What effect does the increase in demand have on the equilibrium quantity and on the efficient quantity?

3. What factors might lead a market to produce an inefficient amount of a product?

CHECKPOINT 6.4

■ **Explain the main ideas about fairness and evaluate claims that competitive markets result in unfair outcomes.**

Practice Problem 6.4

A winter storm cuts the power supply and isolates a small town in the mountains. The people rush to buy candles from the town's store, which is the only source of candles. The store owner decides to ration the candles to one per family but keep the price of a candle unchanged.

a. Who gets to consume the candles?

b. Who receives the consumer surplus on candles?

c. Who receives the producer surplus on candles?

d. Is the outcome efficient?

e. Is the outcome fair according to the utilitarian principle?

f. Is the process fair according to the symmetry principle?

g. If the town's mayor declares a state of emergency and gives every family $100 to cope with the crisis, does this produce a more efficient and fairer outcome?

Solution to Practice Problem 6.4

This problem challenges you to use what you have learned about fairness and think carefully about what is fair and what is unfair.

Quick Review

- *Utilitarianism* A principle that states that we should strive to achieve "the greatest happiness for the greatest number."

- *Symmetry principle* The requirement that people in similar situations be treated similarly.

a.   Who gets to consume the candles?

The answer that each family gets to consume one candle is incorrect because it ignores that candles can be resold. A buyer from the town store will sell his candle if the price exceeds his marginal benefit. The consumers of the candles are those who are willing to pay the most.

b.   Who receives the consumer surplus on candles?

The consumer surplus is received by families that buy and consume the candles. A family that buys and then sells a candle, does not receive any consumer surplus because it does not consume the candle.

c. Who receives the producer surplus on candles?

The town's store owner receives the same producer surplus as normal. The families who initially purchase the candles from the town store and then resell them to other families also receive some producer surplus.

d. Is the outcome efficient?

The outcome is efficient because the families that most highly value the candles are the families that buy and consume the candles.

e. Is the outcome fair according to the utilitarian principle?

The outcome is not fair according to the utilitarian principle. Utilitarians would have the candles shared equally, so that every family gets the same number of candles. But the outcome has the candles shared unequally because some families sell their candles.

f. Is the process fair according to the symmetry principle?

The process is fair according to the symmetry principle because all the exchanges are voluntary. Families that want to sell their candles are free to do so and families that want to buy candles are free to do so.

g. If the town's mayor declares a state of emergency and gives every family $100 to cope with the crisis, does this produce a more efficient and fairer outcome?

When the government provides every family with $100, the demand for candles increases, and the equilibrium price of a candle rises. But the quantity of candles available does not change. To pay the $100, the town council must raise taxes, which might be fair or unfair.

Additional Practice Problem 6.4a

If Bill Gates gives $1,000 to a homeless person, would the transaction be fair? If Mr. Gates is taxed $1,000 by the government and the government gives the $1,000 to the same homeless person, would the transaction be fair?

Solution to Additional Practice Problem 6.4a

If Mr. Gates gives $1,000 to a homeless person, the exchange is considered fair according to the symmetry principle because the exchange is voluntary. The outcome is fair according to the utilitarian principle because there is more equality of income. If Mr. Gates is taxed by the government, the outcome is fair according to the utilitarian principle because there is more equality of income. But the transaction is not fair according to the symmetry principle because the exchange does not occur voluntarily.

■ **Self Test 6.4**

Fill in the blanks

Two views of fairness are that "it's not fair if the ____ (result; income distribution) isn't fair;" and "it's not fair if the ____ (rules; tradeoffs between efficiency and income) aren't fair." _____ (Symmetry; Utilitarianism) is a principle that states that we should strive to achieve "the greatest happiness for the greatest number". According to Robert Nozick, fair-rules ideas require _____ (government intervention; property rights and voluntary exchange).

True or false

1. The symmetry principle is the idea that all people should receive symmetric incomes.

2. The goal of utilitarianism is to achieve the greatest happiness for the greatest number of people.

3. The big tradeoff is the tradeoff between efficiency and happiness.

4. According to the "fair-rules" view of fairness, in times of natural disasters, it is fair to force people to make available necessary goods and services at lower than usual prices.

Multiple choice

1. The requirement that people in similar situations be treated similarly is the _____ principle.

   a. equity

   b. symmetry

   c. market

   d. fairness

2. The principle that states that we should strive to achieve "the greatest happiness for the greatest number" is

   a. equity.

   b. fairness.

   c. market equilibrium.

   d. utilitarianism.

3. Which of the following is an example in which "the big tradeoff" can occur?

   a. the government redistributes income from the rich to the poor

   b. Ford increases the price of a pickup truck

   c. a basketball player signs a $5 million contract

   d. a college lowers tuition

4. The "fair-rules" view of fairness is based on

   a. income transfers from the rich to the poor.

   b. property rights and voluntary exchange.

   c. utilitarianism.

   d. the big tradeoff.

5. An unequal distribution of income is considered fair according to Robert Nozick if

   a. marginal cost equals marginal benefit.

   b. the cost of administering a welfare system is minimized.

   c. property rights are enforced and voluntary exchange occurs.

   d. the economy is producing its maximum total output.

6. Suppose an ice storm strikes eastern Ontario. The price of firewood jumps from $15 a box to $28. If the government buys all the firewood at $28 a box and offers it to consumers for $15 a box, which of the following is true?

   a. There is enough firewood for everyone at $15 a box.

   b. There is a surplus of firewood at $15 a box.

   c. Some people who buy firewood from the government at $15 a box will resell the firewood to consumers who are willing to pay $28 a box, and earn a producer surplus.

   d. Because the government is buying and selling the firewood, the market is efficient.

Short answer

1. In Canada, richer people generally pay a larger fraction of their income as taxes than do poorer people. Is this arrangement fair? Answer from a fair-results view and from a fair-rules view.

2. Suppose that during their working lifetimes, Matt and Pat earned identical incomes as computer programmers. Matt spent all of his income and Pat saved a large portion of hers. Now that they are retired, Pat's income is higher than Matt's because of Pat's saving. Is it fair for Pat's income to be higher than Matt's? Answer from a fair-results view and from a fair-rules view.

3. What is the effect of the big tradeoff in transferring income from people with high incomes to people with low incomes?

4. Is it fair for the government to limit the prices sellers charge for bottled water after a flood destroys a town's water supply?

SELF TEST ANSWERS

■ CHECKPOINT 6.1

Fill in the blanks

<u>Value</u> is what we get and <u>price</u> is what we pay. The benefit a person receives from consuming one more unit of a good is its <u>marginal</u> benefit. The demand curve <u>is</u> a marginal benefit curve. The consumer surplus equals the marginal benefit of a good <u>minus</u> the price paid for it, summed over the quantity consumed.

True or false

1. True; page 138

2. False; page 138

3. True; page 138

4. True; page 139

Multiple choice

1. b; page 138

2. b; page 139

3. d; page 138

4. a; page 138

5. a; page 139

6. b; page 139

Complete the graph

1. a. The marginal benefit from the 20,000th pair of roller blades is $150; page 138.

   b. The marginal benefit from the 40,000 pair of roller blades is $100; page 138.

2. a. The maximum price is $3; page 138.

   b. The marginal benefit is $3. The marginal benefit is the maximum price a consumer is willing to pay for another bag of chips; page 138.

   c. Figure 6.6 shades the area of the consumer surplus; page 139.

■ FIGURE 6.6

Price (dollars per bag of potato chips)

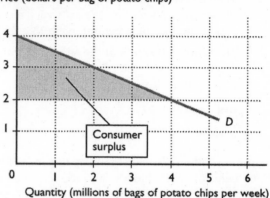

Quantity (millions of bags of potato chips per week)

d. The consumer surplus equals the area of the green triangle in Figure 6.6, which is $1/2 \times (\$4 - \$2) \times 4$ million, which is $4 million; page 139.

Short answer

1. a. The table gives the consumer surpluses.

Price (dollars per MP3 player)	Quantity (millions of MP3 players per year)	Consumer surplus (dollars)
500	4	300
400	8	200
300	12	100
200	16	0
100	20	None

The consumer surplus is zero for the 20 millionth MP3 player because when the price of an MP3 player is $200, the 20 millionth MP3 player is not purchased. For the remaining quantities, the consumer surplus equals marginal benefit, which is the maximum price willing to be paid minus the price; page 139.

b. The consumer surplus decreases as more MP3 players are purchased because the value of an additional MP3 player decreases as more are purchased; page 139.

2. The value of a good is equal to the maximum price a buyer is willing to pay, which also equals the marginal benefit; page 138.

3. The marginal benefit of the slice of pizza equals the price paid plus the consumer surplus on that slice; page 139.

■ **CHECKPOINT 6.2**

Fill in the blanks

Cost is what a seller must give up to produce a good and price is what a seller receives when the good is sold. A supply curve is a marginal cost curve. A firm receives a producer surplus when price is greater than marginal cost.

True or false

1. False; page 141

2. True; page 141

3. False; page 141

4. False; page 142

Multiple choice

1. c; page 141

2. b; page 141

3. d; page 141

4. b; page 142

5. a; page 142

6. d; page 142

Complete the graph

1. a. The minimum price is $1; page 141.

b. The marginal cost is $1. The marginal cost of the 2 millionth bag is the minimum price at which a supplier is willing to produce that bag of chips; page 141.

c. Figure 6.7 shades the area of the producer surplus; page 142.

■ **FIGURE 6.7**
Price (dollars per bag of potato chips)

d. The producer surplus equals the area of the blue triangle in Figure 6.7. Producer surplus is $1/2 \times \$2 \times 4$ million, which equals $4 million; page 142.

Short answer

1. The minimum price for which a firm will produce a slice of pizza equals the marginal cost of producing that slice. It is just worth producing one more slice of pizza if the price for which it can be sold equals its marginal cost. The supply curve tells us this price. So the supply curve is the same as the marginal cost curve; page 141.

2. Producer surplus equals the price of a good minus the marginal cost of producing it, summed over the quantity produced. As the price of a good rises and the supply curve does not shift, the producer surplus increases; page 142.

■ **CHECKPOINT 6.3**

Fill in the blanks

Equilibrium in a competitive market is efficient. Adam Smith believed that each participant in a competitive market is "led by an invisible hand". A public good is a good or service that is consumed simultaneously by everyone, even if they don't pay for it. A price ceiling is a regulation that makes it illegal to charge a price higher than a specified level. Deadweight loss is the decrease in <u>consumer surplus and producer surplus</u> that results from an inefficient level of production.

True or false

1. True; page 144

2. False; page 144

3. False; page 145

4. False; page 148

Multiple choice

1. a; page 144

2. d; page 144

3. c; page 145

4. d; page 147

5. d; page 148

6. c; page 148

Complete the graph

1. In Figure 6.8, the equilibrium quantity of automobiles is 60,000 a week. The efficient quantity of automobiles is also 60,000 a week because that is the quantity at which the marginal benefit equals the marginal cost. The consumer surplus and producer surplus are shown in the figure; pages 144.

■ FIGURE 6.8

Price (thousands of dollars per automobile)

2. When 80,000 automobiles are produced, a deadweight loss occurs. For every automo-

bile that is produced over 60,000, marginal cost exceeds marginal benefit. People are willing to pay less for the marginal car than it costs to produce. The deadweight loss is the area of the light grey triangle in Figure 6.9.

When 40,000 automobiles are produced, a deadweight loss occurs. For each of the 40,000 automobiles produced, marginal benefit exceeds marginal cost. Consumers are willing to pay more for the marginal automobile than it costs to produce. The amount of the deadweight loss is the area of dark grey triangle in Figure 6.9; page 148.

■ FIGURE 6.9

Price (thousands of dollars per automobile)

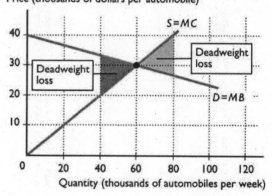

Short answer

1. Adam Smith believed that each participant in a competitive market is "led by an invisible hand to promote an end [the efficient use of resources] which was no part of his intention"; page 145.

2. If the demand for cotton clothing increases, the demand curve for cotton clothing shifts rightward and the equilibrium quantity increases. The demand curve is the marginal benefit curve, so the marginal benefit curve also shifts rightward. The efficient quantity also increases; page 144.

3. The most significant obstacles to achieving an efficient allocation of resources involve externalities, public goods and common re-

sources, and monopoly. Governments influence markets by setting price ceilings, price floors, and production quotas, and taxes and subsidies, which can create inefficiency; page 147.

■ CHECKPOINT 6.4

Fill in the blanks

Two views of fairness are that "it's not fair if the result isn't fair;" and "it's not fair if the rules aren't fair." Utilitarianism is a principle that states that we should strive to achieve "the greatest happiness for the greatest number". According to Robert Nozick, fair-rules ideas require property rights and voluntary exchange.

True or false

1. False; page 151
2. True; page 152
3. False; page 152
4. False; page 153

Multiple choice

1. b; page 151
2. d; page 152
3. a; page 152
4. b; page 153
5. c; page 153
6. c; page 154

Short answer

1. The tax arrangement is fair from a fair-results view. It leads to a greater equality of income. The tax arrangement is not fair from a fair-rules view because the tax is not a voluntary exchange; pages 151-154.

2. From a fair-results view, it is not fair for Pat's income to be substantially higher than Matt's. From a fair-rules view, it is fair because Pat and Matt had the same opportunities; pages 151-154.

3. Income is transferred from people with high incomes to people with low incomes by taxing incomes, which discourages work. It results in the quantity of labour being less than the efficient quantity. Similarly, taxing income from capital discourages saving, which results in the quantity of capital being less than the efficient quantity. The greater the amount of income redistribution through income taxes, the greater is the inefficiency and the smaller is the economic pie; page 152.

4. Limiting the price that can be charged is unfair because it compels the seller to help and such compulsion is unfair; page 154.

Government Influences on Markets

Chapter 7

In Chapter 7 we study how inefficiency is created when the government introduces a price ceiling a price floor, or a production quota.

■ **Explain how a rent ceiling creates a housing shortage, inefficiency, and unfairness.**

A price ceiling is the highest price at which it is legal to trade a particular good, service, or factor of production. A rent ceiling is an example of a price ceiling. A rent ceiling set above the equilibrium rent is ineffective. A housing shortage occurs when a rent ceiling is set below the equilibrium rent because the quantity of housing demanded exceeds the quantity of housing supplied. A black market is an illegal market that operates alongside a government-regulated market. When a rent ceiling creates a shortage of housing, search activity, which is the time spent looking for someone with whom to do business, increases. A rent ceiling creates a deadweight loss and decreases consumer surplus and producer surplus. Rent controls violate the fair-rules view of fairness because they block voluntary exchange. Rent controls violate the fair-results view of fairness because housing is not necessarily provided to the people whose need is greatest.

■ **Explain how the minimum wage creates unemployment, inefficiency, and unfairness.**

A minimum wage law is a government regulation that makes hiring labour for less than a specified wage illegal. A minimum wage law is an example of a price floor. A minimum wage set below the equilibrium wage rate is ineffective. Unemployment occurs when the minimum wage is set above the equilibrium wage rate because the quantity of labour supplied exceeds the quantity of labour demanded. A minimum wage increases job search activity. Some firms and workers might agree to do business at an illegal wage rate below the minimum wage. The minimum wage creates a deadweight loss, delivers an unfair result, and imposes unfair rules.

■ **Explain how production quotas create inefficiency and unfairness.**

A production quota is an upper limit to the quantity of a good that may be produced in a specified period. If the production quota is greater than the equilibrium quantity, nothing changes. If the production quota is less than the equilibrium quantity, the price rises and the quantity demanded equals the quantity produced under the quota. A production quota is inefficient because the marginal benefit exceeds the marginal cost. The consumer is worse off because the quantity produced decreases and the price rises. Consumer surplus shrinks. The producer is better off and producer surplus increases. A deadweight loss is created. Each producer has an incentive to cheat on a voluntary quota. A quota may be fair if it helps struggling producers overcome a natural disaster.

EXPANDED CHAPTER CHECKLIST

When you have completed this chapter, you will be able to

1 Explain how a rent ceiling creates a housing shortage, inefficiency, and unfairness.

- Define rent ceiling and price ceiling.
- Explain why a rent ceiling that exceeds the equilibrium rent is ineffective.
- Illustrate the effects of a rent ceiling set below the equilibrium rent.
- Discuss how a rent ceiling can lead to a black market and increased search activity.
- Discuss the inefficiency and fairness of rent ceilings.

2 Explain how the minimum wage creates unemployment, inefficiency, and unfairness.

- Define minimum wage law and price floor.
- Explain why a minimum wage set below the equilibrium wage rate is ineffective.
- Illustrate the effects of a minimum wage set above the equilibrium wage rate and discuss how a minimum wage can lead to increased job search activity and illegal hiring.
- Discuss the inefficiency and fairness of the minimum wage.

3 Explain how production quotas create inefficiency and unfairness.

- Define production quota.
- Explain why a production quota set above the equilibrium quantity is ineffective.
- Illustrate the effects of a production quota set below the equilibrium quantity.
- Discuss the inefficiency of a production quota.

KEY TERMS

- Black market (page 163)
- Minimum wage law (page 170)
- Price ceiling (page 162)
- Price floor (page 170)
- Production quota (page 175)
- Rent ceiling (page 162)
- Search activity (page 164)

CHECKPOINT 7.1

■ Explain how a rent ceiling creates a housing shortage, inefficiency, and unfairness.

Practice Problem 7.1

The figure shows the rental market for apartments in Halifax, Nova Scotia.

a. What is the rent and how many apartments are rented?

b. If the city council imposes a rent ceiling of $900 a month, what is the rent and how many apartments are rented?

c. If the city council imposes a rent ceiling of $600 a month, what is the rent and how many apartments are rented?

d. With a strictly enforced $600 rent ceiling, is the housing market efficient? Explain why or why not.

e. If the city strictly enforces the rent ceiling, is the housing market fair? Explain why or why not.

f.   If a black market develops, how high could the black market rent be? Explain your answer.

Solution to Practice Problem 7.1

Remember that a rent ceiling is effective only when it is set below the equilibrium price.

Quick Review

*   *Rent ceiling* A government regulation that makes it illegal to charge more than a specified rent for housing.

a.   What is the rent and how many apartments are rented?

In the figure, the equilibrium rent is $800 a month and equilibrium quantity is 3,000 apartments at the intersection of the demand curve, *D*, and the supply curve, *S*.

b.   If the city council imposes a rent ceiling of $900 a month, what is the rent and how many apartments are rented?

A rent ceiling of $900 a month is ineffective because it is above the equilibrium rent. The rent remains at $800 a month and 3,000 apartments are rented.

c.   If the city council imposes a rent ceiling of $600 a month, what is the rent and how many apartments are rented?

The rent ceiling is below the equilibrium rent. In the figure, when the rent falls to $600 a month, the quantity of apartments supplied, which

equals the quantity of apartments rented decreases to 1,000.

d.   With a strictly enforced $600 rent ceiling, is the housing market efficient? Explain why or why not.

The housing market is inefficient because the marginal benefit of the last apartment rented, the 1,000th apartment, exceeds the marginal cost of that apartment. A deadweight loss arises. In the figure the deadweight loss is shown by the grey triangle.

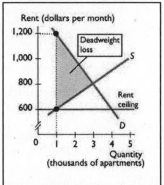

e.   If the city strictly enforces the rent ceiling, is the housing market fair? Explain why or why not.

The housing market is unfair by the fair-rules view because the rent ceiling prevents voluntary exchange. It is unfair by the fair-results view because poorer people do not necessarily get the apartments.

f.   If a black market develops, how high could the black market rent be? Explain your answer.

The black market rent could be as high as $1,200 a month, which equals the willingness of someone to pay for the 1,000th apartment.

Additional Practice Problem 7.1a

The table gives the supply and demand schedules for rounds of golf.

Price (dollars per round of golf)	Quantity demanded	Quantity supplied
	(rounds per week)	
50	2,000	2,800
40	2,300	2,700
30	2,600	2,600
20	2,900	2,500
10	3,200	2,400

a. What is the equilibrium price and equilibrium quantity of rounds of golf?

b. Is there a shortage if the city government imposes a price ceiling of $40 a round of golf? Is there a shortage if the city government imposes a price ceiling of $20 a round of golf?

Solution to Additional Practice Problem 7.1a

a. What is the equilibrium price and equilibrium quantity of rounds of golf?

The equilibrium price is $30 a round of golf and the equilibrium quantity is 2,600 rounds a week.

b. Is there a shortage if the city government imposes a price ceiling of $40 a round of golf?

The price ceiling of $40 a round of golf is above the equilibrium price, so the price remains at $30 a round and the quantity remains at 2,600 rounds a week. There is no shortage. The price ceiling of $20 a round of golf is below the equilibrium price. The price falls to $20 a round. The quantity played equals the quantity supplied at $20, which is 2,500 rounds a week. There is a shortage of 400 rounds a week.

■ **Self Test 7.1**

Fill in the blanks

A price ceiling is the _____ (highest; lowest) price at which it is legal to trade a particular good, service, or factor of production. A rent ceiling is effective if it is set ____ (above; below) the equilibrium rent. A rent ceiling can create a housing ____ (shortage; surplus), which leads to _____ (decreased; increased) search activity. Rent ceilings ____ (are; are not) efficient. The _____ (less; more) inelastic the demand for housing or the supply of housing, the smaller the deadweight loss created by a rent ceiling. Rent ceilings ____ (are; are not) fair. There is _____ (little; plenty of) political support for rent ceilings.

True or false

1. A rent ceiling always lowers the rent paid.

2. When a rent ceiling is higher than the equilibrium rent, a black market emerges.

3. The opportunity cost of a dorm room is equal to its rent.

4. Rent ceilings are efficient because they lower the cost of housing to all renters.

5. The total loss from a rent ceiling exceeds the deadweight loss.

Multiple choice

1. A price ceiling is a government regulation that makes it illegal to charge a price
a. below the equilibrium price.
b. above the equilibrium price.
c. for a good or service.
d. above some specified level.

2. With an effective price ceiling the quantity supplied ____ the quantity demanded and a ____ exists.
a. is less than; surplus
b. is less than; shortage
c. is greater than; surplus
d. is greater than; shortage

3. In a housing market with a rent ceiling set below the equilibrium rent,
a. some people seeking an apartment to rent will not be able to find one.
b. the total cost of renting an apartment will decrease for all those seeking housing.
c. some landlords will not be able to find renters to fill available apartments.
d. None of the above answers are correct.

4. When an effective rent ceiling is imposed
a. the demand for housing decreases.
b. the supply of housing increases.
c. a shortage of housing occurs.
d. a surplus of housing occurs.

5. Rent ceilings
a. increase search activity.
b. result in surpluses.
c. are efficient.
d. benefit producers.

6. The government imposes an effective price ceiling on gasoline. The black market for gasoline is ____ market in which the price ____ the ceiling price.
a. a legal; exceeds
b. an illegal; exceeds
c. a legal; is less than
d. an illegal; is less than

7. A rent ceiling creates a deadweight loss
a. if it is set below the equilibrium rent.
b. if it is set equal to the equilibrium rent.
c. if it set above the equilibrium rent.
d. never.

8. Rent ceilings
a. eliminate the problem of scarcity.
b. allocate resources efficiently.
c. allocate housing to poorer people.
d. benefit renters living in rent-controlled apartments.

Complete the graph

1. The table gives the demand and supply schedules for housing in a small town. In Figure 7.1, label the axes and graph the demand and supply curves. What is the equilibrium rent and quantity of housing?

Rent (dollars per month)	Quantity demanded	Quantity supplied
	(housing units per month)	
900	200	350
800	300	300
700	400	250
600	500	200
500	600	150

■ **FIGURE 7.1**

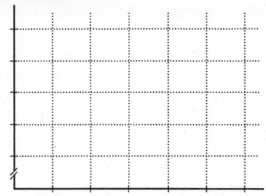

Suppose the government imposes a $600 a month rent ceiling.

a. With the rent ceiling, what is the quantity of housing demanded and the quantity of housing supplied?

b. Indicate the shortage or surplus created by the rent ceiling in Figure 7.1.

Short answer

1. What is a price ceiling?

2. The table gives the demand and supply schedules for milk.

Price (dollars per carton)	Quantity demanded	Quantity supplied
	(cartons per day)	
1.00	200	110
1.25	175	130
1.50	150	150
1.75	125	170
2.00	100	190

a. What is the market equilibrium in the milk market?

b. If the government imposes a price ceiling of $1.25 per carton, what is the price of a carton of milk, what quantity is purchased, and what is the size of the shortage?

c. If the government imposes a price ceiling of $1.75 per carton, what is the price of a carton of milk, what quantity is purchased, and what is the size of the shortage?

3. Are rent ceilings efficient? Are rent ceiling fair?

CHECKPOINT 7.2

■ Explain how the minimum wage creates unemployment, inefficiency, and unfairness.

Practice Problem 7.2

The figure shows the market for tomato pickers in southern Ontario.

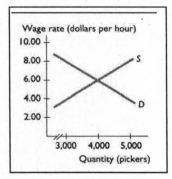

a. What is the equilibrium wage rate of tomato pickers, and what is the equilibrium quantity of tomato pickers employed?

b. Is the market for tomato pickers efficient?

c. If Ontario introduces a minimum wage for tomato pickers of $4 an hour, how many tomato pickers are employed and how many are unemployed?

d. If Ontario introduces a minimum wage for tomato pickers of $8 an hour, how many tomato pickers are employed and how many are unemployed?

e. Is the minimum wage of $8 an hour efficient? Is it fair?

f. Who gains and who loses from the minimum wage of $8 an hour?

Solution to Practice Problem 7.2

Remember that a minimum wage is effective only when it is set above the equilibrium wage rate.

Quick Review

*   *Minimum wage law* A government regulation that makes hiring labour for less than a specified wage illegal.

a. What is the equilibrium wage rate of tomato pickers and what is the equilibrium quantity of tomato pickers employed?

The equilibrium wage rate is $6.00 an hour and the equilibrium quantity of pickers is 4,000 at the intersection of the labour demand curve, *D*, and labour supply curve, *S*.

b. Is the market for tomato pickers efficient?

The market is efficient. At the equilibrium, the marginal benefit to the tomato growers equals the marginal cost borne by the pickers.

c. If Ontario introduces a minimum wage for tomato pickers of $4 an hour, how many tomato pickers are employed and how many are unemployed?

A minimum wage of $4 an hour is less than the equilibrium wage rate. The minimum wage is ineffective. 4,000 pickers are employed and none are unemployed.

d. If Ontario introduces a minimum wage for tomato pickers of $8 an hour, how many tomato pickers are employed and how many are unemployed?

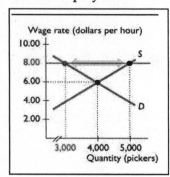

The minimum wage of $8 an hour is above the equilibrium wage rate. In the figure, 3,000 tomato pickers are employed (the quantity of labour demanded when the wage rate is $8 an hour) and 5,000 people would like to work as tomato pickers (the quantity of labour supplied when the wage

rate is $8 an hour). The number of people un-
employed is 5,000 – 3,000, which is 2,000.

**e. Is the minimum wage of $8 an hour effi-
cient? Is it fair?**

The minimum wage of $8 an hour is not effi-
cient because the marginal benefit to growers
(on the demand curve) exceeds the marginal
cost borne by pickers (on the supply curve). A
deadweight loss is created. An additional loss
arises as unemployed tomato pickers search for
jobs. The minimum wage is not fair. It violates
the fair-rules view of fairness because it prevents voluntary exchange. It violates the fair-
results view of fairness because some workers
lose their jobs and are made poorer.

**f. Who gains and who loses from the mini-
mum wage of $8 an hour?**

Tomato pickers who find jobs at the higher
wage rate gain because they earn $8 an hour
rather than $6. Unemployed tomato pickers
lose and all tomato growers lose.

Additional Practice Problem 7.2a

The table gives the supply and demand schedules for sugar.

Price (cents per kilogram)	Quantity demanded	Quantity supplied
	(kilograms of sugar per year)	
10	300	225
15	275	275
20	250	325
25	225	375
30	200	425

a. What is the equilibrium price and quantity
of sugar?

b. If the government imposes a price floor of
25¢ a kilogram, what is the quantity demanded and the quantity supplied? Is
there a shortage or surplus and if so, how
much?

c. Who gains from a price floor of 25¢ a kilogram? Who loses?

Solution to Additional Practice Problem 7.2a

**a. What is the equilibrium price and quan-
tity of sugar?**

The equilibrium price is 15¢ a kilogram and the
equilibrium quantity is 275 kilograms a year.

**b. If the government imposes a price floor of
25¢ a kilogram, what is the quantity demanded and the quantity supplied? Is
there a shortage or surplus and if so, how
much?**

The quantity demanded at 25¢ a kilogram is
225 kilograms and the quantity supplied is 375
kilograms. There is a surplus of 150 kilograms.

**c. Who gains from a price floor of 25¢ a kilo-
gram? Who loses?**

Gainers from the price floor are sugar growers
who sell their sugar at 25¢ a kilogram rather
than 15¢ a kilogram. Losers include sugar producers who cannot sell their sugar and all buyers of sugar.

■ **Self Test 7.2**

Fill in the blanks

A minimum wage is a price _____ (ceiling; floor).
A price floor is the _____ (highest; lowest)
price at which it is legal to trade a particular
good, service, or factor of production. A minimum wage set above the equilibrium wage rate
is _____ (effective; not effective). A minimum
wage _____ (creates; does not create) unemployment and _____ (decreases; increases) job
search activity. An efficient allocation of labour
occurs when the marginal _____ (benefit; cost)
to firms _____ (equals; is greater than) the
marginal _____ (benefit; cost) borne by workers. Labour unions _____ (do not support; support) the minimum wage.

True or false

1. Firms hire labour, so they determine how
much labour to supply in a market.

2. A minimum wage is effective when it is set above the equilibrium wage rate.

3. A minimum wage law can lead to illegal hiring.

4. A minimum wage is fair because low-income workers receive an increase in take-home pay.

5. A minimum wage set above the equilibrium wage rate is efficient.

Multiple choice

1. A price floor

a. sets the maximum price it is legal to charge.

b. is the lowest price at which it is legal to trade a particular good, service, or factor of production.

c. is an illegal price to charge.

d. increases demand.

2. An efficient minimum wage is set

a. above the equilibrium wage rate.

b. below the equilibrium wage rate.

c. equal to the equilibrium wage rate.

d. below $5.

3. A minimum wage set above the equilibrium wage rate

a. increases the quantity of labour supplied.

b. decreases the quantity of labour supplied.

c. shifts the labour supply curve leftward.

d. shifts the labour supply curve rightward.

4. Suppose the current equilibrium wage rate for lifeguards in Halifax is $7.85 an hour. If the government introduces a minimum wage of $8.50 an hour, there is

a. a surplus of lifeguards in Halifax.

b. a shortage of lifeguards in Halifax.

c. no changes in the lifeguard market.

d. an increase in the supply of lifeguards.

5. An increase in an effective minimum wage ____ employment and ____ unemployment.

a. increases; increases

b. increases; decreases

c. decreases; increases

d. decreases; decreases

6. An effective minimum wage

a. increases the quantity of labour demanded.

b. increases job search activity.

c. increases the supply of labour.

d. decreases unemployment.

7. Does the minimum wage create inefficiency when it is set above the equilibrium wage rate?

a. Yes.

b. No.

c. Only if the supply of labour is inelastic.

d. Only if the demand for labour is elastic.

8. When the minimum wage rises, the _____ union labour _____.

a. demand for; increases

b. demand for; decreases

c. supply of; increases

d. supply of; decreases

Complete the graph

1. The table gives the demand and supply schedules for labour in a small town.

Wage rate (dollars per hour)	Quantity demanded	Quantity supplied
	(workers per day)	
4	3,500	2,750
5	3,000	3,000
6	2,500	3,250
7	2,000	3,500
8	1,500	3,750

In Figure 7.2, label the axes. Draw the labour demand curve and the labour supply curve. Indicate the equilibrium wage rate and employment.

FIGURE 7.2

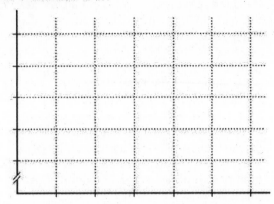

a. What is the effect on the wage rate and levels of employment and unemployment if the government imposes a $4 an hour minimum wage?

b. Indicate any unemployment that arises in Figure 7.2 if the government raises the minimum wage from $4 an hour to $7 an hour.

Short answer

1. Who supports the minimum wage?

2. Do all low-wage workers benefit from a minimum wage?

CHECKPOINT 7.3

■ **Explain how production quotas create inefficiency and unfairness.**

Practice Problem 7.3

The figure shows the market for tomatoes.

a. What are the equilibrium price and quantity of tomatoes?

b. Is the market for tomatoes effi-

cient?

c. If the government introduces a quota for tomato production of 3 billion kilograms a year, what is the price of a kilogram of tomatoes?

d. If the government introduces a quota for tomato production of 1 billion kilograms a year, what is the price of a kilogram of tomatoes?

e. Is the quota of 1 billion kilograms a year efficient?

f. Who gains and who loses from the quota, what are the magnitudes of those gains and losses, and what is the deadweight loss?

g. Could the quota ever be regarded as being fair?

Solution to Practice Problem 7.3

Remember that a quota is effective only when the quota is less than equilibrium quantity.

Quick Review

• *Production quota* An upper limit to the quantity of a good that may be produced in a specified period.

• *Effective quota* When a quota less than the equilibrium quantity is set, the price rises and a deadweight loss is created.

a. **What are the equilibrium price and quantity of tomatoes?**

The equilibrium price and the equilibrium quantity of tomatoes are determined where the demand curve and the supply curve intersect. The equilibrium price is $6.00 a kilogram and the equilibrium quantity of tomatoes is 2 billion kilograms a year.

b. **Is the market for tomatoes efficient?**

Yes, the market is efficient. At the equilibrium, the marginal benefit of consuming the last kilogram of tomatoes equals the marginal cost of producing the last kilogram of tomatoes.

c. **If the government introduces a quota for tomato production of 3 billion kilograms a year, what is the price of a kilogram of tomatoes?**

A quota of 3 billion kilograms of tomatoes a year is greater than the equilibrium quantity, so the quota has no effect. The price remains at $6 a kilogram.

d. **If the government introduces a quota for tomato production of 1 billion kilograms a year, what is the price of a kilogram of tomatoes?**

The quota of 1 billion kilograms of tomatoes a year is less than the equilibrium quantity, so the quota has an effect. The price rises to $8 a kilogram because at this price consumers are willing to buy 1 billion kilograms of tomatoes a year.

e. **Is the quota of 1 billion kilograms a year efficient?**

The quota of 1 billion kilograms of tomatoes a year is inefficient. At 1 billion kilograms a year, the marginal benefit exceeds the marginal cost and a deadweight loss is created. The deadweight loss is the grey triangle in the figure.

f. **Who gains and who loses from the quota, what are the magnitudes of those gains and losses, and what is the deadweight loss?**

Producers gain and consumers lose. Before the quota, producer surplus equals the area of the triangle under the market price of $6 a kilogram and above the supply curve. So the producer surplus before the quota was 1/2 × (2 billion kilograms) × ($4 a kilogram), which is $4 billion dollars. After the quota is imposed, the producer surplus equals the blue area under the price of $8 a kilogram and above the supply curve. The area is 1/2 × (1 billion kilograms) × ($2 a kilogram) + ($4 a kilogram) × (1 billion kilograms), which is $5 billion, so producers gain $1 billion of producer surplus.

Before the quota, consumer surplus equals the area of the triangle above the market price of $6 a kilogram and below the demand curve. So the consumer surplus before the quota was 1/2 × (2 billion kilograms) × ($4 a kilogram), which is $4 billion dollars. After the quota is imposed, the consumer surplus equals the smaller light green triangle. The area of this triangle is ½ × ($2 a kilogram) × (1 billion kilograms), which is $1 billion, so consumers lose $3 billion of consumer surplus.

The deadweight loss is equal to the area of the grey triangle. The area of this triangle is 1/2 × ($4 a kilogram) × (1 billion kilograms), which is $2 billion. The quota has led to a $2 billion deadweight loss.

g. **Could the quota ever be regarded as being fair?**

The quota can be fair only under the fair results concept of fairness and only if producers are poorer than consumers. In this case, the quota raises the incomes of the poor producers. Otherwise, the quota is unfair.

Additional Practice Problem 7.3a
In the practice problem, the government sets the quota. If the quota was voluntary, why would it be difficult for the producers to abide by the quota?

Solution to Additional Practice Problem 7.3a

Each producer has the incentive to produce more than the allotted quota. With the quota in place, the marginal cost of producing another kilogram of tomatoes is $4 and the market price of another kilogram of tomatoes is $8. Producers realize that if they increase production, profit will increase. So if the quota is voluntary, each producer has the incentive to produce more than his or her allotted quota.

■ **Self Test 7.3**

Fill in the blanks

A production quota is ____ (a lower; an upper) limit to the quantity of a good that can be produced in a specified period. A quota that is set at a quantity less than the equilibrium quantity ____ (raises; lowers) the price of the good or service. A quota ____ (increases; decreases) consumer surplus, ____ (increases; decreases) producer surplus, and ____ (creates; does not create) a deadweight loss. It is ____ (easy; difficult) for a voluntary quota to work.

True or false

1. An effective quota must be set at a quantity that is less than the equilibrium quantity.

2. When the government imposes a quota, the government also sets the price that can be charged.

3. By decreasing production, quotas lower the cost of producing the new quantity.

4. Because it decreases production, an effective quota decreases producer surplus in the market.

5. Quotas are efficient because they limit unnecessary production.

Multiple choice

1. A production quota sets
a. an upper limit to the quantity of a good that may be produced in a specified period.
b. a lower limit to the quantity of a good that may be produced in a specified period.
c. an upper limit to the price that may be charged for a good.
d. a lower limit to the price that may be charged for a good.

2. A quota set *above* the equilibrium quantity ____ the price and ____ the quantity produced.
a. raises; increases
b. raises; decreases
c. lowers; increases
d. does not change; does not change

3. A quota set *below* the equilibrium quantity ____ the price and ____ the quantity produced.
a. raises; increases
b. raises; decreases
c. lowers; increases
d. does not change; does not change

4. A quota set below the equilibrium quantity ____ the marginal cost of the good and ____ the price of the good.
a. raises; raises
b. raises; lowers
c. lowers; raises
d. lowers; lowers

5. An effective quota ____ consumer surplus and ____ producer surplus.
a. increases; increases
b. increases; decreases
c. decreases; increases
d. decreases; decreases

6. An effective quota ____ inefficiency and ____ a deadweight loss.

a. leads to; creates

b. leads to; does not create

c. does not lead to; creates

d. does not lead to; does not create

7. A quota is

a. always fair.

b. never fair.

c. possibly fair if producers are richer than consumers.

d. possibly fair if consumers are richer than producers.

8. A voluntary quota is ____ to successfully implement because each producer has the incentive to produce ____ that the allotted quota.

a. easy; more

b. easy; less

c. difficult; more

d. difficult; less

Complete the graph

1. The table gives the demand and supply schedules for wheat.

Price (dollars per basket)	Quantity demanded	Quantity supplied
	(millions of baskets per year)	
3	3,500	2,000
4	3,000	3,000
5	2,500	4,000
6	2,000	5,000
7	1,500	6,000

In Figure 7.3 label the axes. Draw the demand curve and supply curve and indicate the equilibrium price and quantity.

FIGURE 7.3

a. Suppose the government imposes a quota of 5,000 million baskets of wheat a year. What is the effect on the price of wheat, the marginal cost of a basket of wheat, and the quantity produced?

b. With the quota of 5,000 million baskets of wheat, is a deadweight loss created? If so, illustrate it.

c. Suppose the government imposes a quota of 2,000 million baskets of wheat a year. What is the effect on the price of wheat, the marginal cost of a basket of wheat, and the quantity produced?

d. With the quota of 2,000 million baskets of wheat, is a deadweight loss created? If so, illustrate it.

e. Which quota, 5,000 million baskets of wheat a year or 2,000 million baskets of wheat has the largest effect on producer surplus? What is the effect?

Short answer

1. Why must a production quota be set below the equilibrium quantity to be effective?

2. "A quota benefits producers and harms consumers. But there is no overall net effect on society." Comment on this statement. Is it correct or incorrect?

SELF TEST ANSWERS

■ CHECKPOINT 7.1

Fill in the blanks

A price ceiling is the <u>highest</u> price at which it is legal to trade a particular good, service, or factor of production. A rent ceiling is effective if it is set <u>below</u> the equilibrium rent. A rent ceiling can create a housing <u>shortage</u>, which leads to <u>increased</u> search activity. Rent ceilings <u>are not</u> efficient. The <u>more</u> inelastic the demand of housing or the supply of housing, the smaller the deadweight loss created by a rent ceiling. Rent ceilings <u>are not</u> fair. There is <u>plenty of</u> political support for rent ceilings.

True or false

1. False; page 162
2. False; page 163
3. False; page 164
4. False; page 166
5. True; page 166

Multiple choice

1. d; page 162
2. b; pages 162-163
3. a; page 163
4. c; page 163
5. a; page 164
6. b; page 163
7. a; page 166
8. d; page 167

Complete the graph

1. Figure 7.4 shows the demand and supply curves. The equilibrium rent is $800 a month and the quantity is 300 units a month.

■ FIGURE 7.4

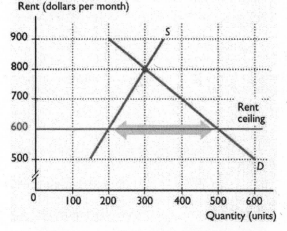

a. The quantity of housing demanded is 500 units a month; the quantity supplied is 200 units a month; pages 162-163.

b. The shortage of 300 units a month is indicated by the arrow; pages 162-163.

Short answer

1. A price ceiling is the highest price at which it is legal to trade a particular good, service, or factor of production. A rent ceiling is an example of a price ceiling; page 162.

2a. The equilibrium price is $1.50 a carton and the equilibrium quantity is 150 cartons a day.

b. The price is $1.25 a carton and 130 cartons a day are purchased. There is a shortage of 45 cartons a day; page 163.

c. The price ceiling is ineffective. The price is $1.50 a carton, 150 cartons a day are purchased, and there is neither a shortage nor a surplus; page 162.

3. Rent ceilings are not efficient. Rent ceilings are not fair. They violate the fair-results view

and the fair-rules view of fairness; pages 166-167.

■ **CHECKPOINT 7.2**

Fill in the blanks

A minimum wage is a price <u>floor</u>. A price floor is the <u>lowest</u> price at which it is legal to trade a particular good, service, or factor of production. A minimum wage set above the equilibrium wage rate is <u>effective</u>. A minimum wage <u>creates</u> unemployment and <u>increases</u> job search activity. An efficient allocation of labour occurs when the marginal <u>benefit</u> to firms <u>equals</u> the marginal <u>cost</u> borne by workers. Labour unions <u>support</u> the minimum wage.

True or false

1. False; page 169
2. True; page 170
3. True; page 171
4. False; page 173
5. False; page 172

Multiple choice

1. b; page 170
2. a; page 170
3. a; page 170
4. a; page 170
5. c; pages 170-171
6. b; page 171
7. a; page 172
8. a; page 173

Complete the graph

1. Figure 7.5 shows the demand curve and the supply curve. The equilibrium wage rate is $5.00 an hour and equilibrium employment is 3,000 workers a day.

■ **FIGURE 7.5**
Wage rate (dollars per hour)

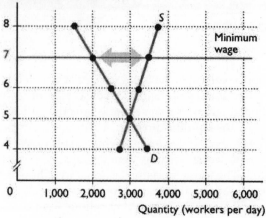

a. The $4 minimum wage is below the equilibrium wage and has no effect; page 170.

b. The $7 minimum wage raises the wage rate to $7. Employment decreases to 2,000 workers. The number of people who would like to work is 3,500. Unemployment equals 3,500 – 2,000, which is 1,500 workers. The amount of unemployment is shown by the arrow in Figure 7.5; page 170.

Short answer

1. The people who find jobs at the minimum wage support the minimum wage because they are better off. Labour unions support the minimum wage because it puts upward pressure on all wage rates including those of union workers; page 173.

2. A minimum wage harms low-wage workers who lose their jobs or cannot find jobs because of the minimum wage; page 173.

■ **CHECKPOINT 7.3**

Fill in the blanks

A production quota is <u>an upper</u> limit to the quantity of a good that can be produced in a specified period. A quota that is set at a quantity less than the equilibrium quantity <u>raises</u> the price of the good or service. A quota <u>decreases</u> consumer surplus, <u>increases</u> producer surplus, and <u>creates</u> a deadweight loss. It is <u>difficult</u> for a voluntary quota to work.

True or false

1. True; page 175

2. False; page 176

3. True; page 176

4. False; page 177

5. False; page 176

Multiple choice

1. a; page 175

2. d; page 175

3. b; page 176

4. c; page 176

5. c; page 177

6. a; page 177

7. d; page 177

8. c; page 177

Complete the graph

1. Figure 7.6 shows the demand and supply curves. The equilibrium price is $4 a basket and the equilibrium quantity is 3,000 million baskets a year.

a. The 5,000 million basket quota for wheat is above the equilibrium quantity and has no effect. The price and marginal cost remain at $4 a basket and the quantity remains at 3,000 million baskets a year; page 175.

b. The quota of 5,000 million baskets of wheat creates no deadweight loss; page 175.

c. The 2,000 million basket quota for wheat is less than the equilibrium quantity and is effective. The price rises to $6 a basket because that is the price that consumers are willing to pay for 2,000 millionth basket. The marginal cost decreases to $3 a basket. The quantity decreases to the quota amount, 2,000 million baskets a year; page 176.

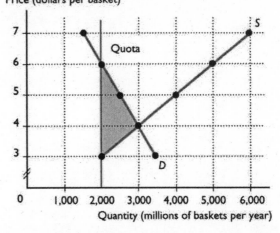

■ FIGURE 7.6

Price (dollars per basket)

d. The quota of 2,000 million baskets of wheat creates a deadweight loss. The deadweight loss is illustrated in Figure 7.6 as the grey triangle; page 177.

e. The quota of 5,000 million baskets of wheat has no effect on producer surplus. The quota of 2,000 million baskets of wheat increases producer surplus; page 177.

Short answer

1. If a production quota is set above the equilibrium quantity, it does not make the equilibrium quantity illegal and is ineffective. If a production quota is set below the equilibrium quantity, it makes the equilibrium quantity illegal and is effective; page 175.

2. The first statement is correct: a quota increases producer surplus (which benefits producers) and decreases consumer surplus (which harms consumers). But the second statement is incorrect. There is a net effect on society because a deadweight loss, which harms society is created,; page 177.

Taxes

Chapter

8

CHAPTER IN PERSPECTIVE

In Chapter 8 we study how taxes affect markets, who pays a tax, the effect of an income tax and a payroll tax, and review ideas about the fairness of taxes.

■ **Describe the effects of sales taxes, the GST, and excise taxes, determine who pays these taxes, and explain why taxes create inefficiencies.**

Taxes raise the price and decrease the quantity of the good that is taxed. Tax incidence is the division of the burden of a tax between the buyer and the seller. For a given elasticity of supply, the buyer pays a larger share of the tax the more inelastic is the demand for the good. And, for a given elasticity of demand, the seller pays a larger share of the tax the more inelastic is the supply of the good. The buyer pays the entire tax when demand is perfectly inelastic or supply is perfectly elastic. The seller pays the entire tax when demand is perfectly elastic or supply is perfectly inelastic. The excess burden of a tax is the amount by which the burden of a tax exceeds the tax revenue received by the government—the deadweight loss from a tax.

■ **Describe the effects of income taxes and social insurance taxes, determine who pays these taxes, and explain which taxes create the greatest inefficiency.**

The marginal tax rate is the percentage of an additional dollar of income that is paid in tax; the average tax rate is the percentage of income that is paid in tax. A progressive tax is a tax whose average rate increases as income increases. A proportional tax is a tax whose average rate is constant at all income levels. A regressive tax is a tax whose average rate decreases as income increases. A tax on labour income decreases employment and creates a deadweight loss. Both the employer and the worker pay part of the tax. A tax on capital income decreases the quantity of capital and creates a deadweight loss. The supply of capital is highly elastic. If the supply of capital is perfectly elastic, firms pay the entire tax. A tax on land or other unique resource does not decrease the quantity and creates no deadweight loss because supply is perfectly inelastic. The entire burden of the tax falls on the owner of the resource. A payroll tax is a tax on employers based on the wages they pay their workers. The incidence of a payroll tax is the same as a social insurance tax on workers because the elasticities of demand and supply, not Parliament, determine who pays the tax.

■ **Review ideas about the fairness of the tax system.**

The benefits principle is the proposition that people should pay taxes equal to the benefits they receive from public services. This arrangement is fair because those who benefit the most pay the most. The ability-to-pay principle is the proposition that people should pay taxes according to how easily they can bear the burden. For fairness, the ability-to-pay principle compares people along vertical and horizontal dimensions. The fairness and efficiency of taxes can conflict, leading to the big tradeoff.

EXPANDED CHAPTER CHECKLIST

When you have completed this chapter, you will be able to

1 Describe the effects of sales taxes, the GST, and excise taxes, determine who pays these taxes, and explain why taxes create inefficiencies.

- Define tax incidence.
- Explain how the incidence of a tax depends on the elasticities of demand and supply.
- Determine who bears the tax if demand is perfectly inelastic or supply is perfectly elastic.
- Determine who bears the tax if demand is perfectly elastic or supply is perfectly inelastic.
- Define the excess burden of a tax and illustrate the deadweight loss from a tax.

2 Describe the effects of income taxes and social insurance taxes, determine who pays these taxes, and explain which taxes create the greatest inefficiency.

- Define taxable income, marginal tax rate, and average tax rate.
- Define progressive tax, regressive tax, and proportional tax.
- Describe how the incidence of an income tax depends upon the elasticity of supply and the elasticity of demand.
- Illustrate the effects of a tax on labour income, capital income, and income from land and other unique resources.
- Show how a payroll tax and a social insurance tax on workers can deliver the same outcome.

3 Review ideas about the fairness of the tax system.

- Discuss the benefits principle and ability-to-pay principle of fairness of taxes.
- Discuss horizontal equity and vertical equity and explain why horizontal and vertical comparisons are difficult to make.

KEY TERMS

- Ability-to-pay principle (page 200)
- Average tax rate (page 191)
- Benefits principle (page 200)
- Excess burden (page 188)
- Horizontal equity (page 200)
- Marginal tax rate (page 191)
- Payroll tax (page 197)
- Progressive tax (page 191)
- Proportional tax (page 191)
- Regressive tax (page 191)
- Taxable income (page 190)
- Tax incidence (page 184)
- Vertical equity (page 201)

CHECKPOINT 8.1

■ Describe the effects of sales taxes, the GST, and excise taxes, determine who pays these taxes, and explain why taxes create inefficiencies.

Practice Problem 8.1

The figure shows the market for softballs. The government imposes a sales tax on softballs of 60 cents a ball.

a. What is the increase in the price that buyers pay for

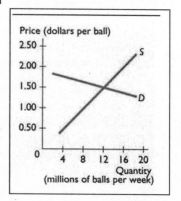

softballs?

b. What is the decrease in the price that sellers receive?

c. What is the decrease in the quantity of softballs?

d. What is the tax revenue from softball sales?

e. Which is more inelastic: the demand for softballs or the supply of softballs? How can you tell?

f. What is the excess burden of the sales tax on softballs?

Solution to Practice Problem 8.1

To work these practice problems, remember that a tax is like an increase in the suppliers' cost. So a tax decreases supply and shifts the supply curve leftward.

Quick Review

- *Effect of a sales tax on the supply curve* A sales tax decreases the supply of the good and the supply curve shifts leftward. The vertical distance between the supply curve without the tax and the supply curve with the tax equals the amount of the tax.

- *Tax incidence and elasticities of demand and supply* For a given elasticity of supply, the more inelastic the demand, the larger the share of a tax paid by the buyer. And, for a given elasticity of demand, the more inelastic the supply, the larger the share of a tax paid by the seller.

a. **What is the increase in the price that buyers pay for softballs?**

The figure shows the effect of the tax. The tax decreases supply. The new supply curve is *S + tax*. The length of the vertical arrow equals the amount of the tax, 60 cents a softball.

The price paid by buyers rises from $1.50 to $1.60, an increase of 10 cents.

b. **What is the decrease in the price that sellers receive?**

The seller receives $1.60 minus the 60 cents tax, which is $1.00 per ball. So the price that sellers receive falls from $1.50 to $1.00, a decrease of 50 cents.

c. **What is the decrease in the quantity of softballs?**

The figure shows that the quantity decreases from 12 million softballs a week to 8 million softballs a week.

d. **What is the tax revenue from softball sales?**

The tax is 60 cents a ball and 8 million balls a week are sold. The tax revenue equals (60 cents) × (8 million balls), which is $4.8 million a week.

e. **Which is more inelastic: the demand for softballs or the supply of softballs? How can you tell?**

The price the seller receives falls from $1.50 to $1.00, so the seller pays 50 cents of the tax. The price the buyer pays rises from $1.50 to $1.60, so the buyer pays 10 cents of the tax. The seller pays more of the tax so the supply is more inelastic than the demand.

f. **What is the excess burden of the sales tax on softballs?**

The excess burden is the deadweight loss of the tax, which equals the area of the grey triangle in the figure. The area of a triangle is 1/2 multiplied by the base multiplied by the height, which is (1/2) × (12 million – 8 million) × ($1.60 – $1.00) = $1.2 million.

Additional Practice Problem 8.1a

Suppose that the initial equilibrium price of a Cole and a Pepsi are the same. The supply of Coke and Pepsi is identical, but the demand for Coke is more elastic than the demand for

Pepsi. The government imposes the same sales tax on Coke and Pepsi.

a. Does the price paid by consumers for a Coke rise by more than, less than, or the same amount as the price paid for a Pepsi?

b. Does the quantity of Coke decrease by more than, less than, or the same amount as the quantity of Pepsi?

c. Does the government collect more than, less than, or the same amount of tax revenue from the tax on Coke as it does from the tax on Pepsi?

Solution to Additional Practice Problem 7.1a

a. **Does the price paid by consumers for a Coke rise by more than, less than, or the same amount as the price paid for a Pepsi?**

   The demand for Coke is more elastic, so consumers play less of the tax imposed on Coke. So, the price paid by consumers for a Coke rises less than the price paid for a Pepsi.

b. **Does the quantity of Coke decrease by more than, less than, or the same amount as the quantity of Pepsi?**

   The quantity of Coke decreases by more than the quantity of Pepsi because the demand for Coke is more elastic than the demand for Pepsi.

c. **Does the government collect more than, less than, or the same amount of tax revenue from the tax on Coke as it does from the tax on Pepsi?**

   The total amount of tax revenue equals the tax multiplied by the quantity sold. Because the decrease in the quantity of Coke is greater than the decrease in the quantity of Pepsi, less Coke than Pepsi is sold after the tax is imposed, and the government collects less tax revenue from the tax on Coke.

■ Self Test 8.1

Fill in the blanks

The tax ____ (elasticity; incidence) is the division of the burden of a tax between the buyer and the seller. A tax is like ____ (a decrease; an increase) in the suppliers' cost. For a given elasticity of supply, the buyer pays a larger share of the tax the more ____ (elastic; inelastic) is the demand for the good. If the supply is perfectly ____ (elastic; inelastic), the seller pays the entire tax. Taxes ____ (create; do not create) a deadweight loss. The excess burden of a tax is the ____ (deadweight loss; surplus) from the tax.

True or false

1. When the government imposes a tax on the sale of a good, the burden of the tax falls entirely on the buyer.

2. For a given elasticity of supply, the more inelastic the demand for a good, the smaller the share of the tax paid by the buyer.

3. When the government taxes a good that has a perfectly elastic supply, the buyer pays the entire tax.

4. A tax on fast-food meals does not create a deadweight loss because the elasticity of supply of fast-food meals equals 1.0.

5. The excess burden of a tax is the deadweight loss from the tax.

Multiple choice

1. Tax incidence refers to

a. how government taxes are spent by the government.

b. the incidences of tax revolts by the tax payers.

c. the amount of a tax minus its burden.

d. the division of the burden of a tax between the buyer and the seller.

2. Neither the supply of nor demand for a good is perfectly elastic or perfectly inelastic. So imposing a tax on the good results in a ____ in the price paid by buyers and ____ in the equilibrium quantity.

a. rise; an increase

b. rise; a decrease

c. fall; an increase

d. fall; a decrease

3. Neither the supply of nor demand for a good is perfectly elastic or perfectly inelastic. So imposing a tax on the good results in a ____ in the price received by sellers and a ____ in the price paid by buyers.

a. rise; rise

b. rise; fall

c. fall; rise

d. fall; fall

4. To determine who bears the greater share of a tax, we compare

a. the number of buyers to the number of sellers.

b. the elasticity of supply to the elasticity of demand.

c. the size of the tax to the price of the good.

d. government tax revenue to business revenue.

5. Suppose the demand for barley is perfectly elastic. The supply curve of barley is upward sloping. If a tax is imposed on barley,

a. barley sellers pay the entire tax.

b. barley buyers pay the entire tax.

c. the government pays the entire tax.

d. the tax is split evenly between barley buyers and sellers.

6. A sales tax ____ consumer surplus and ____ producer surplus.

a. increases; increases

b. increases; decreases

c. decreases; increases

d. decreases; decreases

7. The deadweight loss from a tax is called the ____ the tax.

a. marginal benefit of

b. marginal cost of

c. excess burden of

d. net gain from

8. A sales tax creates a deadweight loss because

a. there is some paperwork opportunity cost of sellers paying the sales tax.

b. demand and supply both decrease.

c. less is produced and consumed.

d. citizens value government goods less than private goods.

Complete the graph

1. The supply curve and the demand curve for pizza slices are shown in Figure 8.1. The price is in dollars per slice and the quantity is thousands of pizza slices per day. Label the axes.

■ FIGURE 8.1

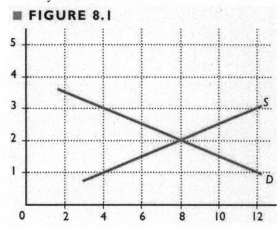

a. What is the equilibrium price and quantity of pizza slices?

b. Suppose the government imposes a sales tax of $2 a slice of pizza. In Figure 8.1, draw the new supply curve after the tax is imposed.

c. After the tax is imposed, what is the price paid by buyers for a slice of pizza? What is the price received by sellers for a slice of pizza? What is the incidence of the tax?

d. In Figure 8.1, darken the area of the dead-weight loss from the tax.

Short answer

Price (dollars per golf ball)	Quantity demanded (golf balls)	Before-tax quantity supplied (golf balls)	After-tax quantity supplied (golf balls)
0.50	1,100	600	0
1.00	1,000	620	0
1.50	900	680	0
2.00	700	700	0
2.50	600	850	____
3.00	300	950	____
3.50	60	1,180	680

1. The above table gives the monthly demand and supply schedules for golf balls at the College Hills Golf Shop. With no tax, what is the equilibrium price and quantity?

Suppose a $2 per ball tax is imposed.

a. Complete the last column of the table.

b. What is the equilibrium price and quantity after the tax is imposed?

c. How much of the tax is paid by the buyer? How much is paid by the seller?

d. How much tax revenue does the government collect?

2. The government decides to tax high blood pressure medicine. The supply by drug companies is elastic; the demand by patients is inelastic. Do the drug companies bear the entire tax burden?

3. What is the relationship between the dead-weight loss from a tax and the excess burden of a tax? Why does a tax create a dead-weight loss?

CHECKPOINT 8.2

■ Describe the effects of income taxes and social insurance taxes, determine who pays these taxes, and explain which taxes create the greatest inefficiency.

Practice Problems 8.2

The table sets out some of Alberta's 2003 taxes.

Tax	Tax rate
Personal income tax	10.0%
Corporate income tax	
Large corporations	12.5%
Small businesses	4.0%
Fuel tax on gasoline	9¢ a litre
Tobacco tax	$32 a carton
Sales tax	0%

Classify each of these taxes as progressive, proportional, and regressive taxes.

2. Explain why Shania Twain pays her own social insurance tax and concert organizers pay none of it.

3. Which tax has the greater excess burden, a tax on land rent or a tax on capital income? Why?

Solution to Practice Problems 8.2

The first Practice Problem gives you practice in recognizing whether a tax is progressive, regressive, or proportional.

Quick Review

• *Progressive tax* A tax whose average rate increases as income increases.

• *Proportional tax* A tax whose average rate is constant at all income levels.

• *Regressive tax* A tax whose average rate decreases as income increases.

1. **Classify each of these taxes as progressive, proportional, and regressive taxes.**

Proportional: The personal income tax rate does not vary with income, so it is a proportional tax.

Regressive: The fuel tax and cigarette tax are excise taxes. These items consume a larger fraction of low income earners' spending and a smaller fraction of high income earners' spending so they are regressive taxes.

Progressive: The corporate income tax is a progressive tax because the tax rate is higher on larger corporations than on small businesses.

2. **Explain why Shania Twain pays her own social insurance tax and concert organizers pay none of it.**

Shania Twain's supply of concerts is most likely perfectly inelastic. When supply is perfectly inelastic, the supplier pays the entire tax. So, Shania Twain pays the entire social insurance tax. Her salary is lower by the amount of the tax, and the concert organizers pay none of the tax.

3. **Which tax has the greater excess burden, a tax on land rent or a tax on capital income? Why?**

A tax on capital income has a much greater excess burden because the supply of capital is very elastic and the supply of land is perfectly inelastic. The highly elastic supply of capital means that a tax imposed on capital income leads to a large decrease in the equilibrium quantity of capital and a large deadweight loss. The perfectly inelastic supply of land means that a tax imposed on land rent leads to no decrease in the equilibrium quantity of land and no deadweight loss.

Additional Practice Problem 8.2a

In Hong Kong, the marginal tax rates on salaries ranges from 2 percent to 20 percent with a maximum average tax of 15 percent, which is reached on incomes of about $59,000. Compare the marginal tax rates in Hong Kong with the Canadian marginal tax rates.

In which country is the personal income tax (tax on salaries) more progressive? Why?

Solution to Additional Practice Problem 8.2a

The personal income tax in Canada is more progressive because the average tax rate increases to higher levels in Canada. Because Hong Kong's marginal tax rates are lower than Canada's marginal tax rates, Hong Kong's average tax rate remains lower than Canada's average tax rate.

■ Self Test 8.2

Fill in the blanks

The percentage of an additional dollar of income that is paid in tax is _____ (a progressive tax; a marginal tax; an average tax) rate. A tax is regressive if the average tax rate _____ (increases; decreases) as income increases. A tax on labour income _____ (creates; does not create) a deadweight loss. If the supply of capital is perfectly elastic, a tax on capital income is paid entirely by the _____ (firms; lenders) and the tax _____ (creates; does not create) a deadweight loss. If the supply of land is perfectly _____ (inelastic; elastic), a tax on income from land is paid entirely by the landowners and the tax _____ (creates; does not create) a deadweight loss. An social insurance tax on workers and a payroll tax both _____ (raise; lower) the wage rate that employees receive and _____ (increase; decrease) employment.

True or false

1. When Hank earns an additional dollar, he pays 30 cents in additional tax. Hank's marginal tax rate is 30 percent.

2. If the average tax rate increases as income increases, the tax is a progressive tax.

3. Sam has $40,000 of taxable income and pays $4,000 income tax. Bert has $50,000 of taxable income and pays $4,500 income tax. Sam and Bert live in a country with a progressive income tax.

4. An income tax on labour creates a dead-weight loss.

5. If the supply of capital is perfectly elastic, a tax on capital income decreases the demand for capital and decreases the interest rate.

Multiple choice

1. The percentage of an additional dollar of income that is paid in tax is the
   a. sales tax.
   b. excise tax.
   c. marginal tax rate.
   d. personal income tax.

2. If the average tax rate is constant as income increases, then the tax is
   a. regressive.
   b. progressive.
   c. proportional.
   d. an average tax.

3. If we tax labour income, the tax
   a. increases the quantity employed because the demand for labour increases.
   b. decreases the quantity employed because the supply of labour decreases.
   c. increases the quantity employed because the supply of labour increases.
   d. decreases the quantity employed because the demand for labour increases.

4. The incidence of an income tax on labour income is generally that the tax is
   a. paid by workers.
   b. paid by employers.
   c. shared between workers and employers.
   d. funded by the deadweight loss.

5. When governments tax capital income, the equilibrium quantity of capital
   a. increases because of the international mobility of capital.
   b. does not change because the supply of capital is perfectly elastic.
   c. decreases.
   d. does not change because the supply of capital is perfectly inelastic.

6. If the supply of capital is perfectly elastic, the incidence of a tax on capital income is
   a. paid entirely by the lenders.
   b. paid entirely by firms.
   c. shared between firms and the lenders.
   d. unknown.

7. A tax on income from land in Calgary is borne entirely by landowners because the
   a. demand for land is perfectly inelastic.
   b. supply of land is perfectly inelastic.
   c. supply of land is perfectly elastic.
   d. demand for land is perfectly elastic.

8. When a social insurance tax is imposed on workers, the level of employment ____ and when a payroll tax is imposed, the level of employment ____.
   a. increases; increases
   b. increases; decreases
   c. decreases; increases
   d. decreases; decreases

Complete the graph

1. Figure 8.2 shows the labour market.
   a. Label the curves. What is the equilibrium wage rate and quantity of labour?
   b. Suppose the government imposes an income tax of $4 an hour on labour income. Illustrate the effect of this tax in the figure.
   c. After the tax is imposed, what is the wage rate paid by firms and what is the amount received by households?

d. If a deadweight loss is created, shade its area. If a deadweight loss is not created, explain why not.

■ **FIGURE 8.2**
Wage rate (dollars per hour)

Quantity of labour (hours per week)

■ **FIGURE 8.3**
Rent (dollars per hectare per year)

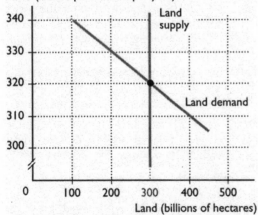

Land (billions of hectares)

2. Figure 8.3 shows the market for land.

a. What is the equilibrium rent and quantity of land?

b. Suppose the government imposes a tax on land income of $10 a hectare. What is the new equilibrium rent paid by renters and what is the amount of rent kept by land-owners? What is the equilibrium quantity of land?

c. If a deadweight loss is created, shade its area. If a deadweight loss is not created, explain why not.

3. Figure 8.4 shows a labour supply curve and labour demand curve. In the figure show the effect of a $5 an hour payroll tax on firms. What is the wage that workers receive before the tax and after the tax? How is the burden of the tax split?

■ **FIGURE 8.4**
Wage rate (dollars per hour)

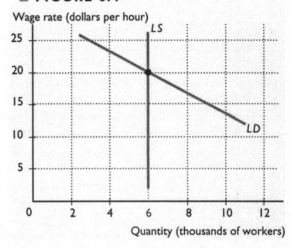

Quantity (thousands of workers)

Short answer

1. Why is the supply of capital highly elastic? Who pays the tax on capital income if the supply of capital is perfectly elastic?

2. Explain why the government cannot mandate that a payroll tax is to be shared equally by the employer and the worker.

CHECKPOINT 8.3

■ **Review ideas about the fairness of the tax system.**

Practice Problem 8.3

In Hong Kong, the marginal income tax rates range from 2 percent to 20 percent. Does Hong Kong place greater weight on the ability-to-pay principle than does Canada? Does Hong Kong place a greater weight on efficiency and a smaller weight on fairness than does Canada?

Solution to Practice Problem 7.3

This Practice Problem gives you practice in recognizing the tradeoff between the fairness of a tax and the efficiency of a tax.

Quick Review

- *Benefits principle* People should pay taxes equal to the benefits they receive from public services.

- *Ability-to-pay principle* People should pay taxes according to how easily they can bear the burden.

  In Hong Kong, the marginal income tax rates range from 2 percent to 20 percent. Does Hong Kong place greater weight on the ability-to-pay principle than does Canada? Does Hong Kong place a greater weight on efficiency and a smaller weight on fairness than does Canada?

The income tax rates in Hong Kong are less than the income tax rates in Canada, so Hong Kong places less weight on the ability-to-pay principle. Taxes create inefficiency and deadweight loss. The lower the tax rate, the less the inefficiency and the smaller the deadweight loss. Because Hong Kong's tax rates are lower than Canada's tax rates, Hong Kong places greater weight on efficiency and less weight on fairness.

Additional Practice Problem 8.3a

"The only fair taxes are user fees, such as toll roads. The gas tax is fair because the funds raised go for road maintenance. All government-provided services need to be funded through user fees. To pay for parks, we need to charge entrance fees. The cost of garbage collection must be based on how much garbage the household creates. Any tax except a user fee is unfair and must be abolished!" Comment on the fairness principle being used. Is it possible for *all* government programs to be funded through user fees?

Solution to Additional Practice Problem 8.3a

The speaker is advocating the benefits principle of taxation, which is the proposition that people should pay taxes equal to the benefits they receive from public services. Although user fees have merit, it is not possible to fund all government programs through user fees. First, for public goods such as national defence, everyone consumes the same amount. It is impossible to determine how much any particular person benefits and therefore not possible to determine the proper fee. Second, some programs are designed to redistribute income to poorer people. It would be ludicrous to tax welfare recipients an amount equal to the benefits they received, which is the case under a user-fee arrangement.

■ Self Test 8.3

Fill in the blanks

The ____ (ability-to-pay; benefits) principle is the proposition that people should pay taxes equal to the benefits they receive from public services. Imposing a higher sales tax on the purchase of jewellery than on food is fair according to the ____ (ability-to-pay; benefit) principle. ____ (Horizontal; Vertical) equity requires that taxpayers with the same ability to pay should pay the same taxes. In Canada, the taxable unit is the _____ (individual; family).

True or false

1. The benefits principle asserts that those people who are harmed by the deadweight loss from a tax should not pay the tax.

2. If the revenue from gasoline taxes is used to pay for road repairs, the tax reflects the ability-to-pay principle.

3. The Canadian income tax system, which uses progressive income taxes, can be considered fair based on the principle of vertical equity.

4. Both vertical and horizontal equity can be achieved when the taxable unit is the family.

5. Canada's income tax system is fair and the U.S. income tax system is unfair.

Multiple choice

1. Which of the following taxes best illustrates the benefits principle of taxation?
   a. sales tax on clothing
   b. state income tax
   c. federal payroll tax
   d. gasoline tax

2. The proposition that people should pay taxes according to how easily they can bear the burden is the ____ principle
   a. regressive tax
   b. benefits
   c. ability-to-pay
   d. fairness

3. If the government imposes a luxury tax on very expensive jewellery, this tax followed the ____ principle.
   a. benefits
   b. ability-to-pay
   c. vertical equity
   d. horizontal equity

4. The proposition that taxpayers with the same ability to pay should pay the same taxes is called
   a. the benefits principle.
   b. the ability-to-pay imperative.
   c. vertical equity.
   d. horizontal equity.

5. Vertical equity implies that
   a. tax rates should be equal for all tax payers.
   b. people with higher incomes should pay more in taxes.
   c. people with higher incomes should pay a lower average tax rate.
   d. All of the above are implied by the principle of vertical equity.

6. Joan's income is $60,000 and she pays $6,000 in taxes. Juan's income is $40,000 and he pays $7,000 in taxes. This situation violates
   a. the benefits principle.
   b. the big tradeoff.
   c. vertical equity.
   d. horizontal equity.

Short answer

1. There are a variety of welfare programs designed to boost the income of poor families. Does it make sense to raise the tax revenue necessary to fund these programs by using the benefits principle of taxation?

2. Is the U.S. tax system fairer than the Canadian tax system?

SELF TEST ANSWERS

■ **CHECKPOINT 8.1**

Fill in the blanks

The tax incidence is the division of the burden of a tax between the buyer and the seller. A tax is like an increase in the suppliers' cost. For a given elasticity of supply, the buyer pays a larger share of the tax the more inelastic is the demand for the good. If the supply is perfectly inelastic, the seller pays the entire tax. Taxes create a deadweight loss. The excess burden of a tax is the deadweight loss from the tax.

True or false

1. False; page 185
2. False; page 185
3. True; page 186
4. False; page 188
5. True; page 188

Multiple choice

1. d; page 184
2. b; page 184
3. c; page 184
4. b; page 185
5. a; page 186
6. d; page 188
7. c; page 188
8. c; page 188

Complete the graph

1. The axes are labelled in Figure 8.5.
a. The price is $2 a slice and the quantity is 8,000 slices a day; page 184.
b. Figure 8.5 shows the supply curve after the tax is imposed; page 185.

c. Buyers pay $3 a slice; sellers receive $1 a slice. The tax is split equally; page 185.

d. The deadweight loss is the grey triangle in Figure 8.5; page 188.

■ **FIGURE 8.5**

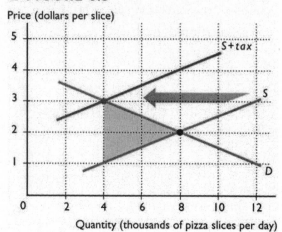

Price (dollars per slice)

Quantity (thousands of pizza slices per day)

Short answer

The equilibrium price is $2.00 a golf ball and the equilibrium quantity is 700 golf balls.

a. The completed supply schedule is in the table; page 184.

Price (dollars per golf ball)	After-tax quantity supplied (golf balls per month)
2.50	600
3.00	620

b. $2.50 a golf ball and 600 golf balls; page 185.

c. The buyer pays $0.50 of the tax. The seller pays $1.50 of the tax; page 185.

d. The tax revenue is $2 a ball × 600 balls, which is $1,200; page 185.

2. The burden of the tax will fall mainly upon buyers, not the drug companies, because demand is inelastic and supply is elastic; page 185.

3. The excess burden of a tax is the same as the deadweight loss. The deadweight loss arises because the tax leads to less of the good or service being produced and consumed; page 188.

■ **CHECKPOINT 8.2**

Fill in the blanks

The percentage of an additional dollar of income that is paid in tax is <u>a marginal tax</u> rate. A tax is regressive if the average tax rate <u>decreases</u> as income increases. A tax on labour income <u>creates</u> a deadweight loss. If the supply of capital is perfectly elastic, a tax on capital income is paid entirely by the <u>firms</u> and the tax <u>creates</u> a deadweight loss. If the supply of land is perfectly <u>inelastic</u>, a tax on income from land is paid entirely by the landowners and the tax <u>does not create</u> a deadweight loss. A social insurance tax on workers and a payroll tax both <u>lower</u> the wage rate that employees receive and <u>decrease</u> employment.

True or false

1. True; page 191
2. True; page 191
3. False; page 191
4. True; page 192
5. False; page 193

Multiple choice

1. c; page 191
2. c; page 191
3. b; page 192
4. c; page 192
5. c; page 193
6. b; page 193
7. b; page 195
8. d; pages 196-197

Complete the graph

1. a. The curves are labelled LD and LS_0 in Figure 8.6. The equilibrium wage rate is $10 an hour and the equilibrium quantity of labour is 35 hours a week; page 192.

   b. The income tax decreases the supply of labour. The labour supply curve shifts leftward from LS_0 to LS_1. The vertical distance between LS_0 and LS_1, indicated by the arrow, is equal to the $4 tax; page 192.

■ **FIGURE 8.6**

Wage rate (dollars per hour)

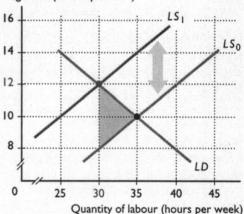

   c. Firms pay a wage rate of $12 an hour; workers receive a wage rate of $8 an hour; page 192.

   d. The deadweight loss is the grey triangle in Figure 8.6; page 192.

2. a. The equilibrium rent is $320 a hectare per year and the equilibrium quantity of land is 300 billion hectares; page 195.

   b. After the tax, renters pay $320 a hectare and landowners keep $310 a hectare. The equilibrium quantity of land is 300 billion hectares, the same as before the tax was imposed; page 195.

   c. There is no deadweight loss created because the equilibrium quantity does not change. The amount produced remains the efficient quantity; page 195.

■ **FIGURE 8.7**

Wage rate (dollars per hour)

Quantity (thousands of workers)

3. Figure 8.7 shows the effect of the tax. The wage rate before the tax is $20 an hour and the wage rate after the tax is $15 an hour. The workers pay all the tax; page 197.

Short Answer

1. Because capital is internationally mobile, its supply is highly (perhaps perfectly) elastic. If the supply of capital is perfectly elastic, firms pay the entire tax on capital income; page 193.

2. The burden of the payroll tax is determined by the elasticity of supply and the elasticity of demand of labour, not by the government splitting the tax. If the demand for labour is more elastic than supply, the burden falls more on the worker and less on the employer. The government can legislate how the tax is collected, but cannot legislate the division of the tax's burden; pages 196-197.

■ **CHECKPOINT 8.3**

Fill in the blanks

The benefits principle is the proposition that people should pay taxes equal to the benefits they receive from public services. Imposing a higher sales tax on the purchase of jewellery than on food is fair according to the ability-to-pay principle. Horizontal equity is the requirement that taxpayers with the same ability to pay should pay the same taxes. In Canada, the taxable unit is the individual.

True or false

1. False; page 200
2. False; page 200
3. True; page 201
4. False; pages 201-202
5. False; page 201

Multiple choice

1. d; page 200
2. c; page 200
3. b; page 200
4. d; page 200
5. b; page 201
6. c; page 201

Short answer

1. If the taxes necessary to fund the various welfare programs were assessed using the benefits principle of taxation, poor families would be required to pay the tax because they are the ones who benefit from the programs. But this outcome would defeat the purpose of the programs, which are designed to increase these families' incomes. The benefits principle of taxation does not work for government programs designed to increase the incomes of the poor; page 200.

2. In Canada, the taxable unit is the individual. In the United States, the taxable unit is the family. Suppose there are two couples making identical total income. In the United States they pay the same income tax. In Canada, each individual pays income tax according to his or her individual income. It is not clear which system is fair. Does horizontal equity require the two family units to be treated alike? Or does it require the four individuals to be treated alike? page 201.

Externalities

CHAPTER IN PERSPECTIVE

An externality in an unregulated market leads to inefficiency and creates a deadweight loss. Chapter 9 explains the role of the government in markets where an externality is present and how government intervention can result in an efficient level of production.

■ **Explain why negative externalities lead to inefficient overproduction and how property rights, pollution charges, or taxes can achieve a more efficient outcome.**

Marginal private cost is the cost of producing an additional unit of a good or service that is borne by the producer of that good or service. Marginal external cost is the cost of producing an additional unit of a good or service that falls on people other than the producer. And marginal social cost, which is the marginal cost incurred by the entire society is the sum of marginal private cost and marginal external cost. Producers take account only of marginal private cost and overproduce when there is a marginal external cost. Sometimes it is possible to reduce the inefficiency arising from an externality by establishing a property right where one does not currently exist. The Coase theorem is the proposition that if property rights exist, only a small number of parties are involved, and transactions costs are low, then private transactions are efficient and the outcome is not affected by who is assigned the property right. When property rights cannot be assigned, the three main methods that governments can use to cope with externalities are emission charges, marketable permits, and taxes.

■ **Explain why positive externalities lead to inefficient underproduction and how public provision, subsidies, vouchers, and patents can achieve a more efficient outcome.**

Marginal private benefit is the benefit from an additional unit of a good or service that the consumer of that good or service receives. Marginal external benefit is the benefit from an additional unit of a good or service that people other than the consumer of the good or service enjoy. And marginal social benefit, which is the marginal benefit enjoyed by society, is the sum of marginal private benefit and marginal external benefit. External benefits from education arise because better-educated people tend to be better citizens, commit fewer crimes, and support social activities. External benefits from research arise because once someone has worked out a basic idea others can copy. When people make decisions about how much schooling to undertake, they undervalue its external benefits and place most emphasis on its private benefits. The result is that if education were provided by private schools that charged full-cost tuition, we would produce too few college graduates. Four devices that governments can use to achieve a more efficient allocation of resources in the presence of external benefits are public provision, private subsidies, vouchers, and patents and copyrights.

EXPANDED CHAPTER CHECKLIST

When you have completed this chapter, you will be able to

1 Explain why negative externalities lead to inefficient overproduction and how property rights, pollution charges, or taxes can achieve a more efficient outcome.

- Give an example of a negative externality and an example of a positive externality.
- Define marginal private cost, marginal external cost, and marginal social cost.
- Draw a figure that shows the relationship between marginal private cost, marginal external cost, and marginal social cost.
- Draw a figure that shows the inefficiency with an external cost.
- Explain the Coase theorem.
- Describe how emission charges, marketable permits, and taxes can lead to efficiency in a market with an external cost.

2 Explain why positive externalities lead to inefficient underproduction and how public provision, subsidies, vouchers, and patents can achieve a more efficient outcome.

- Define marginal private benefit, marginal external benefit, and marginal social benefit.
- Draw a figure that shows the relationship between marginal private benefit, marginal external benefit, and marginal social benefit.
- Draw a figure that shows the inefficiency with an external benefit.
- Describe how public provision, private subsidies, vouchers, and patents and copyrights can lead to efficiency in a market with an external benefit.

KEY TERMS

- Coase theorem (page 214)
- Copyright (page 225)
- Externality (page 208)
- Intellectual property rights (page 225)
- Marginal external benefit (page 220)
- Marginal external cost (page 210)
- Marginal private benefit (page 220)
- Marginal private cost (page 210)
- Marginal social benefit (page 220)
- Marginal social cost (page 210)
- Negative externality (page 208)
- Patent (page 225)
- Positive externality (page 208)
- Property rights (page 213)
- Public provision (page 222)
- Subsidy (page 223)
- Transactions costs (page 214)
- Voucher (page 224)

CHECKPOINT 9.1

■ Explain why negative externalities lead to inefficient overproduction and how property rights, pollution charges, or taxes can achieve a more efficient outcome.

Practice Problem 9.1

The figure illustrates the unregulated market for pesticide. When the factories produce pesticide, they also create waste, which they dump into a lake on the outskirts of the town. The marginal external cost of the dumped waste is equal to the marginal private cost of producing the pesticide, so the marginal social cost of producing the pesticide is double the marginal private cost.

a. What is the quantity of pesticide produced if no one owns the lake?

b. What is the efficient quantity of pesticide?

c. If the residents of the town own the lake, what is the quantity of pesticide produced and how much do the pesticide factories pay to residents of the town?

d. If the pesticide factories own the lake, how much pesticide is produced and how much does the town pay the factories to produce the efficient quantity of pesticide?

e. Suppose that no one owns the lake but the government levies a pollution tax. What is the tax per tonne of pesticide that will achieve the efficient outcome?

Solution to Practice Problem 9.1

This Practice Problem studies the negative production externality of pollution. Part (c) and part (d) use the Coase theorem. According to the Coase theorem, the outcome is efficient if the residents own the lake or if the pesticide factories own the lake.

Quick Review

*   *Marginal private cost* The cost of producing an additional unit of a good or service that is borne by the producer of that good or service.

*   *Marginal external cost* The cost of producing an additional unit of a good or service that falls on people other than the producer.

*   *Marginal social cost* The marginal cost incurred by the entire society—by the producer and by everyone else on whom the cost falls. It is the sum of marginal private cost and marginal external cost.

a. What is the quantity of pesticide produced if no one owns the lake?

If no one owns the lake, the market supply curve is the marginal private cost curve. In the figure the quantity of pesticide produced is the quantity where the demand curve, D = MB, intersects the marginal private cost curve, S = MC. The quantity of pesticide produced is 30 tonnes a week.

b. What is the efficient quantity of pesticide?

At the efficient quantity, the marginal benefit to the factories equals the marginal social cost. The marginal social cost is the sum of the marginal private cost and the marginal external cost. In the figure, the efficient quantity is the quantity where the demand curve, D = MB, intersects the marginal social cost curve, MSC. The efficient quantity is 20 tonnes a week.

c. If the residents of the town own the lake, what is the quantity of pesticide produced and how much do the pesticide factories pay to residents of the town?

The quantity of pesticide produced is the efficient quantity, which is 20 tonnes a week. The factories pay the townspeople the marginal external cost. In the figure, the marginal external cost is the distance between the marginal private cost curve, S = MC, and the marginal social cost curve, MSC. The marginal external cost is $50 a tonne.

d. If the pesticide factories own the lake, how much pesticide is produced and how much does the town pay the factories to produce the efficient quantity of pesticide?

The quantity of pesticide produced is the efficient quantity, which is 20 tonnes a week. The town pays the factories nothing because the factories own the lake and the *MSC* curve becomes the factories' private *MC* curve.

e. Suppose that no one owns the lake but the government levies a pollution tax. What is the tax per tonne of pesticide that will achieve the efficient outcome?

At the efficient quantity of 20 tonnes a week, the marginal external cost is $50 a tonne. A tax of $50 a tonne will set firms' marginal private cost equal to marginal social cost and result in the efficient quantity being produced.

Additional Practice Problem 9.1a

Two factories each emit 10 tonnes of the pollutant sulfur dioxide a week. The cost to eliminate a tonne of sulfur dioxide to Factory A is $4 and the cost to Factory B is $2. The government wants to eliminate 10 tonnes of sulfur dioxide a week.

a. If the government requires that Firm A decrease emissions by 10 tonnes a week, what is the cost of eliminating the pollution?

b. If the government requires that Firm B decrease emissions by 10 tonnes a week, what is the cost of eliminating the pollution?

c. If the government gives each firm 5 marketable permits, each good for 1 tonne of pollution a week, what will occur?

Solution to Additional Practice Problem 9.1a

a. If the government requires that Firm A decrease emissions by 10 tonnes a week, what is the cost of eliminating the pollution?

The cost is $4 a tonne multiplied by 10 tonnes, which is $40 a week.

b. If the government requires that Firm B decrease emissions by 10 tonnes a week, what is the cost of eliminating the pollution?

The cost is $2 a tonne multiplied by 10 tonnes, which is $20 a week.

c. If the government gives each firm 5 marketable permits, each good for 1 tonne of pollution, what will occur?

Firm A will buy permits from Firm B for any price less than $4 a permit; Firm B will sell permits to Firm A for any price greater than $2 a permit. The companies settle on a price and Firm A buys 5 permits from Firm B. Firm B decreases its pollution and incurs a cost of $20 a week.

■ Self Test 9.1

Fill in the blanks

Marginal private cost equals marginal social cost _____ (minus; plus) marginal external cost. A pollution externality creates an _____ (efficient; inefficient) equilibrium. According to the Coase theorem, if property rights exist, only a small number of parties are involved, and transactions costs are low, then private transactions are efficient and the outcome _____ (is; is not) affected by who is assigned the property right. By setting the tax rate equal to the marginal _____ (external; private; social) cost, firms behave in the same way as they would if they bore the cost of the externality directly.

True or false

1. All externalities are negative.

2. Smoking on a plane creates a negative externality.

3. Marginal social cost equals marginal private cost minus marginal external cost.

4. Copper mining creates land pollution. If the copper mining industry is unregulated, then the quantity of copper mined is less than the efficient quantity.

5. The Coase theorem concludes that if property rights to a polluted river are assigned to the polluter, the quantity of pollution will increase.

6. Emission charges allow the government to set the price for a unit of pollution.

7. By issuing marketable permits, the government sets the price for each unit of pollution produced.

8. If the government imposes a pollution tax on lead mining equal to its marginal external cost, the quantity of lead mined will be the efficient quantity.

Multiple choice

1. An externality is
a. something that is external to the economy.
b. a sales tax on a good.
c. a cost or a benefit that arises from production that falls on someone other than the producer; or a cost or benefit that arises from consumption that falls on someone other than the consumer.
d. anything produced in other countries

2. The cost of producing one more unit of a good or service that is borne by the producer of that good or service
a. is the marginal social cost.
b. equals marginal cost minus marginal benefit.
c. is the marginal private cost.
d. is the external cost.

3. The cost of producing an additional unit of a good or service that falls on people other than the producer is
a. the marginal cost.
b. represented by the demand curve.
c. represented by the supply curve.
d. the marginal external cost.

4. Pollution is an example of a
a. negative production externality.
b. negative consumption externality.
c. positive production externality.
d. positive consumption externality.

5. An example of an external cost is
a. second-hand smoke.
b. sulfur emitting from a smoke stack.
c. garbage on the roadside.
d. All of the above answers are correct.

6. The marginal cost of production that is borne by the entire society is the _____ cost.
a. marginal private
b. marginal social
c. marginal external
d. total external

7. The marginal private cost of producing one kilowatt of power is five cents and the marginal social cost of producing each kilowatt is nine cents. The marginal external cost is
a. five cents a kilowatt.
b. nine cents a kilowatt.
c. four cents a kilowatt.
d. zero cents a kilowatt.

8. When the production of a good has a marginal external cost, which of the following will occur in an unregulated market?
a. Overproduction relative to the efficient level will occur.
b. The market price will be less the marginal social cost of the equilibrium quantity.
c. A deadweight loss will occur.
d. All of the above will occur.

9. The Coase theorem is the proposition that if property rights exist, a small number of parties are involved, and transactions costs are low, then private transactions are
a. inefficient.
b. efficient.
c. inequitable.
d. illegal.

10. A marketable permit
a. allows firms to maximize pollution.
b. allows firms to buy and sell the right to pollute at government-controlled prices.
c. eliminates pollution by setting the price of permits above the marginal cost of polluting.
d. allows firms to buy and sell the right to pollute.

11. To work out the emission charge that achieves efficiency, the regulator must determine the _____ cost of pollution at different levels of output.

a.   marginal external

b.   marginal social

c.   total

d.   private

12. If a polluting producer is forced to pay an emission charge or a tax on its output, which of the following occurs?

a.   The quantity supplied along the firm's supply curve will increase.

b.   The firm's demand curve will shift leftward.

c.   The firm's supply curve will shift rightward.

d.   The firm's supply curve will shift leftward.

Complete the graph

1. The table shows the marginal private cost, marginal social cost, and marginal benefit schedules for generating electricity, an activity that creates pollution.

Quantity (megawatts per day)	Marginal private cost	Marginal social cost	Marginal benefit
	(dollars per megawatt)		
1	5	10	50
2	10	20	40
3	15	30	30
4	20	40	20

a.   In Figure 9.1, label the axes and then plot the marginal private cost curve, the marginal social cost curve and marginal benefit curve.

b.   How much electricity will an unregulated market produce? What is the marginal external cost at this amount of production?

c.   What is the efficient amount of electricity? Illustrate the deadweight loss resulting from the market equilibrium.

d.   At the efficient quantity of electricity, what is the marginal external cost? If the government imposes a tax on producing electricity to produce the efficient quantity, what should be the amount of tax?

■ FIGURE 9.1

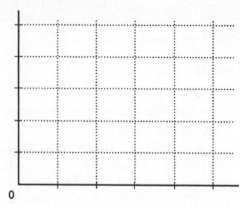

Short answer

1.   If the marginal social cost curve lies above the marginal private cost curve, how do you calculate the marginal external cost?

2.   The table shows the costs of producing pesticide. Complete the table.

Quantity (tonnes per day)	Marginal private cost	Marginal external cost	Marginal social cost
	(dollars per tonne)		
1	100	_____	130
2	120	40	
3	_____	60	210
4	190	_____	280
5	240	120	_____

3.   According to the Coase theorem, when are private transactions efficient?

4.   What is a marketable permit? What is the advantage of a marketable permit over an emission charge?

5.   The production of fertilizer creates water pollution. How do emission charges and taxes result in the efficient quantity of pollution? What information must the government posses to use emission charges or taxes effectively?

CHECKPOINT 9.2

■ **Explain why positive externalities lead to inefficient underproduction and how public provision, subsidies, vouchers, and patents can achieve a more efficient outcome.**

Practice Problem 9.2

The figure shows the marginal private benefit from college education. The marginal cost of a college education is a constant $6,000 per year. The marginal external benefit from a college education is $4,000 per student per year.

a. If colleges are private and government has no involvement in college education, how many people will undertake a college education and what will be the tuition?

b. What is the efficient number of students?

c. If the government decides to provide public colleges, what tuition will these colleges charge to achieve the efficient number of students? How much will taxpayers have to pay?

d. If the government decides to subsidize private colleges, what subsidy will achieve the efficient number of college students?

e. If the government offers vouchers to those who enrol at a college and no subsidy, what is the value of the voucher that will achieve the efficient number of students?

Solution to Practice Problem 9.2

Practice Problem 9.2 studies the important issue of external benefits and education. Because education has external benefits, an unregulated market will result in less than the efficient provision of education.

Quick Review

• *Marginal private benefit* The benefit from an additional unit of a good or service that the consumer of that good or service receives.

• *Marginal external benefit* The benefit from an additional unit of a good or service that people other than the consumer of the good or service enjoy.

• *Marginal social benefit* The marginal benefit enjoyed by society—by the consumers of a good or service and by everyone else who benefits from it. It is the sum of marginal private benefit and marginal external benefit.

a. If colleges are private and government has no involvement in college education, how many people will undertake a college education and what will be the tuition?

If the government has no involvement, the tuition and number of students is determined at the intersection of the supply curve, which is the marginal private cost curve and the demand curve, which is the marginal private benefit curve.

In the figure, tuition equals $6,000 a year and enrolment is 30,000 students a year at the intersection of the $D = MB$ curve and the $S = MC$ curve.

b. What is the efficient number of students?

The efficient number of students is determined at the quantity where marginal cost equals marginal social benefit, which is 50,000 students a year. This quantity is shown in the figure where the $S = MC$ curve and MSB curve intersect.

c. If the government decides to provide public colleges, what tuition will these colleges charge to achieve the efficient number of students? How much will taxpayers have to pay?

The efficient quantity of students is 50,000. The demand curve in the figure, $D = MB$, shows that to have 50,000 students enrol, the tuition must be $2,000 a student. The MC curve shows that the marginal cost for each student is $6,000, so taxpayers must pay $4,000 a student.

d. If the government decides to subsidize private colleges, what subsidy will achieve the efficient number of college students?

To have the efficient quantity of 50,000 students attend college the demand curve shows that tuition must be $2,000. The marginal cost of each student is $6,000, so private colleges must be paid a subsidy of $6,000 − $2,000, which is $4,000 a student. The subsidy is equal to the marginal external benefit.

e. If the government offers vouchers to those who enrol at a college and no subsidy, what is the value of the voucher that will achieve the efficient number of students?

The enrolment is the efficient quantity of 50,000 students when tuition is $2,000. The private college tuition is $6,000, so the value of the voucher must be $6,000 − $2,000, which is $4,000.

Additional Practice Problem 9.2a

A vaccine for chicken pox was recently developed. The government will make the vaccine available if the marginal benefit of vaccination exceeds the marginal cost. The producer of the vaccine reports that the marginal cost of a dose of vaccine is $80. The marginal benefit to the child being vaccinated is estimated to be $30 and an additional marginal benefit to the child's parents is estimated at $60. Based on these data, should the vaccine be made available?

Solution to Additional Practice Problem 9.2a

To determine if the government should make the vaccine available, we need to compare the marginal cost with the marginal social benefit. The marginal social benefit equals the marginal private benefit to the child of $30 plus the marginal external benefit to the parents of $60, which is $90. The marginal social benefit is greater than

the marginal cost, and so the vaccine should be made available.

■ Self Test 9.2

Fill in the blanks

Marginal _____ (external; social) benefit is the benefit enjoyed by society. If the government leaves education to the private market _____ (overproduction; underproduction) occurs. A payment that the government makes to private producers that depends on the level of output is _____ (a subsidy; public provision). The property rights of the creators of knowledge and other discoveries are _____ (intellectual property rights; patents).

True or false

1. The marginal private benefit from a good or service must exceed the marginal external benefit.

2. The expanded job opportunities from a college degree is a marginal private benefit enjoyed by college graduates.

3. A flu vaccination has an external benefit, so the marginal private benefit curve for flu vaccinations lies above the marginal social benefit curve for flu vaccinations.

4. An unregulated market underproduces products with external benefits, such as education.

5. A public community college is an example of public provision of a good that has an external benefit.

6. To overcome the inefficiency in the market for a good with an external benefit, the government can either tax or subsidize the good.

7. Vouchers can help overcome the inefficiency created by a good with an external cost but not the inefficiency created by a good with an external benefit.

8. A patent protects intellectual property rights by giving the patent holder a monopoly.

Multiple choice

1. The benefit the consumer of a good or service receives is the
   a. social benefit.
   b. external benefit.
   c. private benefit.
   d. public benefit.

2. An external benefit is a benefit from a good or service that someone other than the _____ receives.
   a. seller of the good or service
   b. government
   c. foreign sector
   d. consumer

3. When Ronald takes another economics class, other people in society benefit. The benefit to these other people is the marginal ____ benefit of the class.
   a. social
   b. private
   c. external
   d. opportunity

4. Marginal social benefit equals
   a. marginal external benefit.
   b. marginal private benefit.
   c. marginal private benefit minus marginal external benefit.
   d. marginal private benefit plus marginal external benefit.

5. If an external benefit is present, then the
   a. marginal private benefit curve lies above the marginal private cost curve.
   b. marginal social benefit curve lies above the marginal private benefit curve.
   c. marginal social cost curve lies above the marginal private benefit curve.
   d. marginal social benefit is equal to the marginal social cost.

6. In an unregulated market with an external benefit, the
   a. quantity produced is greater than the efficient quantity.
   b. price charged is too high for efficiency.
   c. quantity produced is less than the efficient quantity.
   d. producer is causing pollution but not paying for it.

7. If all education in Canada were provided by private, tuition-charging institutions,
   a. students would consume too much education.
   b. there would be too little education consumed.
   c. the economically efficient level of education would be provided.
   d. the government would provide students with vouchers.

8. Which of the following is a method used by government to cope with the situation in which production of a good creates an external benefit?
   a. removing property rights
   b. paying subsidies
   c. issuing marketable permits
   d. running a lottery

9. If the government provides a subsidy to colleges, then we _____ the marginal _____ of education to find the colleges' supply curve.
   a. subtract the subsidy from; cost
   b. subtract the subsidy from; benefit
   c. add the subsidy to; cost
   d. add the subsidy to; benefit

10. A public university is a service that is an example of

a. patent protection.

b. vouchers.

c. private subsidies.

d. public provision.

11. A voucher is a token that _____ provides to _____.

a. firms; households

b. households; firms

c. the government; households and firms

d. the government; households

12. Which government device is associated with intellectual property rights?

a. public provision

b. private subsidies

c. vouchers

d. patents and copyrights

Complete the graph

1. Figure 9.2 illustrates the market for honey.

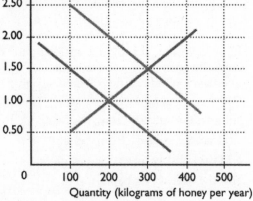

■ **FIGURE 9.2**

Price and cost (dollars per kilogram of honey)

a. Label the curves in the figure.

b. Based on Figure 9.2, does the production of honey create an external cost? An external benefit?

c. What is the efficient quantity of honey? What is the quantity of honey that will be produced in an unregulated market?

d. Shade the area that equals the deadweight loss in an unregulated market.

Short answer

1. When is the efficient quantity produced in a market with an external benefit?

2. Most elementary schools require that children be vaccinated before allowing the child to attend school. Can this policy be justified using economic analysis?

3. Is a private subsidy or a tax the correct government policy for a product that has an external benefit?

4. What is a voucher? How do vouchers work? Why is a voucher a proper policy to deal with the inefficiency created by a good or service that has an external benefit?

SELF TEST ANSWERS

■ CHECKPOINT 9.1

Fill in the blanks

Marginal private cost equals marginal social cost <u>minus</u> marginal external cost. A pollution externality creates an <u>inefficient</u> equilibrium. According to the Coase theorem, if property rights exist, only a small number of parties are involved, and transactions costs are low, then private transactions are efficient and the outcome <u>is not</u> affected by who is assigned the property right. By setting the tax rate equal to the marginal <u>external</u> cost, firms behave in the same way as they would if they bore the cost of the externality directly.

True or false

1. False; page 208

2. True; page 209

3. False; page 210

4. False; page 212

5. False; page 214

6. True; page 215

7. False; page 215

8. True; page 216

Multiple choice

1. c; page 208

2. c; page 210

3. d; page 210

4. a; page 208

5. d; page 210

6. b; page 210

7. c; page 210

8. d; page 212

9. b; page 214

10. d; page 215

11. a; page 215

12. d; page 216

Complete the graph

1. a. Figure 9.3 shows the *MSC, MC,* and *MB* curves; page 212.

■ FIGURE 9.3

Price and cost (dollars per megawatt)

b. An unregulated market will produce 4 megawatts of electricity a day. The marginal external cost at this production level is $20 a megawatt; page 212.

c. The efficient amount of electricity is 3 megawatts a day. The deadweight loss is illustrated in the figure; page 212.

d. At the efficient quantity of electricity, the marginal external cost is $15 a megawatt. The tax is $15 a megawatt. With the tax, 3 megawatts of electricity are produced and the price is $30 a megawatt; page 216.

Short answer

1. The marginal external cost is the distance between the marginal social cost curve and the marginal private cost curve at each quantity of output; page 211.

2. The completed table is below; page 210.

Quantity (tonnes per day)	Marginal private cost	Marginal external cost	Marginal social cost
		(dollars per tonne)	
1	100	<u>30</u>	130
2	120	40	<u>160</u>
3	<u>150</u>	60	210
4	190	<u>90</u>	280
5	240	120	<u>360</u>

3. The Coase theory is the proposition that if property rights exist, only a small number of parties are involved, and transactions costs are low, then private transactions are efficient; page 214.

4. A marketable permit is a permit issued by the government that allows each firm to emit a certain amount of pollution. Firms that have a low marginal cost of reducing pollution sell their permits, and firms that have a high marginal cost of reducing pollution buy permits. To work out the emission charge that achieves efficiency, the government must determine the marginal external cost of pollution at different levels of output and levy a charge on polluters that equals that cost. With marketable permits, the government does not need this information; page 215.

5. Emission charges and taxes are designed to charge polluting firms the cost of their pollution. By forcing the firm to pay this cost, a firm's marginal private cost becomes equal to the marginal social cost. To use emission charges or taxes to overcome the problem of pollution, the government must know the marginal external cost at different levels of output; pages 215-216.

■ CHECKPOINT 9.2

Fill in the blanks

Marginal <u>social</u> benefit is the benefit enjoyed by society. If the government leaves education to the private market <u>underproduction</u> occurs. A payment that the government makes to private producers that depends on the level of output is <u>a</u>

subsidy. The property rights of the creators of knowledge and other discoveries are <u>intellectual property rights</u>.

True or false

1. False; page 220
2. True; page 220
3. False; page 220
4. True; page 221
5. True; page 222
6. False; page 222
7. False; page 222
8. True; page 225

Multiple choice

1. c; page 220
2. d; page 220
3. c; page 220
4. d; page 220
5. b; page 220
6. c; page 221
7. b; page 221
8. b; page 222
9. a; page 223
10. d; page 222
11. d; page 224
12. d; page 225

Complete the graph

1. a. Figure 9.4 labels the curves; page 221.

FIGURE 9.4

Price and cost (dollars per kilogram of honey)

b. The production of honey has an external benefit but no external cost; page 220.

c. The efficient quantity of honey is 300 kilograms a year at the intersection of the *MSB* curve and the *S* = *MC* curve. In an unregulated market, the quantity produced is 200 kilograms a year at the intersection of the *D* = *MB* curve and the *S* = *MC* curve; page 221.

d. Figure 9.4 shades the deadweight loss; page 221.

Short answer

1. The efficient quantity is produced when marginal social benefit equals marginal cost; page 221.

2. Vaccination protects not only the child who is vaccinated, but also makes it less likely for the classmates to catch the disease. So a vaccination has an external benefit. Although the marginal cost of a vaccination may be greater than the marginal private benefit of a vaccination, the marginal social benefit equals the marginal cost and the market is efficient; page 221.

3. The correct government action to deal with a product that has an external benefit is a private subsidy, not a tax; page 222.

4. A voucher is a token that the government gives to households, which they can use to buy specified goods or services. Vouchers increase the demand for the good or service and shift the marginal private benefit curve rightward, closer to the marginal social benefit curve. Vouchers reduce the inefficiency created by a good or service with an external benefit; page 224.

Public Goods and Common Resources

Chapter 10

Chapter 10 studies the types of goods and services that the government provides.

■ **Distinguish among private goods, public goods, and common resources.**

A good, service, or resource is excludable if it is possible to prevent a person from enjoying its benefits and nonexcludable if it is impossible to prevent a person from enjoying its benefits. A good, service, or resource is rival if its consumption by one person decreases its consumption by other people and nonrival if its consumption by one person does not decrease its consumption by other people. A private good is a good or service that can be consumed by only one person at a time and only by those people who have bought it or own it. A private good is excludable and rival. A public good is a good or service that can be consumed simultaneously by everyone and from which no one can be excluded. A public good is nonexcludable and nonrival. A common resource is a resource that is nonexcludable and rival.

■ **Explain the free-rider problem and how public provision can help to overcome that problem.**

A free rider is a person who enjoys the benefits of a good or service without paying for it. The economy's marginal benefit curve for a public good is the vertical sum of the individual marginal benefit curves. The efficient quantity of a public good is the quantity at which marginal benefit equals marginal cost. A private firm would provide too little of a public good. The principle of minimum differentiation is the tendency for competitors to make themselves similar to appeal to the maximum number of clients or voters. Rational ignorance is the decision not to acquire information because the marginal cost of doing so exceeds the expected marginal benefit. Rational ignorance, combined with the bureaucratic goal of budget maximization, can lead to an inefficient overprovision of public goods.

■ **Explain the problem of the commons and review the possible solutions to that problem.**

The problem of the commons is the absence of incentives to prevent the overuse and depletion of a commonly owned resource. Atlantic cod stocks are an example of a common resource. The marginal private benefit of an additional boat is that boat's catch. But the quantity of fish caught by each boat decreases as more boats fish. The marginal social benefit of an additional boat is the change in the total catch that results from that additional boat. Efficiency occurs when the marginal social benefit from a resource equals its marginal cost. But the marginal social benefit is less than the marginal private benefit, so in an unregulated market overuse of the resource occurs. The government can help bring about an efficient use of the common resource by assigning property rights to the resource, or by setting quotas on the amount of the resource that can be used, or by creating a program of individual transferable quotas (ITQ). An individual transferable quota is a production limit that is assigned to an individual who is free to transfer the quota to someone else.

EXPANDED CHAPTER CHECKLIST

When you have completed this chapter, you will be able to

1 Distinguish among private goods, public goods, and common resources.

- Define nonrival, rival, nonexcludable and excludable.
- Define public good, private good, and common resource and discuss how they differ along the two dimensions of rivalry and excludability.

2 Explain the free-rider problem and how public provision can help to overcome that problem.

- Explain the free-rider problem.
- Describe how the marginal benefit for a public good is calculated.
- Explain why the economy's marginal benefit curve for a public good is different from the market demand curve for a private good.
- Show on a figure the efficient quantity of a public good.
- Define the principle of minimum differentiation and explain how it applies to the proposals of political parties.
- Define rational ignorance.
- Explain why the government is large and grows.

3 Explain the problem of the commons and review the possible solutions to that problem.

- Define the problem of the commons.
- Discuss why the marginal private benefit of a common resource exceeds the marginal social benefit of a common resource.
- Illustrate and explain why a common resource is overused.

- Discuss how property rights, quotas, and individual transferable quotas can result in the efficient use of a common resource.

KEY TERMS

- Common resource (page 233)
- Excludable (page 232)
- Free rider (page 235)
- Individual transferable quota (ITQ) (page 249)
- Nonexcludable (page 232)
- Nonrival (page 232)
- Principle of minimum differentiation (page 240)
- Private good (page 232)
- Problem of the commons (page 244)
- Public good (page 233)
- Rational ignorance (page 241)
- Rival (page 232)

CHECKPOINT 10.1

■ Distinguish among private goods, public goods, and common resources.

Practice Problem 10.1

Classify each of the following as a public good, a private good, or a common resource:
a. Measles vaccination
b. Fire protection
c. A Big Mac
d. The St. Lawrence Seaway

Solution to Practice Problem 6.1

The Practice Problem gives practice recognizing public goods, private goods, and common resources.

Quick Review

- *Public good* A public good is nonrival and nonexcludable.

- *Private good* A private good is rival and excludable.

- *Common resource* A common resource is rival and nonexcludable.

Classify each of the following as a public good, a private good, or a common resource:

a. Measles vaccination

A measles vaccination is in part a private good and in part a public good. It is a private good because it is rival since only one person can consume a particular vaccination. It is a public good because a person who is vaccinated benefits others because they are less likely to catch the measles.

b. Fire protection

Fire protection is a public good. It is nonrival because use of fire protection by one person does not decrease the quantity available for someone else. And it is nonexcludable because it is impossible to prevent someone from benefiting from it.

c. A Big Mac

A Big Mac is a private good.

d. The St. Lawrence Seaway

The St. Lawrence Seaway is a common resource. It is rival, because one large oil tanker cannot use the same seaway space as another large oil tanker, and it is nonexcludable.

Additional Practice Problem 10.1a

It's a balmy, pleasant Sunday afternoon on a summer day where the PGA Canadian Open is being played. A variety of goods and services are being consumed. Classify each of the list of goods and services as rival, nonrival, excludable, and nonexcludable. State if any are public or private goods.

a. PGA membership

b. Golf lessons

c. Golf clubs

d. Watching the Canadian Open

e. A pleasant, sunny afternoon

f. Sunset

g. Shrimp eaten at a party following the event

Solution to Additional Practice Problem 10.1a

a. PGA membership

Membership in the PGA is nonrival and excludable.

b. Golf lessons

Golf lessons are rival and excludable and are a private good.

c. Golf clubs

Golf clubs are rival and excludable and are a private good.

d. Watching the Canadian Open

Watching the Canadian is excludable. Whether it is rival depends on whether the tickets are sold out. If it is a sell out, then watching the Canadian Open is rival; in the event that it is not sold out, it is nonrival.

e. A pleasant, sunny afternoon

The pleasant afternoon is nonrival and nonexcludable and so is a public good.

f. Sunset

The sunset is nonrival and nonexcludable and so is a public good.

g. Shrimp eaten at a party following the event

The shrimp are rival and excludable and so are a private good.

■ Self Test 10.1

Fill in the blanks

A good is ____ (rival; nonrival; excludable) if it is possible to prevent someone from enjoying its benefits. A good is ____ (rival; nonrival; excludable) if its use by one person does not decrease the quantity available for someone else. A good that is nonrival and nonexcludable is a ____ (private; public; common) good and a good that is rival and excludable is a ____ (private; public; common) good. A common resource is ____ (rival; nonrival) and ____ (excludable; nonexcludable).

True or false

1. A good is nonexcludable if it is impossible to prevent someone from benefiting from it.

2. A private good is nonrival and nonexcludable.

3. A taco from Taco Bell is a public good.

4. A common resource is nonrival and excludable.

5. Fish in the ocean are rival and nonexcludable.

Multiple choice

1. The fact that Heidi's enjoyment of a sunset does not preclude Mounette from enjoying the same sunset is an example of
   a. a good that is nonrival.
   b. a good that is excludable.
   c. a private good.
   d. the rival nature of consumption.

2. When use of a good decreases the quantity available for someone else, the good is
   a. rival.
   b. nonrival.
   c. excludable.
   d. nonexcludable

3. A private good is ____ and ____.
   a. rival; excludable
   b. rival; nonexcludable
   c. nonrival; excludable
   d. nonrival; nonexcludable

4. If I order a pizza and invite my neighbours to eat it, the pizza is
   a. a private good.
   b. a common resource.
   c. a public good because many people ate it.
   d. either a common resource or a public good depending on whether it is overused or not.

5. A public good is ____ and ____.
   a. rival; excludable
   b. rival; nonexcludable
   c. nonrival; excludable
   d. nonrival; nonexcludable

6. A public good
   a. can only be consumed by one person at a time.
   b. can be consumed simultaneously by everyone.
   c. is any good provided by a company owned by a member of the public.
   d. is any good provided by government.

Short answer

1. What does it mean for a good to be nonexcludable? Nonrival?

2. Describe public goods, private goods, and common resources as excludable, nonexcludable, rival, or nonrival.

CHECKPOINT 10.2

■ **Explain the free-rider problem and how public provision can help to overcome that problem.**

Practice Problems 10.2

1. For each of the following goods, explain whether there is a free-rider problem. If there is no such problem, how is it avoided?
   a. Weed control treatment for lawns
   b. Fire protection
   c. Car licences

d. The Trans-Canada Highway

2. The table provides information about a mosquito control program.

Quantity (square kilometres sprayed per day)	Marginal cost (dollars per day)	Marginal benefit (dollars per day)
0	0	0
1	1,000	5,000
2	2,000	4,000
3	3,000	3,000
4	4,000	2,000
5	5,000	1,000

a. What quantity of spraying would a private mosquito control program provide?

b. What is the efficient quantity of spraying?

c. In a single-issue election on the quantity of spraying, what quantity would the winner of the election provide?

Solution to Practice Problem 10.2

These Practice Problems provide practice recognizing the free-rider problem and identifying the efficient quantity of a public good.

Quick Review

- *Free rider* A person who enjoys the benefits of a good or service without paying for it.

1. **For each of the following goods, explain whether there is a free-rider problem. If there is no such problem, how is it avoided?**

a. **Weed control treatment for lawns**

Weed control treatment is a private good. Whoever wants weed control treatment buys the service.

b. **Fire protection**

Fire protection is a public good. With private provision, people would attempt to be free riders but public provision paid through taxes prevents the free-rider problem.

c. **Car licences**

A car licence is a private good. Whoever wants to drive a car buys a licence.

d. **The Trans-Canada Highway**

The highway is nonrival, nonexcludable, and a public good. Individuals will free ride, though free riding is limited to an extent because users pay vehicle registration fees. They also pay gasoline taxes in proportion to their use of the roadways.

2. **The table provides information about a mosquito control program.**

a. **What quantity of spraying would a private mosquito program provide?**

A private mosquito control program would provide no spraying because people would free ride and not pay for the spraying.

b. **What is the efficient quantity of spraying?**

The efficient quantity of spraying is 3 square kilometres a day because that is the quantity at which the marginal benefit equals the marginal cost.

c. **In a single-issue election on the quantity of spraying, what quantity would the winner of the election provide?**

Voters want the efficient quantity of mosquito spraying, 3 square kilometres a day so each political party proposes 3 square kilometres miles of spraying to gain votes. The outcome is the efficient quantity of spraying.

Additional Practice Problem 10.2a

How do rational ignorance and bureaucrats' goal of budget maximization combine to lead to inefficient overprovision of public goods?

Solution to Additional Practice Problem 10.2a

If voters knew the marginal social benefit and marginal social cost of a public good, they could elect politicians who would deliver the efficient quantity. But voters generally are rationally ignorant about the marginal social benefit and marginal social cost of most public goods. So bureaucrats, who want to increase their budget, and special interest groups, such as the producers of a public good, lobby politicians to provide more than the efficient amount of public goods. Politicians accede to the lobbying because they know that rationally ignorant voters will not realize that too much of the public good is provided.

■ Self Test 10.2

Fill in the blanks

A person who enjoys the benefit of a good or service without paying for it is a ____. The marginal benefit curve for a public good is the ____ (horizontal; vertical) sum of the individual marginal benefit curves. The efficient quantity of a public good is the quantity at which the marginal benefit ____ the marginal cost. ____ (Rational ignorance; The principle of minimum differentiation) is the decision to not acquire information because the marginal cost of doing so exceeds the expected marginal benefit. Bureaucrats try to ____ (maximize; minimize) their budgets.

True or false

1. Beth is a free rider when she is protected by the nation's military but does not pay anything for the protection.

2. The marginal benefit curve for a public good slopes downward.

3. The efficient quantity of a public good is the quantity at which marginal benefit equals marginal cost.

4. A private firm would produce too much of a public good.

5. Rational ignorance can lead to the provision of more than the efficient amount of a public good.

Multiple choice

1. When someone enjoys the benefit of a good or service but does not pay for it, that person
   a. is a free range consumer.
   b. is a free rider.
   c. receives no marginal benefit from the good.
   d. must be consuming an excludable good.

2. The marginal benefit of a public good is the
   a. sum of the marginal benefits of all the individuals at each quantity.
   b. marginal benefit of the individual person who places the lowest value on the good, multiplied by the number of people in the economy.
   c. marginal benefit of the individual person who places the highest value on the good, multiplied by the number of people in the economy.
   d. benefit of the last person's consumption.

3. The marginal benefit curve of a public good
   a. slopes downward.
   b. slopes upward.
   c. is vertical.
   d. is horizontal.

4. The efficient quantity of a public good is
   a. the quantity produced by private firms.
   b. the quantity at which the marginal benefit equals the marginal cost.
   c. impossible to determine because each person's marginal benefit is different.
   d. the quantity at which the marginal benefit exceeds the marginal cost by as much as possible.

5. The efficient quantity of a public good can't be produced by private firms because
   a. only government has the necessary resources.
   b. it is impossible to determine the efficient amount.
   c. consumers have an incentive to free ride and not pay for their share of the good.
   d. private firms aren't large enough.

6. If the two political parties propose similar or identical policies, they are following the principle of

a. rational ignorance.
b. inefficient overprovision.
c. free riding.
d. minimum differentiation.

7. ____ is the decision not to acquire information because the marginal cost of doing so exceeds expected marginal benefit.

a. Rational ignorance
b. The principle of minimum differentiation
c. A free rider decision
d. Consumer ignorance

8. Government bureaucracies over provide public goods and grow larger because of their goal of ____ combined with ____ of the voters.

a. budget maximization; rational ignorance
b. budget minimization; irrational intelligence
c. budget maximization; minimum differentiation
d. budget maximization; irrational exuberance

Complete the graph

1. Three shipping firms serve the west coast of a nation. The table has the firms' marginal benefit schedules for maritime security. Maritime security is a public good and the marginal cost of a unit of maritime security is constant at $120,000.

Quantity (units of maritime security)	Marginal benefit, Firm A (dollars)	Marginal benefit, Firm B (dollars)	Marginal benefit, Firm C (dollars)
1	50,000	50,000	50,000
2	45,000	45,000	45,000
3	40,000	40,000	40,000
4	35,000	35,000	35,000

a. Complete the table below. Then graph the economy's marginal benefit and marginal cost curves in Figure 10.1.

Quantity (units of maritime security)	Marginal benefit (dollars per unit)
1	
2	
3	
4	

b. What is the efficient quantity of maritime security?

c. If all three firms agree to split the cost of maritime security equally, how much would each firm pay per unit and how many units of maritime security would be provided?

d. Suppose that one firm decides to free ride and not pay for any maritime security. How much would each of the two other firms pay per unit and how many units of maritime security would be provided?

■ **FIGURE 10.1**

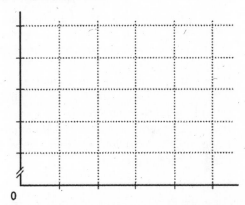

e. In the situation described in part (d), how might government action overcome the problem?

Short answer

1. What is a free rider? Why is free riding not a problem for private goods?

2. How does free riding affect the private provision of a public good? How does rational ignorance affect the public provision of a public good?

CHECKPOINT 10.3

■ Explain the problem of the commons and
review the possible solutions to that problem.

Practice Problem 10.3

In an English village in 1375, cows graze on
common pasture and can produce milk in
the amounts shown in
the table. The mar-
ginal private cost of a
cow is zero.

Number of cows	Milk output (litres per day)
100	300
200	500
300	600
400	600
500	500
600	300
700	0

a. What is the marginal
   private benefit at each
   quantity of cows?
b. What is the
   equilibrium number of
   cows?
c. What is the marginal social benefit at each
   quantity of cows?
d. What are the efficient number of cows and
   quantity of milk to produce?
e. If the common pasture was converted to private land and fenced off, how many cows
   would the landowner keep?
f. If the ITQs were issued for the efficient quantity of milk production, what would be the
   market price of an ITQ?

Solution to Practice Problem 10.3

This Practice Problem gives you practice in determining the difference between the marginal
private benefit and the marginal social benefit for
a common resource. It also tackles policies that
lead to an efficient use of common resources.

Quick Review

• *Problem of the commons* The absence of incentives to prevent the overuse and depletion of
  a commonly owned resource.

a. **What is the marginal private benefit at each
   quantity of cows?**

The table below shows the marginal private
benefit schedule. The marginal private benefit is
the total milk output divided by the number of
cows. At 100 cows, the marginal private benefit
equals 300 litres ÷ 100 cows, which is 3 litres a
cow.

Number of cows	Milk output (litres per day)	Marginal private benefit (litres per cow)	Marginal social benefit (litres per cow)
0	0		
			3.0
100	300	3.0	
			2.0
200	500	2.5	
			1.0
300	600	2.0	
			0.0
400	600	1.5	
			−1.0
500	500	1.0	
			−2.0
600	300	0.5	
			−3.0
700	0	0.0	

b. **What is the equilibrium number of cows?**

The equilibrium number occurs at the quantity
where marginal private benefit equals marginal
cost. The marginal cost is zero, so the equilibrium number of cows is 700 and no milk is produced.

c. **What is the marginal social benefit at each
   quantity of cows?**

The table above shows the marginal social
benefit schedule. The marginal social benefit is
the change in the quantity of milk that results
from an additional cow. An increase in the
number of cows from 100 cows to 200 cows, an
increase of 100 cows increases the quantity of
milk from 300 litres to 500 litres, an increase of
200 litres. Marginal social benefit is equal to 200
litres ÷ 100 cows, which is 2 litres a cow.

d. **What are the efficient number of cows and
   quantity of milk to produce?**

The efficient number of cows occurs at the
quantity where marginal social benefit equals
marginal cost. The marginal cost is zero. The
marginal social benefit equals zero at a quantity
of 350 cows, midway between 300 and 400 cows

in the table. The efficient quantity of cows is 350 and they produce a bit more than 600 litres a day.

e. If the common pasture was converted to private land and fenced off, how many cows would the landowner keep?

If the common pasture was converted to private land, the marginal private benefit becomes equal to the marginal social benefit because the owner's benefit from more cows is the change in milk production. The landowner would keep 350 cows. 350 cows is the quantity that maximizes output.

f. If the ITQs were issued for the efficient quantity of milk production, what would be the market price of an ITQ?

The market price of an ITQ equals the marginal private benefit at the efficient quantity of cows minus the marginal cost. The efficient quantity of cows is 350 and the marginal private benefit at 350 cows is 1.75 litres of milk (midway between the marginal private benefit of 300 cows and of 400 cows). The marginal cost is 0, so the market price of an ITQ is 1.75 litres of milk.

Additional Practice Problem 10.3a

For a common resource, why is the marginal social benefit less than the marginal private benefit?

Solution to Additional Practice Problem 10.3a

The marginal private benefit measures *only* the benefit received by an individual from his or her use of a common resource. But when someone uses a common resource, he or she decreases the benefit received by other users. The marginal social benefit takes account of this decrease. The marginal social benefit is the marginal private benefit minus the decrease in marginal benefit to other users, so the marginal social benefit from a common resource is less than the marginal private benefit.

■ Self Test 10.3

Fill in the blanks

The problem of the commons is the absence of incentives to prevent the ____ (overuse; under use) of a commonly owned resource. The marginal private benefit of an additional fishing boat is the ____ (change in the total fish catch; quantity of fish that one boat can catch). The marginal social benefit of an additional fishing boat is the ____ (change in the total fish catch; quantity of fish that one boat can catch). The marginal private benefit curve for a common resource lies ____ (above; below) the marginal social benefit curve. To use a common resource efficiently, establishing property rights ____ (is; is not) a potential solution. The price of an individual transferable quota equals the marginal ____ (private; social) benefit of the resource at the efficient quantity ____ (plus; minus) the marginal cost of using the resource.

True or false

1. The problem of the commons is the absence of incentives that prevent the overuse and depletion of a commonly owned resource.

2. The marginal social benefit curve of a common resource slopes upward.

3. The efficient use of a common resource occurs at the quantity where marginal private benefit equals marginal cost.

4. At the efficient level of use, the marginal private benefit of a common resource exceeds the marginal social benefit.

5. Property rights and quotas are potential solutions to the problem of the commons.

Multiple choice

1. The problem of the commons is the absence of incentives to
   a. correctly measure the marginal cost.
   b. prevent under use of the common resource.
   c. prevent overuse and depletion of the common resource.
   d. discover the resource.

2. For the common resource of fish, the marginal private benefit of an additional boat is ____ and the marginal social benefit is the ____.
   a. the catch per boat; quantity of fish that one boat can catch
   b. the quantity of fish that one boat can catch; change in the total catch from an additional boat
   c. the change in the total catch from an additional boat; catch per boat
   d. less than the marginal social benefit; change in the total catch from an additional boat

3. For a common resource, the equilibrium with no government intervention is such that ____ equals ____.
   a. marginal private benefit; marginal cost
   b. marginal social benefit; marginal cost
   c. marginal private benefit; marginal social benefit
   d. social benefit; cost

4. For a common resource, the marginal private benefit of the resource is ____ the marginal social benefit.
   a. greater than
   b. equal to
   c. less than
   d. not comparable to

5. For a common resource, the marginal private benefit curve slopes ____ and the marginal social benefit curve slopes ____.
   a. upward; upward
   b. upward; downward
   c. downward; upward
   d. downward; downward

6. For a common resource, efficiency requires that the ____ equals the ____.
   a. marginal private benefit; marginal cost
   b. marginal social benefit; marginal cost
   c. marginal private benefit; marginal social benefit
   d. marginal social cost; marginal cost

7. If the government assigns private property rights to a common resource, then the
   a. resource is under-utilized.
   b. marginal private benefit becomes equal to the marginal social benefit.
   c. government needs to set a quota to achieve efficiency.
   d. None of the above answers is correct.

8. The market price of an individual transferable quota is equal to the _____ at the efficient quantity.
   a. marginal private benefit
   b. marginal social benefit
   c. marginal private benefit minus the marginal cost
   d. marginal social benefit minus the marginal cost

Complete the graph

1. Figure 10.2 shows the marginal cost, marginal private benefit, and marginal social benefit curves for swordfish, a common resource. Label each curve.

   a. What is the equilibrium number of boats and sustainable catch? What is the efficient number of boats and sustainable catch?

b. If the government sets a quota, what quota achieves the efficient outcome?

c. If the government issues individual transferable quotas (ITQ), what is the market price of an ITQ?

■ FIGURE 10.2
Sustainable catch per boat (tonnes per month)

Boats (hundreds)

Short answer

1. What is the problem of the commons and why does it occur? Give an example of how the problem of the commons affects the world's fisheries.

2. For a common resource, why does the marginal private benefit not equal the marginal social benefit? Which is smaller?

3. The table gives the quantity of meat per year and marginal social benefit of grazing sheep on a common pasture. The marginal cost of raising a sheep is 50 kilograms of meat per year.

Number of sheep	Meat (kilograms per year)	Marginal private benefit (kilograms per year)	Marginal social benefit (kilograms per year)
0	0		
10	2,000	____	150
20	3,000	____	50
30	3,000	____	-50
40	2,000	____	-150
50	0	____	

a. Complete the table by calculating the marginal private benefit.

b. In Figure 10.3, plot the marginal cost curve, the marginal private benefit curve, and the marginal social cost curve.

c. What is the equilibrium number of sheep and the equilibrium quantity of meat?

d. What is the efficient number of sheep and the efficient quantity of meat?

e. If the government issues the efficient quantity of individual transfer quotas (ITQ), each of which allows 1 sheep to be grazed on the pasture, how many ITQs does the government issue and what is the market price of an ITQ?

■ FIGURE 10.3
Meat output (kilograms per year)

Sheep (number)

SELF TEST ANSWERS

■ CHECKPOINT 10.1

Fill in the blanks

A good is <u>excludable</u> if it is possible to prevent someone from enjoying its benefits. A good is <u>nonrival</u> if its use by one person does not decrease the quantity available for someone else. A good that is nonrival and nonexcludable is a <u>pub-lic</u> good and a good that is rival and excludable is a <u>private</u> good. A common resource is <u>rival</u> and <u>nonexcludable</u>.

True or false

1. True; page 232
2. False; page 232
3. False; page 232
4. False; page 233
5. True; page 233

Multiple choice

1. a; page 232
2. a; page 232
3. a; page 232
4. a; page 232
5. d; page 233
6. b; page 233

Short answer

1. A good is nonexcludable if it is impossible (or extremely costly) to prevent someone from benefiting from it. For example, the national security provided along Canada's borders benefits everyone. A good is nonrival if its use by one person does not decrease the quantity available for someone else. For example, the national security provided along Canada's borders for you does not decrease the amount of security it provides for your neighbour; page 232.

2. A public good is a good or service that is nonrival and nonexcludable. A private good is a good or service that is rival and excludable. A common resource is a resource that is rival and nonexcludable; pages 232-233.

■ CHECKPOINT 10.2

Fill in the blanks

A person who enjoys the benefit of a good or service without paying for it is a <u>free rider</u>. The marginal benefit curve for a public good is the <u>verti-cal</u> sum of the individual marginal benefit curves. The efficient quantity of a public good is the quantity at which the marginal benefit <u>equals</u> the marginal cost. <u>Rational ignorance</u> is the decision to not acquire information because the marginal cost of doing so exceeds the expected marginal benefit. Bureaucrats try to <u>maximize</u> their budgets.

True or false

1. True; page 235
2. True; page 237
3. True; page 238
4. False; page 238
5. True; page 242

Multiple choice

1. b; page 235
2. a; pages 236-237
3. a; page 237
4. b; page 238
5. c; page 238
6. d; page 240
7. a; page 241
8. a; page 242

Complete the graph

Quantity (units of maritime security)	Economy's marginal benefit (dollars)
1	150,000
2	135,000
3	120,000
4	105,000

1. a. The complete table is above and the completed figure is Figure 10.4; pages 236-237.

■ FIGURE 10.4

Marginal benefit and marginal cost
(thousands of dollars per unit)

b. The efficient quantity is 3 units; page 238.

c. Each firm pays $40,000 and 3 units are provided; page 238.

d. If one firm free rides, the other firms would need to pay $60,000. No maritime security would be provided because $60,000 exceeds each firm's marginal benefit from any quantity; page 238.

e. The government could tax each firm $40,000 per unit and use the tax revenue to provide 3 units of maritime security; page 239.

Short answer

1. A free rider is a person who enjoys the benefits of a good or service without paying for it. Free riding is not a problem for private goods because private goods are excludable; page 235.

2. Because everyone can consume the same quantity of a public good and no one can be excluded from enjoying its benefits, no one has an incentive to pay for it. Everyone has an incentive to free ride. Because of the free-rider problem, private provision would provide too small a quantity of a public good.

   Bureaucrats who maximize their budgets and voters who work in the industry exert a larger influence on public policy than voters who are rationally ignorant. This set of circumstances leads to overprovision; pages 238 and 242.

■ CHECKPOINT 10.3

Fill in the blanks

The problem of the commons is the absence of incentives to prevent the <u>overuse</u> of a commonly owned resource. The marginal private benefit of an additional fishing boat is the <u>quantity of fish that one boat can catch</u>. The marginal social benefit of an additional fishing boat is the <u>change in the total fish catch</u>. The marginal private benefit curve for a common resource lies <u>above</u> the marginal social benefit curve. To use a common resource efficiently, establishing property rights <u>is</u> a potential solution. The price of an individual transferable quota equals the marginal <u>private</u> benefit of the resource at the efficient quantity <u>minus</u> the marginal cost of using the resource.

True or false

1. True; page 244

2. False; page 246

3. False; page 246

4. True; page 246

5. True; page 248

Multiple choice

1. c; page 244

2. b; pages 245-246

3. a; page 245

4. a; pages 246

5. d; page 246

6. b; page 246

7. b; page 248

8. c; page 249

Complete the graph

1. Figure 10.5 labels the curves.; page 247.

a.   The equilibrium number of boats is determined at the intersection of the marginal cost curve and the marginal private benefit curve, so the equilibrium number of boats is 400 and the sustainable catch per boat is 20 tonnes of swordfish a month. The efficient number of boats is determined at the intersection of the marginal cost curve and the marginal social benefit curve, so the efficient number of boats is 200 and the sustainable catch per boat is 60 tonnes of swordfish a month from the marginal social benefit curve; pages 245, 247.

■ FIGURE 10.5

Sustainable catch per boat (tonnes per month)

b. If the government sets the quota at the efficient quantity, the quota for total production is set at the quantity at which marginal social benefit equals marginal cost. Here, that quantity is what 200 boats can produce; page 248.

c. The market price of an individual transferable quota (ITQ) equals the marginal private benefit minus the marginal cost at the efficient level. The government issues ITQs to 200 boats and so the market price of an ITQ is 60 tonnes a month, the marginal private benefit, minus 20 tonnes a month, the marginal cost, which equals a market price of 40 tonnes a month; page 249.

Short answer

1. The problem of the commons is that there is no incentive to prevent the overuse and depletion of a commonly used resource. As more boats fish, the quantity of fish that one boat can catch decreases. But no individual takes account of the *decrease* in the average catch because each person is concerned about what he or she catches As a result, additional boats continue to fish until their marginal private benefit equals the marginal cost of fishing. Each boat considers only its marginal private benefit. With this many

boats fishing, marginal cost is greater than marginal social benefit and the fish stock is depleted; pages 244-245.

2. The marginal private benefit of using a common resource does not equal the marginal social benefit because the marginal private benefit does not take account of the effect that using the resource has on others. As a common resource is used more intensively, each additional person's use decreases everyone else's benefit from the resource. But the marginal private benefit ignores the decrease in other people's benefit. The marginal social benefit takes account of *both* the added benefit to the new user (the marginal private benefit) *and* the decrease in everyone else's benefit. So the marginal social benefit is less than the marginal private benefit; pages 245-246.

Number of sheep	Meat (kilograms per year)	Marginal private benefit (kilograms per year)	Marginal social benefit (kilograms per year)
0	0		
10	2,000	200	150
20	3,000	150	50
30	3,000	100	−50
40	2,000	50	−150
50	0	0	

3. a. The completed table is above. The marginal private benefit of a sheep is the quantity of meat per sheep. For 10 sheep the marginal private benefit is 2,000 kilograms ÷ 10 sheep, which is 200 kilograms; page 245.

   b. Figure 10.6 shows the marginal cost curve, the marginal private benefit curve, and the marginal social benefit curve; pages 245, 247.

   c. The equilibrium number of sheep is determined at the intersection of the marginal private benefit curve and the marginal cost curve. The equilibrium number of sheep is 40. The equilibrium quantity of meat with 40 sheep is 2,000 kilograms a year; page 245.

d. The efficient number of sheep is determined at the intersection of the marginal social benefit curve and the marginal cost curve. The equilibrium number of sheep is 20 sheep. The equilibrium quantity of meat with 20 sheep is 3,000 kilograms a year; page 247.

e. The government issues 20 ITQs because 20 sheep is the efficient number of sheep. The market price of an ITQ is the marginal private benefit at the quantity of ITQs issued minus the marginal cost. The marginal private benefit with 20 ITQs is 150 kilograms of meat a year. The marginal cost is 50 kilograms of meat a year. So the market price of an ITQ is 150 kilograms of meat – 50 kilograms of meat, which is 100 kilograms of meat a year; page 249.

■ **FIGURE 10.6**

Consumer Choice and Demand

Chapter 11

Chapter 11 presents a model of consumer choice based on marginal utility and the fundamental idea that people make rational choices. We use marginal utility theory to derive a demand curve and explain the paradox of value.

■ **Calculate and graph a budget line that shows the limits to a person's consumption possibilities.**

A budget line describes the limits to a consumer's consumption possibilities. A consumer can afford any combination on the budget line and inside it, but she cannot afford any combination outside the budget line. When the price of a good changes, the slope of the budget line changes. The relative price is the price of one good in terms of another good—an opportunity cost. It equals the price of one good divided by the price of another good. The slope of the budget line is the relative price. An increase in the budget shifts the budget line rightward, and a decrease in the budget shifts the budget line leftward.

■ **Explain marginal utility theory and use it to derive a consumer's demand curve.**

Utility is the benefit or satisfaction that a person gets from the consumption of a good or service. Total utility is the total benefit that a person gets from the consumption of a good or service; marginal utility is the change in total utility that results from a one-unit increase in the quantity of a good consumed. As the quantity of a good consumed increases, its total utility increases but its marginal utility decreases. A consumer maximizes total utility when he allocates his entire available budget and makes the marginal utility per dollar spent the same for all goods. The marginal utility per dollar spent is the increase in total utility that comes from the last dollar spent on a good. If the price of a good falls, the marginal utility per dollar spent on that good rises at the current consumption level and the consumer buys more of that good. So when the price of a good falls, there is an increase in the quantity demanded and a movement down along the demand curve.

■ **Use marginal utility theory to explain the paradox of value: Why water is vital but cheap while diamonds are relatively useless but expensive.**

The paradox of value is that water, which is essential to life, is cheap, while diamonds, which are relatively useless, are expensive. We solve this puzzle by distinguishing between total utility and marginal utility. The total utility from water is enormous. But we use so much water that its marginal utility is a small value. We buy few diamonds, so diamonds have a large marginal utility. Diamonds have a high price and a high marginal utility. Water has a low price and a low marginal utility. When the high marginal utility of diamonds is divided by the high price of a diamond, the result is a number that equals the low marginal utility of water divided by the low price of water. Water is cheap but provides a large consumer surplus, while diamonds are expensive but provide a small consumer surplus.

EXPANDED CHAPTER CHECKLIST

When you have completed this chapter, you will be able to

1 Calculate and graph a budget line that shows the limits to a person's consumption possibilities.

- Define and draw a budget line.
- Describe how the slope of the budget line changes when price changes.
- Discus the relationship between the slope of the budget line, opportunity cost, and relative price of a good or service.
- Show the effect of an increase or decrease in the consumer's budget on the budget line.

2 Explain marginal utility theory and use it to derive a consumer's demand curve.

- Define utility and total utility.
- Define and calculate marginal utility.
- Explain the principle of diminishing marginal utility.
- Use the utility-maximizing rule to choose the point on the budget line that maximizes total utility.
- Derive a demand curve using marginal utility theory.
- Describe the relationship between the price elasticity of demand and marginal utility.

3 Use marginal utility theory to explain the paradox of value: Why water is vital but cheap while diamonds are relatively useless but expensive.

- Explain how marginal utility theory resolves the paradox of value.
- Discuss the difference between the price and consumer surplus of water and diamonds.

KEY TERMS

- Budget line (page 256)
- Diminishing marginal utility (page 263)
- Marginal utility (page 263)
- Marginal utility per dollar spent (page 267)
- Relative price (page 259)
- Total utility (page 262)
- Utility (page 262)
- Utility-maximizing rule (page 266)

CHECKPOINT 11.1

■ Calculate and graph a budget line that shows the limits to a person's consumption possibilities.

Practice Problem 11.1

Jerry's burger and magazine budget is $12 a week. The price of a burger is $2, and the price of a magazine is $4.

a. List the combinations of burgers and magazines that Jerry can afford.

b. Draw a graph of Jerry's budget line with the quantity of burgers plotted on the x-axis.

c. What is the relative price of a magazine? Explain your answer.

d. Describe how the budget line in part **b** changes if the following events occur one at a time and other things remain the same:
- The price of a magazine falls.
- The price of a burger rises.
- Jerry's budget for burgers and magazines increases.

Solution to Practice Problem 11.1

This Practice Problem studies the budget line. Remember that when the price of a good changes, the slope of the budget line changes and when the consumer's budget changes, there is a shift of the budget line.

Quick Review

- *Budget line* A line that describes the limits to consumption possibilities and that depends on a consumer's budget and the prices of goods and services.

a. List the combinations of burgers and magazines that Jerry can afford.

The combinations of burgers and magazines that Jerry can afford are listed in the table. To construct this table, select the combinations of burgers and magazines that spend all of Jerry's $12 budget.

Burgers	Magazines
0	3
2	2
4	1
6	0

b. Draw a graph of Jerry's budget line with the quantity of burgers plotted on the *x*-axis.

The figure shows Jerry's budget line. The maximum number of burgers Jerry can buy is 6, where the budget line intersects the *x*-axis and the maximum number of magazines Jerry can buy is 3, where the budget line intersects the *y*-axis.

c. What is the relative price of a magazine? Explain your answer.

The relative price of a magazine equals the price of a magazine divided by the price of a burger, which is $4 per magazine ÷ $2 per burger = 2 burgers per magazine. The relative price of a magazine is the opportunity cost of a magazine, which is the number of burgers that Jerry must forgo to get 1 magazine.

d. Describe how the budget line in part b changes if the following events occur one at a time and other things remain the same:

- **The price of a magazine falls.**

When the price of a magazine falls, and Jerry spends all his budget on magazines, he can buy more magazines. But if Jerry spends all his budget on burgers, he can still buy only 6 burgers a week. The figure shows that Jerry's budget line rotates outward and becomes more steep. Jerry's consumption possibilities have expanded.

- **The price of a burger rises.**

When the price of a burger rises, and Jerry spends all his budget on burgers, he can buy fewer burgers. But if Jerry spends all his budget on magazines, he can still buy 3 magazines a week. The figure shows that Jerry's budget line rotates inward and becomes more steep. Jerry's consumption possibilities have decreased.

- **Jerry's budget for burgers and magazines increases.**

When Jerry's budget for burgers and magazines increases, his consumption possibilities expand. In the figure, Jerry's budget line shifts outward.

Additional Practice Problem 11.1a

Mark is dining at Luigi's Restaurant. He has $30 to spend. Pizza is $15 and a salad is $5.

a.   Graph the budget line with pizza on the *x*-axis.

b.   What is the opportunity cost of a pizza?

c.   What is the relative price of a pizza?

Solution to Additional Practice Problem 11.1a

a.   Graph the budget line with pizza on the *x*-axis.

The figure shows Mark's budget line. The maximum number of pizzas he can buy is 2 and the maximum number of salads he can buy is 6.

b.   What is the opportunity cost of a pizza?

The slope of the budget line is the opportunity cost of a pizza. The slope is (6 salads) ÷ (2 pizzas), which equals 3 salads per pizza.

c.   What is the relative price of a pizza?

The opportunity cost of a pizza is also its relative price. The relative price of a pizza is 3 salads per pizza.

■ Self Test 11.1

Fill in the blanks

A _____ (budget; consumption) line shows the limits to consumption possibilities. The budget line becomes _____ (less; more) steep when the price of the good measured along the *x*-axis increases and everything else remains the same. The slope of the budget line is equal to the _____ (opportunity; relative) price. When income increases, the budget line shifts _____ (inward; outward).

True or false

1.   Dian's budget line shows the limits to what Dian can consume.

2.   A fall in the price of the good measured along the *x*-axis, all other things remaining the same, rotates the budget line inward.

3.   The slope of the budget line measures the opportunity cost of one more unit of the good plotted on the *x*-axis.

4.   The price of one good plus the price of another good equals the relative price.

5.   When Stan's budget increases, his budget line shifts outward.

Multiple choice

1.   A budget line describes

a.   the limits to production possibilities.

b.   the limits to production opportunities.

c.   the slope of the demand curve.

d.   the limits to consumption possibilities.

2.   A budget line

a.   represents combinations of goods a consumer desires.

b.   marks the boundary between what a consumer can and cannot afford.

c.   has a positive slope.

d.   is the same as the production possibilities frontier.

3.   Linda has $10 a month to spend on ice cream cones and chocolate bars. If the price of an ice cream cone is $2 and the price of a chocolate bar is $1, which of the following is a point on Linda's budget line?

a.   4 cones and 0 chocolate bars

b.   1 cone and 8 chocolate bars

c.   3 cones and 1 chocolate bar

d.   5 cones and 10 chocolate bars

4. If a budget line rotates inward and becomes steeper, then the

a. consumer's budget decreased.

b. consumer's budget increased.

c. price of one of the goods decreased.

d. price of one of the goods increased.

5. A steeper budget line means a

a. higher opportunity cost of the good measured on the *x*-axis.

b. lower opportunity cost of the good measured on the *x*-axis.

c. larger income.

d. smaller income.

6. A relative price is the

a. price of a substitute.

b. price of a related good.

c. price of one good divided by the price of another.

d. absolute price of a good.

7. When a consumer's budget increases, the budget line

a. rotates outward and its slope changes.

b. rotates inward and its slope changes.

c. shifts outward and its slope does not change.

d. shifts inward and its slope does not change.

8. Rob buys fishing lures and steaks. If his budget increases, the maximum number of fishing lures he can purchase _____ and the maximum number of steaks he can purchase _____.

a. increases; increases

b. increases; decreases ·

c. decreases; increases

d. decreases; decreases

Complete the graph

1. Jack buys only magazines, which have a price of $3 each, and hamburgers, which have a price of $4 each. Jack's income is $12.

a. In Figure 11.1, draw Jack's budget line.

■ FIGURE 11.1

b. What does the slope of the budget line equal? What is the interpretation of this slope?

c. Can Jack buy 2 magazines and 1 hamburger? Can he buy 2 magazines and 3 hamburgers?

d. Suppose the price of a hamburger falls to $2. In Figure 11.1, draw Jack's new budget line.

e. What does the slope of the new budget line equal? How does the slope compare to your answer to part **b**?

f. Can Jack now buy 2 magazines and 1 hamburger? Can he now buy 2 magazines and 3 hamburgers?

Short answer

1. How is a budget line similar to a production possibilities frontier? How is it dissimilar?

2. What does the slope of a budget line equal?

3. What is the relationship between the relative price of a good and its opportunity cost?

4. If a consumer's budget increases, what happens to the budget line? Does its slope change?

CHECKPOINT 11.2

■ **Explain marginal utility theory and use it to derive a consumer's demand curve.**

Practice Problem 11.2

The table shows Jerry's total utility from burgers and magazines.

Burgers		Magazines	
Quantity per week	Total utility	Quantity per week	Total utility
0	0	0	0
1	14	1	100
2	24	2	120
3	32	3	134
4	38	4	144

a. Calculate Jerry's marginal utility from the second burger in the week.

b. If the price of a burger is $2, calculate the marginal utility per dollar spent on burgers when Jerry buys 2 burgers a week.

c. Calculate Jerry's marginal utility from the second magazine in the week.

d. If the price of a magazine is $4, calculate the marginal utility per dollar spent on magazines when Jerry buys 2 magazines.

e. When the price of a burger is $2, the price of a magazine is $4, and Jerry has $12 a week to spend, Jerry buys 2 burgers and 2 magazines. Does he maximize his total utility? Explain your answer.

Solution to Practice Problem 11.2

The goal of a consumer is to allocate the available budget in a way that maximizes total utility. Total utility is maximized when the sum of the utilities obtained from all goods is as large as possible. This outcome occurs when a person follows the utility-maximizing rule: 1. Allocate the entire available budget and 2. Make the marginal utility per dollar spent the same for all goods.

Quick Review

• *Marginal utility* The change in total utility that results from a one-unit increase in the quantity of a good consumed.

• *Marginal utility per dollar spent* The increase in total utility that comes from the last dollar spent on a good.

a. **Calculate Jerry's marginal utility from the second burger in the week.**

The marginal utility from the second burger equals the total utility from 2 burgers, which is 24 minus the total utility from 1 burger, which is 14. So the marginal utility from the second burger is 24 – 14 = 10 units of utility.

b. **If the price of a burger is $2, calculate the marginal utility per dollar spent on burgers when Jerry buys 2 burgers a week.**

The marginal utility per dollar spent on 2 burgers a week equals the marginal utility of the second burger divided by the price, which is 10 ÷ $2 = 5.

c. **Calculate Jerry's marginal utility from the second magazine in the week.**

The marginal utility from the second magazine equals the total utility from 2 magazines, which is 120 minus the total utility from 1 magazine, which is 100. So the marginal utility from the second magazine is 120 – 100 = 20 units of utility.

d. **If the price of a magazine is $4, calculate the marginal utility per dollar spent on magazines when Jerry buys 2 magazines.**

The marginal utility per dollar spent on 2 magazines a week equals the marginal utility of the second magazine divided by the price, which is 20 ÷ $4 = 5.

e. **When the price of a burger is $2, the price of a magazine is $4, and Jerry has $12 a week to spend, Jerry buys 2 burgers and 2 magazines. Does he maximize his total utility? Explain your answer.**

Jerry maximizes his total utility when he allocates his entire available budget and the marginal utility per dollar spent on burgers equals the marginal utility per dollar spent on magazines. When the price of a burger is $2 and Jerry buys 2 burgers, he spends $4 and when the price of a magazine is $4 and Jerry buys 2 magazines, he spends $8. So Jerry is allocating his entire available budget. Jerry's marginal utility per dollar spent on burgers is 5 from part **b** and his marginal utility per dollar spent on magazines is also 5 from part **d**. So Jerry is maximizing his total utility.

Additional Practice Problem 11.2a

If Jenny is allocating her entire available budget on movies and popcorn, explain the rule she must follow to maximize her total utility.

Solution to Additional Practice Problem 11.2a

If the marginal utility per dollar spent on movies exceeds the marginal utility per dollar spent on popcorn, then Jenny sees more movies and buys less popcorn; if the marginal utility per dollar spent on popcorn exceeds the marginal utility per dollar spent on movies, Jenny buys more popcorn and sees fewer movies. More generally, if the marginal gain from an action exceeds the marginal loss, take the action.

■ Self Test 11.2

Fill in the blanks

The total benefit a person gets from the consumption of a good or service is _____ (marginal; total) utility. The change in total utility that results from a one-unit increase in the quantity of a good consumed is _____ (marginal; elastic) utility. As the quantity of a good consumed increases, total utility _____ (increases; decreases) and marginal utility _____ (increases; decreases). The marginal utility per dollar spent equals the marginal utility of a good _____ (multiplied; divided) by the price of the good. When total utility is maximized, the marginal utility per dollar spent _____ (equals 1; is equal) for all goods. Diminishing marginal utility theory implies that other things remaining the same, the _____ (higher; lower) the price of a good, the smaller is the quantity demanded of that good. If, as the quantity consumed of a good increases, marginal utility decreases quickly, the demand for the good is_____ (elastic; inelastic).

True or false

1. As Katie consumes more sushi, her total utility from sushi increases.

2. As Katie consumes more sushi, her marginal utility from sushi increases.

3. Kim maximizes her utility whenever she allocates her entire available budget.

4. Tommy is allocating his entire available budget. If Tommy's marginal utility per dollar spent on tacos is 8 and the marginal utility per dollar spent on burritos is 10, then Tommy is not maximizing his total utility.

5. Diminishing marginal utility theory implies that other things remaining the same, the higher the price of a good, the greater is the quantity demanded of that good.

Multiple choice

1. In economics, utility
   a. is always increasing.
   b. equals opportunity cost.
   c. is an index of how much a person wants something.
   d. is measured in the same units as relative price.

2. Marginal utility is the
   a. change in total utility that results from a one-unit increase in the quantity of a good consumed.
   b. total benefit from the consumption of a good or service.
   c. quantity of a good a consumer prefers.
   d. average utility per unit consumed.

3. As I drink additional cups of tea at breakfast, my
   a. marginal utility from tea decreases.
   b. total utility from tea increases.
   c. total utility from tea decreases.
   d. Both answers (a) and (b) are correct.

4. Marginal utility per dollar spent is calculated by _____ utility of a good by the price of the good.

a. multiplying marginal

b. dividing marginal

c. multiplying total

d. dividing total

5. When a household maximizes its total utility, then its entire available budget is allocated in such a way that the

a. marginal utility of all goods is equal.

b. marginal utility per dollar spent is equal for all goods.

c. marginal utility is as large as possible for all goods.

d. marginal utility will start decreasing if it consumes fewer goods.

6. Suppose that Jennifer likes pizza and hotdogs. If her marginal utility per dollar spent on pizza is 6 and on hotdogs is 5, Jennifer

a. is maximizing her total utility.

b. could increase her total utility by buying more hotdogs and less pizza.

c. could increase her total utility by buying more pizza and fewer hotdogs.

d. is maximizing her marginal utility.

7. You can use marginal utility theory to find the demand curve by changing

a. the price of one good.

b. income.

c. the utility schedule.

d. the prices of both goods.

8. If, as the quantity consumed of a good increases, marginal utility decreases slowly, the demand for that good is

a. elastic or unit elastic.

b. elastic.

c. unit elastic.

d. inelastic.

Complete the graph

1. Bertha consumes only pop and pizza. The table gives Bertha's total utility from pop and pizza.

a. Complete the table.

Pizza			Pop		
Quantity (slices per day)	Total utility	Marginal utility	Quantity (cans per day)	Total utility	Marginal utility
0	0		0	0	
1	45	___	1	25	___
2	85	___	2	45	___
3	120	___	3	60	___
4	150	___	4	70	___
5	175	___	5	75	___
6	195	___	6	76	___

b. The price of a can of pop is $1 and the price of a slice of pizza is $2. If Bertha's budget is $6, how many cans of pop and slices of pizza does she consume?

c. If the price of a slice of pizza rises to $3, while the price of a can of pop and Bertha's budget do not change, how many cans of pop and slices of pizza does she consume?

d. What are two points on Bertha's demand curve for pizza? Label the axes and then draw her demand curve in Figure 11.2.

■ **FIGURE 11.2**

0

Short answer

1. Carlos drinks Aquafina bottled water. The table gives his total utility from this water. Calculate his marginal utility.

Quantity (bottles of Aquafina per day)	Total utility	Marginal utility
0	0	___
1	25	___
2	45	___
3	60	___
4	70	___
5	75	___
6	76	___

2. Lisa eats tacos and hamburgers. The quantities and marginal utilities for each are in the table below. Lisa's budget is $8.

Tacos		Hamburgers	
Quantity per week	Marginal utility	Quantity per week	Marginal utility
0	0	0	0
1	50	1	80
2	40	2	40
3	30	3	20
4	20	4	10
5	10	5	5

a. If the price of taco is $1 and the price of a hamburger is $2, what quantity of tacos and hamburgers will Lisa purchase?

b. If the price of a taco rises to $2 while neither Lisa's budget nor the price of a hamburger change, what quantity of tacos and hamburgers will Lisa purchase?

c. How does Lisa respond to a change in the price of a taco?

3. What does it mean to "allocate the entire available budget?" How does saving fit into the picture?

4. What is the relationship between a good's marginal utility and its elasticity of demand?

5. What is marginal analysis? Why is making the marginal utility per dollar spent necessary for a consumer to maximize his or her utility?

■ Use marginal utility theory to explain the paradox of value: Why water is vital but cheap while diamonds are relatively useless but expensive.

Practice Problem 11.3

Tony rents 500 videos a year at $3 each and buys 10,000 litres of tap water a year, for which he pays $50. Tony is maximizing total utility. If Tony's marginal utility from water is 0.5 units per litre, what is his marginal utility from a video rental? Which good is the more valuable to Tony: water or videos? Why?

Solution to Practice Problem 11.3

To answer this Practice Problem, remember that when Tony is maximizing his utility that the marginal utility per dollar spent for tap water and videos is equal. And when we are discussing the value of videos and tap water, we are thinking about total utility and consumer surplus.

Quick Review

• *The paradox of value* Why is water, which is essential to life, cheap, but diamonds, which are relative useless, expensive?

Tony rents 500 videos a year at $3 each and buys 10,000 litres of tap water a year, for which he pays $50. Tony is maximizing total utility. If Tony's marginal utility from water is 0.5 units per litre, what is his marginal utility from a video rental? Which good is the more valuable to Tony: water or videos? Why?

Tony is maximizing utility, so the marginal utility per dollar spent on tap water equals the marginal utility per dollar spent on videos. Tony buys 10,000 litres of tap water a year, for which he pays $50. So Tony pays $50 ÷ 10,000 litres, which is $0.005 a litre. Tony's marginal utility per dollar spent for water is 0.5 ÷ $0.005, which is 100.

The price of a video is $3, and the marginal utility of a video divided by the price of a video equals 100. So the marginal utility of a video equals 100 × $3, which is 300 units.

Water most likely generates more total utility for Tony and has a greater consumer surplus. Water is more valuable to Tony.

Additional Practice Problem 11.3a

In Practice Problem 11.3, why does Tony receive a lower marginal utility from his consumption of water?

Solution to Additional Practice Problem 11.3a

Tony rents 500 videos a year and buys 10,000 litres of tap water a year. As the quantity of a good consumed increases, the marginal utility tends to decrease. Because Tony is consuming much more water than videos, his total utility from water is greater than his total utility from videos, but his marginal utility from water is much less than his marginal utility from videos.

■ Self Test 11.3

Fill in the blanks

Marginal benefit is the maximum price a consumer is willing to pay for an extra unit of a good or service when ____ (marginal; total) utility is maximized. The paradox of value is resolved by noting that diamonds have a high price, a ____ (high; low) total utility, and a ____ (high; low) marginal utility. Water provides ____ (more; less) consumer surplus than diamonds.

True or false

1. Katie's demand curve for sushi shows the quantity of sushi she demands at each price when her total utility is maximized.

2. Marginal benefit is the maximum price a consumer is willing to pay for an extra unit of a good or service when total utility is maximized.

3. The paradox of value is that water, which is essential to life, is plentiful while diamonds, which are not essential to life, are much less plentiful.

4. The paradox of value is solved by noting that the total utility from water is small while the marginal utility from water is large.

5. The consumer surplus from water is greater than the consumer surplus from diamonds.

Multiple choice

1. At all points on a demand curve, the
   a. consumer's budget has been allocated to maximize total utility.
   b. quantity describes the quantity demanded at each price when total utility is maximized.
   c. price represents the marginal benefit the consumer gets from an extra unit of a good.
   d. All of the above answers are correct.

2. As more of a good is consumed, the marginal utility of an additional unit ____, so consumers are willing to pay ____ for an additional unit.
   a. decreases; less
   b. increases; less
   c. decreases; more
   d. increases; more

3. The paradox of value refers to the
   a. utility-maximizing rule.
   b. fact that water is vital but cheap while diamonds are relatively useless but expensive.
   c. fact that consumers have different preferences and utility schedules.
   d. law of demand.

4. One reason why water is cheap is because the
   a. marginal utility of water is enormous.
   b. marginal utility of water is small.
   c. marginal utility of water is negative.
   d. total utility of water is small.

5. In the paradox of value between expensive diamonds and inexpensive water, we see that

a. the consumer surpluses are very high for both goods.

b. diamonds have a low consumer surplus while water has a high consumer surplus.

c. diamonds have a high consumer surplus while water has a low consumer surplus.

d. the consumer surpluses are very low for both goods.

Complete the graph

1. Figure 11.3 shows the market for water. Indicate the equilibrium price and then shade in the area of the consumer surplus.

■ **FIGURE 11.3**
Price (dollars per thousand litres)

Quantity (thousands of litres per month)

2. Figure 11.4 shows the market for rubies. Indicate the equilibrium price and then shade in the area of the consumer surplus.

■ **FIGURE 11.4**
Price (thousands of dollars per carat)

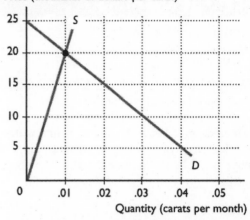

Quantity (carats per month)

3. Based on Figures 11.3 and 11.4, is there more consumer surplus for water or rubies? Which is larger: the marginal utility of a litre of water or a carat of rubies?

Short answer

1. Bobby consumes potato chips and Gatorade and is maximizing his total utility. His marginal utility from the last bag of chips he eats is 40 and his marginal utility from the last bottle of Gatorade he drinks is 60. The price of a bag of chips is $2. What is the price of a bottle of Gatorade?

2. Does the price Bianca is willing to pay for another purse depend on her total utility from purses or her marginal utility? Explain your answer.

3. What is the paradox of value and what is its solution?

SELF TEST ANSWERS

■ CHECKPOINT 11.1

Fill in the blanks

A <u>budget</u> line shows the limits to consumption possibilities. The budget line becomes <u>more</u> steep when the price of the good measured along the *x*-axis increases and everything else remains the same. The slope of the budget line is equal to the <u>relative</u> price. When income increases, the budget line shifts <u>outward</u>.

True or false

1. True; page 256
2. False; page 257
3. True; page 258
4. False; page 259
5. True; page 260

Multiple choice

1. d; page 256
2. b; page 256
3. b; page 256
4. d; page 258
5. a; page 258
6. c; page 259
7. c; page 260
8. a; page 260

Complete the graph

1. a. The budget line in Figure 11.5, which is labelled Hamburgers $4 is Jack's budget line; page 256.

   b. The slope of the budget line equals (–4 magazines ÷ 3 hamburgers), which is –4/3 magazines per hamburger. The slope tells us that the opportunity cost of a hamburger is 4/3 magazines and the relative

price of a hamburger is 4/3 magazines; page 259.

   c. Jack can buy 2 magazines and 1 hamburger. Jack cannot buy 2 magazines and 3 hamburgers because that combination is outside his budget line; page 256.

   d. The new budget line is in Figure 11.5, labelled Hamburgers $2; page 256.

■ FIGURE 11.5

Quantity (magazines per week)

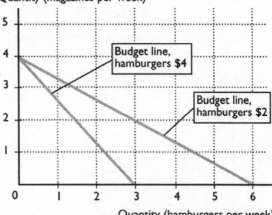

e. The slope of the new budget line is –2/3 magazines per hamburger. Compared to the slope in part **b**, the opportunity cost of a hamburger is lower when its price falls; page 259.

f. Jack can buy 2 magazines and 1 hamburger. Jack also can buy 2 magazines and 3 hamburgers because that combination is now on his budget line; page 256.

Short answer

1. A budget line is similar to a production possibilities frontier. Both curves show a limit to what is feasible. The *PPF* is a technological limit that does not depend on prices. But the budget line does depend on prices. Consumption possibilities change when prices or the available budget change; page 257.

2. The slope of the budget line equals the opportunity cost and the relative price of the good measured along the x-axis; page 258.

3. The relative price is the price of one good in terms of another good. The relative price is an opportunity cost. It equals the price of one good divided by the price of another good; page 259.

4. The budget line shifts outward. Its slope does not change; page 260.

■ **CHECKPOINT 11.2**

Fill in the blanks

The total benefit a person gets from the consumption of a good or service is total utility. The change in total utility that results from a one-unit increase in the quantity of a good consumed is marginal utility. As the quantity of a good consumed increases, total utility increases and marginal utility decreases. The marginal utility per dollar spent equals the marginal utility of a good divided by the price of the good. When total utility is maximized, the marginal utility per dollar spent is equal for all goods. Diminishing marginal utility theory implies that other things remaining the same, the higher the price of a good, the smaller is the quantity demanded of that good. If, as the quantity consumed of a good increases, marginal utility decreases quickly, the demand for the good is inelastic.

True or false

1. True; page 262
2. False; page 263
3. False; page 266
4. True; page 266
5. False; pages 268-269

Multiple choice

1. c; page 262
2. a; page 263
3. d; page 263
4. b; page 267
5. b; page 266
6. c; page 267
7. a; page 268
8. b; page 271

Complete the graph

1. a. The completed table is below; page 263.

Pizza			Pop		
Quantity (slices per day)	Total utility	Marginal utility	Quantity (cans per day)	Total utility	Marginal utility
0	0	0	0	0	0
1	45	45	1	25	25
2	85	40	2	45	20
3	120	35	3	60	15
4	150	30	4	70	10
5	175	25	5	75	5
6	195	20	6	76	1

b. Bertha consumes 2 cans of pop and 2 slices of pizza. This combination allocates all her budget and the marginal utility per dollar spent for pop and pizza both equal 20; page 266.

c. Bertha now consumes 3 cans of pop and 1 slice of pizza. This combination allocates all of her budget and the marginal utility per dollar spent for pop and pizza both equal 15; page 266.

d. One point on her demand curve is $2 and 2 slices of pizza; another point is $3 and 1 slice of pizza. Figure 11.6 shows Bertha's demand curve; page 268.

■ **FIGURE 11.6**

Price (dollars per slice of pizza)

Short answer

1.   The completed table is below; page 263.

Quantity (bottles of Aquafina per day)	Total utility	Marginal utility
0	0	
1	25	25
2	45	20
3	60	15
4	70	10
5	75	5
6	76	1

2a. Lisa will buy 4 tacos and 2 hamburgers because this combination allocates her entire budget and sets the marginal utility per dollar spent on tacos equal to the marginal utility per dollar spent on hamburgers; page 266.

b.   Lisa will buy 2 tacos and 2 hamburgers. This combination allocates her entire budget and sets the marginal utility per dollar spent on tacos equal to the marginal utility per dollar spent on hamburgers; page 266.

c.   When the price of a taco rises, the quantity of tacos demanded decreases; page 268.

3.   To "allocate the entire available budget" means that we use the entire available budget. Using the entire budget doesn't mean not saving anything. The available budget is the amount available after choosing how much to save; page 266.

4.   If, as the quantity consumed of a good increases, marginal utility decreases quickly, the demand for the good is inelastic. The reason is that for a given change in the price, only a small change in the quantity consumed of the good is needed to bring its marginal utility per dollar spent bank to equality with that on all the other items in the consumer's budget.

But if, as the quantity consumed of a good increases, marginal utility decreases slowly, the demand for that good is elastic. In this case, for a given change in the price, a large change in the quantity consumed of the good is needed to bring its marginal utility per dollar spent back to equality with that on all the other items in the consumer's budget; page 270.

5.   Marginal analysis compares the marginal gain from having more of one good with the marginal loss from having less of another good. The "equalize the marginal utility per dollar spent" rule is the result of marginal analysis. Suppose the marginal utility per dollar spent on a blouse exceeds the marginal utility per dollar spent on a purse. Marginal analysis indicates that the consumer increases her total utility by spending a dollar less on purses and spending a dollar more on blouses because the gain in utility from the dollar spent on blouses exceeds the loss in utility from the dollar reduction on purses; page 270.

■   **CHECKPOINT 11.3**

Fill in the blanks

Marginal benefit is the maximum price a consumer is willing to pay for an extra unit of a good or service when <u>total</u> utility is maximized. The paradox of value is resolved by noting that diamonds have a high price, a <u>low</u> total utility, and a <u>high</u> marginal utility. Water provides <u>more</u> consumer surplus than diamonds.

True or false

1. True; page 272
2. True; page 272
3. False; page 272
4. False; page 272
5. True; page 272

Multiple choice

1. d; page 272
2. a; page 272
3. b; page 272
4. b; page 272
5. b; page 272

Complete the graph

1. The equilibrium price is $5 per thousand litres of water. The consumer surplus is the grey area in Figure 11.7; page 272.

■ **FIGURE 11.7**

Price (dollars per thousand litres)

2. The equilibrium price is $20,000 a carat. Figure 11.8 shows the consumer surplus; page 272.

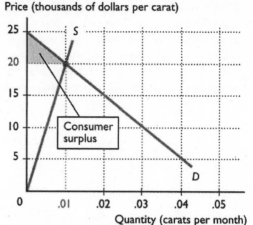

■ **FIGURE 11.8**

Price (thousands of dollars per carat)

3. There is more consumer surplus for water than rubies. Because the price of a carat of rubies is much greater than the price of a litre of water, it must be the case that the marginal utility of a carat of rubies is much greater than the marginal utility of a litre of water; page 272.

Short answer

1. Bobby maximizes his total utility by consuming the combination of chips and Gatorade such that the marginal utility per dollar spent on chips equals the marginal utility per dollar spend on Gatorade. The marginal utility from the last bag of chips is 40 and the price of a bag of chips is $2, so the marginal utility per dollar spent is 40 ÷ $2 = 20. Because the marginal utility of the Gatorade is 60, the price is $3 to make the marginal utility per dollar spent equal to 20; page 272.

2. The price Bianca is willing to pay for another purse depends on marginal utility. Bianca maximizes her total utility by making her marginal utility per dollar spent equal for all goods. If her marginal utility from an additional purse is high, she is willing to pay a high price for the next purse; page 272.

3. The paradox of value is that water, which is essential for life, is cheap while diamonds are relatively useless but expensive. The solution

to the paradox is that people consume a lot of water, so the marginal utility of an additional litre of water is very low. People consume only a few diamonds, so the marginal utility of an additional diamond is quite high. A household maximizes its total utility when the marginal utility per dollar spent is equal for all goods. So water has a low marginal utility and a low price and diamonds have a high marginal utility and a high price; page 272.

Appendix: Indifference Curves

Chapter 11

The appendix uses indifference curves and budget lines to derive a demand curve.

■ **Indifference curves**

An indifference curve is a line that shows combinations of goods among which a consumer is indifferent. All combinations above the indifference curve are preferred to those on the indifference curve and all combinations on the indifference curve are preferred to those below the indifference curve. The marginal rate of substitution, *MRS*, is the rate at which a person will give up good y (the good measured on the y-axis) to get more of good x (the good measured on the x-axis) and at the same time remain on the same indifference curve. The magnitude of the slope of the indifference curve equals the marginal rate of substitution. The marginal rate of substitution diminishes as the consumer moves along an indifference curve, increasing consumption of the good measured on the x-axis and decreasing consumption of the good measured on the y-axis. The consumer is at his best affordable point when he is on his budget line, is on his highest attainable indifference curve, and has a marginal rate of substitution equal to the relative price of the two goods. We can use the indifference curve model to generate a demand curve.

EXPANDED APPENDIX CHECKLIST

1 An indifference curve.

- Define and draw an indifference curve.

- State which consumption combinations are more preferred and which are less preferred to those on an indifference curve.

2 Marginal rate of substitution.

- Define the marginal rate of substitution and explain how the marginal rate of substitution is measured.

- Discuss the key assumption of consumer theory.

3 Consumer equilibrium.

- Describe the best affordable point.

- Discuss when the marginal rate of substitution of equals relative price.

4 Deriving the demand curve.

- Derive a demand curve using indifference curves and budget lines.

KEY TERMS

- Diminishing marginal rate of substitution (page 280)

- Indifference curve (page 279)

- Marginal rate of substitution (page 280)

CHECKPOINT A11.1

Additional Practice Problems A11.1

1. Figure A11.1 shows one of Maria's indifference curves between ice cream cones and milkshakes.

■ FIGURE A11.1

Milkshakes (number per week)

Lightly shade the combinations of cones and milkshakes that are more preferred to those on the indifference curve. More heavily shade the combinations that are less preferred to those on the indifference curve.

2. In Figure A11.1, what is Maria's marginal rate of substitution when she is consuming 4 ice cream cones and 2 milkshakes?

3. In Figure A11.2, what is Maria's best affordable point?

■ FIGURE A11.2

Milkshakes (number per week)

Solution to Additional Practice Problems A11.1

1. **Figure A11.1 shows one of Maria's indifference curves between ice cream cones and milkshakes. Lightly shade the combinations of cones and milkshakes that are more preferred to those on the indifference curve. More heavily shade the combinations that are less preferred to those on the indifference curve.**

Figure A11.3 shows that all combinations above the indifference curve are more preferred to those on it and all combinations below the indifference curve are less preferred to those on it.

■ FIGURE A11.3

Milkshakes (number per week)

2. **In Figure A11.1, what is Maria's marginal rate of substitution when she is consuming 4 ice cream cones and 2 milkshakes?**

Maria's marginal rate of substitution equals the magnitude of the slope of the indifference curve. Use the straight line that touches the combination of 4 ice cream cones and 2 milkshakes and touches the indifference curve at only that point. The magnitude of the slope of this line is 1/2 of a milkshake per ice cream cone, so Maria's marginal rate of substitution is 1/2 of a milkshake per ice cream cone.

3. **In Figure A11.2, what is Maria's best affordable point?**

Figure A11.4 shows Maria's best affordable point. This point is on Maria's budget line and also on the highest attainable indifference curve, I_2.

■ FIGURE A11.4

Milkshakes (number per week)

■ Self Test A11.1

Fill in the blanks

An _____ (equilibrium; indifference) curve is a curve that shows combinations of goods among which a consumer is indifferent. A consumer prefers being on a _____ (lower; higher) indifference curve. The magnitude of the slope of an indifference curve equals the _____ (marginal rate of substitution; rate of consumer equilibrium). The best affordable point occurs at the point on the highest attainable indifference curve where the magnitude of the slope of the budget line _____ (equals; is greater than; is less than) the marginal rate of substitution.

True or false

1. Tara is indifferent among combinations of goods that are on her indifference curve.

2. A consumer is indifferent among combinations on different indifference curves.

3. The marginal rate of substitution is the rate at which a person will give up the good measured on the y-axis to get more of the good measured on the x-axis and at the same time remain indifferent.

4. When Sara is on her budget line, she is always at her best affordable point.

5. Along a demand curve that is derived using indifference curves, the quantity of the good demanded increases when the price rises.

Multiple choice

1. An indifference curve is a line that shows combinations of goods

a. that a consumer prefers one over the other.

b. that have no value.

c. that are affordable.

d. among which a consumer is indifferent.

2. What is the difference between a budget line and an indifference curve?

a. One is measured in dollars while the other is measured in units of goods.

b. One shows what is possible while the other shows what is preferred.

c. One shows a positive relationship and the other shows a negative relationship.

d. There is no difference.

3. In a preference map, combinations on higher indifference curves _____ on a lower indifference curve.

a. always cost more than any combination

b. are preferred to combinations on

c. always cost less than any combination

d. are less preferred than combinations

4.   The marginal rate of substitution is

a.   the consumer surplus.

b.   the same as the consumer's budget line.

c.   equal to the magnitude of the slope of the indifference curve.

d.   equal to the magnitude of the slope of the consumer surplus curve.

5.   At her best affordable point, Erin

a.   is on her budget line.

b.   is on the highest attainable indifference curve.

c.   has a marginal rate of substitution equal to the relative price of the goods.

d.   All of the above answers are correct.

6.   When Ralph is at his best affordable point, the marginal rate of substitution is

a.   greater than the relative price.

b.   equal to the relative price.

c.   less than the relative price.

d.   maximized.

7.   To derive a demand curve using indifference curves, you must change the

a.   consumer's preferences.

b.   consumer's budget.

c.   price of one good, holding the price of the other good and budget constant.

d.   price of both goods simultaneously.

Complete the graph

1.   Figure A11.5 shows two of Brent's indifference curves.

a.   Brent's budget is $40 a month and the price of a movie and renting a DVD are $10 each. Draw Brent's budget line in Figure A11.5. How many DVDs does Brent rent a month?

■ FIGURE A11.5

b.   Draw Brent's new budget line in Figure A11.5 if the price of a DVD rental falls to $5 and everything else remains the same. How many DVDs does Brent now rent per month?

c.   Draw Brent's demand curve in Figure A11.6. How does a fall in the price of a DVD rental change the quantity of DVDs Brent rents?

■ FIGURE A11.6

Short answer

1.   Alberto's marginal rate of substitution between shirts and pants is 2 shirts per pair of pants. As Alberto obtains more pants, what happens to his marginal rate of substitution?

2.   What is the difference between an indifference curve and a demand curve?

SELF TEST ANSWERS

■ CHECKPOINT A1.1

Fill in the blanks

An <u>indifference</u> curve is a curve that shows combinations of goods among which a consumer is indifferent. A consumer prefers being on a <u>higher</u> indifference curve. The magnitude of the slope of an indifference curve equals the <u>marginal rate of substitution</u>. The best affordable point occurs at the point on the highest attainable indifference curve where the magnitude of the slope of the budget line <u>equals</u> the marginal rate of substitution.

True or false

1. True; page 279
2. False; page 279
3. True; page 280
4. False; page 281
5. False; pages 282-283

Multiple choice

1. d; page 279
2. b; pages 279, 282
3. b; pages 279-280
4. c; page 280
5. d; page 281
6. b; page 281
7. c; page 282

Complete the graph

1a. Figure A11.7 shows the budget line. Brent rents 2 DVDs a month; page 282.

b. Figure A11.7 shows the new budget line. Brent now rents 4 DVDs a month; page 282.

■ **FIGURE A11.5**

Movies (number per month)

c. One point on Brent's demand curve is from part **a**. When the price of a DVD rental is $10, the quantity of DVDs Brent rents is 2 a month. The other point is from part **b**. When the price of a DVD rental is $5, Brent rents 4 DVDs a month. Figure A11.8 plots these two points and draws Brent's demand curve. A fall in the price of a DVD rental increases the quantity of DVDs Brent rents; page 282.

■ **FIGURE A11.8**

Price (dollars per DVD rental)

Short answer

1. The marginal rate of 2 shirts per pair of pants means that Alberto is willing to give up 2 shirts in order to get another pair of pants. As Alberto obtains more pants, his marginal rate of substitution decreases; page 280.

2.   An indifference curve is a line that shows combinations of goods among which a consumer is indifferent. A demand curve is a graph of the relationship between the quantity demanded of a good and its price when all other influences on buying plans remain the same. We can use a preference map, which is a series of indifference curves to derive a demand curve; pages 279 and 282.

Chapter

Production and Cost

12

Chapter 12 studies the firm's costs and how these costs vary as the firm varies its output.

■ **Explain how economists measure a firm's cost of production and profit.**

The firm's goal is to maximize profit. The highest-valued alternative forgone is the opportunity cost of a firm's production. A cost paid in money is an explicit cost. A firm incurs an implicit cost when it uses a factor of production but does not make a direct money payment for its use. The return to entrepreneurship is normal profit, which is part of a firm's opportunity cost because it is the cost of not running another firm. A firm's economic profit equals total revenue minus total cost, which is the sum of explicit costs and implicit costs and is the opportunity cost of production.

■ **Explain the relationship between a firm's output and labour employed in the short run.**

The short run is the time frame in which the quantities of some resources are fixed; the long run is the time frame in which the quantities of all resources can be varied. Total product is the maximum quantity of a good that can be produced in a given period. Marginal product is the change in total product that results from a one-unit increase in the quantity of labour employed. As firms hire labour, initially increasing marginal returns occur but eventually decreasing marginal returns set in. Average product is total product divided by the quantity of an input. When marginal product exceeds average product, the average product curve slopes upward and average product increases as more labour is employed. And when marginal product is less than average product, the average product curve slopes downward and average product decreases as more labour is employed.

■ **Explain the relationship between a firm's output and costs in the short run.**

Total cost is the sum of total fixed cost and total variable cost. Marginal cost is the change in total cost that results from a one-unit increase in output. Average total cost is the sum of average fixed cost and average variable cost. The U-shape of the average total cost curve arises from the influence of two opposing forces: spreading total fixed cost over a larger output and decreasing marginal returns. The marginal cost curve intersects the average variable cost and average total cost curves at their minimum points. The average cost curve and the marginal cost curve shift when technology changes or when the price of a factor of production changes.

■ **Derive and explain a firm's long-run average cost curve.**

In the long run, all costs are variable. When a firm changes its plant size, it may experience economies of scale, diseconomies of scale, or constant returns to scale. The long-run average cost curve is a curve that shows the lowest average cost at which it is possible to produce each output when the firm has had sufficient time to change both its plant size and labor employed. The long-run average cost curve slopes downward with economies of scale and upward with diseconomies of scale.

EXPANDED CHAPTER CHECKLIST

When you have completed this chapter, you will be able to

1 Explain how economists measure a firm's cost of production and profit.

- Explain the firm's goal.
- Compare the economic view and the accounting view of cost and profit.
- Define and give examples of explicit cost and implicit cost.
- Define normal profit and explain why it is part of a firm's opportunity cost.
- Define economic profit.

2 Explain the relationship between a firm's output and labour employed in the short run.

- Define short run and long run.
- Define total product and draw a total product curve.
- Define and calculate marginal product.
- Explain why increasing marginal returns and decreasing marginal returns occur.
- Define and calculate average product.
- Use a graph to explain the relationship between marginal product and average product.

3 Explain the relationship between a firm's output and costs in the short run.

- Define total cost, total fixed cost, and total variable cost, and illustrate the total cost curves.
- Define and calculate marginal cost.
- Define average total cost, average variable cost, and average fixed cost, and illustrate the average cost curves and the marginal cost curve.
- Explain why the average total cost curve is U-shaped.

4 Derive and explain a firm's long-run average cost curve.

- Define economies of scale, diseconomies of scale, and constant returns to scale.
- Explain how the long-run average cost curve is constructed and use it to illustrate economies and diseconomies of scale.

KEY TERMS

- Average fixed cost (page 299)
- Average product (page 294)
- Average total cost (page 299)
- Average variable cost (page 299)
- Constant returns to scale (page 306)
- Decreasing marginal returns (page 292)
- Diseconomies of scale (page 306)
- Economic depreciation (page 287)
- Economic profit (page 287)
- Economies of scale (page 305)
- Explicit cost (page 287)
- Implicit cost (page 287)
- Increasing marginal returns (page 292)
- Law of decreasing returns (page 294)
- Long run (page 290)
- Long-run average cost curve (page 306)
- Marginal cost (page 298)
- Marginal product (page 292)
- Normal profit (page 287)
- Short run (page 290)
- Total cost (page 297)
- Total fixed cost (page 297)
- Total product (page 291)
- Total variable cost (page 297)

CHECKPOINT 12.1

■   **Explain how economists measure a firm's cost of production and profit.**

Practice Problem 12.1

Lee is a computer programmer who earned $35,000 in 2001. But Lee loves water sports and in 2002 he opened a body board manufacturing business. At the end of the first year of operation, he submitted the following information to his accountant:

   (i)   He stopped renting out his seaside cottage for $3,500 a year and used it as his factory. The market value of the cottage increased from $70,000 to $71,000.

   (ii) He spent $50,000 on materials, phone, utilities etc.

   (iii) He leased machines for $10,000 a year.

   (iv) He paid $15,000 in wages.

   (v)   He used $10,000 from his savings account at the bank, which pays 5 percent a year interest.

   (vi) He borrowed $40,000 at 10 percent a year from the bank.

   (vii) He sold $160,000 worth of body boards.

   (viii) Normal profit is $25,000 a year.

a.   Calculate Lee's explicit costs and implicit costs.

b.   Calculate Lee's economic profit.

c.   Lee's accountant recorded the depreciation on Lee's cottage during 2002 as $7,000. What did the accountant say Lee's profit or loss was for the year?

Solution to Practice Problem 12.1

This Practice Problem studies the difference between an explicit cost and an implicit cost and the difference between the economic view and the accounting view of cost and profit.

Quick Review

*   *Explicit cost* A cost paid in money.

*   *Implicit cost* An opportunity cost incurred by a firm when it uses a factor of production for which it does not make a direct money payment.

*   *Normal profit* The return to entrepreneurship. Normal profit is part of a firm's opportunity cost because it is the cost of not running another firm.

*   *Economic profit* A firm's total revenue minus total cost.

a.   Calculate Lee's explicit costs and implicit costs.

Lee's explicit costs are $50,000 for materials, phone, utilities etc.; $10,000 to lease machines; $15,000 for wages; and 10 percent of $40,000, which is $4,000 for interest payments. Lee's explicit costs are $79,000.

Lee's implicit costs are: $35,000 for wages forgone; $3,500 that could have been earned as rent for the cottage; forgone bank interest, equal to 5 percent of $10,000, which is $500; normal profit of $25,000; and –$1,000 for the increase in the market value of the cottage. Lee's implicit costs are $63,000.

b.   Calculate Lee's economic profit.

Economic profit is total revenue minus total cost. Total cost is the sum of explicit costs and implicit costs. So Lee's total cost is $79,000 + $63,000, which is $142,000. Lee's economic profit equals $160,000 – $142,000, which is $18,000.

c.   What did the accountant say Lee's profit or loss was for the year?

An accountant calculates profit as total revenue minus explicit costs minus depreciation. Lee's total revenue is $160,000 and his explicit costs are $79,000, so the accountant calculates Lee's profit as $160,000 – $79,000 – $7,000, which is $74,000.

Additional Practice Problem 12.1a

Gary manufactures toy gliders made of balsa wood. Each week, Gary pays $200 in wages, buys balsa wood for $400, pays $50 to lease saws and sanders, and pays $150 in rent for the workspace. To fund his operations, Gary withdrew $162,500 from his savings account at the bank, which paid interest of $250 a week. The normal profit for a glider company is $250 a week. Gary sells $1,500 worth of gliders a week.

a.   How much are the weekly explicit costs?

b.   How much are the weekly implicit costs?

c.   What does an economist compute for the weekly economic profit?

Solution to Additional Practice Problem 12.1a

a.   How much are the weekly explicit costs?

The explicit costs are the money Gary spends on wages, the balsa wood, the leased saws and sanders, and rent. The weekly explicit costs are $200 + $400 + $50 + $150, which equals $800.

b.   How much are the weekly implicit costs?

The implicit costs are the forgone interest and the normal profit. The weekly implicit costs are $250 + $250, which equals $500.

c.   What does an economists compute for the weekly economic profit?

Economic profit is total revenue minus total cost. Total cost is the sum of explicit costs and implicit costs. So Gary's total cost is $800 + $500, which is $1,300. Gary's economic profit equals $1,500 − $1,300, which is $200.

■ Self Test 12.1

Fill in the blanks

The firm's goal is to maximize _____ (growth; market share; profit). A cost paid in money is an _____ (explicit; implicit) cost; a cost incurred when a firm uses a factor of production for which it does not make a direct money payment is an _____ (explicit; implicit) cost. The return to entrepreneurship is _____ (normal; economic) profit and _____ (is; is not) part of the firm's opportunity cost.

A firm's total revenue minus total cost is _____ (normal; economic) profit.

True or false

1.   The firm's goal is to maximize profit.

2.   An accountant measures profit as total revenue minus opportunity cost.

3.   All of a firm's costs must be paid in money.

4.   If a firm earns an economic profit, the return to the entrepreneur exceeds normal profit.

Multiple choice

1.   The goal of a firm is to

a.   maximize profit.

b.   maximize sales.

c.   maximize total revenue.

d.   minimize costs.

2.   For a business, opportunity cost measures

a.   only the cost of labour and materials.

b.   only the implicit costs of the business.

c.   the amount the firm must pay the owners of the factors of production it employs to attract them from their best alternative use.

d.   only the explicit costs the firm must pay.

3.   The cost paid in money to attract a resource from its best alternative use is

a.   normal profit.

b.   an implicit cost.

c.   an explicit cost.

d.   an alternative-use cost.

4.   _____ is an implicit cost.

a.   Wages paid to employees

b.   Interest paid to a bank on a building loan

c.   The value of capital an owner donates to the business

d.   Money paid to a supplier

5. The opportunity cost of a firm using capital that it owns is

a. economic depreciation.

b. depreciation.

c. economic loss.

d. normal loss.

6. The difference between a firm's total revenue and its total cost is ____ profit.

a. explicit

b. normal

c. economic

d. accounting

Short answer

1. What is likely to happen to a firm that does not maximize profit?

2. Bobby quits his job as a dentist to open a model train store. Bobby made $80,000 a year as a dentist. The first year his train store is open, Bobby pays a helper $26,000. He also pays $24,000 in rent, $10,000 in utilities, and buys $200,000 of model trains. Bobby had a good year because he sold all of his model trains for $300,000. Bobby's normal profit is $30,000.

a. What would an accountant calculate as Bobby's profit?

b. What is Bobby's total opportunity cost? What is his economic profit?

3. Why are wages a cost to a business? Why is a normal profit a cost to a business?

CHECKPOINT 12.2

■ **Explain the relationship between a firm's output and labour employed in the short run.**

Practice Problem 12.2

Tom leases a farmer's field and grows pumpkins. Tom hires students to pick and pack the pump-

kins. The table sets out Tom's total product schedule.

Labour (students)	Total product (pumpkins per day)
0	0
1	100
2	220
3	300
4	360
5	400
6	420
7	430

a. Calculate the marginal product of the third student.

b. Calculate the average product of three students.

c. Over what numbers of students does marginal product increase?

d. When marginal product increases, compare average product and marginal product.

Solution to Practice Problem 12.2

This Practice Problem emphasizes the relationship between marginal product and average product. For employment levels at which marginal product exceeds average product, the average product curve slopes upward and average product increases as more labour is employed. For employment levels at which marginal product is less than average product, the average product curve slopes downward and average product decreases as more labour is employed.

Quick Review

• *Marginal product* The change in total product that results from a one-unit increase in the quantity of labour employed. Marginal product equals the change in total product divided by the change in the quantity of labour.

a. **Calculate the marginal product of the third student.**

The marginal product of the third student is the change in total product that results from hiring the third student. The marginal product of the third students equals the total product of 3 students, which is 300 pumpkins a day minus the total product of 2 students, which is 220 pumpkins a day. So the marginal product of the third student is 300 pumpkins a day – 220 pumpkins a day, which is 80 pumpkins a day.

b. **Calculate the average product of three students.**

Average product is calculated as total product divided by the quantity of labour. When Tom hires 3 students, total product is 300 pumpkins a day. So the average product of three students is (300 pumpkins a day) ÷ (3 students), which is 100 pumpkins a day.

c. **Over what numbers of students does marginal product increase?**

The marginal product of the first student is 100 pumpkins a day. The marginal product of the second student is 120 pumpkins a day. And the marginal product of the third student is 80 pumpkins a day. Marginal product increases when Tom hires the first and second students.

d. **When marginal product increases, compare average product and marginal product.**

When Tom hires 1 student, marginal product is 100 pumpkins a day and average product is also 100 pumpkins a day. When Tom hires 2 students, marginal product is 120 pumpkins a day and average product is 110 pumpkins a day. When marginal product increases, average product also increases, and marginal product is greater than average product.

Additional Practice Problem 12.2a

The first five members of the men's basketball squad are each 185 centimetres tall. A sixth player, whose height is 215 centimetres, is added. Has the average height increased or decreased with the addition of this player? A seventh player, whose height is 155 centimetres, is added. What happens to the team's average height? An eighth player, whose height is 185 centimetres, is added. What is the effect on the average height? What is the general rule about how the marginal player's height changes the average height of the team?

Solution to Additional Practice Problem 12.2a

The player who is 215 centimetres tall is above the average height, so adding him to the team increases the average height. The player who is 155 centimetres tall is below the average height, so adding him decreases the average height. When the player who is 185 centimetres tall is added, the team's average height equals 185 centimetres, so his addition has no effect on the average height. The general rule is that when a marginal value lies above the average, the average rises. When the marginal value is below the average, the average falls. And when the marginal value equals the average, the average does not change.

■ Self Test 12.2

Fill in the blanks

The time frame in which the quantities of some resources are fixed is the _____ (long; market; short) run and the time frame in which the quantities of all resources can be changed is the _____ (long; market; short) run. Marginal product equals _____ (total product; the change in total product) divided by the _____ (quantity of labour; change in the quantity of labour). Average product equals _____ (total product; the change in total product) divided by the _____ (quantity of labour; change in quantity of labour). The law of decreasing returns states that as a firm uses more of a _____ (fixed; variable) input, with a given quantity of _____ (fixed; variable) inputs, the marginal product of the _____ (fixed; variable) input eventually decreases. If marginal product exceeds average product, the average product curve slopes _____ (downward; upward).

True or false

1. In the short run, the firm's fixed inputs cannot be changed.

2. Points on and below the total product curve are efficient.

3. Most production processes initially have decreasing marginal returns followed eventually by increasing marginal returns.

4. When the marginal product of labour exceeds the average product of labour, the average product curve is downward sloping.

Multiple choice

1. The short run is a time period during which
a. some of the firm's resources are fixed.
b. all of the firm's resources are fixed.
c. all of the firm's resources are variable.
d. the firm cannot increase its output.

2. In the short run, firms increase output by
a. increasing the size of their plant.
b. decreasing the size of their plant.
c. increasing the amount of labour used.
d. decreasing the amount of labour used.

3. If we compare the short run to the long run, we find that the
a. short run for a firm can be longer than the long run for the same firm.
b. short run is the same for all firms.
c. long run is the time frame in which the quantities of all resources can be changed.
d. long run is the time frame in which all resources are fixed.

4. Marginal product is
a. the total product produced by a certain amount of labour.
b. the change in total product that results from a one-unit increase in the quantity of labour employed.
c. total product divided by the quantity of labour.
d. the amount of labour needed to produce an increase in production.

5. Increasing marginal returns occur when the
a. average product of an additional worker is less than the average product of the previous worker.
b. marginal product of an additional worker exceeds the marginal product of the previous worker.
c. marginal product of labour is less than the average product of labour.
d. total output of the firm is at its maximum.

6. If 25 workers can pick 100 flats of strawberries an hour, then average product is
a. 100 flats an hour.
b. 125 flats an hour.
c. 75 flats an hour.
d. 4 flats an hour.

Complete the graph

1. The table gives the total product schedule at Al's Turkey Town Farm.

Quantity of labour (workers)	Total product (turkeys per day)	Average product (turkeys per worker)	Marginal product (turkeys per worker)
0	0	xx	
			100
1	100	100	
			____
2	300	____	
			____
3	450	____	
			30
4	____	____	
			____
5	____	100	

a. Complete this table. (The marginal product is entered midway between rows to emphasize that it is the result of changing inputs, that is, moving from one row to the next.)

b. In Figure12.1 label the axes and plot the marginal product (*MP*) curve and average product (*AP*) curve. (Plot the *MP* curve midway between the quantities of labour.) Where do the two curves intersect?

■ FIGURE 12.1

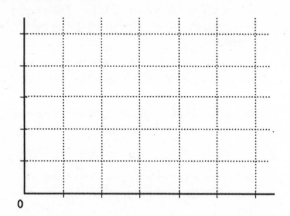

0

Short answer

1. What is the difference between the short run and the long run?
2. A pizzeria opens in your town. As the owner adds workers, what happens to their marginal product? Why?
3. What is the law of decreasing returns?
4. If the marginal product of a new worker exceeds the average product, what happens to the average product?

CHECKPOINT 12.3

■ Explain the relationship between a firm's output and costs in the short run.

Practice Problem 12.3

Tom leases a farmer's field for $120 a day and grows pumpkins. Tom pays students $100 a day to pick and pack the pumpkins. Tom leases capital at $80 a day. The table gives the daily output.

Labour (students)	Output (pumpkins per day)
0	0
1	100
2	220
3	300
4	360
5	400
6	420
7	430

a. Construct the total cost schedule.

b. Construct the average total cost schedule.

c. Construct the marginal cost schedule.

d. At what output is Tom's average total cost a minimum?

Solution to Practice Problem 12.3

This Practice Problem gives you practice in calculating different types of costs. Total cost is the sum of total fixed cost and total variable cost; average total cost equals total cost divided by the quantity produced; and marginal cost is the change in total cost that results from a one-unit increase in output.

Quick Review

- *Total cost* The cost of all the factors of production used by a firm.

- *Marginal cost* The change in total cost that results from a one-unit increase in output.

- *Average total cost* Total cost per unit of output, which equals average fixed cost plus average variable cost.

a. **Construct the total cost schedule.**

Labour	TP	TC	MC	ATC
0	0	200		
			1.00	
1	100	300		3.00
			0.83	
2	220	400		1.82
			1.25	
3	300	500		1.67
			1.67	
4	360	600		1.67
			2.50	
5	400	700		1.75
			5.00	
6	420	800		1.90
			10.00	
7	430	900		2.09

Total cost is the sum of total fixed cost and total variable cost. Tom's total fixed cost is the sum of his lease payments for the field, $120, and for the capital, $80, which equals $200 a day. His total variable cost is the wages of the students, $100 a day per student. For example, if Tom hires 2 students a day, his fixed cost is $200, his variable cost is $200, and his total cost is $400. The *TC* column in the table above shows the total cost schedule.

b. Construct the average total cost schedule.

Average total cost is total cost divided by output. For example, when Tom hires 2 students a day, they pick and pack 220 pumpkins. Tom's total cost is $400. Average total cost is $400 ÷ 220 pumpkins, which is $1.82 a pumpkin. The *ATC* column in the table shows the average total cost schedule.

c. Construct the marginal cost schedule.

The marginal cost is the change in total cost that results from picking and packing an additional pumpkin a day. The total cost of picking and packing 220 pumpkins a day is $400 and the total cost of picking and packing 300 pumpkins a day is $500. The increase in the number of pumpkins is 80, and the increase in total cost is $100. Marginal cost equals $100 ÷ 80 pumpkins, which is $1.25 a pumpkin. The *MC* column in the table above shows the marginal cost schedule.

d. At what output is Tom's average total cost a minimum?

Average total cost is a minimum at the output where average total cost equals marginal cost. The output is 330 pumpkins a day.

Additional Practice Problem 12.3a

Pearl owns a company that produces pools. Pearl has total fixed cost of $2,000 a month and pays each of her workers $2,500 a month. The table shows the number of pools Pearl's company can produce in a month.

a. Complete the left side of the table.

b. Suppose that the wage Pearl pays her workers increases to $3,000 a month. Complete the right side of the table.

c. What was the effect of the wage hike on Pearl's marginal cost?

Labour	Output	TC	MC	TC	MC
0	0	____	____	____	____
1	1	____	____	____	____
2	5	____	____	____	____
3	9	____	____	____	____
4	12	____	____	____	____
5	14	____	____	____	____
6	15	____		____	

Solution to Additional Practice Problem 12.3a

a. Complete the left side of the table.

Labour	Output	TC	MC	TC	MC
0	0	2,000	2,500	2,000	3,000
1	1	4,500	625	5,000	750
2	5	7,000	625	8,000	750
3	9	9,500	833	11,000	1,000
4	12	12,000	1,250	14,000	1,500
5	14	14,500	2,500	17,000	3,000
6	15	17,000		20,000	

The completed table is above. Total cost equals the sum of total fixed cost plus total variable cost. For example, when Pearl hires 6 workers, the total cost is ($2,000) + (6 × $2,500), which is $17,000.

The marginal cost equals the change in total cost divided by the change in output. For example, when output increases from 14 to 15 pools, marginal cost is ($17,000 – $14,500) ÷ (15 – 14), which is $2,500.

b. Suppose that the wage Pearl pays her workers increases to $3,000 a month. Complete the right side of the table.

The completed table is above.

c. What was the effect of the wage hike on Pearl's marginal cost?

The increase in the wage rate increased Pearl's total cost and marginal cost at every level of output.

■ Self Test 12.3

Fill in the blanks

Total cost equals total fixed cost _____ (plus; minus; times) total variable cost. _____ (Marginal; Average) cost is the change in total cost that results from a one-unit increase in output. Average total cost equals average fixed cost _____ (plus; minus; times) average variable cost. The average total cost curve is _____ (S-shaped; U-shaped). When the firm hires the quantity of labour so that the marginal product is at its maximum, marginal cost is at its _____ (maximum; minimum).

True or false

1. In the short run, total fixed cost does not change when the firm changes its output.

2. Marginal cost is always less than average total cost.

3. The average total cost curve is U-shaped because fixed costs are greater than variable costs.

4. An increase in the wage rate shifts the marginal cost curve upward.

Multiple choice

1. Total cost is equal to the sum of total
a. revenue and total cost.
b. variable cost and total product.
c. variable cost and total fixed cost.
d. fixed cost and total product.

2. Total fixed cost is the cost of
a. labour.
b. production.
c. a firm's fixed factors of production.
d. implicit factors of production.

3. Jay set up his hot dog stand near the business district. His total variable cost includes the
a. annual insurance for the hot dog stand.
b. cost of buying the hot dog stand.
c. cost of the hot dogs and condiments.
d. interest he pays on the funds he borrowed to pay for advertising.

4. Marginal cost is equal to
a. the total cost of a firm's production.
b. the difference between total cost and fixed cost.
c. a cost that is not related to the quantity produced.
d. the change in total cost that results from a one-unit increase in output.

5. Average total cost equals
a. marginal cost divided by output.
b. average fixed cost plus average variable cost.
c. total fixed cost plus total variable cost.
d. marginal cost plus opportunity cost.

6. One of the major reasons for the U-shaped average total cost curve is the fact that
a. there are increasing returns from labour regardless of the number of workers employed.
b. there eventually are decreasing returns from labour as more workers are employed.
c. the price falls as output increases.
d. the average fixed cost increases as more output is produced.

Complete the graph

1. Sue hires workers to produce subs at Sue's Sub Shop. Sue pays her workers $10 an hour and has fixed costs of $30 an hour. The table on the next page shows Sue's total product schedule.

Labour	Output	TC	ATC	MC
0	0	___	xx	
				___
1	10	___	___	
				___
2	25	___	___	
				___
3	35	___	___	
				___
4	40	___	___	
				___
5	43	___	___	
				___
6	45	___	___	

a. Complete the table.

b. Plot Sue's *ATC* curve and *MC* curve in Figure12.2. (Plot the marginal cost midway between the quantities.)

■ **FIGURE 12.2**

c. Sue's rent increases and her fixed cost rises to $75 an hour. Complete the following table.

Labour	Output	TC	ATC	MC
0	0	___	xx	
				___
1	10	___	___	
				___
2	25	___	___	
				___
3	35	___	___	
				___
4	40	___	___	
				___
5	43	___	___	
				___
6	45	___	___	

d. Plot Sue's new *ATC* curve and *MC* curve in Figure12.2. (Plot the marginal cost midway between the quantities.)

e. How does the increase in total fixed cost change Sue's average total cost curve? Her marginal cost curve?

2. Label the cost curves in Figure12.3.

■ **FIGURE 12.3**

Total cost (dollars per unit)

Output (units per hour)

Short answer

1. What is the difference between marginal cost and average total cost?

2. Why is the average total cost curve U-shaped?

3. Where does the marginal cost curve intersect the average variable cost curve?

4. What two factors shift the cost curves?

CHECKPOINT 12.4

■ Derive and explain a firm's long-run average cost curve.

Practice Problem 12.4

Tom grows pumpkins. He leases a farmer's field for $120 a day and capital for $80 a day. He hires students at $100 a day. Suppose that Tom now leases 2 fields for $240 a day and twice as much capital for $160 a day. Tom discovers that his output is the numbers in the third column of the table. The numbers in the second column are his output with 1 field and the original amount of capital.

Labour (students per day)	Output with 1 field	Output with 2 fields
	(pumpkins per day)	
0	0	0
1	100	220
2	220	460
3	300	620
4	360	740
5	400	820
6	420	860
7	430	880

a. Find Tom's average total cost curve schedule when he operates with two fields.

b. Make a graph of Tom's average total cost curves using 1 field and 2 fields, and show on the graph Tom's long-run average cost curve.

c. Over what output range will Tom operate with 1 field and over what output range will he operate with 2 fields?

d. What happens to Tom's average total cost curve if he farms 2 fields and doubles his capital?

e. Does Tom experience economies or diseconomies of scale?

Solution to Practice Problem 12.4

This Practice Problem studies the construction of the long-run average cost curve and gives practice in identifying when economies and diseconomies of scale are present.

Quick Review

• *Long-run average cost curve* A curve that shows the lowest average cost at which it is possible to produce each output when the firm has had sufficient time to change both its plant size and labour employed.

a. **Find Tom's average total cost curve schedule when he operates with two fields.**

Total cost is the fixed cost of $400 a day plus the variable cost of $100 a day for each student hired. Average total cost is the total cost divided by output. The average total cost curve schedule is shown in the table.

Output (pumpkins per day)	Average total cost (dollars per pumpkin)
0	xx
220	2.27
460	1.30
620	1.13
740	1.08
820	1.10
860	1.16
880	1.25

b. **Make a graph of Tom's average total cost curves using 1 field and 2 fields and show on the graph Tom's long-run average cost curve.**

The figure shows Tom's two average total cost curves. The average total cost curve with 1 field is labelled ATC_1 and uses the average total costs from Practice Problem 11.3. The average total cost curve with 2 fields is labelled ATC_2. Tom's long-run average cost curve is the lower segments of these two ATC curves, highlighted in the figure.

c. **Over what output range will Tom operate with 1 field and over what output range will he operate with 2 fields?**

Tom will operate with 1 field if he produces up to 300 pumpkins a day because for this range of output, his average total cost is less with 1 field. For more than 300 pumpkins a day, Tom will operate with 2 fields.

d. What happens to Tom's average total cost curve if he farms 2 fields and doubles his capital?

Tom's average total cost increases at lower levels of output (up to 300 pumpkins a day) and decreases at higher levels of output (greater than 300 pumpkins a day).

e. Does Tom experience economies or diseconomies of scale?

Tom experiences economies of scale because as he increases his plant, the average total cost of picking and packing a pumpkin decreases.

Additional Practice Problem 12.4a

Describe economies of scale and diseconomies of scale along a long-run average cost curve.

Solution to Additional Practice Problem 12.4a

When economies of scale are present, the *LRAC* curve slopes downward. When the *LRAC* curve is horizontal, constant returns to scale are present. And when the *LRAC* curve slopes upward, diseconomies of scale are present.

■ Self Test 12.4

Fill in the blanks

In the long run, a firm ____ (can; cannot) vary its quantity of labour and ____ (can; cannot) vary its quantity of capital. Economies of scale occur if when a firm increases its plant size and labour employed by the same percentage, the firm's average total cost ____ (increases; decreases). When the firm has ____ (economies; diseconomies) of scale, its long-run average cost curve slopes upward.

True or false

1. All costs are fixed in the long run.

2. When a firm increases its plant size and labour, greater specialization of capital and labour can lead to economies of scale.

3. Constant returns to scale occur if when the firm increases its plant size and labour employed by the same percentage, output increases by the same percentage.

4. The long-run average cost curve is derived from the marginal cost curves for different possible plant sizes.

Multiple choice

1. Economies of scale is a condition in which
   a. marginal cost decreases as production increases.
   b. total cost increases as production is increased by increasing all inputs by the same percentage.
   c. marginal product increases as labour increases and capital decreases.
   d. when a firm increases its plant size and labour employed by the same percentage, its output increases by a larger percentage and its average total cost decreases.

2. The main source of economies of scale is
   a. better management.
   b. constant returns to plant.
   c. specialization.
   d. long-run cost curves eventually sloping downward.

3. Diseconomies of scale can occur as a result of which of the following?
   a. increasing marginal returns as the firm increases its size
   b. lower total fixed cost as the firm increases its size
   c. management difficulties as the firm increases its size
   d. greater specialization of labour and capital as the firm increases its size

4. Constant returns to scale occur when an increase in plant size

a. increases total cost.

b. does not change total cost.

c. increases average total cost.

d. does not change average total cost.

5. A firm's long-run average cost curve shows the ____ average cost at which it is possible to produce each output when the firm has had ____ time to change both its labour force and its plant.

a. highest; sufficient

b. lowest; sufficient

c. lowest; insufficient

d. highest insufficient

6. Economies of scale and diseconomies of scale explain

a. cost behaviour in the short run.

b. profit maximization in the long run.

c. the U-shape of the long-run average cost curve.

d. the U-shape of the short-run cost curves.

Complete the graph

1. In Figure12.4, darken the firm's long-run average cost curve.

■ **FIGURE 12.4**

Short answer

1. Describe how a long-run average cost curve is constructed.

2. What are economies of scale? What leads to economies of scale?

SELF TEST ANSWERS

■ CHECKPOINT 12.1

Fill in the blanks

The firm's goal is to maximize <u>profit</u>. A cost paid in money is an <u>explicit</u> cost; a cost incurred when a firm uses a factor of production for which it does not make a direct money payment is an <u>implicit</u> cost. The return to entrepreneurship is <u>normal</u> profit and <u>is</u> part of the firm's opportunity cost. A firm's total revenue minus total cost is <u>economic</u> profit.

True or false

1. True; page 286
2. False; page 286
3. False; page 287
4. True; page 287

Multiple choice

1. a; page 286
2. c; pages 286-287
3. c; page 287
4. c; page 287
5. a; page 287
6. c; page 287

Short answer

1. A firm that does not seek to maximize profit is either eliminated or bought by firms that do seek that goal; page 286.

2a. An accountant calculates profit as total revenue minus explicit costs. Bobby's explicit costs are $26,000 + $24,000 + $10,000 + $200,000, which equals $260,000. The accountant calculates profit as $300,000 − $260,000, which is $40,000; page 286.

b. Bobby's opportunity cost is the sum of his explicit costs and his implicit costs. Bobby's explicit costs are $260,000. His implicit costs are the sum of his income forgone as a dentist, $80,000 and normal profit, $30,000. So Bobby's implicit costs are $110,000. Total opportunity cost is $260,000 + $110,000, which is $370,000. Bobby's economic profit is $300,000 − $370,000, which is −$70,000. Bobby incurs an economic loss; page 287.

3. Wages are a cost because they are paid to hire a factor of production, labour. A normal profit is a cost because it is paid to obtain the use of another factor of production, entrepreneurship; page 287.

■ CHECKPOINT 12.2

Fill in the blanks

The time frame in which the quantities of some resources are fixed is the <u>short</u> run and the time frame in which the quantities of all resources can be changed is the <u>long</u> run. Marginal product equals <u>the change in total product</u> divided by the <u>change in the quantity of labour</u>. Average product equals <u>total product</u> divided by the <u>quantity of labour</u>. The law of decreasing returns states that as a firm uses more of a <u>variable</u> input, with a given quantity of <u>fixed</u> inputs, the marginal product of the <u>variable</u> input eventually decreases. If marginal product exceeds average product, the average product curve slopes <u>upward</u>.

True or false

1. True; page 290
2. False; page 292
3. False; page 292
4. False; page 294

Multiple choice

1. a; page 290
2. c; page 290
3. c; page 290

4. b; page 292

5. b; page 292

6. d; page 294

Complete the graph

1. a. The completed table is below; pages 292, 294.

Quantity of labour (workers)	Total product (turkeys per day)	Average product (turkeys per worker)	Marginal product (turkeys per worker)
0	0	xx	
			100
1	100	100	
			<u>200</u>
2	300	<u>150</u>	
			<u>150</u>
3	450	<u>150</u>	
			30
4	<u>480</u>	120	
			20
5	<u>500</u>	100	

b. Figure 12.5 plots the *MP* curve and the *AP* curve. The curves intersect where the *AP* curve is at its maximum; page 266.

■ FIGURE 12.5

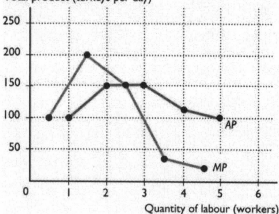

Total product (turkeys per day)

Short answer

1. The short run is the time frame in which the quantities of some resources are fixed. The long run is the time frame in which the quantities of *all* resources can be changed; page 290.

2. As the pizzeria initially adds workers, the marginal product of each additional worker exceeds the marginal product of the previous worker. The marginal product increases because the workers can specialize—some workers can make the pizzas and others can deliver them. As more workers are added, eventually the marginal product of each additional worker is less than the marginal product of the previous worker. The marginal product decreases because more workers are using the same equipment, so there is less productive work for each new worker; page 292.

3. The law of decreasing returns states that as a firm uses more of a variable input, with a given quantity of fixed inputs, the marginal product of the variable input eventually decreases; page 294.

4. If the marginal product of a new worker exceeds the average product, then hiring the worker will increase the average product; page 294.

■ CHECKPOINT 12.3

Fill in the blanks

Total cost equals total fixed cost <u>plus</u> total variable cost. <u>Marginal</u> cost is the change in total cost that results from a one-unit increase in output. Average total cost equals average fixed cost <u>plus</u> average variable cost. The average total cost curve is <u>U-shaped</u>. When the firm hires the quantity of labour so that the marginal product is at its maximum, marginal cost is at its <u>minimum</u>.

True or false

1. True; page 297

2. False; page 300

3. False; page 301

4. True; page 302

Multiple choice

1. c; page 297

2. c; page 297

3. c; page 297

4. d; page 298

5. b; page 299

6. b; page 301

Complete the graph

1. a. The completed table is below; page 299.

Labour	Output	TC	ATC	MC
0	0	30	xx	
				1.00
1	10	40	4.00	
				0.67
2	25	50	2.00	
				1.00
3	35	60	1.71	
				2.00
4	40	70	1.75	
				3.33
5	43	80	1.86	
				5.00
6	45	90	2.00	

b. Figure12.6 plots the curves as ATC_0 and MC; page 300

■ FIGURE 12.6

Average and marginal cost (dollars per sub)

c. The completed table is in the next column; page 299.

d. Figure12.6 plots the curves as ATC_1 and MC; page 300.

Labour	Output	TC	ATC	MC
0	0	75	xx	
				1.00
1	10	85	8.50	
				0.67
2	25	95	3.80	
				1.00
3	35	105	3.00	
				2.00
4	40	115	2.88	
				3.33
5	43	125	2.91	
				5.00
6	45	135	3.00	

e. The average cost curve shifts upward; the marginal cost curve does not change; page 302.

2. The labelled figure, Figure12.7, is below; page 298.

■ FIGURE 12.7

Total cost (dollars per unit)

Short answer

1. Marginal cost is the change in total cost that results from a one-unit increase in output. Average total cost is total cost per unit of output, which equals average fixed cost plus average variable cost; pages 298-299.

2. When output increases, the firm spreads its total fixed costs over a larger output and its average fixed cost decreases—its average fixed cost curve slopes downward.

   Decreasing marginal returns means that as output increases, ever larger amounts of labour are needed to produce an additional unit of output. So average variable cost eventually increases, and the *AVC* curve eventually slopes upward.

Initially as output increases, both average fixed cost and average variable cost decrease, so average total cost decreases and the *ATC* cure slopes downward. But as output increases further and decreasing marginal returns set in, average variable cost begins to increase. Eventually, average variable cost increases more quickly than average fixed cost decreases, so average total cost increases and the *ATC* curve slopes upward; page 301.

3. The marginal cost curve intersects the average variable cost at the point where the average variable cost is at its minimum; page 300.

4. Cost curves shift if there is a change in technology or a change in the price of a factor of production; page 302.

■ CHECKPOINT 12.4

Fill in the blanks

In the long run, a firm <u>can</u> vary its quantity of labour and <u>can</u> vary its quantity of capital. Economies of scale occur if when a firm increases its plant size and labour employed by the same percentage, the firm's average total cost <u>decreases</u>. When the firm has <u>diseconomies</u> of scale, its long-run average cost curve slopes upward.

True or false

1. False; page 305

2. True; page 305

3. True; page 306

4. False; page 306

Multiple choice

1. d; page 305

2. c; page 305

3. c; page 306

4. d; page306

5. b page 306

6. c; page 306

Complete the graph

1. Figure12.8 darkens the firm's long-run average cost curve; page 306.

■ FIGURE 12.8

Average total cost (dollars per unit)

Short answer

1. A long-run average cost curve is a curve that shows the lowest average cost at which it is possible to produce each output when the firm has had sufficient time to change both its plant size and labour employed. Suppose that Alfred can operate with four different sizes of plant. The segment of each of the four average total cost curves for which that plant has the lowest average total cost is the scallop-shaped curve that is the long-run average cost curve; page 306.

2. Economies of scale is a condition in which, when a firm increases its plant size and labour employed by the same percentage, its output increase by a larger percentage and its average total cost decreases. The main source of economies of scale is greater specialization of both labour and capital; page 305.

Chapter 13

Perfect Competition

Chapter 13 studies perfect competition, the market that arises when demand for a product is large relative to the output of a single producer.

■ **Explain a perfectly competitive firm's profit-maximizing choices and derive its supply curve.**

Perfect competition exists when: many firms sell an identical product to many buyers; there are no restrictions on entry into (or exit from) the market; established firms have no advantage over new firms; and sellers and buyers are well informed about prices. A firm in perfect competition is a price taker—it cannot influence the price of its product. The market demand curve is downward sloping. A perfectly competitive firm faces a perfectly elastic demand. Marginal revenue is the change in total revenue that results from a one-unit increase in the quantity sold. In perfect competition, marginal revenue equals price. A firm maximizes its profit at the output level at which total revenue exceeds total cost by the largest amount. Another way to find the profit-maximizing output is to use marginal analysis. A firm maximizes its profit at the output level at which marginal revenue equals marginal cost. The shutdown point is the output and price at which the firm just covers its total variable cost. A firm's supply curve is the upward-sloping part of its marginal cost curve above minimum average variable cost.

■ **Explain how output, price, and profit are determined in the short run.**

The market supply curve in the short run shows the quantity supplied at each price by a fixed number of firms. Market demand and market supply determine the price and quantity bought and sold. Each firm takes the price as given and produces its profit-maximizing output. A perfectly competitive firm earns an economic profit when price exceeds average total cost and incurs an economic loss when price is less than average total cost.

■ **Explain how output, price, and profit are determined in the long run.**

Economic profit is an incentive for new firms to enter a market, but as they do so, the price falls and the economic profit of each existing firm decreases. Economic loss is an incentive for firms to exit a market, but as they do so, the price rises and the economic loss of each remaining firm decreases. In the long run, a firm earns a normal profit and there is no entry or exit. External economies are factors beyond the control of an individual firm that lower its average total cost as the *market* output increases. External diseconomies are factors beyond the control of a firm that raise the firm's average total cost as *market* output increases. In a market undergoing technological change, firms that adopt the new technology make an economic profit. So new-technology firms have an incentive to enter. Firms that stick with the old technology incur economic losses. They either exit the market or switch to the new technology. Competition eliminates economic profit in the long run.

EXPANDED CHAPTER CHECKLIST

When you have completed this chapter, you will be able to

1 Explain a perfectly competitive firm's profit-maximizing choices and derive its supply curve.

- Describe the four market types.

- Explain why a firm in perfect competition is a price taker.

- Describe the market demand curve and a firm's demand curve in perfect competition.

- Define marginal revenue.

- Discuss how a perfectly competitive firm determines its profit-maximizing output.

- Explain when a firm makes a decision to temporarily shutdown and locate the shutdown point on a graph.

- Derive and draw a firm's short-run supply curve.

2 Explain how output, price, and profit are determined in the short run.

- Derive the market supply curve in the short run.

- Illustrate a perfectly competitive firm that is earning an economic profit and calculate the amount of the economic profit.

- Illustrate a perfectly competitive firm that is incurring an economic loss and calculate the amount of the economic loss.

3 Explain how output, price, and profit are determined in the long run.

- Illustrate the case of a perfectly competitive firm in long-run equilibrium, when it earns only a normal profit.

- Explain how economic profit attracts entry, and discuss the effect entry has on the mar-

ket supply, the price, and the existing firms' economic profit.

- Explain how economic loss creates exit, and discuss the effect exit has on the market supply, the price, and the surviving firms' economic loss.

- Define external economies and external diseconomies and explain their effect on the long-run equilibrium price.

- Define and graph the long-run market supply curve.

- Describe the forces at work in markets with technological change.

KEY TERMS

- External diseconomies (page 330)
- External economies (page 330)
- Long-run market supply curve (page 331)
- Marginal revenue (page 315)
- Monopolistic competition (page 314)
- Monopoly (page 314)
- Oligopoly (page 314)
- Perfect competition (page 314)
- Price taker (page 315)
- Shutdown point (page 319)

CHECKPOINT 13.1

■ Explain a perfectly competitive firm's profit-maximizing choices and derive its supply curve.

Practice Problems 13.1

1. Sarah's Salmon Farm produces 1,000 fish a week. The marginal cost is $30 a fish, average variable cost is $20 a fish, and the market price is $25 a fish. Is Sarah maximizing profit? Explain why or why not. If Sarah is not maximizing profit, to do so, will she in-

crease or decrease the number of fish she produces in a week?

2. Trout farming is a perfectly competitive industry, and all trout farms have the same cost curves. The market price is $25 a fish. To maximize profit, each farm produces 200 fish a week. Average total cost is $20 a fish, and average variable cost is $15 a fish. Minimum average variable cost is $12 a fish.

a. If the price falls to $20 a fish, will trout farms continue to produce 200 fish a week? Explain why or why not.

b. If the price falls to $12 a fish, what will the trout farmer do?

c. What is one point on the trout farm's supply curve?

Solution to Practice Problems 13.1

To answer these Practice Problems remember that a perfectly competitive firm maximizes profit when it produces the output such that marginal revenue equals marginal cost. Also remember that a firm shuts down when price is less than minimum average variable cost.

Quick Review

- *A firm's short-run supply curve* A perfectly competitive firm's short-run supply curve has two separate parts. At prices that exceed minimum average variable cost, the supply curve is the same as the marginal cost curve above the shutdown point. And at prices below minimum average variable cost, the supply curve runs along the vertical axis.

- *Shutdown point* The output and price at which the firm just covers its total variable cost.

1. **Sarah's Salmon Farm produces 1,000 fish a week. The marginal cost is $30 a fish, average variable cost is $20 a fish, and the market price is $25 a fish. Is Sarah maximizing profit? Explain why or why not. If Sarah is not maximizing profit, to do so, will she increase or decrease the number of fish she produces in a week?**

The profit-maximizing output occurs when marginal revenue equals marginal cost. And for a firm in perfect competition, marginal revenue equals price. When Sarah produces 1,000 fish a week, marginal cost is $30 a fish and marginal revenue, which equals price is $25 a fish. To maximize profit, Sarah must decrease the quantity of fish until she reaches the output at which marginal cost is $25 a fish.

2. **Trout farming is a perfectly competitive industry, and all trout farms have the same cost curves. The market price is $25 a fish. To maximize profit, each farm produces 200 fish a week. Average total cost is $20 a fish, and average variable cost is $15 a fish. Minimum average variable cost is $12 a fish.**

a. **If the price falls to $20 a fish, will trout farms continue to produce 200 fish a week? Explain why or why not.**

Trout farms will produce fewer than 200 fish per week. In the figure, the initial marginal revenue curve is MR_0. Trout farms produce 200 fish because that is the quantity that sets marginal revenue equal to

marginal cost. When the price falls to $20 a fish, the marginal revenue curve shifts downward to MR_1. At the lower marginal revenue, trout farms cut their production to less than 200 fish a week, at the quantity where MC and MR_1 intersect.

b. **If the price falls to $12 a fish, what will the trout farmer do?**

At $12 a fish, trout farmers cut production to the output where marginal cost equals $12. But $12 is minimum average variable cost, so trout farmers are at the shutdown point. Farms are indifferent between producing the profit-maximizing output and producing nothing. Regardless of their decision, they incur an economic loss equal to total fixed cost.

c. **What is one point on the trout farm's supply curve?**

At prices less than $12 a fish, the quantity supplied is zero fish. At $12 a fish, the quantity supplied might be zero or it may be the quantity determined at the intersection of the marginal cost curve and the marginal revenue curve at the price of $12. And at a price of $25 a fish, the quantity supplied is 200 fish.

Additional Practice Problem 13.1a

Suppose that Sarah, of Sarah's Salmon Farm in Practice Problem 13.1 cuts her production to a point where marginal revenue is greater than marginal cost. Explain why she is not maximizing profit.

Solution to Additional Practice Problem 13.1a

If marginal revenue exceeds marginal cost, then the extra revenue from selling one more fish exceeds the extra cost incurred to produce it. So if Sarah produces one more fish, then the marginal revenue that she receives from selling that fish is greater than the cost to produce that fish. To maximize economic profit, Sarah should increase her output until she reaches the point where the marginal revenue she receives from a fish equals the marginal cost to produce it.

■ Self Test 13.1

Fill in the blanks

The conditions that define perfect competition arise when the market demand for the product is _____(large; small) relative to the output of a single producer. A perfectly competitive firm faces an ____ (elastic; inelastic) demand. The change in total revenue that results from a one-unit increase in the quantity sold is marginal____ (cost; price; revenue). When a perfectly competitive firm maximizes profit, marginal revenue equals ____ (average variable; marginal) cost. When a firm shuts down, it incurs a loss equal to its total ____ (variable; fixed) cost. A firm will shut down if price is less than ____ (marginal; average total; minimum average variable) cost. A perfectly competitive firm's supply curve is its marginal ____ (cost; revenue) curve above minimum average ____ (total; variable) cost.

True or false

1. A perfectly competitive market has many firms.

2. A firm in perfect competition is a price taker.

3. To maximize profit, a perfectly competitive firm makes the vertical difference between its marginal revenue curve and marginal cost curve as large as possible.

4. Stan's U-Pick blueberry farm, a perfectly competitive firm, will shut down if its total revenue is less than its total cost.

5. A perfectly competitive firm's short-run supply curve is its average total cost curve above minimum average variable cost.

Multiple choice

1. The four market types are

a. perfect competition, imperfect competition, monopoly, and oligopoly.

b. oligopoly, monopsony, monopoly, and imperfect competition.

c. perfect competition, monopoly, monopolistic competition, and oligopoly.

d. oligopoly, oligopolistic competition, monopoly, and perfect competition.

2. Perfect competition exists when

a. many firms sell an identical product to many buyers.

b. there are no restrictions on entry into (or exit from) the market, and established firms have no advantage over new firms.

c. sellers and buyers are well informed about prices.

d. All of the above.

3. A perfectly competitive firm is a price taker because

a. many other firms produce the same product.

b. only one firm produces the product.

c. many firms produce a slightly differentiated product.

d. a few firms compete.

4. The demand curve faced by a perfectly competitive firm is

a. horizontal.

b. vertical.

c. downward sloping.

d. upward sloping.

5. The marginal revenue curve faced by a wheat producer in Saskatchewan is

a. downward sloping.

b. the same as his demand curve.

c. upward sloping.

d. U-shaped.

6. A perfectly competitive firm maximizes its profit by producing at the point where

a. total revenue equals total cost.

b. marginal revenue equals marginal cost.

c. total revenue equals marginal revenue.

d. total cost is at its minimum.

7. If the market price is lower than a perfectly competitive firm's average total cost, the firm will

a. immediately shut down.

b. continue to produce if the price exceeds average fixed cost.

c. continue to produce if the price exceeds minimum average variable cost.

d. shut down if the price exceeds average fixed cost.

8. One part of a perfectly competitive firm's supply curve is its

a. marginal cost curve below the shutdown point.

b. entire marginal cost curve.

c. marginal cost curve above the shutdown point.

d. average variable cost curve above the shutdown point.

Complete the graph

1. Figure 13.1 shows a perfectly competitive fish firm's cost curves.

■ **FIGURE 13.1**

Price and cost (dollars per fish)

a. Label the curves.

b. If the market price is $40 a fish, what is the firm's equilibrium output and price?

c. If the market price is $20 a fish, what is the firm's equilibrium output and price?

d. What is the firm's shutdown price?

e. Darken the firm's supply curve.

Short answer

1. What are the conditions that define perfect competition?

2. What is a "price taker?" Why are perfectly competitive firms price takers?

3. What is the difference between a perfectly competitive firm's demand curve and the market demand curve?

4. Willy, a perfectly competitive wheat farmer, can sell 999 baskets of wheat for $3 each or 1,000 baskets for $3 each. What is Willy's marginal revenue and total revenue if he sells 1,000 baskets of wheat?

5. Peter owns Peter's Porkers, a small hog farm. The table gives Peter's total cost schedule. Peter is in a perfectly competitive market and can sell each hog for $200.

Quantity (hogs)	Total cost (dollars)	Total revenue (dollars)	Eco- nomic profit (dollars)
0	300	——	——
1	350	——	——
2	425	——	——
3	575	——	——
4	825	——	——
5	1,200	——	——

a. Complete the table.

b. What is Peter's profit-maximizing number of hogs and what price will Peter set?

c. When Peter increases his production from 2 hogs to 3 hogs, what is the marginal cost? Is it profitable for Peter to increase production?

d. When Peter increases his production from 3 hogs to 4 hogs, what is the marginal cost? Is it profitable for Peter to increase production?

e. What is the marginal cost of the third hog?

6. When will a firm temporarily shut down?

CHECKPOINT 13.2

■ Explain how output, price, and profit are determined in the short run.

Practice Problems 13.2

Tulip growing is a perfectly competitive industry, and all tulip growers have the same cost curves. The market price of tulips is $25 a bunch, and each grower maximizes profit by producing 2,000 bunches a week. The average total cost of producing tulips is $20 a bunch, and the average variable cost is $15 a bunch. Minimum average variable cost is $12 a bunch.

a. What is the economic profit that each grower is making in the short run?

b. What is the price at the grower's shutdown point?

c. What is each grower's profit at the shutdown point?

Solution to Practice Problem 13.2

In the short run, a firm can make an economic profit or incur an economic loss. This Practice Problem gives you practice in calculating economic profit.

Quick Review

• *Economic profit* A firm earns an economic profit when price exceeds average total cost.

• *Economic loss* A firm incurs an economic loss when price is less than average total cost.

Tulip growing is a perfectly competitive industry, and all tulip growers have the same cost curves. The market price of tulips is $25 a bunch, and each grower maximizes profit by producing 2,000 bunches a week. The average total cost of producing tulips is $20 a bunch, and the average variable cost is $15 a bunch. Minimum average variable cost is $12 a bunch.

a. **What is the economic profit that each grower is making in the short run?**

The economic profit on each bunch of tulips is the price minus average total cost, which is $25 – $20 = $5. Each grower produces 2,000 bunches a week, so each grower's total economic profit is (2,000 bunches) × ($5), which is $10,000 a week.

b. **What is the price at the grower's shutdown point?**

The shutdown point is at a price equal to the minimum average variable cost. The shutdown point is at a price of $12 a bunch.

c. What is each grower's profit at the shut-down point?

At the shutdown point, the grower incurs an economic loss equal to total fixed cost.

$ATC = AVC + AFC$. So $AFC = ATC - AVC$. When 2,000 bunches are grown, $ATC = \$20$ a bunch and $AVC = \$15$ a bunch, so $AFC = \$20$ a bunch − $\$15$ a bunch, which is $\$5$ a bunch. Total fixed cost equals quantity times average fixed cost, which is (2,000 bunches a week) × ($\$5$) = $\$10,000$ a week. So the economic loss at the shutdown point is $\$10,000$ a week.

Additional Practice Problem 13.2a

Quantity (roses per week)	Average total cost (dollars per rose)	Marginal cost (dollars per rose)
100	2.00	1.50
200	1.50	1.50
300	1.67	2.50
400	2.00	5.00

1. Growing roses is a perfectly competitive industry. There are 100 rose growers and all have the same cost curves. The table above gives the costs of one of the growers, Rosita's Roses. Minimum average variable cost is $1.50 a rose. The table to the right has the market demand schedule for roses.

Price (dollars per rose)	Quantity demanded (roses per week)
1.00	50,000
1.50	45,000
2.00	40,000
2.50	30,000
3.00	20,000

a. Plot the market supply curve and the market demand curve in the figure to the right.

b. What is the equilibrium price of a rose?

c. How many roses does Rosita produce? What is her economic profit or loss?

Price and cost (dollars per rose)

Solution to Additional Practice Problem 13.2a

a. Plot the market supply curve and the market demand curve in the figure.

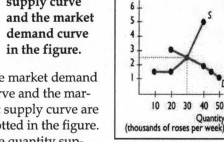

Price and cost (dollars per rose)

The market demand curve and the market supply curve are plotted in the figure. The quantity supplied in the market at any price is the sum of the quantities supplied by each firm at that price. Because each firm is identical, the market quantity supplied is 100 times the quantity supplied by any one firm. The firm's supply curve is its marginal cost curve above the minimum average variable cost. For example, when the price is $2.50 a rose, Rosita's marginal cost schedule shows she will supply 300 roses a week. So the quantity supplied in the market equals 100 × (300 roses a week), which is 30,000 roses a week.

b. What is the equilibrium price of a rose?

The figure shows that the equilibrium price of a rose is $2.50.

c. How many roses does Rosita produce? What is her economic profit or loss?

Rosita produces 300 roses a week and makes an economic profit. Her economic profit per rose equals the price of a rose minus the average total cost, which is $2.50 − $1.67 = $0.83. Rosita produces 300 roses a week, so total economic profit is (300 roses a week) × ($0.83) = $249 a week.

■ **Self Test 13.2**

Fill in the blanks

In a perfectly competitive industry, the quantity supplied in the market at any price is ____ (determined by the market demand curve; equal to the sum of the quantities supplied by all firms at that price). A firm earns an economic profit when price exceeds ____ (marginal revenue; average total cost). A firm _____ (can; cannot) incur an economic loss in the short run.

True or false

1. The market supply curve in the short run shows the quantity supplied at each price by a fixed number of firms.

2. Market supply in a perfectly competitive market is perfectly elastic at all prices.

3. A perfectly competitive firm earns an economic profit if price equals average total cost.

4. In a perfectly competitive industry, a firm's economic profit is equal to price minus marginal revenue multiplied by quantity.

5. A perfectly competitive firm incurs an economic loss if price is less than the marginal cost.

Multiple choice

1. If the market supply curve and the market demand curve intersect at 600,000 units and there are 10,000 identical firms in the market, then each firm is producing
   a. 600,000 units.
   b. 60,000,000,000 units.
   c. 60,000 units.
   d. 60 units.

2. A perfectly competitive firm earns an economic profit in the short run if price is
   a. equal to marginal cost.
   b. equal to average total cost.
   c. greater than average total cost.
   d. greater than marginal cost.

3. For a perfectly competitive firm earning an economic profit, which of the following is correct?
   a. price equals marginal revenue
   b. marginal revenue equals marginal cost
   c. price is greater than average total cost
   d. All of the above are correct.

4. The market for apples in British Columbia is perfectly competitive. An apple producer earning a normal profit could earn an economic profit if the _____ cost of selling apples _____.
   a. average total; does not change
   b. average total; increases
   c. average total; decreases
   d. marginal; does not change

5. Juan's Software Service Company is in a perfectly competitive industry. Juan's makes 1,000 service calls a month. Juan has total fixed cost of $25,000 a month, the average variable cost for 1,000 service calls is $45, and marginal revenue is $75. What is his economic profit?
   a. $5,000 a month
   b. $25,000 a month
   c. $45,000 a month
   d. It is impossible to determine with the information given.

6. If a perfectly competitive firm finds that price is less than its average total cost, then the firm
   a. will raise its price to increase its economic profit.
   b. will lower its price to increase its economic profit.
   c. is earning an economic profit.
   d. is incurring an economic loss.

7. A perfectly competitive video-rental firm in Red Deer will incur an economic loss if the average total cost of each video rental is

a. greater than the marginal revenue of each rental.

b. less than the marginal revenue of each rental.

c. equal to the marginal revenue of each rental.

d. equal to zero.

8. In the short run, a perfectly competitive firm

a. must make an economic profit.

b. must suffer an economic loss.

c. must earn a normal profit.

d. might make an economic profit, incur an economic loss, or make a normal profit.

Complete the graph

1. Is the lawn maintenance firm illustrated in Figure 13.2 earning an economic profit or incurring an economic loss? Shade the area that shows the economic profit or economic loss. What is the amount of economic profit or economic loss?

■ FIGURE 13.2

Price and cost (dollars per lawn)

Short answer

1. In a perfectly competitive market, how is the market supply calculated?

2. If price is less than average total cost, is the firm earning an economic profit or incurring an economic loss?

CHECKPOINT 13.3

■ **Explain how output, price, and profit are determined in the long run.**

Practice Problem 13.3

Tulip growing is a perfectly competitive industry, and all tulip growers have the same cost curves. The market price of tulips is $15 a bunch, and each grower maximizes profit by producing 1,500 bunches a week. The average total cost of producing tulips is $21 a bunch. Minimum average variable cost is $12 a bunch, and the minimum average total cost is $18 a bunch. Tulip growing is a constant cost industry.

a. What is a tulip grower's economic profit in the short run?

b. How does the number of tulip growers change in the long run?

c. What is the price in the long run?

d. What is the economic profit in the long run?

Solution to Practice Problem 13.3

A perfectly competitive firm earns a normal profit in the long run. A firm will not incur an economic loss in the long run because it will shut down. And a perfectly competitive firm cannot earn an economic profit in the long run because the presence of an economic profit attracts entry, which drives down the price and eliminates economic profit. Competitive firms cannot prevent entry into their market and so they cannot protect an economic profit.

Quick Review

• *Entry* Economic profit is an incentive for new firms to enter a market, but as they do so, the price falls and the economic profit of each existing firm decreases.

- *Exit* Economic loss is an incentive for firms to exit a market, but as they do so, the price rises and the economic loss of each remaining firm decreases.

Tulip growing is a perfectly competitive industry, and all tulip growers have the same cost curves. The market price of tulips is $15 a bunch, and each grower maximizes profit by producing 1,500 bunches a week. The average total cost of producing tulips is $21 a bunch. Minimum average variable cost is $12 a bunch, and the minimum average total cost is $18 a bunch. Tulip growing is a constant cost industry.

a. **What is a tulip grower's economic profit in the short run?**

The tulip growers are incurring an economic loss because price is less than average total cost. The price is $15 a bunch and average total cost is $21 a bunch, so the economic loss is $21 – $15, which is $6 a bunch. Each tulip grower producers 1,500 bunches a week, so the economic loss is 1,500 bunches × $6, which is $9,000 a week. Notice that the tulip growers continue to produce because price is greater than minimum average variable cost.

b. **How does the number of tulip growers change in the long run?**

Because firms are incurring an economic loss, some firms exit the market and the number of tulip growers decreases.

c. **What is the price in the long run?**

As tulip growers exit the market, the market supply decreases, and the price rises. The price rises as long as growers are exiting, and growers exit as long as they incur an economic loss. The growers stop exiting when they earn a normal profit, which occurs when price equals minimum average total cost. So in the long run, the price rises to $18 a bunch.

d. **What is the economic profit in the long run?**

In a perfectly competitive market, the economic profit in the long run is zero. In the long run, the tulip growers will make normal profit.

Additional Practice Problem 13.3a

Growing roses is a perfectly competitive industry. Initially there are 100 rose growers and all have the same cost curves.

Quantity (roses per week)	Average total cost (dollars per rose)	Marginal cost
100	2.00	1.50
200	1.50	1.50
300	1.67	2.50
400	2.00	5.00

The above table gives the costs of one of the growers, Rosita's Roses. The table to the right gives the market demand schedule for roses. The equilibrium price for a rose is $2.50.

Price (dollars per rose)	Quantity demanded (roses per week)
1.00	50,000
1.50	45,000
2.00	40,000
2.50	30,000
3.00	20,000

a. Plot Rosita's marginal cost curve and marginal revenue curve in the figure to the right.

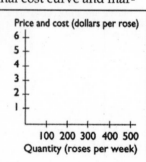

Is Rosita earning an economic profit or incurring an economic loss?

b. As time passes, what occurs in the market?

c. What is the long-run price of a rose? What is Rosita's profit in the long run? In the long run, how many growers are in the market?

Solution to Additional Practice Problem 13.3a

a. **Plot Rosita's marginal cost curve and marginal revenue curve in the figure. Is Rosita earning an economic profit or incurring an economic loss?**

The figure shows Rosita's marginal cost curve and marginal revenue curve. She is producing 300 roses a week and earning an economic profit because the price of a rose exceeds the average total cost.

b.   As time passes, what occurs in the market?

Because rose growers are earning an economic profit, more rose growers enter the market. The supply of roses increases. The equilibrium price of a rose falls and the market equilibrium quantity increases.

c.   What is the long-run price of a rose? What is Rosita's profit in the long run? In the long run how many growers are in the market?

The long-run price of a rose will be $1.50, which is the minimum average total cost and rose growers earn a normal profit. When the price of a rose is $1.50, the quantity demanded is 45,000 roses a week. At a price of $1.50, each grower produces 200 roses a week. So there will be 225 growers, each producing 200 roses a week.

■ Self Test 13.3

Fill in the blanks

In the long run, a perfectly competitive firm ____ (can; cannot) earn an economic profit. In the long run, a perfectly competitive firm ____ (does not produce; produces) the quantity at minimum average total cost. Entry into an industry shifts the market ____ (demand; supply) curve ____ (rightward; leftward). Firms exit an industry when they are ____ (making a normal profit; incurring an economic loss). In a market with external diseconomies, the long-run supply curve is ____ (upward; downward) sloping. A technological change results in perfectly competitive firms ____ (temporarily; permanently) earning an economic profit.

True or false

1. When price equals average total cost, the firm earns a normal profit.

2. Entry into a perfectly competitive market lowers the price.

3. In the long run, a firm incurring an economic loss exits a perfectly competitive market.

4. External economies are factors that lower a firm's costs as its output increases.

5. New technology shifts a firm's cost curves upward.

Multiple choice

1. In the long run, new firms enter a perfectly competitive market when

a. normal profits are greater than zero.

b. economic profits are equal to zero.

c. normal profits are equal to zero.

d. economic profits are greater than zero.

2. In a perfectly competitive market, if firms are earning an economic profit, the economic profit

a. attracts entry by more firms, which lowers the market price.

b. can be earned both in the short run and the long run.

c. is less than the normal profit.

d. leads to a decrease in demand.

3. When firms leave a perfectly competitive market, the market

a. supply curve shifts leftward.

b. supply curve does not change.

c. demand curve shifts rightward.

d. supply curve shifts rightward.

4. In the long run, as firms exit a perfectly competitive industry, the economic losses of the surviving firms

a. increase.

b. decrease until they equal zero.

c. decrease until economic profits are earned.

d. do not change.

5. Factors outside the control of a firm that raise the firm's costs as market output increases are

a. internal economies.

b. external diseconomies.

c. external economies.

d. internal diseconomies.

6. In the long run, a firm in a perfectly competitive market will

a. earn zero economic profit, that is, it will earn a normal profit.

b. earn zero normal profit but it will earn an economic profit.

c. remove all competitors and become a monopolistically competitive firm.

d. incur an economic normal loss.

7. In a market with no external economies or diseconomies, the long-run market supply curve is

a. perfectly elastic.

b. perfectly inelastic.

c. positively sloped.

d. negatively sloped.

8. Technological change brings a ____ to firms that adopt the new technology.

a. permanent economic profit

b. temporary economic profit

c. permanent economic loss

d. temporary economic loss

Complete the graph

1. Through the point in Figure 13.3, draw one long-run market supply curve for an industry with external economies and another for an industry with external diseconomies.

■ **FIGURE 13.3**

Price (dollars per unit)

2. Figure 13.4 shows cost curves for two firms in the maple syrup industry undergoing technological change. Firm 1 uses the old technology and has average total cost curve ATC_1 and marginal cost curve MC_1. Firm 2 uses the new technology and has average total cost curve ATC_2 and marginal cost curve MC_2. Initially the price of the product is $6 a can.

a. At the price of $6 a can, do firm 1 and firm 2 earn an economic profit, normal profit, or incur an economic loss?

b. As more firms adopt the new technology, what happens to market supply and price? Do firms 1 and 2 earn an economic profit, normal profit, or incur an economic loss?

c. In the long run, what will be the new price? Will the firms earn an economic profit, a normal profit, or incur an economic loss?

■ **FIGURE 13.4**

Price and cost (dollars per can)

Short answer

1. Why are perfectly competitive firms unable to earn an economic profit in the long run? Why won't they incur an economic loss in the long run?

2. What are external economies and external diseconomies? What relationship do they have to the long-run market supply curve?

SELF TEST ANSWERS

■ CHECKPOINT 13.1

Fill in the blanks

The conditions that define perfect competition arise when the market demand for the product is large relative to the output of a single producer. A perfectly competitive firm faces an elastic demand. The change in total revenue that results from a one-unit increase in the quantity sold is marginal revenue. When a perfectly competitive firm maximizes profit, marginal revenue equals marginal cost. When a firm shuts down, it incurs a loss equal to its total fixed cost. A firm will shut down if price is less than minimum average variable cost. A perfectly competitive firm's supply curve is its marginal cost curve above minimum average variable cost.

True or false

1. True; page 314

2. True; page 315

3. False; page 318

4. False; page 319

5. False; page 319

Multiple choice

1. c; page 314

2. d; page 314

3. a; page 315

4. a; pages 315-316

5. b; pages 315-316

6. b; page 318

7. c; page 319

8. c; page319

Complete the graph

1a. Figure 13.5 labels the curves; page 320.

b. Output is 35 fish and the price is $40 a fish; page 318.

c. Output is 30 fish and the price is $20 a fish; page 318.

d. The shutdown price is $10 a fish; page 319.

e. The firm's supply curve is darkened in Figure 13.5; page 319.

■ FIGURE 13.5

Price and cost (dollars per fish)

Short answer

1. Perfect competition exists when: many firms sell an identical product to many buyers; there are no restrictions on entry into (or exit from) the market; established firms have no advantage over new firms; and sellers and buyers are well informed about prices; page 314.

2. A price taker is a firm that cannot influence the price of the good or service it produces. Perfectly competitive firms are price takers because there are many competing firms, each selling an identical product. Any individual firm is such a small part of the market that its actions cannot affect the price; page 315.

3. A perfectly competitive firm's demand is perfectly elastic because all sellers produce goods that are perfect substitutes. So the firm's demand curve is horizontal. The mar-

ket demand curve is downward sloping; pages 315-316.

4. Willy's marginal revenue equals the price of a basket of wheat, which is $3. His total revenue equals price multiplied by quantity, which is $3,000; page 315.

5a. The completed table is below; page 317.

Quantity (hogs)	Total cost (dollars)	Total revenue (dollars)	Economic profit (dollars)
0	300	0	–300
1	350	200	–150
2	425	400	–25
3	575	600	25
4	825	800	–25
5	1,200	1,000	–200

b. The profit maximizing number of hogs is 3. Peter charges $200 a hog; page 316.

c. Marginal cost is the change in total cost that results from increasing production from 2 to 3 hogs. Marginal cost is $150. It is profitable to increase production because marginal revenue exceeds marginal cost; page 318.

d. The marginal cost is $250. Increasing production is not profitable because marginal cost exceeds marginal revenue; page 318.

e. The marginal cost of the third hog is $200, which is the average of the marginal cost of increasing production from 2 to 3 hogs and increasing production from 3 to 4 hogs. Because marginal cost of the third hog equals marginal revenue, 3 hogs is the profit-maximizing output; page 318.

6. If a firm shuts down, it incurs an economic loss equal to total fixed cost. If the firm produces some output, it incurs an economic loss equal to total fixed cost plus total variable cost minus total revenue. If total revenue exceeds total variable cost, the firm's economic loss is less than total fixed cost. So it pays the firm to produce. But if total revenue is less than total variable cost, the firm's economic loss exceeds total fixed cost. So the firm shuts down temporarily; page 319.

■ **CHECKPOINT 13.2**

Fill in the blanks

In a perfectly competitive industry, the quantity supplied in the market at any price is equal to the sum of the quantities supplied by all firms at that price. A firm earns an economic profit when price exceeds average total cost. A firm can incur an economic loss in the short run.

True or false

1. True; page 322

2. False; page 322

3. False; page 323

4. False; page 323

5. False; page 324

Multiple choice

1. d; page **322**

2. c; page 323

3. d; page 323

4. c; page 323

5. a; page 323

6. d; page 324

7. a; page 324

8. d; pages 323-324

Complete the graph

1. The firm is earning an economic profit. Figure 13.6 illustrates the economic profit.

■ FIGURE 13.6

Price and cost (dollars per lawn)

Economic profit per lawn equals the price minus average total cost, which is $30 – $20 = $10 per lawn. The quantity is 35 lawns, so economic profit is ($10 a lawn) × (35 lawns a week), which is $350 a week; page 323.

Short answer

1. The market supply in the short run is the quantity supplied at each price by a fixed number of firms. The quantity supplied at a given price is the sum of the quantities supplied by all firms at that price. For example, if there are 100 firms in the geranium market and each produces 50 geraniums when the price is $3, then the quantity supplied in the market at $3 is 5,000 geraniums; page 322.

2. The firm is incurring an economic loss. If price is less than average total cost, the firm is incurring an economic loss on each unit produced and has an overall economic loss; page 324.

■ CHECKPOINT 13.3

Fill in the blanks

In the long run, a perfectly competitive firm <u>cannot</u> earn an economic profit. In the long run, a perfectly competitive firm <u>produces</u> the quantity at minimum average total cost. Entry into an industry shifts the market <u>supply</u> curve <u>rightward</u>. Firms exit an industry when they are <u>incurring an</u>

<u>economic loss</u>. In a market with external diseconomies, the long-run supply curve is <u>upward</u> sloping. A technological change results in perfectly competitive firms <u>temporarily</u> earning an economic profit.

True or false

1. True; page 326
2. True; page 327
3. True; page 328
4. False; page 330
5. False; page 332

Multiple choice

1. d; page 327
2. a; page 327
3. a; page 328
4. b; page 328
5. b; page 330
6. a; page 326
7. a; page 330
8. b; page 332

Complete the graph

1. Figure 13.7 shows the two long-run market supply curves. LS_1 slopes downward, reflecting the presence of external economies. LS_2 slopes upward, reflecting the presence of external diseconomies; page 330.

■ FIGURE 13.7

Price (dollars per unit)

2a. At the price of $6 a can, the marginal revenue curve is MR_0 in Figure 13.8. Firm 1 produces 20 cans a week and earns a normal profit because the $6 price equals average total cost. Firm 2 produces 35 cans a week and earns an economic profit because the $6 price exceeds average total cost; pages 326-327.

■ FIGURE 13.8

Price and cost (dollars per can)

b. Market supply increases and the price falls. Firm 1 now incurs an economic loss and firm 2 earns a smaller economic profit; page 332.

c. In the long run, the new price will be $4 a can because that is the minimum of the new average total cost. Firm 1 will either have adopted the new technology and be earning

a normal profit or will have exited the industry. Firm 2 will earn a normal profit; page 332.

Short answer

1. Perfectly competitive firms cannot earn an economic profit in the long run because the existence of an economic profit invites entry by new firms. As these new firms enter, the market supply increases, driving down the price and eventually eliminating the economic profit. No firm will incur an economic loss in the long run because it will exit; pages 326-327.

2. External economies are factors beyond the control of an individual firm that lower its average total cost as the *market* output increases. External diseconomies are factors outside the control of a firm that raise the firm's average total cost as *market* output increases. An industry with external economies has a downward-sloping long-run market supply curve and an industry with external diseconomies has an upward-sloping long-run market supply curve; pages 330-331.

Monopoly

CHAPTER IN PERSPECTIVE

Chapter 14 studies how a monopoly chooses its price and quantity and discusses whether a monopoly is efficient or fair.

■ **Explain how monopoly arises and distinguish between single-price monopoly and price-discriminating monopoly.**

A monopoly is a market with a single supplier of a good or service that has no close substitutes and in which natural or legal barriers to entry prevent competition. A monopolist faces a tradeoff between price and the quantity sold. A single-price monopoly is a monopoly that must sell each unit of its output for the same price to all its customers. A price-discriminating monopoly is a monopoly that is able to sell different units of a good or service for different prices.

■ **Explain how a single-price monopoly determines its output and price.**

The demand curve for a monopoly is the downward-sloping market demand curve. For a single-price monopoly, marginal revenue is less than price, so the marginal revenue curve lies below the demand curve. A monopoly maximizes profit by producing the quantity at which marginal revenue equals marginal cost and finds the highest price at which it can sell this output on the demand curve. A monopoly never profitably produces an output in the inelastic range of its demand curve.

■ **Compare the performance of a single-price monopoly with that of perfect competition.**

Compared to perfect competition, a single-price monopoly produces a smaller output and charges a higher price. A monopoly is inefficient because it creates a deadweight loss. A monopoly redistributes consumer surplus so that the producer gains and the consumers lose. Rent seeking is the act of obtaining special treatment by the government to create economic profit or to divert consumer surplus or producer surplus away from others. Rent seeking restricts competition and often creates a monopoly.

■ **Explain how price discrimination increases profit.**

To be able to price discriminate a firm must be able to identify and separate different types of buyers and sell a product that cannot be resold. Price discrimination converts consumer surplus into economic profit. Perfect price discrimination charges every consumer the maximum price the consumer is willing to pay. Perfect price discrimination eliminates consumer surplus but is efficient.

■ **Explain how monopoly regulation influences output, price, economic profit, and efficiency.**

Monopolies exist and have a potential advantage over a competitive alternative because of economies of scale and incentives to innovate. A marginal cost pricing rule sets price equal to marginal cost and the monopoly produces the efficient quantity. An average cost pricing rule, which sets price equal to average cost, covers a firm's costs and provides a normal profit but is inefficient.

EXPANDED CHAPTER CHECKLIST

When you have completed this chapter, you will be able to

1 **Explain how monopoly arises and distinguish between single-price monopoly and price-discriminating monopoly.**

- Define monopoly and state the two conditions under which monopoly arises.
- Define barrier to entry, natural monopoly and legal monopoly.
- Describe how a price-discriminating monopoly differs from single-price monopoly.

2 **Explain how a single-price monopoly determines its output and price.**

- Calculate marginal revenue and explain why marginal revenue is less than price for a single-price monopoly.
- Explain the relationship between marginal revenue and elasticity.
- Use a total revenue curve and a total cost curve to find the profit-maximizing level of output for a single-price monopoly.
- Describe a single-price monopoly's output and price decision.

3 **Compare the performance of a single-price monopoly with that of perfect competition.**

- Compare the output and price of perfect competition and single-price monopoly.
- Discuss the efficiency and fairness of monopoly.
- Define rent seeking and discuss its effects.

4 **Explain how price discrimination increases profit.**

- State the two conditions necessary for price discrimination.

- Explain why a firm practices price discrimination.
- Define perfect price discrimination and explain how a perfectly price-discriminating monopoly chooses its level of output.
- Discuss the relationship between price discrimination and efficiency.

5 **Explain how monopoly regulation influences output, price, economic profit, and efficiency.**

- List two potential advantages of monopoly over perfect competition.
- Define and illustrate a marginal cost pricing rule and an average cost pricing rule.

KEY TERMS

- Average cost pricing rule (page 361)
- Barrier to entry (page 340)
- Legal monopoly (page 341)
- Marginal cost pricing rule (page 361)
- Natural monopoly (page 340)
- Perfect price discrimination (page 356)
- Price-discriminating monopoly (page 342)
- Rent seeking (page 351)
- Single-price monopoly (page 342)

CHECKPOINT 14.1

■ Explain how monopoly arises and distinguish between single-price monopoly and price-discriminating monopoly.

Practice Problems 14.1

1. Monopoly arises in which of the following situations?

a. Coca-Cola cuts its price below that of Pepsi-Cola in an attempt to increase its market share.

b. A single firm, protected by a barrier to entry, produces a personal service that has no close substitutes.

c. A barrier to entry exists, but some close substitutes for the good exist.

d. A firm offers discounts to students and seniors.

e. A firm can sell any quantity it chooses at the going price.

f. The government issues Mike Weir, Inc. an exclusive licence to produce golf balls.

g. A firm experiences economies of scale even when it produces the quantity that meets the entire market demand.

2. Which of the cases **a** to **f** in problem 1 are natural monopolies and which are legal monopolies? Which can price discriminate, which cannot, and why?

Solution to Practice Problems 14.1

To answer these Practice Problems remember that a monopoly arises when there are no close substitutes and barriers to entry exist.

Quick Review

- *Barrier to entry* A natural or legal constraint that protects a firm from competitors.

1. Monopoly arises in which of the following situations?

a. Coca-Cola cuts its price below that of Pepsi-Cola in an attempt to increase its market share.

A monopoly is a market with a single firm. More than one firm exists so there is no monopoly.

b. A single firm, protected by a barrier to entry, produces a personal service that has no close substitutes.

A monopoly is a market with a single supplier of a good or service that has no close substitutes and in which natural or legal barriers to entry prevent competition. Part **b** describes a monopoly.

c. A barrier to entry exists, but some close substitutes for the good exist.

A monopoly does not arise because close substitutes for the good exist.

d. A firm offers discounts to students and seniors.

Firms other than a monopoly can price discriminate, so price discrimination by itself is not proof of a monopoly.

e. A firm can sell any quantity it chooses at the going price.

When a firm can sell any quantity it chooses at the going price, demand for the good that the firm produces is perfectly elastic. This situation occurs when the firm is in perfect competition.

f. The government issues Mike Weir, Inc. an exclusive licence to produce golf balls.

When the government grants a licence, it is creating a legal monopoly.

g. A firm experiences economies of scale even when it produces the quantity that meets the entire market demand.

When a firm experiences economies of scale when it produces the quantity that meets the entire market demand, it produces that quantity at a lower price than two or more firms could. This firm is a natural monopoly.

2. Which of the cases in a to f in problem 1 are natural monopolies and which are legal monopolies? Which can price discriminate, which cannot, and why?

A natural monopoly is a monopoly that arises because one firm can meet the entire market demand at a lower price than two or more firms could. So **g** describes a natural monopoly and **b** could be a natural monopoly, but the type of barrier to entry is not specified.

A legal monopoly is a market in which competition and entry are restricted by the concentration of ownership of a natural resource or by the granting of a public franchise, government licence, patent, or copyright. So **f** describes a legal monopoly and **b** could be a legal monopoly, but the type of barrier to entry is not specified.

Monopoly **b** can price discriminate because a personal service cannot be resold. Monopoly **f** cannot price discriminate because golf balls can be resold. There is not enough information given about the type of good in monopoly **g** to determine if monopoly **g** can price discriminate.

Additional Practice Problem 14.1a

Describe the monopoly in the Canadian postal delivery market.

Solution to Additional Practice Problem 14.1a

There are legal barriers to entry in the market for the delivery of first class mail. Canada Post has the legal monopoly to deliver first class mail. But this monopoly is being weakened by substitutes such as the fax machine and courier services.

■ Self Test 14.1

Fill in the blanks

One of the requirements for monopoly is that there _____ (are; are no) close substitutes for the good. A _____ (legal; natural) monopoly exists when one firm can meet the entire market demand at a lower price than two or more firms could. A monopoly that is able to sell different units of a good or service for different prices is a _____ (legal-price; natural-price; price-discriminating) monopoly.

True or false

1. A legal barrier creates a natural monopoly.

2. A firm experiences economies of scale along a downward-sloping long-run average cost curve.

3. A monopoly always charges all customers the same price.

Multiple choice

1. A monopoly market has
   a. a few firms.
   b. a single firm.
   c. a few firms, but two dominate the market.
   d. only two firms in it.

2. The two types of barriers to entry in a monopoly market are
   a. legal and illegal.
   b. natural and legal.
   c. natural and illegal.
   d. natural and unnatural.

3. A natural monopoly is one that arises from
   a. patent law.
   b. copyright law.
   c. a firm buying up a natural resource.
   d. economies of scale.

4. A legal barrier is created when a firm
   a. has economies of scales.
   b. is granted a public franchise, government licence, patent, or copyright.
   c. produces a unique product or service.
   d. produces a standardized product or service.

5. A pizza producer who sets the price of a second pizza far below the first is an example of
   a. monopoly.
   b. a barrier to entry.
   c. behaviour that is not profit maximizing.
   d. price discrimination.

Short answer

1. What conditions define monopoly?

2. What are the two types of barriers to entry?

3. What are the two pricing strategies a monopoly can use?

CHECKPOINT 14.2

■ **Explain how a single-price monopoly determines its output and price.**

Practice Problem 14.2

Minnie's Mineral Springs is a single-price monopoly. The first two columns of the table show the demand schedule for Minnie's spring water, and the middle and third columns show the firm's total cost schedule.

Price (dollars per bottle)	Quantity (bottles per hour)	Total cost (dollars per hour)
10	0	1.00
9	1	1.50
8	2	2.50
7	3	5.50
6	4	10.50
5	5	17.50

a. Calculate Minnie's total revenue schedule and marginal revenue schedule.

b. Sketch Minnie's demand curve and marginal revenue curve.

c. Calculate Minnie's profit-maximizing output, price, and economic profit.

d. If the owner of the water source that Minnie uses increases the fee that Minnie pays by $15.50 an hour, what are Minnie's new profit-maximizing output, price, and economic profit?

e. If instead of increasing the fee that Minnie pays by $15.50 an hour, the owner of the water source increases the fee that Minnie pays by $4.00 a bottle, what are Minnie's new profit-maximizing output, price, and economic profit?

Solution to Practice Problem 14.2

To answer this Practice Problem, remember that a monopoly maximizes profit by producing the output at which marginal revenue equals marginal cost and charges the maximum price that consumers are willing to pay for that output.

Quick Review

*   *Marginal revenue* The change in total revenue that results from a one-unit increase in the quantity sold.

a. **Calculate Minnie's total revenue schedule and marginal revenue schedule.**

Total revenue equals price times quantity sold and is reported in the middle column of the table. Marginal revenue is equal to the change in total revenue when Minnie increases her output by 1 bottle an hour and is reported in the third column in the table.

Quantity (bottles per hour)	Total revenue (dollars per hour)	Marginal revenue (dollars per bottle)
0	0	
		9
1	9	
		7
2	16	
		5
3	21	
		3
4	24	
		1
5	25	

b. **Sketch Minnie's demand curve and marginal revenue curve.**

The demand curve and marginal revenue curve are in the figure to the right. The marginal revenue curve lies below the demand curve.

Price and marginal revenue (dollars per bottle)

b. **Calculate Minnie's profit-maximizing output, price, and economic profit.**

The figure plots the marginal revenue curve, the marginal cost curve, and the demand curve. To

Price and cost (dollars per bottle)

find Minnie's marginal cost, find the change in total cost when output increases by 1 bottle. For example, when Minnie increases production from 2 bottles to 3 bottles an hour, total cost increases from $2.50 an hour to $5.50 an hour. So the marginal cost of increasing production from 2 to 3 bottles an hour is $3.00. The profit-maximizing output is 3 bottles an hour, where marginal revenue equals marginal cost. Minnie can sell 3 bottles an hour at $7 a bottle, so her total revenue is $21. And her total cost of producing 3 bottles an hour is $5.50. Minnie's economic profit is $21.00 – $5.50, which is $15.50 an hour.

d. **If the owner of the water source that Minnie uses increases the fee that Minnie pays by $15.50 an hour, what are Minnie's new profit-maximizing output, price, and economic profit?**

When the fee increases, Minnie's fixed cost increases, but her marginal cost does not change. The profit-maximizing output and price remain the same. But economic profit falls to zero.

e. **If instead of increasing the fee that Minnie pays by $15.50 an hour, the owner of the water source increases the fee that Minnie pays by $4.00 a bottle, what are Minnie's new profit-maximizing output, price, and economic profit?**

Minnie's marginal cost increases by $4 a bottle. Marginal revenue now equals marginal cost when Minnie produces 2 bottles an hour. Minnie sells each bottle at a price of $8, so her total revenue is $16 an hour. Total cost is $10.50 an hour. Minnie's economic profit is $16.00 – $10.50, which is $5.50 an hour.

Additional Practice Problem 14.2a

The following table gives part of Minnie's total cost schedule from Practice Problem 14.2.

a. Complete the table.

Quantity (bottles per hour)	Total cost (dollars per hour)	Average total cost (dollars per bottle)	Marginal cost (dollars per bottle)
0	1.00		
			____
1	1.50	____	
			____
2	2.50	____	
			____
3	5.50	____	
			____
4	10.50	____	

b. Using information in the table and in Practice Problem 14.2, plot Minnie's demand curve, marginal revenue curve, average total cost curve, and marginal cost curve. Indicate the equilibrium quantity and price, and show Minnie's economic profit.

Price and cost (dollars per bottle)

Solution to Additional Practice Problem 14.2a

a. **Complete the table.**

The completed table is below.

Quantity (bottles per hour)	Total cost (dollars per hour)	Average total cost (dollars per bottle)	Marginal cost (dollars per bottle)
0	1.00		
			0.50
1	1.50	1.50	
			1.00
2	2.50	1.25	
			3.00
3	5.50	1.83	
			5.00
4	10.50	2.63	

b. **Using information in the table and in Practice Problem 14.2, plot Minnie's demand curve, marginal revenue curve, average total cost curve, and marginal cost curve. Indicate the equilibrium quantity and price, and show Minnie's economic profit.**

The completed figure is to the right. The equilibrium quantity is the quantity where the *MR* and *MC* curves intersect, which is 3 bottles an hour. The price is $7 a bottle from the demand curve. The economic profit is equal to the area of the blue rectangle.

■ Self Test 14.2

Fill in the blanks

For each level of output, marginal revenue for a single-price monopoly is ____ (greater than; equal to; less than) price. When demand is inelastic, marginal revenue is ____ (positive; negative). A single-price monopoly maximizes profit by producing the quantity at which marginal revenue ____ (is greater than; equals; is less than) marginal cost and then finds the highest price it can sell that output by using the ____ (demand; marginal revenue; average total cost) curve.

True or false

1. For a single-price monopoly, marginal revenue exceeds price.

2. A monopoly can profitably produce an output in the inelastic range of its demand curve.

3. A single-price monopoly maximizes profit by producing the quantity that makes marginal revenue equal to marginal cost.

Multiple choice

1. For a single-price monopoly, price is ____ marginal revenue.
   a. greater than
   b. less than
   c. equal to
   d. unrelated to

2. A single-price monopoly can sell 1 unit for $9.00 or 2 units for $8.50 a unit. The marginal revenue from selling the second unit is
   a. $17.50.
   b. $17.00.
   c. $8.50.
   d. $8.00.

3. When demand is elastic, marginal revenue is
   a. positive.
   b. negative.
   c. zero.
   d. increasing as output increases.

4. A single-price monopoly produces where
   a. the difference between marginal revenue and marginal cost is as large as possible.
   b. marginal revenue equals marginal cost.
   c. average total cost is at its minimum.
   d. the marginal cost curve intersects the demand curve.

5. A monopolist charges a price that
   a. is determined by the intersection of the marginal revenue and marginal cost curves.
   b. minimizes marginal cost.
   c. is determined by its demand curve.
   d. is independent of the amount produced.

Complete the graph

1. The table gives the demand schedule for the monopoly seller of hamburgers in small town.

Quantity (hamburgers per hour)	Price (dollars per hamburger)	Marginal revenue (dollars per hamburger)
1	8.00	
		——
2	7.00	
		——
3	6.00	
		——
4	5.00	
		——
5	4.00	

Complete the table by calculating the marginal revenue and then draw the demand curve and marginal revenue curve in Figure 14.1.

2. Figure 14.2 shows a monopoly. Label the curves. Identify the quantity produced by labelling it Q and the price charged by labelling it P. Is the monopoly earning an economic profit or incurring an economic loss? Shade the area that shows the economic profit or economic loss.

■ **FIGURE 14.1**
Price and marginal revenue (dollars per hamburger)

■ **FIGURE 14.2**
Price and cost (dollars per unit)

Short answer

1. What is the relationship between the elasticity of demand and marginal revenue?

2. Both perfectly competitive and monopoly firms maximize their profit by producing where $MR = MC$. Why do both use the same rule?

3. Why can a monopoly earn an economic profit in the long run?

CHECKPOINT 14.3

■ **Compare the performance of a single-price monopoly with that of perfect competition.**

Practice Problems 14.3

Township is a small isolated community served by one newspaper that can meet the market demand at a lower cost than two or more newspapers could. There is no local radio or TV station and no Internet access. The *Township Gazette* is the only source of news. The figure shows the marginal cost of printing the *Township Gazette* and the demand for it. The *Township Gazette* is a profit-maximizing, single-price monopoly.

a. How many copies of the *Township Gazette* are printed each day?

b. What is the price of the *Township Gazette*?

c. What is the efficient number of copies of the *Township Gazette*?

d. What is the price at which the efficient number of copies could be sold?

e. Is the number of copies printed the efficient quantity? Explain why or why not.

f. On a graph, show the consumer surplus that is redistributed from consumers to the *Township Gazette*.

g. On a graph, show the deadweight loss that arises from the monopoly of the *Township Gazette*.

Solution to Practice Problem 14.3

Single-price monopolies create a deadweight loss. The key to this Practice Problem is to remember that a monopoly produces where *MR* = *MC* but efficiency requires production where *MB* = *MC*.

Quick Review

• *Monopoly and competition compared* Compared to perfect competition, a single-price monopoly produces a smaller output and charges a higher price.

• *Monopoly and efficiency* A single-price monopoly creates a deadweight loss.

a. How many copies of the *Township Gazette* are printed each day?

The marginal revenue curve extends from the intersection of the demand curve and the *y*-axis to the *x*-axis, halfway between the origin and the point where the demand curve intersects the *x*-axis. To

maximize profit, the firm produces 150 papers a day, the quantity at which marginal revenue equals marginal cost.

b. What is the price of the *Township Gazette*?

Using the demand curve, the price that corresponds to the quantity of 150 newspapers a day is 70¢ a newspaper.

c. What is the efficient number of copies of the *Township Gazette*?

The efficient quantity is the quantity where marginal benefit equals marginal cost. The demand curve is the marginal benefit curve, so the efficient quantity is 250 newspapers a day.

d. What is the price at which the efficient number of copies could be sold?

From the demand curve, 250 newspapers a day will be bought at 50¢ each.

e. Is the number of copies printed the efficient quantity? Explain why or why not.

The *Township Gazette* is not printing the efficient quantity. The marginal benefit of the 150th newspaper is greater than the marginal cost.

f. On a graph, show the consumer surplus that is redistributed from consumers to the *Township Gazette*.

The redistributed consumer surplus is the blue rectangle in the figure.

g. On a graph, show the deadweight loss that arises from the monopoly of the *Township Gazette*.

The grey triangle in the figure shows the deadweight loss from the monopoly.

Additional Practice Problem 14.3a

Throughout the future suppose that the *Township Gazette's* economic profit is $2 million. If the *Township Gazette* is put up for sale and bidding is a competitive process, what do you expect will be the price for which the newspaper is sold?

Solution to Additional Practice Problem 14.3a

Bidders will be willing to pay up to $2 million for the *Township Gazette* because if they can buy it for any price less than $2 million, they will receive an economic profit. Because the bidding is competitive, the price of the *Township Gazette* will be bid up to $2 million, and the winning bidder will earn a normal profit. This result demonstrates a rent-seeking equilibrium in which rent seeking costs exhaust economic profit.

■ Self Test 14.3

Fill in the blanks

Compared to perfect competition, a single-price monopoly produces a ____ (larger; smaller) output and charges a ____ (higher; lower) price. A single-price monopoly ____ (creates; does not create) a deadweight loss. The act of obtaining special treatment by the government to create an economic profit is called ____ (government-surplus; rent seeking). Rent seeking ____ (decreases; increases) the amount of deadweight loss.

True or false

1. A single-price monopoly charges a higher price than a perfectly competitive industry would charge.

2. A monopoly redistributes consumer surplus so that the consumers gain and the producer loses.

3. The buyer of a monopoly always makes an economic profit.

Multiple choice

1. If a perfectly competitive industry is taken over by a single firm that operates as a single-price monopoly, the price will ____ and the quantity will ____.
a. fall; decrease
b. fall; increase
c. rise; decrease
d. rise; increase

2. Comparing single-price monopoly to perfect competition, we see that ____ consumer surplus.
a. monopoly increases the amount of
b. monopoly has the same amount of
c. perfect competition has no
d. monopoly decreases the amount of

3. Is a single-price monopoly efficient?
a. Yes, because it creates a deadweight loss.
b. No, because it creates a deadweight loss.
c. Yes, because producer surplus decreases.
d. Yes, because consumers surplus decreases.

4. Monopolies are
a. always fair but not efficient.
b. efficient but might or might not be fair.
c. inefficient and might or might not be fair.
d. both fair and efficient.

5. In equilibrium, rent seeking eliminates the
a. deadweight loss.
b. economic profit.
c. consumer surplus.
d. demand for the product.

Complete the graph

1. Figure 14.3 shows the ostrich farming market after one farmer buys all of the farms and operates as a single-price monopoly. Label the curves and show the deadweight loss. What is the competitive price and quantity? What is the monopoly price and quantity?

■ FIGURE 14.3
Price and cost (dollars per ostrich)

Quantity (thousands of ostriches per year)

Short answer

1. How does the quantity produced and the price set by a single-price monopoly compare to those in a perfectly competitive market?

2. What happens to consumer surplus with a single-price monopoly?

3. What is rent seeking? How does rent seeking affect society?

CHECKPOINT 14.4

■ **Explain how price discrimination increases profit.**

Practice Problems 14.4

Village, a small isolated town, has one veterinarian. For a 30-minute consultation, the veterinarian charges a rich person twice as much as a poor person.

a. Does the veterinarian practise price discrimination?

b. Does the veterinarian's pricing system redistribute consumer surplus? If so, explain how.

c. Is the veterinarian using resources efficiently? Explain your answer.

d. If the veterinarian decided to charge everyone the maximum price that he or she would be willing to pay, what would be the consumer surplus?

e. In part **d**, is the market for veterinarian service in Village efficient?

Solution to Practice Problem 14.4

To answer this Practice Problem, remember that the key idea behind price discrimination is to convert consumer surplus into economic profit.

Quick Review

- *Price discrimination* Charging different prices for a single good or service because the willingness to pay varies across buyers.

a.   Does the veterinarian practise price discrimination?

Charging different prices to rich and poor people for the same service is price discrimination.

b.   Does the veterinarian's pricing system redistribute consumer surplus? If so, explain how.

The veterinarian is setting the price closer to the maximum each consumer is willing to pay. Each consumer receives less consumer surplus, which is converted into economic profit.

c.   Is the veterinarian using resources efficiently? Explain your answer.

The veterinarian is not using resources efficiently. Price discrimination creates a deadweight loss unless the monopolist can practise perfect price discrimination.

d.   If the veterinarian decided to charge everyone the maximum price that he or she would be willing to pay, what would be the consumer surplus?

The veterinarian is now practicing perfect price discrimination. All of the consumer surplus would be converted into economic profit and consumer surplus would be zero.

e.   In part d, is the market for veterinarian service in Village efficient?

The demand curve becomes the marginal revenue curve in perfect price discrimination. The demand curve is also the marginal benefit curve. The veterinarian provides services until marginal revenue equals marginal cost, which is the same thing as when marginal benefit equals marginal cost and resource use is efficient.

Additional Practice Problem 14.4a

Why is the price to attend a movie less on a weekday evening than on a weekend evening?

Solution to Additional Practice Problem 14.4a

The movie cinema is practising price discrimination between two groups of buyers. Each group has a different average willingness to pay. By having two different prices, the movie cinema maximizes profit by converting consumer surplus into economic profit.

■ Self Test 14.4

Fill in the blanks

It is _____ (sometimes; never) possible for a monopoly to charge different customers different prices. The key idea behind price discrimination is to convert _____ (consumer surplus; producer surplus) into economic profit. Price discrimination results in consumers with a higher willingness to pay paying a _____ (higher; lower) price than consumers with a lower willingness to pay. Perfect price discrimination results in _____ (maximum; zero) consumer surplus.

True or false

1. Price discrimination lowers a firm's profit.

2. Price discrimination converts producer surplus into consumer surplus.

3. With perfect price discrimination, the demand curve is the marginal revenue curve.

Multiple choice

1. A firm that price discriminates

a. divides buyers into different groups according to their willingness to pay.

b. sells a good that cannot be resold.

c. identifies into which group a buyer falls .

d. All of the above answers are correct.

2. Which of the following is <u>NOT</u> price discrimination?

a. different prices based on different production costs

b. charging business flyers a higher airfare than tourists

c. charging consumers who buy a larger quantity a lower price

d. pricing on the basis of some easily distinguishable characteristic of buyers

3. When a monopolist price discriminates, it

a. increases the amount of consumer surplus.

b. decreases the monopolist's economic profit.

c. converts consumer surplus into economic profit.

d. converts economic profit into consumer surplus.

4. If a monopolist is able to perfectly price discriminate, consumer surplus is

a. equal to zero.

b. maximized.

c. unchanged from what it is with a single-price monopoly.

d. unchanged from what it is in a perfectly competitive industry.

5. With perfect price discrimination, the quantity of output produced by the monopolist is _____ the quantity produced by a perfectly competitive industry.

a. greater than

b. less than

c. equal to

d. almost always greater than

Complete the graph

1a. In Figure 14.4, show the economic profit earned by a dry cleaner that owns a single-price monopoly.

b. Calculate the economic profit earned by a perfect price discriminating monopoly and show the economic profit in the figure.

■ FIGURE 14.4

Price and cost (dollars per article of clothing)

Short answer

1. Explain the effect of price discrimination on consumer surplus and economic profit.

2. When does a price discriminating monopoly produce the efficient quantity of output?

CHECKPOINT 14.5

■ **Explain how monopoly regulation influences output, price, economic profit, and efficiency.**

Practice Problem 14.5

The local water company is a natural monopoly. The figure shows the demand for water and the water company's cost of providing water.

a. If the company is an unregulated profit-maximizer:

   i. What is the price of water?

ii. What quantity of water would be supplied?

iii. What would be the dead-weight loss?

b. If the company is regulated to make normal profit:

   i. What is the price of water?

   ii. What quantity of water would be supplied?

   iii. What would be the deadweight loss?

c. If the company is regulated to be efficient:

   i. What is the price of water?

   ii. What quantity of water would be supplied?

   iii. What would be the deadweight loss?

Solution to Practice Problem 14.5

This Practice Problem studies the implications of monopoly regulation.

Quick Review

- *Marginal cost pricing rule* A price rule for a natural monopoly that sets price equal to marginal cost.

- *Average cost pricing rule* A price rule for a natural monopoly that sets the price equal to average cost and enables the firm to cover its costs and earn a normal profit.

a. **If the company is an unregulated profit-maximizer:**

   i. **What is the price of water?**

   ii. **What quantity of water would be supplied?**

   iii. **What would be the deadweight loss?**

The firm produces where marginal revenue equals marginal cost. In the figure, the price of water is 6 cents a litre, the quantity of water supplied is 2,000 litres a day, and the deadweight loss is $40 a day, which is the area of the grey triangle.

b. **If the company is regulated to make a normal profit:**

i.   **What is the price of water?**

ii. **What quantity of water would be supplied?**

iii. **What would be the deadweight loss?**

The company is regulated using an average cost pricing rule. In the figure, the price is 4 cents a litre and the quantity supplied is 3,000 litres a day, at the intersection of the long-run average cost curve and the demand curve. The deadweight loss is the area of the grey triangle, which is $10 a day.

c. **If the company is regulated to be efficient:**

i.   **What is the price of water?**

ii. **What quantity of water would be supplied?**

iii. **What would be the deadweight loss?**

The company is regulated using a marginal cost pricing rule. In the figure, the price is 2 cents a litre and the quantity supplied is 4,000 litres a day at the intersection of the marginal cost curve and the demand curve. Deadweight loss is zero.

Additional Practice Problem 14.5a

If you are the owner of the natural monopoly would you want to be regulated or unregulated? If regulated, would you prefer an average cost pricing rule or a marginal cost pricing rule?

Solution to Additional Practice Problem 14.5a

You would prefer not to be regulated. If you are not regulated, price is greater than average total cost and you earn an economic profit. And, if you are regulated, you would prefer the average cost pricing rule. With this rule you earn a normal profit. If a marginal cost pricing rule is imposed, you incur an economic loss.

■ Self Test 14.5

Fill in the blanks

_____ (Economies of scale; Incentives to innovate) can lead to natural monopoly. Efficiency is attained if a natural monopoly is regulated using _____ (a marginal; an average) cost pricing rule. _____ (A marginal; An average) cost pricing rule allows a natural monopoly to earn a normal profit.

True or false

1. Large firms with monopoly power innovate more than smaller competitive firms, which lack monopoly power.

2. A natural monopoly regulated using a marginal cost pricing rule incurs an economic loss.

3. A natural monopoly that is regulated using an average cost pricing rule incurs an economic loss.

Multiple choice

1. If a single firm can meet the entire market demand at a lower price than a larger number of smaller firms can, the single firm is

   a. price discriminating.

   b. a natural monopoly.

   c. a legal monopoly.

   d. efficient when profit maximizing.

2. What are the potential advantages of monopoly over competition for the economy?

   a. There are none.

   b. Monopolists earn more profit.

   c. Monopolies have a higher rate of productivity growth.

   d. Economies of scale and incentives to innovate are potential advantages.

3. When the government regulates a natural monopoly, the government

   a. determines the price the monopoly charges.

   b. insures that there is enough competition.

   c. always uses the marginal cost pricing rule.

   d. All of the above answers are correct.

4. With a marginal cost pricing rule, a natural monopoly produces an ____ amount of output and ____.

   a. efficient; earns an economic profit

   b. efficient; incurs an economic loss

   c. inefficient; earns an economic profit

   d. inefficient; incurs an economic loss

5. With an average cost pricing rule, a natural monopoly produces an ____ amount of output and ____.

   a. efficient; earns an economic profit

   b. efficient; incurs an economic loss

   c. inefficient; earns a normal profit

   d. inefficient; earns an economic profit

Short answer

1. Why is creating competition in a market with a natural monopoly wasteful?

2. Describe the slope of the natural monopoly's long-run average cost curve at the point where it intersects the demand curve.

3. What are the two ways to regulate a natural monopoly? What are their advantages and disadvantages?

SELF TEST ANSWERS

■ CHECKPOINT 14.1

Fill in the blanks

One of the requirements for monopoly is that there <u>are no</u> close substitutes for the good. A <u>natural</u> monopoly exists when one firm can meet the entire market demand at a lower price than two or more firms could. A monopoly that is able to sell different units of a good or service for different prices is a <u>price-discriminating</u> monopoly.

True or false

1. False; page 340
2. True; page 340
3. False; page 342

Multiple choice

1. b; page 340
2. b; page 340
3. d; page 340
4. b; page 341
5. d; page 342

Short answer

1. Monopoly occurs when there is a market with a single supplier selling a good or service that has no close substitutes and in which the firm is protected by either a natural or a legal barrier to entry; page 340.

2. Barriers to entry are anything that protects a firm from the entry of new competitors. Barriers to entry are either natural barriers (the result of economies of scale) or legal barriers (the result of government actions); pages 340-341.

3. A monopoly can sell each unit of its output for the same price to all its customers or it can price discriminate by selling different units of its good or service at different prices; page 342.

■ CHECKPOINT 14.2

Fill in the blanks

For each level of output, marginal revenue for a single-price monopoly is <u>less than</u> price. When demand is inelastic, marginal revenue is <u>negative</u>. A single-price monopoly maximizes profit by producing the quantity at which marginal revenue <u>equals</u> marginal cost and then finds the highest price it can sell that output by using the <u>demand</u> curve.

True or false

1. False; page 344
2. False; pages 345-346
3. True; page 346

Multiple choice

1. a; page 344
2. d; page 344
3. a; page 345
4. b; page 346
5. c; page 346

Complete the graph

1. The completed table is below.

Quantity (hamburgers per hour)	Price (dollars per hamburger)	Marginal revenue (dollars per hamburger)
1	8.00	
		<u>6.00</u>
2	7.00	
		<u>4.00</u>
3	6.00	
		<u>2.00</u>
4	5.00	
		<u>0.00</u>
5	4.00	

Figure 14.5 plots the demand curve and marginal revenue curve; page 344.

■ FIGURE 14.5
Price and marginal revenue (dollars per hamburger)

2. The curves, quantity, price, and economic profit are labelled in Figure 14.6; page 347.

■ FIGURE 14.6
Price and cost (dollars per unit)

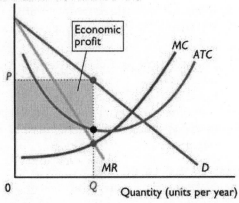

Short answer

1. If demand is elastic, marginal revenue is positive; if demand is unit elastic, marginal revenue is zero; and if demand is inelastic, marginal revenue is negative; page 345.

2. Both competitive and monopoly firms maximize profit by producing where $MR = MC$ because for *any* firm, a unit of output is produced if $MR > MC$ and is not produced if $MR < MC$. As long as $MR > MC$, *any* firm continues to produce additional output until it reaches the point at which $MR = MC$; page 346.

3. A monopoly can earn an economic profit in the long run because it is protected by a barrier to entry. Other firms might want to enter the market to earn an economic profit, but they cannot do so; page 347.

■ CHECKPOINT 14.3
Fill in the blanks

Compared to perfect competition, a single-price monopoly produces a smaller output and charges a higher price. A single-price monopoly creates a deadweight loss. The act of obtaining special treatment by the government to create an economic profit is called rent seeking. Rent seeking increases the amount of deadweight loss.

True or false

1. True; page 349
2. False; page 350
3. False; page 351

Multiple choice

1. c; page 349
2. d; page 350
3. b; page 350
4. c; page 350
5. b; page 352

Complete the graph

1. Figure 14.7 shows that the perfectly competitive price is $20 an ostrich and the quantity is 30,000 ostriches a year. The monopoly price is $30 an ostrich and the quantity is 20,000 ostriches a year. The deadweight loss is the area of the grey triangle; page 350.

■ **FIGURE 14.7**

Price and cost (dollars per ostrich)

Short answer

1. The price set by a monopoly firm exceeds the price in a competitive market and the quantity produced by a monopoly is less than the quantity produced in a competitive market; page 349.

2. Consumer surplus decreases with a single-price monopoly. Consumer surplus decreases because the monopoly produces less output and charges a higher price; page 350.

3. Rent seeking is the act of obtaining special treatment by the government to create economic profit or to divert consumer surplus or producer surplus away from others. Rent seeking harms society because in a competitive rent-seeking equilibrium, the amount of the deadweight loss increases; page 352.

■ **CHECKPOINT 14.4**

Fill in the blanks

It is <u>sometimes</u> possible for a monopoly to charge different customers different prices. The key idea behind price discrimination is to convert <u>consumer surplus</u> into economic profit. Price discrimination results in consumers with a higher willingness to pay paying a <u>higher</u> price than consumers with a lower willingness to pay. Per-

fect price discrimination results in <u>zero</u> consumer surplus.

True or false

1. False; page 354
2. False; page 354
3. True; page 357

Multiple choice

1. d; page 354
2. a; page 354
3. c; page 354
4. a; pages 356–357
5. c; page 358

Complete the graph

1. a. The economic profit is the blue rectangle in Figure 14.8. The economic profit equals the area of the blue rectangle, which is $60 a day; page 355.

   b. The economic profit is increased by the addition of the two grey areas. The economic profit is now the sum of the initial economic profit plus the additional economic profit, which is a total of $120 a day; page 357.

■ **FIGURE 14.8**

Price and cost (dollars per article of clothing)

Quantity (articles of clothing per day)

Short answer

1. Price discrimination decreases consumer surplus and increases economic profit. Price discrimination allows the firm to charge a price closer to the maximum the consumer is willing to pay, which is the marginal benefit of the good. Consumer surplus is converted into economic profit; page 354.

2. With perfect price discrimination, the monopoly increases output to the point at which price equals marginal cost. This output is identical to that of perfect competition. Deadweight loss with perfect price discrimination is zero. So perfect price discrimination produces the efficient quantity; page 358.

■ **CHECKPOINT 14.5**

Fill in the blanks

Economies of scale can lead to natural monopoly. Efficiency is attained if a natural monopoly is regulated using a marginal cost pricing rule. An average cost pricing rule allows a natural monopoly to earn a normal profit.

True or false

1. False; page 360
2. True; page 361
3. False; page 361

Multiple choice

1. b; page 360
2. d; page 360
3. a; page 361
4. b; page 361
5. c; page 361

Short answer

1. A natural monopoly is a situation in which a single firm can produce at a lower average cost than a larger number of smaller firms can. Where significant economies of scale exist, it would be wasteful not to have a monopoly. So creating competition in a market that is a natural monopoly would be wasteful; page 360.

2. The average total cost curve is sloping downward at the point where it intersects the demand curve; page 361.

3. A natural monopoly can be regulated using a marginal cost pricing rule or an average cost pricing rule. The marginal cost pricing rule is a price rule for a natural monopoly that sets price equal to marginal cost. The advantage of this rule is that the firm produces the efficient quantity. The disadvantage is that the firm incurs an economic loss. An average cost pricing rule is a price rule for a natural monopoly that sets the price equal to average cost and enables the firm to cover its costs and earn an normal profit. The advantage of this rule is that the firm earns a normal profit. The disadvantage is that the firm produces less than the efficient quantity of output and a deadweight loss is created; pages 360-361.

Monopolistic Competition and Oligopoly

CHAPTER IN PERSPECTIVE

Chapter 15 studies the two market structures that lie between the extremes of perfect competition and monopoly: monopolistic competition and oligopoly.

■ **Explain how price and quantity are determined in monopolistic competition.**

Monopolistic competition is a market structure in which a large number of firms compete; each firm produces a differentiated product; firms compete on product quality, price, and marketing; and firms are free to enter and exit. The four-firm concentration ratio and the Herfindahl-Hirschman Index are indexes that measure the extent to which a market is dominated by a small number of firms. A firm in monopolistic competition maximizes profit by producing the output at which marginal revenue equals marginal cost. The price is determined by the demand curve. Entry and exit result in zero economic profit and excess capacity in long-run equilibrium. In monopolistic competition price exceeds marginal cost—a sign of inefficiency—but the inefficiency arises from product differentiation—a gain for consumers.

■ **Explain why selling costs are high in monopolistic competition.**

To maintain economic profit, firms in monopolistic competition innovate and develop new products, and incur huge costs to ensure that buyers appreciate the differences between their own products and those of their competitors. Selling costs such as advertising increase a firm's total cost, but they might lower average total cost if they increase the quantity sold by a large enough amount.

■ **Explain the dilemma faced by firms in oligopoly.**

An oligopoly is a market structure in which a small number of firms compete and natural or legal barriers restrict the entry of new firms. Firms in oligopoly would make the same economic profit as a monopoly if they could act together to restrict output to the monopoly level. Each firm can make a larger economic profit by increasing production, but this action decreases the economic profit of the other firms.

■ **Use game theory to explain how price and quantity are determined in oligopoly.**

Game theory is the tool economists use to analyze strategic behaviour. Games have rules, strategies, and payoffs. The prisoners' dilemma is a game between two prisoners that shows why it is hard to cooperate, even when it would be beneficial to both players to do so. The equilibrium of a game occurs when each player takes the best possible action given the action of the other player. This equilibrium concept is called Nash equilibrium. The equilibrium of the prisoners' dilemma game is not the best outcome. An oligopoly game is like the prisoners' dilemma. In a repeated game, a punishment strategy can produce a monopoly output, price, and economic profit.

EXPANDED CHAPTER CHECKLIST

When you have completed this chapter, you will be able to

1 Explain how price and quantity are determined in monopolistic competition.

- Describe monopolistic competition.
- Define product differentiation.
- Calculate the four-firm concentration ratio and the Herfindahl-Hirschman Index.
- Illustrate the firm's profit-maximizing decision in monopolistic competition in the short run and in the long run.
- Discuss efficiency of monopolistic competition.
- Illustrate the excess capacity of firms in monopolistic competition.

2 Explain why selling costs are high in monopolistic competition.

- Explain why firms in monopolistic competition are continuously developing new products.
- Discuss the efficiency of product innovation.
- Illustrate how an increase in sales brought about by advertising can lower average total cost.

3 Explain the dilemma faced by firms in oligopoly.

- Define oligopoly and explain how one firm's actions can decrease the profits of other firms.
- Define cartel and explain why collusion usually breaks down.

4 Use game theory to explain how price and quantity are determined in oligopoly.

- Define game theory and discuss the three features of games.

- Describe the prisoners' dilemma.
- Define Nash equilibrium and be able to recognize the Nash equilibrium in a payoff matrix.
- Explain why a repeated game might lead to the monopoly outcome.

KEY TERMS

- Capacity output (page 373)
- Cartel (page 380)
- Duopoly (page 380)
- Four-firm concentration ratio (page 370)
- Game theory (page 385)
- Herfindahl-Hirschman Index (page 370)
- Nash equilibrium (page 386)
- Payoff matrix (page 386)
- Prisoners' dilemma (page 385)
- Product differentiation (page 368)
- Strategies (page 386)

CHECKPOINT 15.1

■ Explain how price and quantity are determined in monopolistic competition.

Practice Problem 15.1

Natti is a dot.com entrepreneur who has established a Web site at which people can design and buy a pair of cool sunglasses. Natti pays $4,000 a month for her Web server and Internet connection. The glasses that her customers design are made to order by another firm, and Natti pays this firm $50 a pair. Natti has no other costs. The table shows the demand schedule for Natti's sunglasses.

Price (dollars per pair)	Quantity demanded (pairs per month)
250	0
200	50
150	100
100	150
50	200
0	250

a. Calculate Natti's profit-maximizing output, price, and economic profit.

b. Do you expect other firms to enter the Web sunglasses business and compete with Natti?

c. What happens to the demand for Natti's sunglasses in the long run?

d. What happens to Natti's economic profit in the long run?

Solution to Practice Problem 15.1

Firms in monopolistic competition are similar to firms in perfect competition because both industries have no barriers to entry. When answering this Practice Problem remember that when possible, firms enter a market if they expect to earn an economic profit.

Quick Review

• *The firm's profit-maximizing decision* A firm in monopolistic competition produces the quantity at which marginal revenue equals marginal cost. The price is determined by the demand curve.

a. Calculate Natti's profit-maximizing output, price, and economic profit.

Natti will produce the quantity where marginal cost equals marginal revenue. The marginal cost is $50. The table shows Natti's marginal revenue.

Price (dollars per pair)	Quantity demanded (pairs per month)	Total revenue (dollars per month)	Marginal revenue (dollars per pair)
250	0	0	
			200
200	50	10,000	
			100
150	100	15,000	
			0
100	150	15,000	
			–100
50	200	10,000	
			–200
0	250	0	

When 100 pairs of sunglasses are produced, marginal revenue is $50 a pair (which is the average of $100 and $0). To maximize profit, Natti produces 100 pairs of sunglasses and sets a price

of $150 a pair. Economic profit equals total revenue minus total cost. Natti's total revenue is 100 pairs × $150 a pair, which is $15,000. Total cost is the fixed cost of $4,000 plus variable cost of 100 pairs × $50 a pair, which is $5,000. So total cost is $9,000. Natti's economic profit is $15,000 – $9,000, which is $6,000 a month.

b. Do you expect other firms to enter the Web sunglasses business and compete with Natti?

Natti is earning an economic profit, so other firms will enter because they have an incentive to do so.

c. What happens to the demand for Natti's sunglasses in the long run?

As other firms enter, the demand for Natti's sunglasses will decrease. Natti's demand curve will shift leftward.

d. What happens to Natti's economic profit in the long run?

As the demand for Natti's sunglasses decreases her economic profit decreases. In the long run, Natti earns zero economic profit.

Additional Practice Problem 15.1a

The table gives some hypothetical data on sales in the fast-food hamburger market.

Firm	Sales (millions of dollars)	Market share (percent)
McDonald's	1,200	_____
Burger King	600	_____
Wendy's	600	_____
Harvey's	300	_____
A&W	100	_____
Other 20 smaller firms	800	_____

Complete the table and then calculate the four-firm concentration ratio. Based on the hypothetical concentration ratio, in what market structure would you classify the fast-food hamburger market?

Solution to Additional Practice Problem 15.1a

To calculate the market shares, first calculate the total sales within the market, which is $3,600 million. A firm's market share equals 100 times its sales divided by the total sales. The market shares are in the table below.

Firm	Sales (millions of dollars)	Market share (percent)
McDonald's	1,200	33.3
Burger King	600	16.7
Wendy's	600	16.7
Harvey's	300	8.3
A&W	100	2.8
Other 20 smaller firms	800	22.2

The four-firm concentration ratio is the percentage of the value of sales accounted for by the four largest firms in the industry, which is 33.3 percent + 16.7 percent + 16.7 percent + 8.3 percent = 75.0 percent. The fast-food hamburger market is an oligopoly.

■ Self Test 15.1

Fill in the blanks

In monopolistic competition there are a _____ (large; small) number of firms producing _____ (identical; differentiated) products. The square of the percentage market share of each firm summed over the 50 largest firms is the _____ (50-firm concentration ratio; Herfindahl-Hirschman Index). A firm in monopolistic competition produces the quantity where marginal revenue _____ (is greater than; equals; is less than) marginal cost. In the long run, a firm in monopolistic competition _____ (can; cannot) earn an economic profit. A firm in monopolistic competition _____ (does not have; has) excess capacity in the long run.

True or false

1. A firm in monopolistic competition faces a downward-sloping demand curve.

2. The larger the four-firm concentration ratio, the more competitive the industry.

3. A firm in monopolistic competition can make an economic profit in the short run.

4. In a broader view of efficiency, monopolistic competition brings gains for consumers.

Multiple choice

1. In monopolistic competition there
   a. are a large number of firms.
   b. are several large firms.
   c. is one large firm.
   d. might be many, several, or one firm.

2. Product differentiation means
   a. making a product that has perfect substitutes.
   b. making a product that is entirely unique.
   c. the inability to set your own price.
   d. making a product that is slightly different from the products of competing firms.

3. If the four-firm concentration ratio for the market for pizza is 28 percent, then this industry is best characterized as
   a. a monopoly.
   b. monopolistic competition.
   c. an oligopoly.
   d. perfect competition.

4. A monopolistically competitive firm maximizes profit by equating
   a. price and marginal revenue.
   b. price and marginal cost.
   c. demand and marginal cost.
   d. marginal revenue and marginal cost.

5. In the long run, a firm in monopolistic competition
   a. earns a normal profit.
   b. produces at minimum average total cost.
   c. has deficient capacity.
   d. None of the above answers is correct.

6. At a firm's capacity output

a. marginal cost is at a minimum.

b. average total cost is at a minimum.

c. profit is maximized.

d. marginal revenue is at a maximum.

Complete the graph

1. Figure 15.1 shows the demand curve and marginal revenue curve for Seaside Pizza, a firm in monopolistic competition. Draw the average total cost curve and marginal cost curve so that Seaside's output is 40 pizzas a day and its economic profit is $160 a day. Is this a short-run or long-run equilibrium?

■ **FIGURE 15.1**
Price and cost (dollars per pizza)

2. Figure 15.2 shows the demand curve and marginal revenue curve for Surf Pizza, a firm in monopolistic competition. Draw the average total cost curve and marginal cost curve so that Surf's output is 20 pizzas a day and its economic profit is $0. Does your figure illustrate a short-run or long-run equilibrium?

Short answer

1. What conditions define monopolistic competition?

2. Industry A has 1 firm with a market share of 57 percent and 43 other firms, each with a market share of 1 percent. Industry B has 4 firms, each with a market share of 15 percent, and 40 other firms, each with a market share of 1 percent.

a. Calculate the four-firm concentration ratio for the two industries.

b. Calculate the Herfindahl-Hirschman Index for the two industries.

3. Why do firms in monopolistic competition earn zero economic profit in the long run?

4. Is monopolistic competition efficient?

■ **FIGURE 15.2**
Price and cost (dollars per pizza)

CHECKPOINT 15.2

■ **Explain why selling costs are high in monopolistic competition.**

Practice Problem 15.2

Bianca bakes delicious cookies. Her total fixed cost is $40 a day, and her average variable cost is $1 a bag. Few people know about Bianca's Cookies, and she is maximizing her profit by selling 10 bags a day for $5 a bag. Bianca thinks that if she spends $50 a day on advertising, she can increase her market and sell 25 bags a day for $5 a bag.

a. If Bianca's belief about the effect of advertising is correct, can she increase her economic profit by advertising?

b. If she advertised, would her average total cost increase or decrease at the quantity produced?

c. If Bianca's belief about the effect of advertising is correct, would she continue to sell her cookies for $5 a bag, or would she raise or lower her price?

Solution to Practice Problem 15.2

The Practice Problem helps you to understand why firms in monopolistic competition advertise.

Quick Review

*   *Selling costs* Selling costs such as advertising expenditures might lower average total cost if they increase the quantity sold by a large enough amount and they might increase demand.

a. If Bianca's belief about the effect of advertising is correct, can she increase her economic profit by advertising?

If Bianca does not advertise she sells 10 bags a day for $5 a bag and her total revenue is $50 a day. Her total fixed cost is $40 a day and her total variable cost is $10 a day, so total cost is $50 a day. Bianca's economic profit is $50 − $50, which is zero.

If Bianca advertises, she sells 25 bags a day for $5 a bag and her total revenue is $125 a day. Her total fixed cost is $90 a day, the sum of her original total fixed cost and advertising cost, and her total variable cost is $25 a day. Total cost is $115 a day. Bianca's economic profit is $125 − $115, which is $10 a day. So Bianca can increase her economic profit by advertising.

b. If she advertised, would her average total cost increase or decrease at the quantity produced?

Average total cost is total cost divided by quantity. Before advertising, average total cost is $50 ÷ 10 bags, which is $5 a bag. After advertising, average total cost is $115 ÷ 25 bags, which is $4.60 a bag. Advertising decreases her average total cost.

c. If Bianca's belief about the effect of advertising is correct, would she continue to sell her cookies for $5 a bag, or would she raise or lower her price?

The price at which Bianca sells her cookies depends on how her demand curve shifts. And when the demand curve shifts, the marginal revenue curve also shifts. Bianca produces the quantity where marginal revenue equals marginal cost and the price is taken from the demand curve. We do not have sufficient information to determine if she would raise or lower her price.

Additional Practice Problem 15.2a

The table gives the cost of producing a pair of Nike running shoes.

a. The cost of producing and shipping a pair of Nikes to Canada is $32. The remaining costs are selling costs. What percentage of the retail price are selling costs?

b. When the shoes reach Canada, selling costs in Canada are the result of activity at Nike Headquarters and local retailers. What proportion of the $110 price are attributable to Nike and what proportion to local retailers?

Cost	Expenditure (dollars)
Asia	
Material	14.25
Capital	4.75
Labour	4.25
Profit	2.75
Shipping	0.75
Import duty	5.25
Nike	
Distribution	8.00
Advertising	6.25
R and D	0.50
Profit	10.00
Local	
Labour	14.75
Shop rent	14.00

Solution to Additional Practice Problem 15.2a

a. What percentage of the retail price are selling costs?

Selling costs account for ($78 ÷ $110) × 100, which is 70.9 percent of the price.

b. What proportion of the $110 price is attributable to Nike and what proportion to local retailers?

Nike accounts for ($24.75 ÷ $110) × 100, which is 22.5 percent of the price and local retailers account for ($53.25 ÷ $110) × 100, which is 48.4 percent of the price.

■ Self Test 15.2

Fill in the blanks

Firms in monopolistic competition _____ (are; are not) continuously developing new products. In monopolistic competition, product improvement _____ (does; does not) equal its efficient level. Advertising costs _____ (are; are not) large in monopolistic competition. Advertising costs are a _____ (fixed; variable) cost and shift the average total cost curve _____ (downward; upward). Monopolistic competition _____ (definitely is; might be; definitely is not) efficient.

True or false

1. Firms in monopolistic competition innovate without regard to cost.

2. Firms in monopolistic competition often undertake extensive advertising.

3. Because advertising increases demand for a firm's product, increasing the amount of advertising shifts the firm's cost curves downward.

4. Whether monopolistic competition is inefficient depends in part on the value people place on product variety.

Multiple choice

1. To enjoy economic profits, firms in monopolistic competition must continuously
   a. shut down.
   b. exit the industry.
   c. innovate and develop new products.
   d. declare bankruptcy.

2. A firm in monopolistic competition that introduces a new and differentiated product will temporarily have a _____ demand for its product and be able to charge a _____ price.
   a. less elastic, lower
   b. less elastic, higher
   c. more elastic, lower
   d. more elastic, higher

3. The decision to innovate
   a. depends on the marketing department's needs.
   b. depends on whether the firm wants to benefit its customers.
   c. is based on the marginal cost and the marginal revenue of innovation.
   d. None of the above answers is correct.

4. Advertising costs and other selling costs are
   a. efficient.
   b. fixed costs.
   c. variable costs.
   d. marginal costs.

5. For a firm in monopolistic competition, selling costs
   a. increase costs and reduce profits.
   b. increase demand and increase profits.
   c. can change the quantity produced and lower the average total cost.
   d. can lower total cost.

6. The efficiency of monopolistic competition
   a. is as clear-cut as the efficiency of perfect competition.
   b. depends on whether the gain from extra product variety offsets the selling costs and the extra cost arising from excess capacity.
   c. comes from its excess capacity.
   d. is eliminated in the long run.

Short answer

1. Why do firms in monopolistic competition engage in innovation and product development?

2. How might advertising lower average total cost?

3. Is advertising and product differentiation efficient?

CHECKPOINT 15.3

■ Explain the dilemma faced by firms in oligopoly.

Practice Problem 15.3

Isolated Island has two natural gas wells, one owned by Tom and the other owned by Jerry. Each well has a valve that controls the rate of flow of gas, and the marginal cost of producing gas is zero. The table gives the demand schedule for gas on this island. What will the price of gas be on Isolated Island if Tom and Jerry

Price (dollars per unit)	Quantity demanded (units per day)
12	0
11	1
10	2
9	3
8	4
7	5
6	6
5	7
4	8
3	9
2	10
1	11
0	12

a. Form a cartel and maximize their joint profit?

b. Are forced to sell at the perfectly competitive price?

c. Compete as duopolists?

Solution to Practice Problem 15.3

This Practice Problem compares the price and output of monopoly, duopoly, and perfect competition.

Quick Review

- *Duopoly* A market in which there are only two firms.

- *Cartel* A group of firms acting together to limit output, raise price, and increase economic profit.

a. What will be the price if Tom and Jerry form a cartel and maximize their joint profit?

Tom and Jerry will charge the monopoly price and produce the monopoly quantity. A monopoly produces the quantity at which marginal revenue equals marginal cost. Marginal cost is zero. Marginal revenue is zero when total revenue is at its maximum. The table shows that total revenue is at a maximum when 6 units a day are produced. And from the demand schedule, the highest price at which 6 units a day can be sold is $6 a unit.

Price (dollars per unit)	Quantity demanded (units per day)	Total revenue (dollars per day)
12	0	0
11	1	11
10	2	20
9	3	27
8	4	32
7	5	35
6	6	36
5	7	35
4	8	32
3	9	27
2	10	20
1	11	11
0	12	0

b. What will be the price if Tom and Jerry are forced to sell at the perfectly competitive price?

In perfect competition, marginal revenue equals price. Firms produce at the point where marginal revenue equals marginal cost. Marginal cost equals zero, so price is also zero.

c. What will be the price if Tom and Jerry compete as duopolists?

When Tom and Jerry compete as duopolists, they will increase production beyond the monopoly output and the price will fall. But they will not increase production to the point where the price falls to zero.

Additional Practice Problem 15.3a

Suppose Tom and Jerry from Practice Problem 15.3 agree to operate as a monopoly. Tom and Jerry agree that each will produce 3 units. There are no fixed costs.

a. What is Tom's profit? Jerry's profit? The combined profit?

b. Suppose Tom decides to cheat on the agreement by producing 4 units. Jerry sticks to the agreement. If 7 units are produced, what is the price? What is Tom's profit? Jerry's profit? The combined profit?

c. Why would Tom consider cheating on the agreement he made with Jerry?

Solution to Additional Practice Problem 15.3a

a. What is Tom's profit? Jerry's profit? The combined profit?

Profit is equal to total revenue. Combined profit is equal to $6 × 6 units a day, which is $36 a day. Tom's profit is $18 a day, and Jerry's profit is also $18 a day.

b. Suppose Tom decides to cheat on the agreement by producing 4 units. Jerry sticks to the agreement. If 7 units are produced, what is the price? What is Tom's profit? Jerry's profit? The combined profit?

If 7 units are produced, the price is $5 a unit. Tom's profit on his 4 units is $20 and Jerry's profit on his 3 units is $15. Combined profit is $35.

c. Why would Tom consider cheating on the agreement he made with Jerry?

Tom considers cheating because cheating increases *his* profit. Tom realizes that when he alone cheats, his profit will be more, $20 versus $18. Jerry's profit falls more than Tom's rises but Tom is concerned only about his own profit.

■ Self Test 15.3

Fill in the blanks

In an oligopoly a ____ (large; small) number of firms compete. A ____ (cartel; duopoly) is a group of firms acting together to limit output, raise price, and increase economic profit. When a duopoly charges the perfectly competitive price, each firm receives _____ (no; positive) economic profit. When a duopoly charges the monopoly price, economic profit is _____ (maximized; minimized).

True or false

1. Oligopoly is a market in which a small number of firms compete.

2. The aim of a cartel is to lower price, increase output, and increase economic profit.

3. In a duopoly, the highest price that the firms might set is the perfectly competitive price.

4. A duopoly is currently making the same economic profit as a monopoly. If one firm increases its output, the economic profit of the other firm will increase.

Multiple choice

1. An oligopoly is a market structure in which
    a. many firms each produce a slightly differentiated product.
    b. one firm produces a unique product.
    c. a small number of firms compete.
    d. many firms produce an identical product.

2. The problem for a firm in an oligopoly is that
    a. there are barriers to entry.
    b. one firm's profits are affected by other firms' actions.
    c. they can produce either identical or differentiated goods.
    d. there are too many of them for any one firm to influence price.

3. Collusion results when a group of firms

a. act separately to limit output, lower prices, and decrease economic profits.

b. act together to limit output, raise the price, and increase economic profit.

c. in Canada legally fix prices.

d. None of the above answers is correct.

4. A market with only two firms is called a

a. duopoly.

b. two-firm monopolistic competition.

c. two-firm monopoly.

d. cartel.

5. Cartel agreements are difficult to maintain because

a. each member firm can increase its own profit by cutting its price and selling more.

b. forming a cartel is legal but frowned upon throughout the world.

c. supply will decrease because of the high cartel price.

d. None of the above answers are correct.

6. The greatest amount of economic profit is earned by a cartel when the cartel produces the

a. monopoly level of output.

b. perfectly competitive level of output.

c. output level that maximizes total revenue.

d. output level that minimizes total cost.

Complete the graph

1. Anytown has two newspapers that have a duopoly in the local market. The table contains information on market demand and marginal revenue for newspapers. Marginal cost of a newspaper is 20 cents.

a. Graph the demand curve, marginal revenue curve, and marginal cost curve in Figure 15.3.

Quantity (thousands of newspapers per day)	Price (cents)	Marginal revenue (cents)
0	60	60
2	50	40
4	40	20
6	30	0
8	20	−20

■ FIGURE 15.3

Cost and price (cents per newspaper)

b. What price and quantity represent the competitive outcome?

c. What price and quantity represent the monopoly outcome?

d. What price and quantity represent the duopoly outcome?

Short answer

1. In oligopoly, one firm's profit-maximizing actions might decrease its competitors' profits. Why is this fact a problem for firms in oligopoly?

2. What is a cartel? Why might a firm have the incentive to cheat on a collusive agreement to limit production and boost prices?

3. From the standpoint of efficiency, is it better to have firms successfully form a cartel or to have the cartel collapse and have the competitive outcome?

CHECKPOINT 15.4

■ **Use game theory to explain how price and quantity are determined in oligopoly.**

Practice Problem 15.4

Bud and Wise are the only two makers of aniseed beer, a new-age product designed to replace root beer. Bud and Wise are trying to figure out how much of this new beer to produce. They each know that if they both limit production to 10,000 litres a day, they will make the maximum attainable joint profit of $200,000 a day—$100,000 a day each. They also know that if either of them produces 20,000 litres a day while the other produces 10,000 a day, economic profit will be $150,000 for the one that produces 20,000 litres and an economic loss of $50,000 for the one that sticks with 10,000 litres. And they also know that if they both increase production to 20,000 litres a day, they will both earn zero economic profit.

a. Construct a payoff matrix for the game that Bud and Wise must play.

b. Find the Nash equilibrium.

c. What is the equilibrium if this game is played repeatedly?

Solution to Practice Problem 15.4

To find the Nash equilibrium of a game, place yourself in the position of the first player. Ask yourself "what if" your opponent takes one action: What will you do? Then ask "what if" the opponent takes the other action: Now what will you do? This analysis allows you to determine the first player's action. Then place yourself in the position of the second player and repeat the "what if" analysis to determine the second player's action.

Quick Review

• *Game theory* The tool that economists use to analyze *strategic behaviour*—behaviour that recognizes mutual interdependence and takes account of the expected behaviour of others.

• *Nash equilibrium* An equilibrium in which each player takes the best possible action given the action of the other player.

a. **Construct a payoff matrix for the game that Bud and Wise must play.**

A payoff matrix is a table that shows payoffs for every possible action by each player given every possible action by the other player. The payoff matrix is above. The number in each square is the economic profit in thousands of dollars.

b. **Find the Nash equilibrium.**

To find Wise's strategy, ask what Wise will do for each of Bud's choices. If Bud produces 10,000 litres (the first column of the payoff matrix), Wise produces 20,000 litres because that gives Wise a larger profit. If Bud produces 20,000 litres (the second column of the payoff matrix), Wise produces 20,000 litres because that gives him a larger profit. Regardless of Bud's action, Wise produces 20,000 litres. Similar reasoning shows that Bud also produces 20,000 litres. So the Nash equilibrium is for each to produce 20,000 litres and earn zero economic profit.

c. **What is the equilibrium if this game is played repeatedly?**

In a repeated game, Bud and Wise produce the monopoly output of 10,000 litres a day each and earn the maximum economic profit. This outcome occurs if they use a tit-for-tat strategy.

Additional Practice Problem 15.4a

Bud and Wise from Practice Problem 15.4 are playing a repeated game and each is using a tit-for-tat strategy. Yesterday, both produced 10,000 litres but today Bud produces an additional 10,000 litres. What takes place today and in the future?

Solution to Additional Practice Problem 15.4a

Today, Bud earns an economic profit of $150,000 and Wise incurs an economic loss of $50,000. But on the second day Wise will produce 20,000 litres. Bud goes back to producing 10,000 litres to induce Wise to produce 10,000 on the third day. So on the second day, Wise earns an economic profit of $150,000 and Bud incurs an economic loss of $50,000. Over the two days, Wise earns an economic profit of $100,000 and Bud earns an economic profit of $100,000. If the two firms had both produced 10,000 litres a day, over two days each would have made an economic profit of $200,000. The tit-for-tat strategy will result in both firms producing 10,000 litres a day in the future and earning monopoly profit.

■ Self Test 15.4

Fill in the blanks

Game theory is the main tool that economists use to analyze _____ (rational; strategic) behaviour. Games feature ____, ____, and ____. The Nash equilibrium is ____ (always; not always) the best possible equilibrium for the players. Game theory shows that duopolists ____ (can; cannot) always reach the best possible equilibrium. In a ____ (repeated; single-play) game, a tit-for-tit strategy can be used. The ____ (larger; smaller) the number of firms, the harder it is for an oligopoly to maintain the monopoly output.

True or false

1. Game theory is used to analyze strategic behaviour.

2. A prisoners' dilemma has no equilibrium.

3. A Nash equilibrium is the best outcome for all players in a prisoners' dilemma game.

4. The monopoly outcome is more likely in a repeated game than in a one-play game.

Multiple choice

1. One of the main tools economists use to analyze strategic behaviour is
   a. the Herfindahl-Hirschman Index.
   b. game theory.
   c. product differentiation.
   d. collusion.

2. Game theory reveals
   a. that the equilibrium might not be the best solution for the parties involved.
   b. that oligopoly firms are interdependent.
   c. that each player looks after his or her own self-interest.
   d. All of the above answers are correct.

3. A Nash equilibrium occurs
   a. when each player acts without considering the actions of the other player.
   b. when each player takes the best possible action given the action of the other player.
   c. only when players use the tit-for-tat strategy.
   d. only when the game is played in Nashville.

4. The prisoners' dilemma game
   a. shows that prisoners are better off if they cooperate.
   b. shows it is easy to cooperate.
   c. has an equilibrium in which both prisoners are made as well off as possible.
   d. All of the above answers are correct.

5. Oligopolists can achieve an economic profit
   a. always in the long run.
   b. if the firms cooperate.
   c. only if demand for their products is inelastic.
   d. only if demand for their products is elastic.

6. When duopoly games are repeated over time and a tit-for-tat strategy is used,

a. the competitive outcome prevails.

b. the monopoly outcome can prevail.

c. both firms begin to make economic losses.

d. one firm goes out of business.

Complete the graph

1. Intel and AMD undertake research and development. If each spends $2 billion, economic profit is zero. If each spends $1 billion, economic profit is $500 million each. If one spends $2 billion and the other spends $1 billion, the one spending $2 billion has a $1,500 million economic profit and the other has a $100 million economic loss.

a. Complete the payoff matrix below.

b. What is the Nash equilibrium of this game?

Intel's strategies

AMD's strategies

Short answer

1. What are strategies in game theory?

2. Why don't the players cooperate in a prisoners' dilemma? In a duopolists' dilemma?

3. How does the number of players in a game affect its outcome?

SELF TEST ANSWERS

■ CHECKPOINT 15.1

Fill in the blanks

In monopolistic competition there are a <u>large</u> number of firms producing <u>differentiated</u> products. The square of the percentage market share of each firm summed over the 50 largest firms is the <u>Herfindahl-Hirschman Index</u>. A firm in monopolistic competition produces the quantity where marginal revenue <u>equals</u> marginal cost. In the long run, a firm in monopolistic competition <u>cannot</u> earn an economic profit. A firm in monopolistic competition <u>has</u> excess capacity in the long run.

True or false

1. True; page 369

2. False; page 370

3. True; page 371

4. True; page 373

Multiple choice

1. a; page 368

2. d; page 368

3. b; page 370

4. d; page 371

5. a; page 372

6. b; page 373

Complete the graph

1. Figure 15.4 shows the average total cost curve and the marginal cost curve so that Seaside Pizza's output is 40 pizzas a day and economic profit is $160 a day. The figure shows a short-run equilibrium because Seaside is earning an economic profit; page 371.

■ FIGURE 15.4

Price and cost (dollars per pizza)

2. Figure 15.5 shows the average total cost curve and the marginal cost curve so that Surf Pizza's output is 20 pizzas a day and economic profit is zero. The figure shows a long-run equilibrium because Surf is earning zero economic profit; page 372.

■ FIGURE 15.5

Price and cost (dollars per pizza)

Short answer

1. Monopolistic competition occurs when a large number of firms compete; each firm produces a differentiated product; the firms compete on product quality, price, and mar-

keting; and firms are free to enter and exit; page 368.

2a. The four-firm concentration ratios are the same for both industries, 60 percent; page 370.

b. The Herfindahl-Hirschman Index is 3,292 for Industry A and 940 for Industry B; page 370.

3. There is no restriction on entry in monopolistic competition, so if firms in an industry are making an economic profit, other firms have an incentive to enter the industry. The entry of new firms decreases the demand for each firm's product. The demand curve and marginal revenue curve shift leftward. When all firms in the industry are earning zero economic profit, there is no incentive for new firms to enter and the industry is in long-run equilibrium; page 372.

4. In monopolistic competition, price exceeds marginal revenue and marginal revenue equals marginal cost, so price exceeds marginal cost—a sign of inefficiency. But this inefficiency arises from product differentiation that consumers value and for which they are willing to pay. So the loss that arises because marginal benefit exceeds marginal cost must be weighed against the gain that arises from greater product variety; page 373.

■ **CHECKPOINT 15.2**
Fill in the blanks

Firms in monopolistic competition <u>are</u> continuously developing new products. In monopolistic competition, product improvement <u>does not</u> equal its efficient level. Advertising costs <u>are</u> large in monopolistic competition. Advertising costs are a <u>fixed</u> cost and shift the average total cost curve <u>upward</u>. Monopolistic competition <u>might be</u> efficient.

True or false

1. False; page 375
2. True; page 376
3. False; page 377

4. True; page 378

Multiple choice

1. c; page 375
2. b; page 375
3. c; page 375
4. b; page 377
5. c; page 377
6. b; page 378

Short answer

1. Firms innovate and develop new products to increase demand for their product and earn an economic profit; page 375.

2. Although advertising increases a firm's costs, it might also increase sales. If the quantity sold increases by a large enough amount, it can lower average total cost because the greater fixed cost is spread over a greater output; page 377.

3. The bottom line on the question of whether advertising and product differentiation are efficient is ambiguous. Advertising and product differentiation provide consumers with variety, which is a benefit. But this benefit needs to be weighed against the costs of advertising and product differentiation as well as the possibility that the actual differences between products may be very small; page 378.

■ **CHECKPOINT 15.3**
Fill in the blanks

In an oligopoly a <u>small</u> number of firms compete. A <u>cartel</u> is a group of firms acting together to limit output, raise price, and increase economic profit. When a duopoly charges the perfectly competitive price, each firm receives <u>no</u> economic profit. When a duopoly charges the monopoly price, economic profit is <u>maximized</u>.

True or false

1. True; page 380

2. False; page 380

3. False; page 382

4. False; page 382

Multiple choice

1. c; page 380

2. b; page 380

3. b; page 380

4. a; page 380

5. a; pages 381-383

6. a; pages 381-383

Complete the graph

1. a. The curves are graphed in Figure 15.6.

   b. The competitive equilibrium is 8,000 newspapers a day and a price of 20¢ a newspaper; page 381.

   c. The monopoly equilibrium is 4,000 newspapers a day and a price of 40¢ a newspaper; page 381.

■ FIGURE 15.6

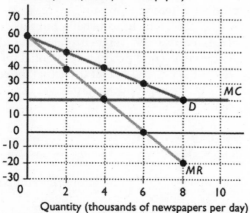

Cost and price (cents per newspaper)

Quantity (thousands of newspapers per day)

   d. The exact price and quantity can't be predicted, but it will be somewhere between the competitive and monopoly outcomes. The price will be between 40¢ and 20¢ a newspaper and the output will be between 4,000 and 8,000 newspapers a day; page 382.

Short answer

1. The point that one firm's actions can decrease another firm's profits is what makes cooperation difficult in an oligopoly. While the firms might be better off cooperating, each firm trying to increase its profit takes actions that lead the profits of its competitors to decrease, so that all the firms wind up worse off; pages 382-383.

2. A cartel is a group of firms acting together to limit output, raise price, and increase economic profit. Every firm has the incentive to cheat on an output-limiting agreement because if it and it alone cheats by boosting its output and cutting its price, its economic profit will increase; pages 380, 383.

3. From the standpoint of efficiency, it is better off to have a cartel collapse and obtain the competitive outcome because the competitive outcome is efficient. If the cartel is successful, the monopoly outcome inflicts a deadweight loss on society; page 381.

■ CHECKPOINT 15.4

Fill in the blanks

Game theory is the main tool that economists use to analyze strategic behaviour. Games feature rules, strategies, and payoffs. The Nash equilibrium is not always the best possible equilibrium for the players. Game theory shows that duopolists cannot always reach the best possible equilibrium. In a repeated game, a tit-for-tit strategy can be used. The larger the number of firms, the harder it is for an oligopoly to maintain the monopoly output.

True or false

1. True; page 385

2. False; page 386

3. False; page 387

4. True; page 388

Multiple choice

1. b; page 385
2. d; page 386
3. b; page 386
4. a; page 387
5. b; page 388
6. b; page 388

Complete the graph

1. a. The completed payoff matrix is below. The payoffs are in millions of dollars; page 386.

Intel's strategies

| | Spend $1 billion | Spend $2 billion |

b. The Nash equilibrium is for both Intel and AMD to spend $2 billion on research and development and each earn zero economic profit; pages 387-388.

Short answer

1. Strategies are all of the possible actions of each player. In the prisoner's dilemma, the two strategies are confess to the bank robbery and deny having committed the bank robbery; page 386.

2. In the prisoners' dilemma game, the players do not cooperate because they do not see cooperation as being in their best interest. Regardless of what the second player does, the first player is better off confessing. Similarly, regardless of what the first player does, the second player is better off confessing. Because it is in each players separate interest to confess rather than cooperate by denying, both players confess. In the duopolists' dilemma game, the players do not cooperate for precisely the same reason they do not cooperate in the prisoners' dilemma game; pages 387-388.

3. The more players in a game, the harder it is to maintain the monopoly outcome; page 388.

Regulation and Competition Law

Chapter 16

Chapter 16 studies government regulation of monopoly and oligopoly and Canada's competition laws. The chapter discusses the Competition Act and looks at some examples of how the Competition Act works.

■ **Explain the effects of regulation of natural monopoly and oligopoly.**

Regulation consists of rules administered by a government agency to influence economic activity by determining prices, product standards and types, and the conditions under which new firms may enter an industry. Two broad economic theories of regulation are public interest theory and capture theory. Public interest theory is the theory that regulation seeks an efficient use of resources. Capture theory is the theory that regulation helps producers to maximize economic profit. A natural monopoly is an industry in which one firm can supply the entire market at a lower price than two or more firms can. A marginal cost pricing rule, which sets price equal to marginal cost achieves an efficient use of resources in a regulated industry. A natural monopoly that is regulated to set price equal to marginal cost incurs an economic loss. A natural monopoly that is regulated with an average cost pricing rule, which sets price equal to average total cost covers its total cost. But the quantity is less than the efficient quantity and a deadweight loss arises. A regulation that sets the price at a level that enables a regulated firm to earn a specified target percent return on its capital is a rate of return regulation. This rate of return is part of the opportunity cost of the natural monopoly and is included in the firm's average total cost. So rate of return regulation is similar to average cost pricing.

■ **Describe Canada's competition law and explain three competition policy debates.**

Competition law is the body of law that regulates and prohibits certain kinds of market behaviour, such as monopoly and monopolistic practices. Canada's competition law dates from the Combines Investigation Act of 1889. Canada's competition law today is defined in the Competition Act of 1986. The Competition Act established a Competition Bureau and a Competition Tribunal. The Competition Act distinguishes between practices that are criminal—conspiracy to fix prices, bid-rigging, other anticompetitive price-fixing actions, and false advertising—and non-criminal—mergers, abuse of a dominant market position, refusal to deal, and other actions designed to limit competition such as exclusive dealing. Price fixing is always a violation of the competition law, but other practices, such as resale price maintenance, tying arrangements, and predatory pricing are more controversial. Resale price maintenance is an agreement between a manufacturer and a distributor on the price at which a product may be resold. A tying arrangement is an agreement to sell one product only if the buyer agrees to buy another, different product. Predatory pricing is setting a low price to drive competitors out of business with the intention of setting a monopoly price when the competition has gone.

EXPANDED CHAPTER CHECKLIST

When you have completed this chapter, you will be able to

1 Explain the effects of regulation of natural monopoly and oligopoly.

- Define regulation and discuss how regulation has changed since the early 1980s.

- Discuss the two economic theories of regulation.

- Explain the marginal cost pricing rule and show that it achieves an efficient output in a regulated industry.

- Explain the average cost pricing rule and show the deadweight loss that it creates.

- Describe how rate of return regulation can lead to managers of a firm exaggerating the firm's costs.

- Discuss regulation of an oligopoly, and describe how an oligopoly is regulated according to the public interest theory and the capture theory.

2 Describe Canada's competition law and explain three competition policy debates.

- Define competition law.

- Discuss the Competition Act of 1986 and distinguish between practices that are criminal and non-criminal.

- Discuss resale price maintenance, tying arrangements, and predatory pricing.

- Give examples to show how the Competition Act works.

KEY TERMS

- Average cost pricing rule (page 399)
- Capture theory (page 397)
- Competition law (page 406)
- Deregulation (page 396)
- Earnings sharing regulation (page 402)
- Marginal cost pricing rule (page 399)
- Predatory pricing (page 408)
- Price cap regulation (page 402)
- Public interest theory (page 397)
- Rate of return regulation (page 400)
- Regulation (page 396)
- Resale price maintenance (page 407)
- Tying arrangement (page 408)

CHECKPOINT 16.1

■ Explain the effects of regulation of natural monopoly and oligopoly.

Practice Problem 16.1

An unregulated natural monopoly bottles Elixir, a unique health product that has no substitutes. The monopoly's total fixed cost is $150,000, and its marginal cost is 10 cents a bottle. The figure illustrates the demand for Elixir.

a. How many bottles of Elixir does the monopoly sell?

b. What is the price of a bottle of Elixir?

c. Is the monopoly's use of resources efficient?

d. How might government regulate the monopoly in the public interest?

e. If the government introduces a marginal cost pricing rule, what will be the price of a bottle of Elixir, the quantity of Elixir sold, and the monopoly's profit?

Solution to Practice Problem 16.1

This Practice Problem will help you to understand how regulation changes price and output in a natural monopoly. Remember that an unregulated monopoly produces the quantity where marginal revenue equals marginal cost and the price is determined by the demand curve.

Quick Review

• *Marginal cost pricing rule* A rule that sets price equal to marginal cost to achieve an efficient output in a regulated industry.

• *Public interest theory* The theory that regulation seeks an efficient use of resources.

An unregulated natural monopoly bottles Elixir, a unique health product that has no substitutes. The monopoly's total fixed cost is $150,000, and its marginal cost is 10 cents a bottle.

a. How many bottles of Elixir does the monopoly sell?

The monopoly produces the quantity at which marginal revenue equals marginal cost. In the figure, marginal revenue equals marginal cost when 1.0 million bottles a year are produced.

b. What is the price of a bottle of Elixir?

The price is 30 cents a bottle. The demand curve shows that 30 cents a bottle is the highest price at which the monopoly can sell the 1 million bottles.

c. Is the monopoly's use of resources efficient?

The monopoly's use of resources is inefficient. When resource use is efficient, the firm produces the quantity at which price equals marginal cost. The efficient quantity is 2 million bottles a year.

d. How might government regulate the monopoly in the public interest?

The government can regulate the monopoly using a marginal cost pricing rule or an average cost pricing rule.

e. If the government introduces a marginal cost pricing rule, what will be the price of a bottle of Elixir, the quantity of Elixir sold, and the monopoly's profit?

If the monopoly is regulated using a marginal cost pricing rule, the price is set equal to marginal cost, which is 10 cents a bottle. When the price is 10 cents a bottle, the quantity demanded is 2.0 million bottles a year. The monopoly covers its total variable cost, but not its total fixed cost. So the monopoly incurs an economic loss of $150,000 a year.

Additional Practice Problem 16.1a

If the monopoly in Practice Problem 16.1 is regulated, which type of regulation would the owner of the monopoly prefer?

Solution to Practice Problem 16.1a

The owner of the monopoly would prefer a rate of return regulation. A rate of return regulation sets the price at a level that enables a regulated firm to earn a specified target percent return on its capital. So with a rate of return regulation, the monopoly does not incur an economic loss. A rate of return regulation, if based on a correct assessment of the producer's average total cost, results in a price that favours the consumer and does not enable the monopoly to maximize profit. But it may be possible for the managers of a firm to exaggerate the firm's cost and earn an economic profit.

■ **Self Test 16.1**

Fill in the blanks

The theory that regulation seeks an efficient use of resources is the _____ (capture; public interest) theory and the theory that regulation helps producers maximize economic profit is the _____ (capture; public interest) theory. Since the early 1980s, the government has _____ (increased; reduced) the amount of regulation in the Canadian economy. With _____ (an average; a marginal) cost pricing rule, a natural monopoly incurs an economic loss. Rate of return regulation makes price _____ (equal to; greater than; less than) average total cost. According to the capture theory, regulation of cartels _____ (maximizes; minimizes) economic profit.

True or false

1. Regulatory rules are administered by the regulated company.

2. Public interest theory assumes that the political process introduces regulation that eliminates deadweight loss.

3. The capture theory predicts that regulations benefit large interest groups.

4. In a regulated industry, firms are free to determine the price they charge but the regulating agency determines the production technology they must use.

5. A regulated natural monopoly produces the efficient quantity of output when it is regulated by a marginal cost pricing rule.

6. Rate of return regulation sets the price at a level that allows the regulated firm to earn a specified target percent return on its capital.

7. With rate of return regulation, the managers of a firm have an incentive to exaggerate the firm's costs.

8. According to public interest theory, oligopoly is regulated to ensure a competitive outcome.

Multiple choice

1. Regulation

a. consists of rules administered by a government agency.

b. is a theory that resources are used efficiently.

c. consists of rules administered by private industry to avoid government interference.

d. is a theory that firms maximize profits if government agencies assist.

2. Deregulation is the process of _____ restrictions on prices, product standards and types, and entry conditions.

a. increasing

b. not changing

c. evaluating

d. removing

3. The theory that regulation seeks an efficient use of resources is the _____ theory.

a. public interest

b. producer surplus

c. consumer surplus

d. capture

4. Which of the following best describes the capture theory of regulation?

a. Regulation seeks an efficient use of resources.

b. Regulation is aimed at keeping prices as low as possible.

c. Regulation helps producers to maximize economic profit.

d. All of the above describe the capture theory.

5. The first regulation in Canada was the

a. Canadian Wheat Act of 1883.

b. War Measures Act of 1914.

c. Railway Act of 1888.

d. Conscription Act of 1917.

6. At a level of output where regulators force a natural monopoly to set a price that is equal to marginal cost, the firm will be

a. earning a normal profit.

b. earning an economic profit.

c. incurring an economic loss.

d. earning a normal profit.

7. If a natural monopoly is told to set price equal to average total cost, then the firm

a. is not able to set marginal revenue equal to marginal cost.

b. automatically also sets price equal to marginal cost.

c. will earn a substantial economic profit.

d. will incur an economic loss.

8. Rate of return regulation is designed to allow a natural monopoly to

a. earn an economic profit.

b. earn a normal profit.

c. underestimate its average total cost.

d. compete with any firm entering the market.

9. When a regulatory agency uses rate of return regulation, the

a. agency is able to eliminate the deadweight loss.

b. regulated firm has no incentive to cut costs.

c. regulated firm's profit must be maximized for the market to be efficient.

d. the regulated firm must receive a government subsidy.

10. According to the capture theory, regulation serves the interest of the

a. consumer.

b. government.

c. producer.

d. government and the producer.

11. Under a rate of return regulation, the managers of a firm try to make their apparent costs _____ the true costs.

a. equal

b. exceed

c. less than

d. less than or equal to

12. A price cap regulation is

a. a price floor.

b. a price ceiling.

c. a regulation that gives a firm an incentive to operate inefficiently.

d. also called an earnings sharing regulation.

Complete the graph

1. Figure 16.1 shows both the actual and exaggerated average total cost curves of a cable TV company that is a regulated monopoly. Also given are the demand curve, marginal revenue curve, and marginal cost curve.

■ **FIGURE 16.1**

Answer questions (a) through (c) based on the assumption that regulators know the true costs of production.

a. What price would the regulator set using the marginal cost pricing rule?

b. What price would the regulator set using the average cost pricing rule?

c. What price would the firm set if it was unregulated?

d. Now assume that the monopoly successfully
exaggerates its cost of production. What
price would the regulator set using the average cost pricing rule?

2. A small town has only five restaurants. Figure 16.2 shows the demand curve, marginal
revenue curve, marginal cost curve, and average total cost curve for the restaurant market in this town.

a. What are the competitive price and quantity?

b. What price and quantity would result if the
firms colluded and acted like a monopoly?

c. Suppose the restaurants are regulated. What
price and quantity would prevail under
the public interest theory?

d. If the restaurants are regulated, what price
and quantity would prevail under the capture theory?

■ FIGURE 16.2

Price and cost (dollars per meal)

Short answer

1. Why doesn't the government regulate all
industries?

2. What is the public interest theory of regulation? The capture theory?

3. What is the advantage of using a marginal
cost pricing rule to regulate a natural monopoly? The disadvantage?

4. What is rate of return regulation? Does it
attempt to set the regulated firm's price
equal to its marginal cost or its average total
cost? If a firm regulated using rate of return
regulation exaggerates its costs, what occurs?

CHECKPOINT 16.2

■ **Describe Canada's competition law and
explain three competition policy debates.**

Practice Problems 16.2

1. The Competition Bureau allowed the
merger of the Toronto-Dominion Bank and
Canada Trust in 2000 only if the banks
agreed to sell their branches in three local
markets (Kitchener, Port Hope, and Brantford, Ontario). Why did the Competition
Bureau require these branches to be sold
and not others?

2. The Competition Bureau examines any
merger in which the merged company has a
share of the Canadian market that exceeds
35 percent. The Competition Bureau is reviewing the proposed mergers of two drugstore chains that will give the merged company 39 percent of the Canadian market and
of two furniture manufacturers that will
give the merged company 50 percent of the
Canadian market.

Explain why the Competition Bureau would
be more concerned about the merger of the
drugstore chains than the merger of the furniture firms.

Solution to Practice Problems 16.2

These Practice Problems will help you to understand many of the issues surrounding mergers.

Quick Review

- *Competition law* The body of law that regulates and prohibits certain kinds of market behaviour, such as monopoly and monopolistic practices.

1. **The Competition Bureau allowed the merger of the Toronto-Dominion Bank and Canada Trust in 2000 only if the banks agreed to sell their branches in three local markets (Kitchener, Port Hope, and Brantford, Ontario). Why did the Competition Bureau require these branches to be sold and not others?**

The merger between Toronto-Dominion Bank and Canada Trust reduced competition significantly in Kitchener, Port Hope, and Brantford, Ontario. In all other market areas, consumers had an adequate choice even after the merger.

2. **The Competition Bureau examines any merger in which the merged company has a share of the Canadian market that exceeds 35 percent. The Competition Bureau is reviewing the proposed mergers of two drugstore chains that will give the merged company 39 percent of the Canadian market and of two furniture manufacturers that will give the merged company 50 percent of the Canadian market.**

   Explain why the Competition Bureau would be more concerned about the merger of the drugstore chains than the merger of the furniture firms.

The market share of the merged furniture manufacturers, which is 50 percent of the Canadian market would be larger than the market share of the merged drugstore chains, which is 39 percent of the Canadian market. But foreign furniture manufacturers would still compete with Canadian producers. It is less likely that drugstores compete with foreign producers, so the merger of the drugstores would decrease competition in the Canadian drugstore market.

Additional Practice Problem 16.2a

Is resale price maintenance efficient or inefficient?

Solution to Additional Practice Problem 16.2a

Resale price maintenance is inefficient if it enables dealers to operate a cartel and charge the monopoly price. Resale price maintenance might be efficient if it enables a manufacturer to induce dealers to provide the efficient standards of service in selling a product.

■ Self Test 16.2

Fill in the blanks

Canada's competition law dates from the _____ (Combines Investigation Act; Competition Act). Under the Competition Act conspiracy to fix prices and false advertising are _____ (criminal; non-criminal) offences and abuse of a dominant market position and refusal to deal are _____ (criminal; non-criminal) offences. Price fixing is _____ (always; sometimes) a violation of the competition law. An agreement to sell one product only if the buyer agrees to buy another, different product is _____ (an efficient; a tying) arrangement. In recent years, Air Canada has been accused of practicing _____ (predatory pricing; resale price maintenance) against smaller regional airlines.

True or false

1. Canada's competition law dates from the Competition Act of 1889.

2. The Competition Act distinguishes between practices that are criminal and non-criminal.

3. Resale price maintenance is also called horizontal price-fixing.

4. A tying arrangement occurs when two firms agree to sell a similar good at a similar price.

5. Economists believe that predatory pricing occurs regularly.

6. Following the merger of Air Canada with Canadian Airlines in April 2000, the Competition Bureau agreed to allow Air Canada to undercut the fares of small regional airlines.

7. It is not possible to recognize price-fixing practices that are international in scope.

8. The federal government has the final power to approve or reject bank mergers in Canada.

Multiple choice

1. Canada's competition law today is defined in the
   a. Tribunal Act of 1967.
   b. Competition Act of 1986.
   c. Combines Investigation Act of 1889.
   d. Canadian Charter.

2. Which of the following are criminal offences under the Competition Act?
   a. false advertising
   b. abuse of a dominant market position
   c. refusal to deal
   d. All of the above answers are correct.

3. Canada's competition law dates from
   a. 1867.
   b. 1889.
   c. 1967.
   d. 1986.

4. Which of the following are non-criminal offences under the Competition Act?
   a. abuse of a dominant market position
   b. exclusive dealing
   c. refusal to deal
   d. All of the above answers are correct.

5. The Competition Bureau and the Competition Tribunal were established by the
   a. Department of Finance.
   b. Combines Investigation Act.
   c. Competition Act.
   d. British North American Act.

6. Resale price maintenance
   a. agreements are legal under the Competition Act.
   b. agreements are agreements to sell one product only if the buyer agrees to buy another, different product at a specified price.
   c. always create an efficient use of resources.
   d. occurs when a manufacturer agrees with a distributor on the price at which the product will be resold.

7. Economists are sceptical that predatory pricing occurs because
   a. a firm that cuts its price below the profit-maximizing level loses during the low-price period
   b. even if the firm succeeds in driving its competitors out of business, new competitors will enter as soon as the price is increased.
   c. any potential gain from a monopoly position is temporary.
   d. All of the above answers are correct.

8. When NutraSweet tried to gain a monopoly, the Competition Tribunal ruled its action unduly limited competition. As a result, there was _____ in competition and a _____ in the price of aspartame in Canada.
   a. an increase; rise
   b. an increase; fall
   c. a decrease; rise
   d. a decrease; fall

9. Since Air Canada merged with Canadian airlines, the Competition Bureau has asked the Competition Tribunal to issue orders

a. prohibiting Air Canada from competing in regional markets.

b. prohibiting Air Canada from undercutting the fares of small regional airlines.

c. that allow Air Canada to compete in regional markets.

d. that allow Air Canada to purchase other small regional airlines.

10. Price-fixing practices

a. are a non-criminal offence under the Competition Act.

b. are the main reason why bank mergers in Canada in 1998 were disallowed.

c. do not cross international borders.

d. are international in scope.

11. In 1998, the federal government _____ allow the merger between the Royal Bank and Bank of Montreal and _____ allow the merger between the Canadian Imperial Bank of Commerce and the Toronto-Dominion Bank.

a. did not; did not

b. did not; did

c. did; did not

d. did; did

12. In Canada, the _____ has the final power to approve or reject bank mergers.

a. Bank of Canada

b. Competition Bureau

c. federal government

d. Competition Tribunal

Short answer

1. What is competition law?

2. The Competition Act distinguishes between two practices. Identify and describe each practice.

3. Give two examples of price-fixing practices that are international in scope.

4. Why are economists sceptical that predatory pricing occurs?

5. What did the Competition Bureau conclude about the planned merger between the Royal Bank and the Bank of Montreal and between the Canadian Imperial Bank of Commerce and the Toronto-Dominion Bank in 1998?

SELF TEST ANSWERS

■ CHECKPOINT 16.1

Fill in the blanks

The theory that regulation seeks an efficient use of resources is the public interest theory and the theory that regulation helps producers maximize economic profit is the capture theory. Since the early 1980s, the government has reduced the amount of regulation in the Canadian economy. With a marginal cost pricing rule, a natural monopoly incurs an economic loss. Rate of return regulation makes price equal to average total cost. According to the capture theory, regulation of cartels maximizes economic profit.

True or false

1. False; page 396
2. True; page 397
3. False; page 397
4. False; page 397
5. True; page 399
6. True; page 400
7. True; page 401
8. True; page 403

Multiple choice

1. a; page 396
2. d; page 396
3. a; page 397
4. c; page 397
5. c; page 396
6. c; page 399
7. a; page 399
8. b; page 400
9. b; page 400
10. c; page 397
11. b; page 401

12. b; page 402

Complete the graph

1a. Using marginal cost pricing, the regulator will set a price of $10 a month; page 399.
b. Using average cost pricing, the regulator will set a price of $20 a month; page 399.
c. The firm sets the profit-maximizing price of $30 a month; page 398.
d. If the firm successfully exaggerates its costs, the regulator will set a price of $30 a month; page 401.
2a. The competitive price is $8 a meal and the competitive quantity is 300 meals a day; page 403.
b. The monopoly price is $12 a meal and the quantity is 200 meals a day; page 403.
c. The price is $8 a meal and the quantity is 300 meals a day, the same as the competitive outcome; page 403.
d. The price is $12 a meal and the quantity is 200 meals a day, the same as the monopoly outcome; page 403.

Short answer

1. The government does not regulate all industries because not all industries need to be regulated. Competitive industries do not need regulation because competition produces an efficient outcome. But a natural monopoly is not a competitive industry and so government regulation might help move the monopoly towards efficiency; pages 396, 398.

2. The public interest theory of regulation is the theory that regulation seeks an efficient use of resources. The capture theory of regulation is the theory that regulation helps producers to maximize economic profit; page 397.

3. The advantage of using a marginal cost pricing rule is that the firm produces the efficient

quantity of output. The disadvantage is that the firm incurs an economic loss; page 399.

4. Rate of return regulation is a regulation that sets the price at a level that enables a regulated firm to earn a specified target percent return on its capital. The target rate of return is determined with reference to what is normal in competitive industries. This rate of return is part of the opportunity cost of the natural monopoly and is included in the firm's average total cost. So rate of return regulation attempts to set the price equal to average total cost. If the firm successfully exaggerates its costs, the regulators allow the firm to increase the price it charges so that it can cover all of its now higher, exaggerated costs; pages 400-401.

■ CHECKPOINT 16.2

Fill in the blanks

Canada's competition law dates from the Combines Investigation Act. Under the Competition Act, conspiracy to fix prices and false advertising are criminal offences and abuse of a dominant market position and refusal to deal are non-criminal offences. Price fixing is always a violation of the competition law. An agreement to sell one product only if the buyer agrees to buy another, different product is a tying arrangement. In recent years, Air Canada has been accused of practicing predatory pricing against smaller regional airlines.

True or false

1. False; page 406

2. True; page 407

3. False; page 407

4. False; page 408

5. False; page 409

6. False; page 409

7. False; page 410

8. True; page 410

Multiple choice

1. b; page 406

2. a; page 407

3. b; page 406

4. d; page 407

5. c; page 406

6. d; page 407

7. d; page 408

8. b; page 409

9. b; page 409

10. d; page 410

11. a; page 410

12. c; page 410

Short answer

1. Competition law is the body of law that regulates and prohibits certain kinds of market behaviour, such as monopoly and monopolistic practices; page 406.

2. The Competition Act distinguishes between practices that are criminal and non-criminal. Conspiracy to fix prices, bid-rigging, other anti-competitive price-fixing actions, and false advertising are criminal offences. Mergers, abuse of a dominant market position, refusal to deal, and other actions designed to limit competition such as exclusive dealing are non-criminal offences; page 407.

3. Producers based in Japan, the Untied States, and Canada were charged with conspiracy to raise prices for thermal fax paper. In 1996, the New Oji Paper Company pleaded guilty to one charge of conspiracy to set prices. This prosecution was the first of a Japan-based manufacturer for a price fixing in Canada.

   And in 1999, three European and two Japanese pharmaceutical companies were fined a total of $88.5 million for fixing the prices of various vitamins; page 410.

4. A firm that cuts its price below the profit-maximizing level loses during the low-price period. Even if it succeeds in driving its

competitors out of business, new competitors
will enter as soon as the price is increased. So
any potential gain from a monopoly position
is temporary. No case of predatory pricing
has been definitively found; page 408.

5. The Competition Bureau reviewed the
merger plans of the Royal Bank and the Bank
of Montreal and the merger plans of the Canadian Imperial Bank of Commerce and the
Toronto-Dominion Bank and found that they
would likely lead to a substantial lessening
of competition in some banking services;
page 410.

Demand and Supply in Factor Markets

Chapter 17

CHAPTER IN PERSPECTIVE

This chapter studies demand, supply, and equilibrium in factor markets.

■ **Describe the anatomy of the markets for labour, capital, and land.**

The four factors of production are labour, capital, land, and entrepreneurship. The wage rate is the price of labour, the interest rate is the price of capital, and rent is the price of land. A labour market is a collection of people and firms who are trading labour services. A capital market is a collection of people and firms who are lending and borrowing to finance the purchase of physical capital. A commodity market is a market in which raw materials are traded.

■ **Explain how the value of marginal product determines the demand for a factor of production.**

The demand for a factor of production is derived from the demand for the goods and services it is used to produce. The value of marginal product is the value to a firm of hiring one more unit of a factor of production. To maximize profit, a firm hires labour up to the point at which the value of marginal product equals the wage rate. A firm's demand for labour curve is also its value of marginal product curve. The demand for labour depends on the price of the firm's output, the prices of other factors of production, and technology.

■ **Explain how wage rates and employment are determined.**

An individual's labour supply curve can be backward bending at higher wage rates so that an increase in the wage rate decreases the quantity of labour supplied. The key factors that change the supply of labour are the adult population, preferences, and time in school and training. The labour market equilibrium determines the wage rate and employment.

■ **Explain how interest rates, borrowing, and lending are determined.**

Other things remaining the same, the higher the interest rate, the smaller is the quantity of capital demanded. The quantity of financial capital supplied results from people's saving decisions. Other things remaining the same, the higher the interest rate, the greater is the quantity of saving supplied. Capital market equilibrium occurs at the interest rate where the quantity of capital demanded equals the quantity of capital supplied.

■ **Explain how rents and natural resource prices are determined.**

Natural resources are either renewable or nonrenewable. The quantity of land is fixed, so the supply of each particular block of land is perfectly inelastic. Economic rent is the income received by *any* factor of production over and above the amount required to induce a given quantity of the factor to be supplied. The known quantity of a nonrenewable resource increases over time because advances in technology enable ever less accessible sources of the resource to be discovered.

EXPANDED CHAPTER CHECKLIST

When you have completed this chapter, you will be able to

1 Describe the anatomy of the markets for labour, capital, and land.

- Identify the four factors of production.
- Describe labour markets, capital markets, and land markets.

2 Explain how the value of marginal product determines the demand for a factor of production.

- Explain why the demand for a factor of production is a derived demand.
- Calculate the value of marginal product.
- Explain how a firm decides the number of workers to hire.
- Explain the relationship between the value of marginal product curve and the demand for labour curve.
- State the factors that change the demand for labour.

3 Explain how wage rates and employment are determined.

- Describe an individual's labour supply curve.
- List the key factors that change the supply of labour.
- Illustrate labour market equilibrium.

4 Explain how interest rates, borrowing, and lending are determined.

- Explain the relationship between the interest rate and the quantity of capital demanded.
- Discuss the two main factors that change the demand for capital.

- Explain the relationship between the interest rate and the quantity of saving supplied.
- Discuss the main influences on the supply of saving.
- Use a graph to find the equilibrium interest rate and quantity of financial capital.

5 Explain how rents and natural resource prices are determined.

- Define the two categories of natural resources and give examples of each.
- Illustrate the market for land.
- Define economic rent and illustrate the components of a factor's income.

KEY TERMS

- Bond (page 419)
- Bond market (page 419)
- Capital market (page 419)
- Commodity market (page 420)
- Derived demand (page 421)
- Economic rent (page 436)
- Factor price (page 418)
- Financial capital (page 419)
- Job (page 418)
- Labour market (page 418)
- Nonrenewable natural resources (page 435)
- Renewable natural resources (page 435)
- Stock market (page 419)
- Value of marginal product (page 421)

CHECKPOINT 17.1

■ **Describe the anatomy of the markets for labour, capital, and land.**

Practice Problem 17.1

To stage the 2004 Olympic Games, the Athens Organizing Committee
a. Borrowed money and sold sponsorships.
b. Built an Olympic Village and other venues.
c. Hired and trained several thousand volunteers and security guards.
d. Sold more than 7 million tickets.
e. Built environmentally friendly water and waste-recycling plants in the Olympic facilities.
f. Set up an Internet site to receive 1 million hits a day.

Which of these items are not factors of production? Divide those that are factors of production into land, labour, physical capital, human capital, financial capital, and entrepreneurship.

Solution to Practice Problem 17.1

To answer this Practice Problem, you need to know the definitions of the four factors of production.

Quick Review

• *Factors of production* The four factors of production are labour, capital, land, and entrepreneurship.

To stage the 2004 Olympic Games, the Athens Organizing Committee

a. Borrowed money and sold sponsorships.

Borrowing money and selling sponsorships is acquiring financial capital.

b. Built an Olympic Village and other venues.

The Olympic Village and other venues are physical capital.

c. Hired and trained several thousand volunteers and security guards.

The volunteers and guards are labour and the skill they acquire is human capital.

d. Sold more than 7 million tickets.

The tickets sold are not a factor of production.

e. Built environmentally friendly water and waste-recycling plants in the Olympic facilities.

Water and waste-recycling plants are physical capital.

f. Set up an Internet site to receive 1 million hits a day.

The Internet site exists on a server and so it, as well as the server, is physical capital.

In addition, the Athens Organizing Committee is entrepreneurship.

Additional Practice Problem 17.1a

What is the difference between a stock and a bond?

Solution to Additional Practice Problem 17.1a

A share in the stock of a company is an entitlement to a share in the profits of the company. A bond is a promise to pay specified sums of money on specified dates.

■ **Self Test 17.1**

Fill in the blanks

The factors of production are ____, ____, ____, and ____. The funds that firms use to buy and operate physical capital are ____ (financial; stock) capital. The market in which raw materials are traded is the ____ (capital; commodity; labour) market.

True or false

1. The amount that an entrepreneur is paid is determined in a factor market.
2. Stocks and bonds are traded in a stock market.

3. As a factor of production, coal is considered to be land.

Multiple choice

1. The four factors of production that produce goods and services are
a. labour, capital, profits, and land.
b. money, labour, rent, and profit.
c. labour, capital, land, and entrepreneurship.
d. wages, interest, rent, and profit.

2. Individuals that create firms and hire labour, capital, and land in factor markets are called
a. politicians.
b. bureaucrats.
c. exploiters.
d. entrepreneurs.

3. The wage rate paid to labour is
a. a factor output.
b. a factor price.
c. a factor input.
d. an input of the workforce.

4. _____ capital consists of the funds that firms use to buy and operate capital.
a. Human
b. Physical
c. Financial
d. Logistical

5. Which of the following would be traded in the commodity market?
a. 1,200 shares of Coca-Cola stock
b. bonds issued by Cisco
c. interest-bearing securities of the federal government
d. petroleum

Short answer

1. For what are factors of production used?

2. What is the difference between capital and financial capital?

3. Trees are categorized as what type of factor of production?

CHECKPOINT 17.2

■ **Explain how the value of marginal product determines the demand for a factor of production.**

Practice Problem 17.2

Kaiser's Ice Cream Parlour hires workers to produce smoothies. The market for smoothies is perfectly competitive, and smoothies sell for $4 each. The labour market is competitive, and the wage rate is $40 a day. The table shows the workers' total product, *TP*.

Workers	Smoothies per day
1	7
2	21
3	33
4	43
5	51
6	55

a. Calculate the marginal product of hiring the fourth worker.

b. Calculate the value of marginal product of the fourth worker.

c. How many workers will Kaiser's hire to maximize its profit?

d. How many smoothies a day will Kaiser's produce to maximize its profit?

e. If the price of a smoothie rises to $5, how many workers will Kaiser's hire?

f. Kaiser's installs a new soda fountain that increases the productivity of workers by 50 percent. If the price remains at $4 a smoothie and the wage rate rises to $48 a day, how many workers does Kaiser's now hire?

Solution to Practice Problem 17.2

To answer this Practice Problem, remember that to maximize profit, a firm hires labour up to the point at which the value of marginal product equals the wage rate.

Quick Review

- *Value of marginal product* The value to a firm of hiring one more unit of a factor of production, which equals price of a unit of output multiplied by the marginal product of the factor of production.

a. **Calculate the marginal product of hiring the fourth worker.**

The marginal product of hiring the fourth worker equals the total product of hiring four workers, which is 43 smoothies minus the total product of hiring three workers, which is 33 smoothies. So the marginal product of hiring the fourth worker is 10 smoothies.

b. **Calculate the value of marginal product of the fourth worker.**

To calculate the value of marginal product of the fourth worker, multiply the marginal product of the fourth worker by the price of a smoothie. The value of the marginal product of the fourth worker is 10 smoothies a day × $4, which is $40 a day.

c. **How many workers will Kaiser's hire to maximize its profit?**

To maximize its profit, Kaiser hires up to the point at which the value of marginal product equals the wage rate. The wage rate is $40 a day and the answer to part **b** shows that the value of marginal product of the fourth worker is also $40 a day. So Kaiser's hires 4 workers.

d. **How many smoothies a day will Kaiser's produce to maximize its profit?**

To maximize its profit, Kaiser's hires 4 workers and the 4 workers produce 43 smoothies a day. So when Kaiser's produces 43 smoothies a day it maximizes its profit.

e. **If the price of a smoothie rises to $5, how many workers will Kaiser's hire?**

The increase in the price of a smoothie increases the value of marginal product. The value of marginal product of the fourth worker is now 10 smoothies a day × $5, which is $50 a day. And

the value of marginal product of the fifth worker is 8 smoothies a day × $5.00, which is $40 a day. To maximize its profit, Kaiser hires up to the point at which the value of marginal product equals the wage rate. The wage rate is $40 a day, so when the price of a smoothie increases to $5, Kaiser's hires 5 workers.

f. **Kaiser's installs a new soda fountain that increases the productivity of workers by 50 percent. If the price remains at $4 a smoothie and the wage rate rises to $48 a day, how many workers does Kaiser's now hire?**

A worker's marginal product is now 50 percent higher than before. The marginal product of the 5th worker increases from 8 smoothies a day to 12 smoothies a day. The value of marginal product of the fifth worker is 12 smoothies a day × $4, which is $48 a day. To maximize its profit, Kaiser hires up to the point at which the value of marginal product equals the wage rate. The wage rate is $48 a day, so when the productivity of workers increases by 50 percent, Kaiser's hires 5 workers.

Additional Practice Problem 17.2a

In Practice Problem 17.2, what is Kaiser's total revenue if it hires 3 workers,? What is Kaiser's total revenue if it hires 4 workers? If Kaiser's hires a fourth worker, what is the change in Kaiser's total revenue? How does the increase in Kaiser's total revenue compare to the value of marginal product?

Solution to Additional Practice Problem 17.2a

When Kaiser's hires 3 workers, Kaiser's produces 33 smoothies a day. Total revenue is 33 smoothies a day × $4, which is $132 a day. When Kaiser's hires 4 workers, Kaiser's produces 43 smoothies a day. Total revenue is 43 smoothies a day × $4, which is $172 a day. Kaiser's total revenue increases by $40 when Kaiser hires the fourth worker. The change in Kaiser's total revenue equals the value of marginal product of the fourth worker.

■ Self Test 17.2

Fill in the blanks

The value of marginal product equals the marginal product of the factor of production times the ____ (factor's price; price of a unit of output). The quantity of labour demanded by a firm is the quantity at which the value of the marginal product of labour equals the ____ (wage rate; price of a unit of output). When the price of the firm's output increases, the demand for labour ____ (decreases; increases).

True or false

1. The demand for labour is derived from the demand for the goods and services that the labour is hired to produce.

2. A firm's demand for labour curve is also its value of marginal product curve.

3. A rise in the wage rate decreases the quantity of labour demanded.

Multiple choice

1. The demand for a factor of production is derived from the

   a. supply of the factors.

   b. price of the factors.

   c. supply of the good the factor is used to produce.

   d. demand for the goods and services the factor is used to produce.

2. Which of the following is true?

   a. The value to a firm of hiring another worker is the worker's value of marginal product.

   b. A firm hires more workers if the wage rate is greater than the value of marginal product.

   c. The value of marginal product is the cost of hiring a worker.

   d. The value of marginal product increases as more workers are hired.

3. The value of the marginal product of labour is equal to the marginal product of the factor ____ the price of a unit of output.

   a. divided by

   b. multiplied by

   c. minus

   d. plus

4. The rule for maximizing profit is to hire labour up to the point at which the value of marginal product ____ the wage rate.

   a. equals

   b. is greater than

   c. is less than

   d. is a mirror image of

5. An increase in the price of a firm's output leads to a ____ the demand for labour curve.

   a. movement up along

   b. movement down along

   c. rightward shift of

   d. leftward shift of

Complete the graph

1. Gene's Lawn Service hires workers to mow lawns. The market for mowing lawns is perfectly competitive and Gene charges $25 a lawn. The table shows the workers' marginal product schedule.

Quantity of labour (workers)	Marginal product (lawns per worker)	Value of marginal product 1 (dollars per day)	Value of marginal product 2 (dollars per day)
1	13	____	____
2	12	____	____
3	11	____	____
4	10	____	____
5	9	____	____

   a. Calculate the value of marginal product for each quantity of workers and record your answers in the "Value of marginal product 1" column. In Figure 17.1, plot Gene's demand for labour curve and label it LD_1.

b. Suppose the price of mowing a lawn rises to $30 a lawn. Calculate the new value of marginal product and record your answers in the "Value of the marginal product 2" column. In Figure 17.1, plot Gene's new demand for labour curve and label it LD_2. How did the increase in the price of mowing a lawn change Gene's demand for labour curve?

■ FIGURE 17.1

Wage rate (dollars per day)

Short answer

1. Why does the value of marginal product decrease as more workers are employed?

2. What is the relationship between the demand for labour curve and the value of marginal product curve?

3. What factors change the demand for labour and shift the demand for labour curve?

CHECKPOINT 17.3

■ Explain how wage rates and employment are determined.

Practice Problem 17.3

Fast-food outlets in Greenville hire both teenagers and retirees. In Greenville, the following events occur one at a time and other things re-

main the same. Explain the influence of each event on the market for fast-food workers.

a. A new theme park opens and hires teenagers to sell tickets for its rides.

b. The new theme park becomes the hottest tourist attraction in the province.

c. Retirees from around the province flock to Greenville and make it their home.

d. The demand for hamburgers and fries decreases and as a result the price of a hamburger and fries decreases.

e. New technology in the fast-food industry decreases the marginal product of fast-food workers.

Solution to Practice Problem 17.3

To answer this Practice Problem use a labour demand–labour supply graph to determine the effect of each influence on the equilibrium wage rate and the level of employment.

Quick Review

- *Changes in the demand for labour* The demand for labour depends on the price of the firm's output, the prices of other factors of production, and technology.

- *Change in the supply of labour* The key factors that change the supply of labour are the adult population, preferences, and time in school and training.

a. **A new theme park opens and hires teenagers to sell tickets for its rides.**

Some teenage workers prefer to work in the theme park, so the supply of fast-food labour decreases. In the figure, which shows the market for fast-food workers, the supply of labour curve shifts leftward from LS_0 to LS_1. The wage rate rises and the number of fast-food workers employed decreases.

b. **The new theme park becomes the hottest tourist attraction in the province.**

As the number of tourists increases, the demand for fast food increases and the demand for fast-food workers increases. In the figure, the demand for labour curve shifts rightward from LD_0 to LD_1. The wage rate rises and the number of fast-food workers employed increases.

c. **Retirees from around the province flock to Greenville and make it their home.**

The influx of retirees increases the supply of labour. In the figure, the supply of labour curve shifts rightward from LS_0 to LS_1. The wage rate falls and the number of fast-food workers employed increases.

d. **The demand for hamburgers and fries decreases and as a result the price of a hamburger and fries decreases.**

A decrease in the price of a hamburger and fries decreases the value of marginal product of labour. The demand for labour decreases, and the demand for labour curve shifts leftward from LD_0 to LD_1. The wage rate falls and the number of fast-food workers employed decreases.

e. **New technology in the fast-food industry decreases the marginal product of fast-food workers.**

A decrease in the marginal product of fast-food workers decreases the value of marginal product of labour. The demand for labour decreases. In the figure that answers part **d** the demand for labour curve shifts leftward from LD_0 to LD_1. The wage rate falls and the number of fast-food workers employed decreases.

Additional Practice Problem 17.3a

Why does an individual's labour supply curve bend backward?

Solution to Additional Practice Problem 17.3a

To see how the wage rate influences the quantity of labour supplied, think about Emma's labour supply decision. Emma enjoys leisure time, but if her boss offers her $12 an hour, Emma chooses to work 30 hours a week. This wage rate is high enough to make Emma regard this use of her time as the best available to her. If Emma were offered a lower wage rate, she would not be willing to give up so much leisure. If Emma were offered a higher wage rate, she would want to work even longer hours, but only up to a point. If Emma is offered $25 an hour, she would be willing to work a 40-hour week. But if the wage rate is increased above $25 an hour, Emma would cut back on her work hours and take more leisure. Emma's labour supply curve eventually bends backward.

■ Self Test 17.3

Fill in the blanks

An individual's ____ (demand; supply) of labour curve bends backward. An increase in the adult population ____ (decreases; increases) the supply of labour. If the wage rate exceeds the equilibrium wage rate, the quantity of labour supplied is ____ (greater; less) than the quantity of labour demanded.

True or false

1. An individual's supply of labour curve shows that the quantity of labour supplied always increases when the wage rate rises.

2. An increase in college enrolment decreases the supply of low-skilled labour.

3. If the wage rate is less than the equilibrium wage rate, the wage rate will rise to eliminate the surplus of labour.

Multiple choice

1. An individual's labour supply curve eventually bends backward because at a high enough wage rate,
a. people are willing to work more hours.
b. employers are willing to hire more workers.
c. people desire more leisure time.
d. very few workers are hired.

2. How does an increase in the adult population change the market supply of labour?
a. It will become more inelastic.
b. The supply of labour decreases.
c. The supply of labour increases.
d. None of the above answers is correct.

3. The supply of labour curve shifts leftward if
a. the population increases.
b. the demand for labour curve shifts leftward.
c. the supply of labour increases.
d. None of the above answers is correct.

4. If the wage rate is above the equilibrium wage rate, the quantity of labour demanded is ____ the quantity of labour supplied.
a. greater than
b. less than
c. equal to
d. the negative of

5. The more people who remain in school for full-time education and training, the _____ is the _____ low-skilled labour.
a. smaller; demand for
b. smaller; supply of
c. larger; supply of
d. larger; demand for

Complete the graph

1. Figure 17.2 shows Hank's supply of labour curve. At what wage rate does an increase in the wage rate decrease the quantity of labour Hank supplies?

■ **FIGURE 17.2**

2. Figure 17.3 shows the labour market for webmasters. Suppose that more companies start conducting more business on the Internet. In Figure 17.3, illustrate the effect in the market for webmasters. What happens to the equilibrium wage rate and number of webmasters?

■ **FIGURE 17.3**

Wage rate (dollars per hour)

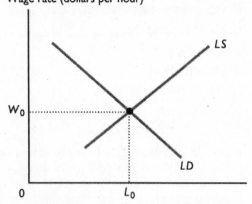

Quantity of labour (number of webmasters)

Short answer

1. How does an increase in the adult population change the supply of labour?

2. If more people decide to obtain an advanced education, after they graduate what is the effect on the supply of high-skilled labour? What is the effect on the equilibrium wage rate for high-skilled workers?

CHECKPOINT 17.4

■ **Explain how interest rates, borrowing, and lending are determined.**

Practice Problem 17.4

Wendy plans to open a Starbucks coffee shop. To do so, she will need $50,000 to buy the franchise and $20,000 to outfit the coffee shop. Wendy has $15,000 in her bank account, and the current interest rate is 5 percent a year.

a. What is Wendy's opportunity cost of opening the coffee shop?

b. What is the quantity of financial capital that Wendy plans to get from the capital market?

c. What is the quantity of financial capital that Wendy plans to provide herself?

d. If demand for financial capital increases just when Wendy plans to go to the capital market, what will happen to her opportunity cost of the coffee shop? Explain your answer.

e. If the supply of financial capital increases just when Wendy plans to go to the capital market, what will happen to her opportunity cost of the coffee shop? Explain your answer.

Solution to Practice Problem 17.4

When answering this Practice Problem, remember that the market for financial capital is similar to other markets. It is the interaction of demand and supply that determine the equilibrium interest rate and quantity of capital.

Quick Review

• *Factors that change the demand for capital* Two main factors that change the demand for capital are population growth and technological change.

• *Influences on the supply of saving* The main influences on the supply of saving are population, average income, and expected future income.

a. **What is Wendy's opportunity cost of opening the coffee shop?**

Wendy's opportunity cost is the interest she pays on the $55,000 she borrows plus the forgone interest on the $15,000 she provides. With an interest rate of 5 percent a year, her borrowing costs are ($55,000) × (0.05), which is $2,750 a year and the interest forgone equals ($15,000) × (0.05), which is $750. The total opportunity cost is $3,500 a year.

b. **What is the quantity of financial capital that Wendy plans to get from the capital market?**

Wendy needs $70,000 and she has $15,000. So the quantity of financial capital she plans to get from the capital market is the difference between $70,000 and $15,000, which is $55,000.

c. **What is the quantity of financial capital that Wendy plans to provide herself?**

Wendy plans to provide $15,000 herself.

d. **If demand for financial capital increases just when Wendy plans to go to the capital market, what will happen to her opportunity cost of the coffee shop? Explain your answer.**

If the demand for financial capital increases, the equilibrium interest rate rises. The interest rate that Wendy has to pay for her financial capital will exceed 5 percent a year and the opportunity cost of her coffee shop will increase.

e. **If the supply of financial capital increases just when Wendy plans to go to the capital market, what will happen to her opportunity cost of the coffee shop? Explain your answer.**

If the supply of financial capital increases, the equilibrium interest rate falls. The interest rate that Wendy has to pay for her financial capital will be less than 5 percent a year and the opportunity cost of her coffee shop will decrease.

Additional Practice Problem 17.4a

Describe the capital market equilibrium over time.

Solution to Additional Practice Problem 17.4a

Over time, the demand for capital and the supply of capital increase. Population growth increases the demand for capital. As the increased population earns a larger income, the supply of capital increases. Technological advances increase the demand for capital, and bring higher incomes. The supply of capital increases. The quantity of capital increases because the demand for capital and supply of capital increase, but the interest rate does not persistently increase or decrease.

■ Self Test 17.4

Fill in the blanks

The higher the interest rate, the ____ (greater; smaller) the quantity of capital demanded. The quantity of financial capital ____ (demanded; supplied) results from people's saving decisions. An increase in average income ____ (increases; decreases) the supply of capital. As the population grows, the demand for physical capital ____ (decreases; increases).

True or false

1. Technological change increases the demand for all types of capital.

2. A rise in the interest rate decreases the quantity of capital supplied.

3. If a household's current income is low and its expected future income is high, the household will have a low level of saving.

Multiple choice

1. The demand for financial capital stems from
a. an individual's need to pay for benefits.
b. a firm's requirement to pay for union wages.
c. a firm's demand for physical capital.
d. a firm's demand for labour.

2. When the interest rate falls, the ____ financial capital ____.
a. demand for; increases
b. demand for; decreases
c. quantity demanded of; increases
d. quantity demanded of; decreases

3. The quantity of financial capital supplied results from people's ____ decisions.
a. saving
b. spending
c. investing
d. employment

4. The higher the interest rate, the

a. more incentive people have to consume.

b. less incentive people have to save.

c. higher the opportunity cost of current consumption.

d. lower the opportunity cost of current consumption.

5. If a household's current income is _____ and its expected future income is low, it will have _____.

a. zero; a high level of saving

b. high; a negative level of saving

c. high; no saving

d. high; a high level of saving

Short answer

1. How does technological change affect the demand for capital?

2. What is the source of the supply of financial capital?

3. If people expect an increase in future income, what is the effect on the interest rate?

CHECKPOINT 17.5

■ **Explain how rents and natural resource prices are determined.**

Practice Problem 17.5

Which of the following items are nonrenewable natural resources, which are renewable natural resources, and which are not natural resources? Explain your answers.

a. Beaches on Prince Edward Island

b. The CN Tower

c. Diamond mines in northern Canada

d. The Great Lakes

e. National parks

f. Douglas fir forests in British Columbia

g. Oil reserves under the Atlantic Ocean off Newfoundland

h. The Lion's Gate Bridge in Vancouver

Solution to Practice Problem 17.5

To answer this Practice Problem, remember the distinction between renewable natural resources and nonrenewable natural resources.

Quick Review

*   *Renewable natural resources* Natural resources that can be used repeatedly.

*   *Nonrenewable natural resources* Natural resources that can be used only once and that cannot be replaced once they have been used.

a. Beaches on Prince Edward Island

The beaches are a gift of nature, which can be used repeatedly, so they are a renewable natural resource.

b. The CN Tower

The CN Tower is a national landmark, but it is not a national resource.

c. Diamond mines in northern Canada

A diamond mine is a gift of nature. Once the diamond is mined, it cannot be used repeatedly, so it is a nonrenewable natural resource.

d. The Great Lakes

The Great Lakes are a gift of nature. They can be used repeatedly, so they are a renewable natural resource.

e. National parks

The national parks are a gift of nature. They can be used repeatedly, so they are a renewable natural resource.

f. Douglas fir forests in British Columbia

The national parks are a gift of nature. They can be used repeatedly, so they are a renewable natural resource.

g. Oil reserves under the Atlantic Ocean off Newfoundland

The oil reserves are a gift of nature. They cannot be used repeatedly, so they are a nonrenewable natural resource.

h. The Lion's Gate Bridge in Vancouver

The Lion's Gate Bridge is a national landmark, but it is not a national resource.

Additional Practice Problem 17.5a

As a nonrenewable natural resource is used, what happens to the supply and its price?

Solution to Additional Practice Problem 17.5a

Using a natural resource decreases its supply, which causes its price to rise. But new technologies that lead to the discovery of previously unknown reserves increase supply, which causes the price to fall. Also, new technologies that enable a more efficient use of a nonrenewable natural resource decrease the demand for the resource, which causes its price to fall.

■ Self Test 17.5

Fill in the blanks

The supply of each particular block of land is perfectly _____ (elastic; inelastic). Economic rent can be earned by _____ (only land; any factor of production). Over time, advances in technology _____ (increase; decrease) the known quantity of a natural resource.

True or false

1. Forestland is a renewable natural resource.

2. The demand for land is perfectly elastic, and the supply of land is perfectly inelastic.

3. The price of a natural resource always rises over time.

Multiple choice

1. A natural resource is renewable if it
   a. never has to rest.
   b. can be used repeatedly.
   c. cannot be replaced once it has been used.
   d. is available at a price of zero.

2. Oil is an example of
   a. a nonrenewable natural resource.
   b. a renewable natural resource.
   c. physical capital.
   d. a resource for which the true value of the resource cannot be measured.

3. The supply of each particular block of land is
   a. perfectly elastic.
   b. unit elastic.
   c. elastic.
   d. perfectly inelastic.

4. Economic rent is the income over and above
   a. opportunity cost.
   b. average cost.
   c. factor income.
   d. marginal cost.

5. The income required to induce the supply of a given quantity of a factor of production is
   a. the value of marginal product.
   b. its marginal cost.
   c. its opportunity cost.
   d. its economic rent.

Complete the graph

1. The table shows the demand for land. The supply of land is 20,000 square hectares.

Rent (dollars per hectare per month)	Land (thousands of hectares)
400	10
350	20
300	30
250	40
200	50

a. In Figure 17.4, label the axes and graph the market for land.

b. Find the equilibrium rent and quantity and indicate the economic rent and opportunity cost.

■ FIGURE 17.4

Rent (dollars per hectare per month)

Short answer

1. Why is petroleum considered a nonrenewable natural resource?

2. John Travolta receives $18 million to act in a movie. Suppose Mr. Travolta would act in a movie as long as he received $100,000. What are his opportunity cost and economic rent?

SELF TEST ANSWERS

■ CHECKPOINT 17.1

Fill in the blanks

The factors of production are <u>labour</u>, <u>capital</u>, <u>land</u>, and <u>entrepreneurship</u>. The funds that firms use to buy and operate physical capital are <u>financial</u> capital. The market in which raw materials are traded is the <u>commodity</u> market.

True or false

1. False; page 418
2. False; page 419
3. True; page 420

Multiple choice

1. c; page 418
2. d; page 418
3. b; page 418
4. c; page 419
5. d; page 420

Short answer

1. Factors of production are used to produce goods and services; page 418.

2. Capital consists of tools, instruments, machines, buildings, and other constructions that have been produced in the past and that businesses now use to produce goods and services. Financial capital is the funds that firms use to buy and operate physical capital; page 419.

3. Trees are categorized as land; page 420.

■ CHECKPOINT 17.2

Fill in the blanks

The value of marginal product equals the marginal product of the factor of production times the <u>price of a unit of output</u>. The quantity of labour demanded by a firm is the quantity at which the value of the marginal product of labour equals

the <u>wage rate</u>. When the price of the firm's output increases, the demand for labour <u>increases</u>.

True or false

1. True; page 421
2. True; page 422
3. True; page 423

Multiple choice

1. d; page 421
2. a; page 421
3. b; page 421
4. a; page 422
5. c; page 424

Complete the graph

1. a. The completed table is below. Figure 17.5 plots the demand for labour curve, LD_1.

Quantity of labour (workers)	Marginal product (lawns per worker)	Value of marginal product 1 (dollars per day)	Value of marginal product 2 (dollars per day)
1	13	<u>325</u>	<u>390</u>
2	12	<u>300</u>	<u>360</u>
3	11	<u>275</u>	<u>330</u>
4	10	<u>250</u>	<u>300</u>
5	9	<u>225</u>	<u>270</u>

■ **FIGURE 17.5**

Wage rate (dollars per day)

b. In Figure 17.5, the demand for labour curve shifts rightward; pages 421–424.

Short answer

1. As more of the factor of production is employed, marginal product decreases, and value of marginal product, which equals the price of a unit of the output multiplied by the marginal product of the factor of production also decreases; page 421.

2. The demand for labour curve and the value of marginal product curve are the same; page 423.

3. Three factors change the demand for labour and shift the demand for labour curve: a change in the price of the firm's output, a change in the prices of other factors of production, and a change in technology; page 424.

■ **CHECKPOINT 17.3**

Fill in the blanks

An individual's <u>supply</u> of labour curve bends backward. An increase in the adult population <u>increases</u> the supply of labour. If the wage rate exceeds the equilibrium wage rate, the quantity of labour supplied is <u>greater than</u> the quantity of labour demanded.

True or false

1. False; page 426

2. True; page 428

3. False; page 428

Multiple choice

1. c; page 426

2. c; page 428

3. d; page 428

4. b; page 428

5. b; page 428

Complete the graph

1. Figure 17.6 shows that for wage rates exceeding $30 an hour, Hank decreases the quantity of labour he supplies as the wage rate rises; page 426.

■ **FIGURE 17.6**

Wage rate (dollars per hour)

2. In Figure 17.7 the demand for Webmasters increases. The demand for labour curve shifts rightward from LD_0 to LD_1. The equilibrium wage rate rises and the quantity of webmasters employed increases; page 428.

■ FIGURE 17.7

Wage rate (dollars per hour)

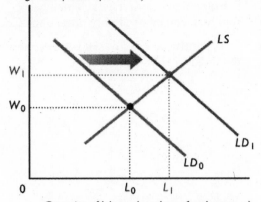

Quantity of labour (number of webmasters)

Short answer

1. An increase in the adult population increases the supply of labour; page 428.

2. As more people obtain advanced degrees the supply of high-skilled labour increases. The equilibrium wage rate for high-skilled labour falls; page 428.

■ CHECKPOINT 17.4

Fill in the blanks

The higher the interest rate, the _smaller_ the quantity of capital demanded. The quantity of financial capital _supplied_ results from people's saving decisions. An increase in average income _increases_ the supply of capital. As the population grows, the demand for physical capital _increases_.

True or false

1. False; page 431
2. False; page 431
3. True; page 432

Multiple choice

1. c; page 431
2. c; page 431
3. a; page 431
4. c; page 431
5. d; page 432

Short answer

1. Advances in technology increase the demand for some types of physical capital and decrease the demand for other types. For example, the development of desktop computers increased the demand for office computing equipment and decreased the demand for electric typewriters; page 431.

2. The supply of financial capital results from people's saving; page 431.

3. If people expect an increase in future income, they save less now and the supply of capital decreases. The equilibrium interest rate rises; pages 432-433.

■ CHECKPOINT 17.5

Fill in the blanks

The supply of each particular block of land is perfectly _inelastic_. Economic rent can be earned by _any factor of production_. Over time, advances in technology _increase_ the known quantity of a natural resource.

True or false

1. True; page 435
2. False; page 435
3. False; page 437

Multiple choice

1. b; page 435
2. a; page 435
3. d; page 435
4. a; page 436
5. c; page 436

Complete the graph

1. a. Figure 17.8 shows the completed figure; page 435.

■ **FIGURE 17.8**

b. Equilibrium rent is $350 a hectare and the equilibrium quantity is 20,000 hectares. Figure 17.8 shows the economic rent. Opportunity cost is zero; page 436.

Short answer

1. Petroleum is a nonrenewable natural resource. It can be used only once; page 435.

2. Opportunity cost is $100,000 and economic rent is $17.9 million; page 436.

Inequality and Redistribution

CHAPTER IN PERSPECTIVE

Chapter 18 studies economic inequality—its extent, sources, and potential remedies. The chapter looks at taxes and government programs that redistribute incomes and studies their effect on economic equality in Canada.

■ **Describe the inequality in income and wealth in Canada and explain why wealth inequality is greater than income inequality.**

A Lorenz curve is a curve that graphs the cumulative percentage of income (or wealth) against the cumulative percentage of households. The farther the Lorenz curve is from a 45° line, the greater is the inequality. The wealthiest 20 percent of Canadians own 70 percent of the total wealth in the country. The distributions of income and wealth have become more unequal during the past two decades. Statistics Canada measures the number of poor households by calculating the number of households that lie below a low-income cutoff—the income at or below which a household spends 20 percentage points more of its income on food, shelter, and clothing than does the average household. A low-income household in Canada is likely to be a single-parent mother, under 24 years old, with no job, living in Quebec with her children. Because the wealth distribution data excludes human capital, the income distribution is a more accurate measure of economic inequality than the wealth distribution. A typical household's income changes over time. It starts out low, grows to a peak when the household's workers reach retirement age, and then falls after retirement. So because different households are at different stages in the life cycle, measured inequality overstates actual inequality.

■ **Explain how economic inequality arises.**

High-skilled labour has a higher value of marginal product than low-skilled labour, so at a given level of employment, firms are willing to pay a higher wage rate to a high-skilled worker than to a low-skilled worker. The vertical distance between the high-skilled worker's supply curve and the low-skilled worker's supply curve is the compensation for the cost of acquiring skill. The equilibrium wage rate of high-skilled labour is higher than that of low-skilled labour.

■ **Explain the effects of taxes, social security, and welfare programs on economic inequality.**

Governments in Canada redistribute income by using income taxes, income maintenance programs, and subsidized services. Income taxes in Canada are progressive. The three major income maintenance programs are social security programs, unemployment compensation, and welfare programs. Taxes and government benefits reduce the degree of inequality that the market generates. The redistribution of income creates the big tradeoff between equity and efficiency. A negative income tax provides every household with a guaranteed minimum annual income and taxes all income above the guaranteed minimum at a fixed rate.

EXPANDED CHAPTER CHECKLIST

When you have completed this chapter, you will be able to

1 Describe the inequality in income and wealth in Canada and explain why wealth inequality is greater than income inequality.

- Describe the distribution of income and wealth in Canada and discuss how these distributions have changed during the past two decades.

- Draw and interpret a Lorenz curve.

- Define low-income cutoff and describe the lowest-income household in Canada.

- Explain why income is a more accurate measure of economic inequality than wealth.

2 Explain how economic inequality arises.

- Discuss the demand for high-skilled labour and low-skilled labour.

- Discuss the supply of high-skilled labour and low-skilled labour.

- Illustrate the market for high-skilled labour and the market for low-skilled labour.

- Explain the impact on economic inequality of bequests and assortative mating.

3 Explain the effects of taxes, social security, and welfare programs on economic inequality.

- Describe how income taxes, income maintenance programs, and subsidized services redistribute income.

- Define market income and money income.

- Explain how government actions change the distribution of income.

- Explain the big tradeoff and give two reasons why redistribution decreases the size of the economic pie.

- Discuss the negative income tax.

KEY TERMS

- Lorenz curve (page 445)
- Low-income cutoff (page 447)
- Market income (page 459)
- Money income (page 459)
- Negative income tax (page 462)

CHECKPOINT 18.1

■ Describe the inequality in income and wealth in Canada and explain why wealth inequality is greater than income inequality.

Practice Problem 18.1

Table 18.1 on page 444 of your textbook shows the distribution of income in Canada. The table below shows the distribution of income in Peru and in Sweden.

	Peru		Sweden	
Households	Income (percentage)	Households	Income (percentage)
Lowest 20 percent	4.0	Lowest 20 percent	9.5
Second 20 percent	4.3	Second 20 percent	15.5
Third 20 percent	8.3	Third 20 percent	19.0
Fourth 20 percent	15.2	Fourth 20 percent	23.1
Highest 20 percent	68.2	Highest 20 percent	32.9

a. Draw the Lorenz curves for Canada, Peru, and Sweden.

b. Compare the distributions of income in Peru and Sweden with that in Canada. Which distribution is more unequal? Which is more equal?

Solution to Practice Problem 18.1

A Lorenz curve graphs the cumulative percentage of income (or wealth) against the cumulative percentage of households. To answer this Practice Problem, calculate the cumulative percentages.

Quick Review

- *Lorenz curve* A curve that graphs the cumulative percentage of income (or wealth) against the cumulative percentage of households. The farther the Lorenz curve is from a 45° line, the greater is the inequality.

a. Draw the Lorenz curves for Canada, Peru, and Sweden.

To draw the Lorenz curves, we first need to calculate the cumulative percentage of households and the cumulative percentage of income. The table below shows these calculations for Peru and Sweden.

Peru		Sweden	
Households (cumulative percentage)	Income (cumulative percentage)	Households (cumulative percentage)	Income (cumulative percentage)
20	4.0	20	9.5
40	8.3	40	25.0
60	16.6	60	44.0
80	31.8	80	67.1
100	100.0	100	100.0

The figure shows the Lorenz curves, which plot the cumulative percentage of income against the cumulative percentage of households for Canada, Peru, and Sweden.

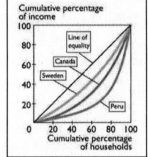

b. Compare the distributions of income in Peru and Sweden with that in Canada. Which distribution is more unequal? Which is more equal?

The closer the Lorenz curve is to the line of equality, the more equally is income distributed. Peru's Lorenz curve lies further from the line of equality than does Canada's so the distribution of income in Canada is more equal than that in Peru. Sweden's Lorenz curve lies closer to the line of equality than does Canada's, so the distribution of income in Canada is less equal than that in Sweden.

Additional Practice Problem 18.1a

The figure shows the Lorenz curves for three nations, A, B, and C. In which nation is income distribution most unequal? The most equal? In which nation is average income the highest?

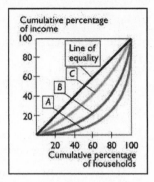

Solution to Additional Practice Problem 18.1a

The closer the Lorenz curve is to the line of equality, the more equally is income distributed. Nation A's Lorenz curve lies furthest from the line of equality so the distribution of income in nation A is most unequal. Nation C's Lorenz curve lies closest to the line of equality so the distribution of income in nation C is most equal. The Lorenz curve does not give information about average income, so it is impossible to know in which nation average income is the highest.

■ Self Test 18.1

Fill in the blanks

In Canada in 2001, the median household income was approximately ____ ($27,000; $47,000; $57,000). The poorest 20 percent of households received about ____ (4; 12) percent of total income and the richest 20 percent received about ____ (26; 46) percent of total income. A Lorenz curve for income graphs the ____ (percentage; cumulative percentage) of income against the cumulative percentage of households. During the past two decades, the distributions of income and wealth in Canada have become ____ (less; more) unequal. The income at or below which a household spends 20 percentage points more of its income on food, shelter, and clothing than does the average household is the ____ (low-income cutoff; poverty level). Wealth distribution is a ____ (less; more) accurate measure of economic inequality than income distribution because wealth distribution data _____ (excludes; includes) human capital.

True or false

1. The Lorenz curve always lies above the line of equality.

2. In Canada, the distribution of income is more equal than the distribution of wealth.

3. Between 1980 and 2001, the share of the total income received by the richest 20 percent of households has decreased.

4. The highest-income household in Canada is likely to be a married couple with two full-time jobs, between 45 and 54 years old, college-educated, and living in Ontario.

5. Inequality of annual income overstates the degree of lifetime inequality.

Multiple choice

1. The median income is the income that

a. is equal to the average income.

b. is most often observed.

c. is in the middle so that 50 percent of households have incomes above the median and 50 percent have incomes below the median.

d. defines the low-income cutoff.

2. The median household income in Canada in 2001 was approximately

a. $57,000.

b. $40,000.

c. $62,000.

d. $22,000.

3. Which of the following is correct about Canada?

a. Income is equally distributed.

b. Wealth is equally distributed.

c. Income is equally distributed but wealth is unequally distributed because of inheritances.

d. Both wealth and income are unequally distributed.

4. If wealth distribution is more unequal than income distribution, the

a. Lorenz curve for income is farther away from the 45° line than the Lorenz curve for wealth.

b. government has imposed a higher tax rate on income.

c. Lorenz curve for wealth is farther away from the 45° line than the Lorenz curve for income.

d. None of the above answers is correct.

5. In Canada between 1980 and 2001, the share of total income received by the richest 20 percent of households increased by _____ percentage points.

a. 1.0

b. 4.0

c. 11.5

d. 25.0

6. In Canada between 1984 and 1999, the median wealth of the richest 20 percent of households _____ and the median wealth of the poorest 40 percent of households _____.

a. increased; decreased

b. did not change; did not change

c. did not change; increased

d. increased; had almost no change

7. If the average household spends 35 percent of its income on food, shelter, and clothing, the low-income cutoff is the income at which a household spends _____ percent of its income on these items.

a. 35

b. 25

c. 15

d. 55

8. The inequality of annual income

a. overstates the degree of lifetime inequality.

b. understates the degree of lifetime inequality.

c. cannot change from one year to the next.

d. None of the above answers is correct.

Complete the graph

1. The table has data for the nation of Beta. Complete the table. In Figure 18.1, plot the Lorenz curve for Beta.

Household percentage	Percentage of income	Cumulative percentage of income
Lowest 20 percent	5.0	____
Second 20 percent	9.0	____
Third 20 percent	20.0	____
Fourth 20 percent	26.0	____
Highest 20 percent	40.0	____

■ FIGURE 18.1

Short answer

1. Can a Lorenz curve for income ever lie above the line of equality? Why or why not?

2. What does the distance between a Lorenz curve for income and the line of equality tell about the distribution of income?

3. How has the distribution of income and wealth changed in Canada during the last two decades? Why have these distributions changed?

4. What is the low-income cutoff?

5. What is the relationship between income and wealth? Why does the Lorenz curve for income differ from that for wealth?

6. Is the distribution of annual or lifetime income more equal? Why?

CHECKPOINT 18.2

■ **Explain how economic inequality arises.**

Practice Problem 18.2

In Canada in April 2001, 83,000 people had full-time managerial and professional jobs that paid an average of $840 a week. At the same time, 125,000 people had full-time sales positions that paid an average of $340 a week.

a. Explain why managers and professionals are paid more than salespeople.

b. Explain why, despite the higher weekly wage, fewer people are employed as managers and professionals than as salespeople.

c. If Internet shopping becomes very popular and the range of goods and services available on the Internet expands rapidly, what changes do you expect will occur in the market for salespeople?

Solution to Practice Problem 18.2

This Practice Problem studies the relationship between skill differentials and the wage rate. Remember that high-skilled labour has a higher value of marginal product than low-skilled labour and skills are costly to obtain.

Quick Review

- *Demand for high-skilled labour and low-skilled labour* The vertical distance between the demand curve for low-skilled labour and the demand curve for high-skilled labour is equal to the value of marginal product of skill.

- *Supply of high-skilled labour and low-skilled labour* The vertical distance between the supply curve of low-skilled labour and the supply curve of high-skilled labour is equal to the compensation that high-skilled workers require for the cost of acquiring the skill.

a. **Explain why managers and professionals are paid more than salespeople.**

The typical manager or professional has incurred a higher cost of education and on-the-job training than the typical salesperson. In the figure, the supply curve of managers and professionals, S_H, lies above the supply curve of salespeople, S_L, and the vertical distance between the two curves is the compensation for the cost of acquiring skill. The better education and more on-the-job training result in managers and professionals having more human capital and a higher value of marginal product than salespeople. So the demand curve for managers and professionals, D_H, lies above the demand curve for salespeople, D_L, and the vertical distance between the two curves is equal to the value of marginal product of skill.

The demand for and supply of each type of workers determine the wage rate. In the figure, managers and professionals receive a higher wage rate than salespeople.

b. **Explain why, despite the higher weekly wage, fewer people are employed as managers and professionals than as salespeople.**

The figure shows that the combination of demand and supply leads to fewer managers and professionals employed than salespeople.

c. **If Internet shopping becomes very popular and the range of goods and services available on the Internet expands rapidly, what changes do you expect will occur in the market for salespeople?**

The demand for salespeople will decrease, the demand curve for salespeople will shift leftward, and fewer people will work in sales. The equilib-

rium wage rate will depend on what happens to the supply of salespeople.

Additional Practice Problem 18.2a

What is the opportunity cost of acquiring a skill?

Solution to Additional Practice Problem 18.2a

The opportunity cost of acquiring a skill includes actual expenditures on tuition and books, as well as costs in the form of lost or reduced earnings while the skill is being acquired. When a person goes to school full time, that cost is the total earnings forgone. When a person receives on-the-job training, he or she is paid a lower wage than one who is doing a comparable job but not undergoing training. In this case, the cost of acquiring the skill is equal to the wage paid to a person not being trained minus the wage paid to a person being trained.

■ Self Test 18.2

Fill in the blanks

The demand curve for high-skilled workers lies ____ (above; below) the demand curve for low-skilled workers and the supply curve of high-skilled workers lies ____ (above; below) the supply curve of low-skilled workers. The wage rate paid high-skilled workers is ____ (greater; less) than the wage rate paid low-skilled workers. The tendency for people to marry within their own socioeconomic class is called ____ (bequests; assortative mating) and makes the distribution of wealth ____ (less; more) equal.

True or false

1. At a given wage rate, the quantity of high-skilled labour demanded exceeds the quantity of low-skilled labour demanded.

2. The horizontal distance between the demand curve for high-skilled labour and the demand curve for low-skilled labour measures the value of marginal product of skill.

3. The greater the cost of acquiring a skill, the greater is the vertical distance between the

supply curve of high-skilled labour and the supply curve of low-skilled labour.

4. The equilibrium wage rate paid high-skilled workers exceeds that paid to low-skilled workers.

5. Economists agree that prejudice causes wage differentials.

6. Intergenerational transfers of wealth, such as bequests, increase economic equality.

Multiple choice

1. Differences in skills

a. arise partly from differences in education and partly from differences in on-the-job training.

b. can lead to large differences in earnings.

c. result in different demand curves for high-skilled and low-skilled labour.

d. All of the above answers are correct.

2. Other things being equal, the demand curve for low-skilled workers ____ the demand curve for high-skilled workers.

a. lies below

b. lies above

c. is the same as

d. is not comparable to

3. The cost of acquiring a skill accounts for why the

a. demand for high-skilled workers is different than the demand for low-skilled workers.

b. supply of high-skilled workers is different than the supply of low-skilled workers.

c. demand for high-skilled workers is different than the supply of high-skilled workers.

d. None of the above answers is correct.

4. The vertical distance between the supply curve of neurosurgeons and the supply curve of fast-food servers represents the

a. difference in the demand for these two occupations.

b. compensation that neurosurgeons require for the cost of acquiring their skill.

c. difference in the value of the marginal product of the two professions.

d. difference in on-the-job training.

5. The wage rate that high-skilled workers receive is ____ the wage rate that low-skilled workers receive.

a. more than

b. the same amount as

c. less than

d. some amount that is not comparable to

6. If discrimination against women decreases their value of marginal product, then you would expect women to have a ____ wage rate than men and there will be ____ high-paying jobs for women.

a. lower; more

b. higher; fewer

c. lower; fewer

d. higher; more

7. The inequality in the distribution of income and wealth is increased by

a. the fact that debts cannot be bequeathed.

b. saving to redistribute an uneven income over the life cycle.

c. marrying outside one's own socioeconomic class.

d. donating money to charities.

8. An example of assortative mating is when

a. the right person for the job is always hired.

b. opposites attract.

c. wealthy individuals marry wealthy partners.

d. None of the above answers is correct.

Complete the graph

■ FIGURE 18.2

Wage rate (dollars per hour)

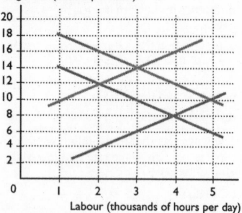

Labour (thousands of hours per day)

1. Figure 18.2 shows demand and supply curves for high-skilled and low-skilled workers.

a. Label the demand curve for the high-skilled workers D_H and the demand curve for low-skilled workers D_L. Label the supply curves similarly, using S_H and S_L.

b. What is the value of marginal product of skill?

c. What is the compensation required for the cost of acquiring the skill?

d. What is the equilibrium wage rate for high-skilled workers and low-skilled workers?

Short answer

1a. How does the demand for high-skilled workers compare to the demand for low-skilled workers? How does the supply of high-skilled workers compare to the supply of low-skilled workers?

b. How does the wage rate of high-skilled workers compare to the wage rate of low-skilled workers?

c. How does the quantity of high-skilled workers employed compare to the quantity of low-skilled workers employed?

2. What is assortative mating?

CHECKPOINT 18.3

■ Explain the effects of taxes, social security, and welfare programs on economic inequality.

Practice Problem 18.3

The first table shows the distribution of market income in an economy.

Households	Income (millions of dollars per year)
Lowest 20 percent	5
Second 20 percent	10
Third 20 percent	18
Fourth 20 percent	28
Highest 20 percent	39

The government redistributes income by collecting income taxes and paying benefits as shown in the following table.

Households	Income tax (percent)	Benefit (millions of dollars)
Lowest 20 percent	0	10
Second 20 percent	10	8
Third 20 percent	18	3
Fourth 20 percent	28	0
Highest 20 percent	39	0

a. Calculate the income shares of each 20 percent of households after tax and redistribution.

b. Draw the Lorenz curve for this economy before and after taxes and benefits.

Solution to Practice Problem 18.3

This problem emphasizes how the redistribution of income moves the Lorenz curve closer to the line of inequality.

Quick Review

• *Market income* A household's income earned from the markets for factors of production and with no government redistribution.

- *Money income* Market income plus money benefits paid by the government.

a. Calculate the income shares of each 20 percent of households after tax and redistribution.

To calculate the income shares, first multiply market income by the tax rate to find the taxes paid. The table below summarizes the calculations and shows the benefits received.

Households	Market income	Taxes paid	Benefits received
	(millions of dollars)		
Lowest 20 percent	5	0.0	10
Second 20 percent	10	1.0	8
Third 20 percent	18	3.2	3
Fourth 20 percent	28	7.8	0
Highest 20 percent	39	15.2	0

Then subtract the taxes paid and add the benefits received to the market income. Divide the result by total income, as shown in the following table.

Households	Income after taxes and benefits (millions of dollars)	Income (percentage of total income)
Lowest 20 percent	15.0	16.0
Second 20 percent	17.0	18.1
Third 20 percent	17.8	19.0
Fourth 20 percent	20.2	21.5
Highest 20 percent	23.8	25.4

b. Draw the Lorenz curve for this economy before and after taxes and benefits.

The table shows the cumulative percentage of income before taxes and benefits and after taxes and benefits.

	Cumulative percentage of income	
	before	after
Lowest 20 percent	5.0	16.0
Second 20 percent	15.0	34.1
Third 20 percent	33.0	53.1
Fourth 20 percent	61.0	74.6
Highest 20 percent	100.0	100.0

These cumulative percentages are plotted in the Lorenz curves in the figure.

Additional Practice Problem 18.3a

Why does the economy in the Practice Problem have a smaller total income following the collection of income taxes and distribution of benefits?

Solution to Additional Practice Problem 18.3a

Prior to the collection of income taxes and distribution of benefits, total income is $100 million. Following the collection of income taxes and distribution of benefits, total income is $93.8 million. The redistribution of income creates the big tradeoff between equity and efficiency. A dollar collected from a rich person does not translate into a dollar received by a poor person. A portion of each dollar is used up in the process of redistribution.

■ Self Test 18.3

Fill in the blanks

A household's _____ (market; money) income is the income earned from the markets for factors of production and with no government redistribution. The distribution of income after taxes and benefits is _____ (more; less) equal than the distribution of market income. Redistribution of income creates the big tradeoff between _____ (equity; tax revenue) and _____ (efficiency; redistribution). The long-term solution to the problem of single mothers on welfare in Canada is _____ (acquiring human capital; increasing welfare payments). _____ (A negative income; An income) tax provides every household with a guaranteed minimum annual income and taxes all income above the guaranteed minimum at a fixed rate.

True or false

1. Canadian federal and provincial taxes are progressive.

2. Subsidized services from the government go to only households with below-average incomes.

3. The distribution of income after taxes and benefits is more equal than the market distribution of income.

4. The redistribution of income creates the big tradeoff between earning an income and losing welfare benefits.

5. Under a negative income tax, some households would receive more money from the government than they would pay in taxes.

Multiple choice

1. Which of the following is a way income is redistributed in Canada?
a. subsidized services
b. income taxes
c. income maintenance programs
d. All of the above.

2. A _____ tax is one that taxes income at an average rate that increases with the level of income.
a. regressive
b. progressive
c. flat
d. consumption

3. A _____ tax is one that taxes income at a constant rate, regardless of the level of income.
a. regressive
b. proportional
c. progressive
d. both a and b

4. The three major types of income maintenance programs are
a. social security programs, unemployment compensation, and welfare programs.
b. minimum wage laws, unemployment compensation, and agricultural price supports.
c. student loans, rent control, and welfare programs.
d. welfare programs, minimum wage laws, and social security programs.

5. A household's income earned in factor markets before tax and with no government redistribution is
a. money income.
b. welfare.
c. market income.
d. exploitative income.

6. Which of the following measures shows the most equality?
a. money income
b. market income
c. income after taxes and benefits
d. wealth

7. When government redistributes income, one dollar collected from a rich person translates into _____ dollar received by a poor person.
a. one
b. less than one
c. more than one
d. Any of these is likely to occur.

8. With a negative income tax that has a $10,000 guaranteed minimum income and a 25 percent tax rate, a household that has a market income of $16,000

a. "pays" income tax of –$6,000.

b. pays income tax of $6,000.

c. "pays" income tax of –$4,000.

d. pays income tax of $14,000.

Short answer

1. Would progressive or regressive income taxes redistribute more money from the rich to the poor? Why?

2. What are Canada's three major income maintenance programs?

3. Currently the government more heavily taxes high-income households and transfers money to low-income households. What are the likely reactions of the recipients of the money? Of the taxpayers? How do these reactions reflect the big tradeoff?

4. Suppose a negative income tax plan is passed so that a household is guaranteed an income of $20,000 and market income is taxed at a rate of 25 percent.

a. What is the total income of a household that has a market income of $20,000?

b. What is the total income of a household that has a market income of $60,000?

c. What is the break-even income?

SELF TEST ANSWERS

■ CHECKPOINT 18.1

Fill in the blanks

In Canada in 2001, the median household income was approximately $57,000. The poorest 20 percent of households received about 4 percent of total income and the richest 20 percent received about 46 percent of total income. A Lorenz curve for income graphs the cumulative percentage of income against the cumulative percentage of households. During the past two decades, the distributions of income and wealth in Canada have become more unequal. The income at or below which a household spends 20 percentage points more of its income on food, shelter, and clothing than does the average household is the low-income cutoff. Wealth distribution is a less accurate measure of economic inequality than income distribution because wealth distribution data excludes human capital.

True or false

1. False; page 445
2. True; page 445
3. False; page 446
4. True; page 447
5. True; page 450

Multiple choice

1. c; page 444
2. a; page 444
3. d; page 445
4. c; page 445
5. b; page 446
6. d; page 446
7. d; page 447
8. a; page 450

Complete the graph

1. The completed table and the Lorenz curve are in the next column; page 445.

Household percentage	Percentage of income	Cumulative percentage of income
Lowest 20 percent	5.0	5.0
Second 20 percent	9.0	14.0
Third 20 percent	20.0	34.0
Fourth 20 percent	26.0	60.0
Highest 20 percent	40.0	100.0

■ FIGURE 18.3

Cumulative percentage of income

Short answer

1. A Lorenz curve for income can never lie above the line of equality. The Lorenz curve plots the cumulative percentage of income against the cumulative percentage of households. Because the households are arranged by order of income, the cumulative percentage of income is always less (except at 0 percent and 100 percent) than the cumulative percentage of households; page 445.

2. The farther away the Lorenz curve is from the line of equality, the less equal is the distribution of income; page 445.

3. Both the distribution of income and wealth have become less equal in Canada during the past two decades. The distribution of income changed because the better educated in the higher income groups have benefited more from recent rapid technological changes. The distribution of wealth changed because the

wealthiest households have a larger proportion of their wealth invested in stocks and they have benefited from the extraordinary performance of the stock market in the 1990s; pages 446-447.

4. The low-income cutoff is the income at or below which a household spends 20 percentage points more of its income on food, shelter, and clothing than does the average household; page 447.

5. Income is the flow of earnings that results from the stock of wealth. The Lorenz curves for income and wealth show that income is distributed more equally than wealth. The wealth distribution excludes human capital, so the income distribution is a more accurate measure of economic inequality than the wealth distribution; page 449.

6. The distribution of lifetime income is more equal than the distribution of annual income because in any given year, different households are at different stages in the life cycle; page 450.

■ **CHECKPOINT 18.2**

Fill in the blanks

The demand curve for high-skilled workers lies <u>above</u> the demand curve for low-skilled workers and the supply curve of high-skilled workers lies <u>above</u> the supply curve of low-skilled workers. The wage rate paid high-skilled workers is <u>greater</u> than the wage rate paid low-skilled workers. The tendency for people to marry within their own socioeconomic class is called <u>assortative mating</u> and makes the distribution of wealth <u>less</u> equal.

True or false

1. True; page 452
2. False; page 452
3. True; page 452
4. True; page 453
5. False; page 455

6. False; page 456

Multiple choice

1. d; page 452
2. a; page 452
3. b; page 452
4. b; page 452
5. a; page 453
6. c; page 455
7. a; page 456
8. c; page 456

Complete the graph

1.a. Figure 18.4 labels the curves.

■ **FIGURE 18.4**

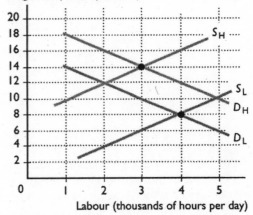

Wage rate (dollars per hour)

b. The value of marginal product of skill is $4 an hour because that is the vertical distance between the demand curve for high-skilled workers and the demand curve for low-skilled workers; page 452.

c. The compensation required for the cost of acquiring the skill is $8 an hour because that is the vertical distance between the supply curve for high-skilled workers and the supply curve for low-skilled workers; pages 452-453.

d. The equilibrium wage rate for high-skilled workers is $14 an hour and the equilibrium wage rate for low-skilled workers is $8 an hour; page 453.

Short answer

1a. Because the value of the marginal product of high-skilled workers exceeds that of low-skilled workers, the demand for high-skilled workers exceeds the demand for low-skilled workers. Because skills are costly to attain, the supply of high-skilled workers is less than the supply of low-skilled workers; pages 452-453.

b. The demand for high-skilled workers exceeds the demand for low-skilled workers and the supply of high-skilled workers is less than the supply of low-skilled workers. So the wage rate received by high-skilled workers exceeds the wage rate received by low-skilled workers; page 453.

c. The quantity of high-skilled workers employed compared to the quantity of low-skilled workers employed depends on the positions of the demand and supply curves of both types of labour. The demand curve for high-skilled labour lies to the right of the demand curve for low-skilled labour. The supply curve of high-skilled labour lies to the left of the supply curve of low-skilled labour. Because the positions of these curves determine the quantity of labour employed, we cannot say with certainty how the quantity of high-skilled workers employed compares with the quantity of low-skilled workers employed; page 453.

2. Assortative mating is the tendency for people to marry within their own socioeconomic class. Assortative mating makes the distribution of wealth less equal because very wealthy people tend to marry other very wealthy people; page 456.

■ **CHECKPOINT 18.3**

Fill in the blanks

A household's <u>market</u> income is the income earned from the markets for factors of production and with no government redistribution. The distribution of income after taxes and benefits is <u>more</u> equal than the distribution of market income. Redistribution of income creates the big tradeoff between <u>equity</u> and <u>efficiency</u>. The long-term solution to the problem of single mothers on welfare in Canada is <u>acquiring human capital</u>. <u>A negative income</u> tax provides every household with a guaranteed minimum annual income and taxes all income above the guaranteed minimum at a fixed rate.

True or false

1. True; page 458
2. False; page 459
3. True; page 460
4. False; page 461
5. True; page 462

Multiple choice

1. d; page 458
2. b; page 458
3. b; page 458
4. a; page 458
5. c; page 459
6. c; page 460
7. b; page 461
8. a; page 462

Short answer

1. A progressive income tax will redistribute more income away from the rich to the poor. A progressive income tax has a higher average tax rate as income rises. As a result, the rich pay a greater amount of taxes than do the poor because the rich have more income

and because the average tax rate on that income is higher; page 458.

2. The three types of income maintenance programs are social security programs, unemployment compensation, and welfare programs; page 458.

3. The recipients of the money payments likely will work less. If they were to work more, they might earn enough to move into a higher tax bracket and lose the money the government is giving to them. The taxpayers also will tend to work less. These effects illustrate the force of the big tradeoff: by making incomes more equal, the government program decreases people's incentives to work, decreases economic efficiency, and decreases the nation's income; page 461.

4. a. The household receives its $20,000 guaranteed income. Then, on its market income of $20,000, it pays ($20,000) × (25 percent) = $5,000 in taxes, leaving $15,000 in income after taxes. Its total income is $20,000 + $15,000 = $35,000. This household receives a negative income tax payment of $15,000; page 462.

   b. The household receives its $20,000 guaranteed income. Then, on its market income of $60,000, it pays ($60,000) × (25 percent) = $15,000 in taxes, leaving $45,000 in income after taxes. Its total income is $20,000 + $45,000 = $65,000. This household receives a negative income tax payment of $5,000; page 462.

   b. The break-even income is $80,000. With a market income of $80,000, the household pays $20,000 in taxes, exactly equal to its payment from the government. Households with incomes less than $80,000 receive funds from the government and households with income greater than $80,000 make payments to the government; page 462.